Development Finance

Debates, dogmas and new directions

Stephen Spratt

 Routledge
Taylor & Francis Group

LONDON AND NEW YORK

First published 2009
by Routledge
2 Park Square, Milton Park, Abingdon, Oxon OX14 4RN

Simultaneously published in the USA and Canada
by Routledge
270 Madison Ave, New York, NY 10016

Routledge is an imprint of the Taylor & Francis Group, an informa business

Typeset in Times New Roman by
Swales & Willis Ltd, Exeter, Devon
Printed and bound in Great Britain by
CPI Antony Rowe, Chippenham, Wiltshire

British Library Cataloguing in Publication Data
A catalogue record for this book is available from the British Library

Library of Congress Cataloging in Publication Data
Spratt, Stephen.
Development finance : debates, dogmas and new directions / Stephen
Spratt.
p. cm.
Includes bibliographical references and index.
1. Finance–Developing countries. 2. Economic development–
Finance. 3. International finance. I. Title.
HG195.S68 2008
332′.042091724–dc22
2008009767

ISBN10: 0–415–42318–X (hbk)
ISBN10: 0–415–42317–1 (pbk)
ISBN10: 0–203–89144–9 (ebk)

ISBN13: 978–0–415–42318–2 (hbk)
ISBN13: 978–0–415–42317–5 (pbk)
ISBN13: 978–0–203–89144–5 (ebk)

Contents

vi *Contents*

Figures

Tables

Boxes

1 An introduction to the financial system in theory and in practice

Introduction

The aim of this book is to introduce and analyse the issues and debates surrounding development finance, at both a global and local level. Although the area is relatively new, at least in the form of a distinct subject in its own right, the question of the relationship between the financial sector and economic development and growth has a long and occasionally volatile history.

The development of an effective financial system has been seen as an essential prerequisite for growth at some points, and an unproductive parasite on the real economy at others. The contemporary debate, for the most part, subscribes to the first of these perspectives, though some still support the 'parasitic view'. Those reading this book for the first time are also likely to take a relatively optimistic view of what the financial system can achieve – there would be little point studying the subject if this were not so. Similarly, this book takes a broadly optimistic stance on the debate – there would be little point writing it if this were not the case.

However, it is important to stress at the outset that, as with much in the fields of economics, finance and development, there is rarely only one answer to any question. The answers arrived at may owe as much to the ideological predispositions of their authors as to conclusive empirical evidence. It is important to bear this in mind as you work through this book, which is structured so as to equip you with the skills and confidence to critically analyse the issues for yourself – ultimately, to reach your own conclusions.

Having said that, whilst we do not have all the answers, it is not the case that we know nothing. Theoretical positions have evolved, changed direction, gone up blind alleys (and back again) and been informed by real-world experience for at least a hundred years. It is from this real-world experience that we have, perhaps, the most to learn: we have seen what has worked and what has not, though we may not always know exactly why these outcomes have occurred.

In this first chapter, however, we start with some financial theory and some basic facts with the aim of establishing a framework for the rest of the book. Chapter 2 considers the relationship between finance, development, growth and poverty alleviation. The third chapter reviews both the theory and practice of the trend towards financial liberalisation that began in the early 1970s, whilst Chapter 4 provides an overview of the key features of the domestic financial system in developing countries. Chapter 5 examines the debate around reform of the domestic financial system, focusing on the link between financial sector development, economic growth and poverty reduction. Chapter 6 then moves to the external financial system and compares trends and key issues in official development assistance (i.e. aid) and private sector flows. Chapter 7 considers the incidence and causes of financial crises and debt crises in developing countries, whilst Chapter 8 assesses reforms to the global system, under the aegis of the 'international financial architecture'. Chapter 9 examines the linkages between the domestic financial sector, private sector development and growth in developing countries. The final chapter pulls these different strands together, and considers the options facing policy-makers in developing countries, and ends with a discussion of what countries could do, and what obstacles they may face in proactively developing a financial system that can facilitate high and sustained rates of growth and, ultimately, the elimination of extreme poverty.

First, however, we must answer some basic questions, before seeing how others have answered them in the past.

The most fundamental question to answer is simply, what is the financial system actually for? In principle, the role of the financial system is largely the same as in Walter Bagehot's description of the London money market in 1864: 'It is an organisation of credit, by which the capital of A, who does not want it, is transferred to B, who does want it' (Bagehot, 1978: 422).

Whilst this remains the ostensible purpose of the international financial system, the reality is now very different. In particular, the scale, complexity and interrelatedness of financial markets today has created a plethora of profitable opportunities that are not a 'means to an end', but have become an end in themselves. Total world economic output in 2005 was estimated at between US$55 trillion and US$60 trillion per year. These are big numbers, but they are dwarfed by turnover in the global financial markets – the spot foreign exchange market alone sees more than US$450 trillion in turnover per year, or almost ten times the real economic output of the global economy.

Before returning to this issue, however, the next section considers how, in principle, the financial system performs the functions described by Bagehot almost 150 years ago.

1.1 How do financial systems do this, in theory?

Bagehot described how the nineteenth-century London money market channelled surplus financial resources to capital-scarce borrowers looking to invest. The first function of the financial system is therefore:

(a) *To mobilise savings and allocate credit* – banks, as well as other financial institutions, act as intermediaries between savers and borrowers/investors. Thus households with surplus resources place these resources with banks, which in turn sift through potential borrowers and allocate credit to its most productive use. Similarly, asset management companies and 'contractual savings' institutions[1] also mobilise savings and allocate these funds as investments, usually in public capital markets.

As well as channelling resources indirectly from the capital-rich to the capital-poor through third-party financial intermediaries, the financial system also enables the process to occur directly:

(b) *It enables individuals to directly provide surplus resources through the capital markets* – individuals and institutions with surplus capital to invest can directly participate in the capital markets of the financial system through providing debt financing to companies by purchasing corporate bonds, or by providing equity finance to companies through the purchase of shares.

In addition to these key functions, the financial sector also organises and implements various aspects of the 'plumbing' of the national economic system. Perhaps the most important of these is:

(c) *The provision of clearing and settlement services* – if the national economic system is seen in terms of an engine, then clearing and settlement systems can be viewed as the fuel that enables the machine to function. Specifically, businesses and individuals are able to settle financial balances, whether they be cheques or credit and debit cards for smaller balances usually associated with individuals or small businesses or large value payments between financial institutions, which are generally settled centrally within the national central bank.

As well as providing these vital functions for the private sector, the financial system is both overseen and used by national governments in a variety of ways.

(d) *Governments regulate the activities of the financial system* – the government has an indispensable role in terms of setting and enforcing the regulation of financial institutions, whether directly or through specialist agencies set up by government to undertake this role. The international system, in contrast, does not have one regulator, but relies on coordinating the activities of national regulators.

(e) *Governments also borrow from the financial system* – the government issues sovereign bonds, which are purchased by the financial system (both nationally and internationally), thereby providing the funds needed to finance government expenditure (i.e. to finance fiscal deficits).

(f) *Governments may also take a more direct role in the financial system* – both historically and today, many governments have sought to intervene directly in the functioning of domestic financial systems. Examples of such activities include directing the allocation of credit through development banks and/or directly owning or controlling a section of the commercial banking sector.

Ultimately, therefore, the ostensible purpose of the financial system remains as described by Bagehot above, and the system performs these functions within a regulatory framework implemented and enforced by national governments. However, it is important to reiterate that, at least in principle, the system does not simply allocate surplus capital to *any* borrower, but to the most productive possible use. In theory, this efficient allocation therefore maximises the productive use of capital.

Later we will consider the theoretical principles and assumptions behind this perspective in some detail. Before this, however, the next section highlights the key features of the financial system's infrastructure, before discussing the most important financial institutions that operate within this framework.

1.2 What are the key features of the financial system?

1.2.1 Capital markets

(a) *Bond markets* (or 'fixed income' markets) enable corporations and governments to borrow directly from investors in the capital markets through the issuance of bonds. Bonds are issued in the 'primary market', and then traded in the 'secondary market'. The resultant debt provides investors that purchase the bonds with a regular stream of income payments through 'coupons' (i.e. interest payments) for the life of the debt, as well as the payment of the debt's 'principal' upon maturity. The magnitude of the coupon is set at the time of issuance, hence the term 'fixed-interest'. In the secondary markets, a fall in the price of the bond therefore results in an increase in the rate of interest, or 'yield' paid, as the fixed coupon payment becomes a larger percentage of the price of the bond. The reverse is obviously true of a rise in the price of a bond. In terms of the pricing of risk, therefore, falling demand for a bond – perhaps due to market perceptions of deteriorating credit quality of the issuer – leads to falling prices and higher interest rates. The higher interest rate therefore reflects the perceived increase in the risk attached to the bond. Bonds may have any maturity, and in general terms the shorter the maturity the lower the rate of interest. Other factors that influence the level of interest attached to a bond are (a) the creditworthiness of the issuer (be it corporate or sovereign), and (b) specific features that may be attached to the bond to alter its nature (more will be said of these features below, but a bond without such additions is known as 'vanilla')

(b) *Equity markets* enable investors to obtain a percentage of the ownership of the company in question. There are two forms of equity market: (1) 'public equity markets' (share markets/stock exchanges) are where companies 'list' their shares for trading purposes, with the total value of the company's outstanding shares termed 'market capitalisation'. Investors that purchase a company's shares are entitled to a share of the company's profits in proportion to their stake in the form of 'dividends', which are usually paid annually. Although in many markets – particularly developed ones – anyone can invest in public equity markets, in practice major institutional investors play a dominant role. In the UK, for example, just 14% of the total market capitalisation of the London Stock Exchange is held by private individuals (i.e. 'retail investors'), with the remainder being held by financial institutions (i.e. 'institutional investors'). (2) The second form of equity market is 'private equity', where shares are not listed on a public market, but are sold directly to investors.

In terms of pricing, the value of both bonds and equities can be described as the present value of future revenues derived from the financial instrument. For bonds: 'The value of a bond is the present value of the promised cash flows on the bond, discounted at an interest rate that reflects the default risk in these cash flows' (Damodaran, 2002: 887). For equities, value can be determined either 'intrinsically' or 'extrinsically'. Intrinsic valuation refers to the fundamental value of the equities, which is usually determined in a similar way to that described for bonds above: future (net) revenues of the company in question are discounted back to arrive at a 'net present value' (NPV) today, which is then simply divided by the number of shares issues to produce the 'fair value' of each share today. There are a variety of models that have been designed to perform this function, but the most commonly used are some variant on the standard discounted cash flow (DCF) model.

A key distinction between bond and equity markets relates to the nature of risk. In bond markets, it is the issuer who carries the primary risk, since payments must be met regardless of the financial circumstances of the company. In equity markets, however, the risk is primarily held by the investor, since dividend payments will be linked to the financial performance of the company so that in a bad year no payment will be made. Put another way, if a company raises finance in the bond market debt accrues, but if it raises finance in the equity markets it does not.

1.2.2 *Other financial markets*

(a) *Money markets* provide a market for short-term debt securities, such as bankers' acceptances, commercial paper and government bills with short maturities. Money market securities are generally used to provide liquidity to companies and banks – including overnight loans to meet their reserve requirements as usually determined by the central bank. As such, they are associated with low rates of interest, which reflect the very short maturities involved, and the low credit risk (zero in the face of government) of the participants in the market.

(b) *Derivatives markets* provide instruments for the handling of financial risks, where participants in the derivatives markets purchase instruments that enable themselves to 'hedge' themselves against future movements in asset prices. A derivative is therefore a financial contract whose value is *derived* from a financial instrument such as a stock or bond, an asset (such as a commodity), a currency or a market index (such as the FTSE 100, for example). Derivatives may be traded on market exchanges, such as the Mercantile Exchange in Chicago (CME), the Chicago Board of Trade (CBOT) or the London International Financial Futures and Options Exchange (LIFFE). Derivatives may also be bought or sold privately on an 'over-the-counter' (OTC) basis between major financial institutions. By 2004, average *daily* turnover in the global derivatives market was estimated at $2.4 trillion, with the largest form of contract relating to interest rates, followed by foreign exchange (FX), equities and commodity-related contracts.

(c) *FX markets* trade currencies internationally. By 2004, global FX markets saw average daily turnover of US$1.8 trillion, which is broadly equivalent to the annual GDP of the United Kingdom. Historically, the FX market has been rather an ad hoc affair, with no central market. However, since 2002 an increasing proportion of global FX trades have been transacted and settled through the Continuous-Linked-Settlement (CLS) Bank, which by 2006 processed more than half of all global FX trades. CLS Bank was established to reduce settlement risk in international FX transactions, which is particularly problematic given that such trades often involve more than one time-zone. That is, as both sides of an FX trade have to be settled for the transaction to be complete, it is possible for an institution in one time-zone to settle its side of the trade, only for its counterparty in another time-zone subsequently to default on its side of the trade. Settlement risk of this kind in FX markets is often described as Herstatt Risk after a German bank in the early 1970s.[2]

From a national/international perspective, capital and money markets are almost entirely national, whereas derivatives and FX markets are more international in nature. In terms of participants, 'retail' investors (i.e. the general investing public, as opposed to financial institutions) may provide financing directly to borrowers through any of these markets (though in practice they tend to focus on equity markets). Alternatively, however, they may provide funds indirectly through financial institutions, which may operate on a national or international basis depending on the scope and scale of their activities:

1.2.3 Commercial financial institutions

(a) *Commercial banks* take deposits from the public and lend money on a short- to medium-term commercial basis to individual and corporate borrowers. The difference between the interest rate paid to savers and that charged to borrowers is called the 'spread'. Crucially, commercial banks transform short-term liabilities (i.e. current account deposits that can be withdrawn on demand) into long-term assets (i.e. loans of longer maturity).

(b) *Investment banks/merchant banks* undertake a broader range of financial services, which are generally related to the business and financial institutions sectors. These forms of banks assist businesses in finding and structuring various forms of finance, including the issuance of corporate bonds and the 'underwriting' these issues (i.e. they agree to purchase any unsold bonds). Investment banks also arrange mergers and acquisitions (M&A) and may invest their own capital by taking equity positions (public or private) in selected businesses.

(c) *Universal banks* perform all the functions of commercial banks, combined with the services offered by investment banks.

(d) *Mortgage banks/building societies* specialise in providing finance for the purchase of property, both residential and commercial. (Although these distinctions between types of banks remain, the last two decades have seen considerable erosion of the 'functional boundaries' between the different types of bank and non-bank financial institutions.)

(e) *'Contractual savings' institutions* such as pension funds and insurance companies pool and invest the savings of their members to generate sufficient funds to meet their liabilities (i.e. pension liabilities and paying insurance claims). The investment and asset management activities involved in this function may be performed 'in-house' or may be outsourced to a third-party asset management company.

(f) *Asset management companies* provide 'portfolio management' services for retail and institutional investors (including pension funds) by accessing the public (and private) financial markets described above.

(g) *Venture capitalists/private equity companies* provide seed (or growth) capital for new (or expanding) businesses.

(h) *Finance companies* have less clearly defined activities than banks, and are frequently established to circumvent restrictive regulation. They are generally regulated far less stringently than commercial banks in particular, as they do not take deposits from the general public.

1.2.4 Quasi-commercial financial institutions

(a) *State development banks* are directly owned by governments (either wholly or partially) and are used to direct credit to those sectors of the economy identified by government as priorities. The finance may be on either concessional or commercial terms.

(b) *Mutual/cooperative banks* are collectively owned by their members and operate on a basis that is not strictly commercial but is designed to maximise the benefits to these members. They are therefore often able to pay higher rates of interest to savers and charge borrowers lower rates of interest than purely commercial banks.

(c) *Post office savings banks* provide basic financial services, often to those on low incomes.

(d) *Credit unions/friendly societies* are also owned by their members, where savings are pooled and credit granted to members on low incomes.

(e) *Microfinance institutions* may be organised as a bank, cooperative, credit union etc. Aims vary, but providing the poor with access to financial services is a core feature.

1.2.5 Governmental financial institutions

Central banks have a monopoly of 'fiat money' issuance (i.e. paper money, which is not backed by gold, for example). Central banks also:

- Provide liquidity on a day-to-day basis, which is often used to control the money supply.
- Act as the lender-of-last resort (LOLR) to the domestic banking system, thereby providing sufficient confidence to prevent bank runs. A bank run occurs where depositors simultaneously attempt to withdraw their deposits, perhaps because of fears over the solvency of the bank. As described above, however, banks transform these 'demand deposits' into longer-term loans (i.e. they borrow short-term and lend long-term). Furthermore, banks also multiply these deposits – so that a £10 deposit can form the basis of £100 worth of loans, for example – on the assumption that only a certain proportion of depositors (10% in this example) will seek to withdraw their funds at the same time. A bank run where many (or all) depositors seek to do so, however, can lead to the insolvency and closure of a bank, as the bank is unable to meet its depositors' requests simultaneously. By standing ready to provide liquidity to banks to enable them to meet their obligations (i.e. the LOLR function) the central bank is able to 'short-circuit' bank runs, many of which are generated and amplified by the knowledge that not all depositors will be able to access their money. If it is known that the central bank stands behind the commercial banks in this respect, depositors have no incentive to rush to withdraw their money before other depositors are able to do so.

As well as these features of all central banks they *may*:

- Own or oversee national payment and settlement systems (see above).
- Provide prudential regulation/supervision of the banking (and broader financial) sector.
- Provide (or require banks to provide) deposit insurance, which, as the name suggests, insures depositors' money held in banks. The purpose of deposit insurance is broadly similar to that of the LOLR function described above: by guaranteeing individuals' money held in banks, deposit insurance schemes may prevent the onset of bank runs. In the USA, for example, deposit insurance schemes are operated by the Federal Deposit Insurance Corporation (FDIC), which was established in the wake of the Wall Street Crash of 1929 when large numbers of American banks were forced to close as a result of panic-fuelled bank runs.
- Determine and/or execute monetary policy. The past decade has seen increasing moves towards independence of central banks with regard to executing monetary policy. In the UK, for example, the Bank of England was given responsibility for setting UK interest rates in 1997 by the incoming Labour government. The Bank works within a framework established by the UK Treasury, with the remit of hitting an 'inflation target' of 2.5%, and alters interest rates to achieve this end. The European Central Bank (ECB) is charged with keeping inflation at or near 2%, though, unlike the UK, the ECB's target is not symmetrical.[3] The US Federal Reserve has similar independence, though it does not aim for an explicit inflation target and also takes economic growth considerations into account.
- Determine and/or execute exchange rate policy. Since the 1970s, many countries – particularly developed countries – have avoided targeting specific exchange rates, preferring a free-floating currency,[4] with the onus of macroeconomic management placed on monetary policy as described above. However, many other countries – particularly developing countries – maintain a fixed or managed exchange rate, which the central bank often has the role of managing.

1.3 How do financial markets differ from other markets?

In some ways, the financial markets are similar to any other market for goods or services. However, in certain key respects, they are fundamentally different. The key areas of distinction in this respect relate to time and the management of risk:

1   Fundamentally, financial markets differ from other markets in that they generally involve delivery in the future as opposed to the present.

Consider the difference between buying a car today with your own money in cash and borrowing the money to buy the care on hire purchase over a period of some years. The key difference is that the future is inherently *uncertain*, which carries risks. The interest rate paid on the borrowed money is a reflection of this risk. This is the 'time value of money', which is the term used to describe the fact that a rational individual will value £100 today more than £100 in six months' time.

2   Financial markets also allow *transfers across time* – individuals can choose to defer part of their consumption until the future (through saving), while businesses and governments without sufficient funds can invest today (through borrowing), in the hope of generating more income in the future. Consumption and investment can both therefore be 'smoothed' through time through the use of the financial markets.

3   Financial markets also *transfer and manage risk* by channelling funds from risk-averse savers to risk-taking investors. Depositors receive a rate of interest from the bank, whilst the interest rate charged to risk-taking investors who borrow is a reflection of the following risks:

- credit risk – the danger of default (applicable to individuals, companies *and* some governments);
- market risk – the risk of loss caused by sudden changes in asset prices;
- liquidity risk – the risk of being unable to sell financial assets quickly without loss;
- systemic risk – the risk of contagion from another bank or commercial institution.

All financial institutions are subject to some or all of these risks to differing extents, depending on the nature of their activities. Indeed, many financial institutions, particularly banks, largely emerged, historically, to mitigate these risks.

For example, banks are able to reduce credit risk through gathering information on borrowers *ex ante*, and monitoring them *ex post*. In the absence of the banking sector acting as an intermediary, individuals would have to perform this function themselves if they wished to lend their surplus resources. Furthermore, if they did do this, they would face severe liquidity risk in the event that they wished to withdraw their funds. Banks enable individuals to obtain the benefits of such investment (i.e. a rate of interest), while retaining the option of withdrawing their funds at any time (i.e. liquidity risk is dramatically reduced). Banks are also able to greatly reduce market risk through holding a widely diversified portfolio of investments across a range of different markets, both geographically and sectorally.

Thus far, we have examined the key features of the financial system, and the most important markets and institutions that comprise it. We have also considered the various functions that, at least in theory, the financial system is designed to perform in the context of a national economy. However, the ability (and suitability) of the financial system to perform most – if not all – of these functions rests on certain key assumptions about how the system fundamentally operates. As we shall see below, many of these assumptions remain disputed today, and this was also the case historically. Therefore, in order to unpick the rationales that lie behind the 'facts' described above, and to provide a framework for thinking about the later chapters in this book, the following sections provide, first, some theory and, second, an account of the evolution of the different schools of thought, both economic and financial, that have made major contributions to our understanding of these issues.

1.4 Financial theory and the major schools of thought in historical perspective

1.4.1 Some fundamental theory

In principle, as we have seen, the international financial markets have evolved as the intermediary between those who possess surplus funds and those who wish to borrow. The view that the market, rather than the state for example, is the best performer of this role is most famously expressed in the Efficient Market Hypothesis (EMH), which underpins many of the assumptions made about how markets, particularly financial markets, work.

The hypothesis postulates that capital markets will be optimal in terms of *allocative efficiency* if prices fully and accurately reflect all the relevant information, thereby ensuring that price signals correctly direct equilibria. There are three levels of efficiency in this respect:

1   The first is the 'weak form' of the EMH: this requires prices to fully reflect historical performance and volatility; it renders 'technical analysis' (market actors obtaining abnormal profits through the analysis of historical price trends) impossible, since all this information is already fully reflected in the market price.
2   The second level is the 'semi-strong form' of the EMH: this requires prices to reflect all the information contained in the weak form as well as all currently available information; it thus renders 'fundamental analysis' (market actors obtaining abnormal profits through the analysis of current information such as balance sheets or dividend payments) impossible.
3   The third level of efficiency described is the 'strong form' of the EMH: this requires all the information which is known to any market actor to be fully reflected in the price; it renders all abnormal profits unobtainable since not even those with inside information are able to capitalise as the information is already reflected in the market price.

Malkiel (1987) assesses the evidence on the EMH, and concludes that the weak form is completely confirmed by the evidence and is widely accepted as valid. Whereas some studies have contradicted the semi-strong form, the great majority support the view that new information is incorporated into prices with great speed. The strong form in its pure sense is rejected, however, since it is clear that traders with inside information are able to make abnormal profits.

However, for Malkiel, the evidence suggests that the market overall comes quite close to strong-form efficiency and he concludes that:

> If there is truly some area of pricing inefficiency that can be discovered by the market and dependably exploited, then profit-maximising traders and investors will eventually through their purchases and sales bring market prices in line so as to eliminate the possibility of extraordinary return.
>
> (1987: 122)

This argument echoes a seminal contribution in this area by Milton Friedman (1953), which contends that the arbitraging activities of rational investors will ensure that prices cannot deviate from equilibrium levels to any significant degree. In practical terms, the argument is that investors will sell overvalued assets and buy undervalued assets, thereby ensuring that market prices reflect fundamental or 'fair' value. This was a key argument used by those arguing for floating exchange rates in the late 1960s and early 1970s, where it was argued that floating rates would not be excessively volatile, but would tend towards equilibrium fair value due to the activities of rational investors.

Numerous challenges have been made to the widespread acceptance of the EMH. Tobin (1984) is highly sceptical on the efficiency of the financial markets. He distinguishes four efficiency tests that can be levelled at the financial markets:

1   The first is *Information-Arbitrage Efficiency*, which asks whether all publicly available information is reflected in market prices: in this sense Tobin agrees that financial markets are indeed highly efficient.
2   The second test is *Fundamental-Valuation Efficiency*, which asks whether prices fully reflect future expected earnings: he concludes that, in this sense, the financial markets are not efficient as they fluctuate far more than can be justified by changes in fundamentals.
3   The third test is *Full-Insurance Efficiency*, which assesses whether market actors are able to fully insure for themselves the delivery of goods and services in all future contingencies: again, Tobin concludes that financial markets in this sense are not efficient.
4   The final test is *Functional Efficiency*, which asks whether markets perform their functions efficiently: Tobin asserts that, in contrast to the ostensible purpose of the financial markets – as described by Bagehot – 'very little of the work done by the securities industry, as gauged by the

volume of market activity, has to do with the financing of real investment in any direct way' (p. 11).

Tobin (1984) ultimately concludes that: 'we are throwing more and more of our resources, including the cream of our youth, into financial activities remote from the production of goods and services, into activities that generate high private rewards disproportionate to their social productivity' (p. 14).

In many ways this distinction is the key theoretical dividing line. Supporters of the EMH see the financial markets as optimally efficient processors of information, senders of price signals and allocators of global capital. To the extent that this is not the case, however, this is seen as primarily a function of government restrictions and controls that prevent the system playing its optimising role.

Others argue that whilst financial markets may be efficient in some senses, they are a long way from the benign vision set out above. Moreover, the reason for this shortfall is not the result of controls placed upon the system, but is an inherent feature of the financial markets themselves. This emphasis on the perfectibility of markets on the one hand is contrasted with the view of those who stress the prevalence of market failure and the potential for government to correct these failures, such as Stiglitz (1994) for example.

For supporters of the EMH, therefore, the international financial system could function in an optimal manner if allowed to develop without distorting interventions. For those who stress the importance of market failure and market inefficiency, however, this is an illusion. Rather, the negative features of untrammelled financial markets need to be restrained and positive features actively promoted by interventions by government and other official agencies.

A related distinction is the role played by the price mechanism. For supporters of the EMH, prices in free and open markets reflect 'true' or fundamental values, which is based upon all relevant existing knowledge, and will only change when new information appears or old information is revised. Unfortunately, however, this view does not seem to square with the observable volatility of financial markets. This is the primary basis of challenges to the EMH position: economic fundamentals – of companies or countries – do not change to anything like the extent that market prices do. This is true of all markets, but is particularly the case in emerging and developing countries.

Whilst this may appear a rather abstract distinction, it has wide-reaching implications. If one accepts some version of the efficient market position, then countries wishing to access the international financial markets should, in addition to ensuring that their economies are organised in a sustainable manner, adopt international norms of regulation and supervision to ensure that their markets are compatible with the international system. In addition, relevant data should be released in a timely and accurate fashion, thereby enabling the markets to take a balanced, rational view on the basis of the best possible information. From this perspective, emerging and developing markets would represent only one part of a globally diversified portfolio: that is, the asset class is no different from any other. Furthermore, from this perspective, incidents of turmoil or financial crises are largely a rational response to deteriorating fundamentals in the economies concerned, with the catalyst being new information that highlights this point.

Alternatively, if one accepts that the (perhaps excessive) volatility of financial markets is not simply the rational response of investors to new information, but an inherent aspect of the international financial system, then developing and emerging economies should exercise caution. In particular, in the absence of fundamental reforms to counteract these tendencies, countries should be wary of completely liberalising their financial systems with respect to the financial markets. Rather, they would be better advised to adopt a selective approach, wherein flows that contribute towards developmental objectives in a sustainable manner (i.e. stable, longer-term flows) are encouraged, whilst short-term, reversible flows that could contribute towards instability and crises are discouraged.

Domestically, the same issues apply. A belief in the inherent superiority and efficiency of the market mechanism suggests that government should (a) concentrate on establishing the 'rule of the game' in terms of a level playing field for market participants, (b) ensure obstacles to financial and private sector development are removed, and (c) avoid further interventions in the economic or financial sectors, which by definition will be sub-optimal when compared with the 'invisible hand' of efficient markets.

In many ways, this distinction describes the debate over virtually all aspects of financial markets (and perhaps economics in general) today. However, as we shall see, the distinction and the debate are far from new.

1.4.2 Some history

(a) John Maynard Keynes

Before Keynes, the assumption had been that, whilst markets can fail, these failures were anomalous events – indeed, the late nineteenth century is often cited as the last great period of free capital movement globally and general optimism about the nature and role of free markets.

In contrast, Keynes (1936) argued that imperfections are inherent in markets and that there is no innate tendency towards the production of optimal outcomes – aggregate demand is just as likely to be such as to produce a low-growth, high-unemployment equilibrium than any other. Therefore, to ensure the desirable outcomes of high levels of growth and employment, it is necessary for governments to intervene in the economy. It seems probable that in the absence of the global effects of the Great Depression, Keynes's views would not have had the impact that they did.

For Keynes, changes in market structure and the nature of economic activity had created a highly precarious environment. Originally enterprises were owned and run by the same entrepreneurs. In these times investments were commonly irrevocable. However, the divorce between ownership and control and the emergence of stock markets altered this situation radically.

Stock market valuations offer the investor the opportunity to reappraise her investments on a daily basis as prices fluctuate both absolutely and relative to each other. This introduced liquidity into the economic system, enabling investors to withdraw their investments at any stage.

For Keynes, these developments had a number of significant consequences:

- Firstly, the quantity of real knowledge of the businesses concerned – in terms of their genuine long-term prospects – is inevitably reduced; investors may know little or nothing about a venture other than the value of its stock.
- Secondly, and as a result of the first consequence, day-to-day fluctuations in profits have an unwarranted impact on the share price.
- Thirdly, 'a conventional valuation which is established as the outcome of the mass psychology of a large number of ignorant individuals is liable to change violently as the result of a sudden fluctuation of opinion due to factors which do not really make much difference to the prospective yield' (p. 154).
- Fourthly, Keynes argues that although one would expect these destabilising forces to be offset by the activities of professional and knowledgeable investors, this does not occur because investors: 'are concerned, not with what an investment is really worth to a man who buys it for keeps, but with what the market will value it at, under the influence of mass psychology, three months or a year hence' (p. 155).[5]

Keynes describes the activity of forecasting the 'psychology of the market' as speculation and the long-term forecasting of future yields as enterprise. It is not seen as inevitable that the former will predominate in the market, but Keynes predicts that, as markets develop, this will increasingly be the case. 'Speculators may do no harm as bubbles on a steady stream of enterprise. But the situation is serious when enterprise becomes the bubble on a whirlpool of speculation' (p. 159).

(b) Irving Fischer, the Great Depression, Bretton Woods and the Keynesian consensus

Another strand of thought to emerge at this time focused on observable real-world impacts of the Great Depression. The approach viewed financial crises as an integral part of the business cycle – not anomalies or a rational response to deteriorating economic circumstances as had previously been assumed.

Fisher (1933) attempted to determine the root cause of the length and depth of the Great Depression, where he saw the crucial factor as the level of debt in the economy. Fisher argued that upswings in the economy, instigated by some exogenous event, encouraged increasing levels of indebtedness as greater investment opportunities emerged.

Higher levels of investment are then financed through higher levels of debt, which also funds the growth of speculation in asset markets with the aim of obtaining capital gains through rising asset prices. The increase in borrowing raises the money supply and therefore the rate of inflation. This rise in prices reduces the value of the debt, which encourages ever more borrowing.

At a crucial point a crisis is provoked when the level of debt becomes 'overindebtedness' and borrowers are no longer able to meet their liabilities. To overcome this problem 'distress selling' occurs where borrowers liquidate their assets in an attempt to meet the demands of creditors. If selling of this kind is widespread enough, the previous inflation becomes deflation and the cycle reverses itself. Falling prices then cause the level of outstanding debt to increase and, as the value of collateral falls with the price level, creditors call in loans and fears of bank insolvencies trigger off bank runs. This process continues, economic activity declines and unemployment rises. Ultimately, bankruptcies rectify the excessive levels of debt and recovery can begin.

The key point to make is that the Great Depression shook people's faith in the ability of free financial markets to deliver optimal outcomes. Furthermore, many commentators believed that the international financial and economic effects of this event led directly to the onset of the Second World War. Consequently, when representatives of forty-four countries gathered at Bretton Woods in New Hampshire in 1944, the aim was to construct an international economic system that would reduce the instability of the financial system. Unlike what had preceded it – and the situation today – the time was one of faith in the power of the state to achieve desirable goals that the market, left to itself, was now seen as incapable of producing: the goal was stability and the establishment of confidence in future events.

The reforms instituted at Bretton Woods ushered in a long period of stability, with currencies holding to their pegs (other than infrequent realignments) for the better part of thirty years. International movement of capital was greatly restricted in relation to what had existed previously. Indeed, at Bretton Woods Keynes had argued that the imposition of stringent capital controls should be obligatory on all countries, not least because of the damage he thought that unfettered capital flows could do. In this, he was overruled by the US representative Harry Dexter White, and the final outcome was that the IMF would allow such controls but not insist upon them.

(c) Structuralism

The distrust of markets that encouraged the post-war Bretton Woods reforms was not restricted to industrial countries. In Latin America the structuralist school of thought began to develop within the Economic Commission for

Latin America (ECLAC) from its launch in 1947, and under the leadership of its first executive secretary, Raul Prebisch.

The structuralist approach to development was focused on the 'centre-periphery' paradigm, which sought to explain the unequal nature of the world economic system. In a radical departure from classical trade theory, structuralists did not view developing countries that focused on primary commodity exports as rationally exploiting their comparative advantage in these sectors. Before the 1930s, the dominant development position had been one of export-led growth – not unlike today – but the global recession of the 1930s greatly reduced export markets, and led to a questioning of this approach.

The structuralists argued that the industrial revolution in the 'centre' had dramatically increased the productivity of the factors of production (land, labour, capital) in these economies. In contrast, the industrial sector in the periphery was tiny and was reliant on the import of capital goods from the centre. Furthermore, the Prebisch-Singer hypothesis (the 'decline in the net barter terms of trade') suggested that the prices of primary commodities were falling relative to manufactured goods and would continue to do so. Consequently, developing countries had to export more and more commodities simply to be able to import the same quantity of capital goods. Wages in the periphery were kept low by a large pool of surplus labour in agriculture and the lack of unionisation, whilst wages in the centre were driven up by unionisation and productivity improvements.

The upshot of all this was that the periphery was trapped in commodity production and export to serve the centre and had no prospect of developing the vibrant industrial sector needed to get out of this situation. To address this, the structuralists proposed 'import-substitution industrialisation' (ISI) where high tariffs were placed on industrial imports, except for the essential hi tech capital goods needed to drive the industrialisation process. The aim was to move the economy onto a virtuous circle of industrialisation, rising productivity, wages and employment.

Initially, structuralists encouraged capital inflows to fund at least part of this development. However, as the fruits of the ISI process failed to develop, the structuralist position came in for strong criticism in the 1960s, not least from within its own ranks. The position on foreign capital inflows accordingly began to change, with some arguing that foreign investors ended up controlling the key industrialising sectors of the economy. This led to restrictions on capital flows into the Latin American region. For structuralists, therefore, the external system – both trade and financial – did not represent an opportunity for poorer countries to develop, but rather was a constraint on this development.

Structuralism (and the related ideology of 'developmentalism') had much in common with the Keynesian consensus that dominated the industrial economies in the post-war period. However, like them it was ultimately swept away in the 1970s. For the structuralists in Latin America, the emergence of authoritarian military regimes in the southern cone countries was the proximate cause of this. The ultimate cause, however, was the fact that these regimes were inspired by monetarist policies and the 'new right' who were able to point to the manifest failures of structuralist policies and therefore undermine the assumptions that underpinned these policies.

(d) Monetarism and the return of faith in markets

Kindleberger (1978) distinguishes two distinct schools of thought in financial theory, which, he argues, have been identifiable since the seventeenth century. These schools were described in 1810 as the Currency School and the Banking School and, for Kindleberger, can be broadly identified with the modern schools of monetarism and Keynesianism.

The long-standing argument between the two schools has been over the Currency School's (monetarist) desire to control the money supply and the Banking School's (Keynesian) desire to expand it. This argument represents the articulation of the two aims of maintaining the credibility, and therefore functionality of the stock of money, and the expansion of credit to foster higher levels of economic growth. Monetarists see the money supply (M) as exogenous to real income (Y), prices (P) and interest rates (R) so that an increase in M will result in an increase in P but Y cannot change (too much money chasing too few goods). Keynesians also subscribed to this 'quantity theory of money' in principle. However, they argued that increasing M could increase Y, since the economy may spend long periods below full employment equilibrium and Y *can* be increased up to this level. From a structuralist or post-Keynesian perspective, however, M is *endogenous* to the economy: i.e. it responds to the credit needs of the economy. Artificially restricting the money supply therefore only serves to artificially restrict the growth of the economy.

This debate has witnessed the dominance of one school or the other at different times: the post-war adoption of expansionary demand-management policies by many countries was a significant victory for the intellectual off-spring of the Banking School, for example. From a monetarist perspective the expansion of the money supply through government borrowing, ostensibly to raise effective demand during economic downturns, was a recipe for disaster. They argued that the long-run impact of this approach would inevitably lead to an inflationary spiral, an argument that ultimately proved to be correct.

Crudely, monetarists placed greater faith in the ability of free markets in general, and the price mechanism in particular, to produce optimal outcomes. In contrast, they had little faith in the state's ability to successfully take on this role.

The monetarist revival gathered pace throughout the 1960s and was there-fore well positioned to offer an alternative explanation of the events that were to unfold in the 1970s. This decade saw the collapse of the system of fixed exchange rates, the demise of Keynesianism as the dominant, global economic ideology, and the return to the instability that the optimists at Bretton Woods thirty years earlier had hoped to eradicate. These huge changes in the economic landscape moved the parameters within which theory had been operating and led to the emergence of new schools of thought, as well as the evolution of older ones.

The Bretton-Woods system of fixed exchange rates supported by extensive capital controls offered few opportunities for profit in international financial markets. However, capital controls began to be loosened from 1958 and the consequence was a steady rise in the scale and complexity of international flows of capital. These increases put rising pressure on the parities of inter-national currencies and were a significant factor in the eventual collapse of the system. In 1971 the Nixon administration in the US, no longer able to maintain the fixed rate between the dollar and gold, unilaterally severed the link and thus removed the foundation of the international system of fixed exchange rates.

Interestingly, these developments were accompanied by a rapid rise in the use of derivatives to hedge risk as volatility increased in global markets, contrary to the predictions of Friedman (1953) that floating exchange rates would be relatively stable.

(e) Neo-liberalism

Neo-liberalism is primarily associated with the Chicago School of Econom-ics, which also emphasised the efficiency of markets and free competition, and stressed the primary role of individuals in determining optimal economic outcomes. In contrast, government interventions in markets were viewed with suspicion, being largely seen as distorting markets and preventing these optimal outcomes from occurring.

Neo-liberals argued that there was no need for government to intervene in the economy to ensure full employment, for example, since in a free market situation prices will adjust to ensure adequate supply and to ensure that all the factors of production are employed – that is, markets *automatically* adjust to full employment and attempts to use monetary or fiscal policy to achieve these ends merely create inflation.

The elections of Margaret Thatcher in 1979 and Ronald Reagan in 1980 saw this ideological perspective come to the fore. Although early pure monet-arist policies such as control of the money supply were soon abandoned, the focus on the optimal nature of market outcomes continued. This has developed into a coherent body of thought, which has clear policy prescrip-tions at both the domestic and international level.

In domestic terms, the agenda has been dominated by proposals to mimic the 'Anglo-Saxon' model. Relevant domestic policy proposals in this regard include:

- the deregulation of domestic financial markets;
- privatisation;
- reductions in the power of trade unions;

- smaller government;
- lower tax rates;
- opening of international goods and capital markets.

Internationally, the 1990s saw the birth and rise of the 'Washington Consensus', which in turn advocated:

- privatisation;
- free trade;
- export-led growth;
- financial capital mobility;
- deregulated labour markets;
- macroeconomic prudence.

In all of these proposed policy measures, the common theme is that intervention in markets is usually counterproductive; regulation should be light; and markets should be freed to enable them to produce the optimal outcomes that theory suggests. The efficient market hypothesis is perhaps the most obvious example of this perspective, but the general faith in markets and distrust of state intervention cuts across all sectors of the financial and real economies.

Clearly, these policy proposals come from a coherent ideological position. However, they were also informed by observations of what works and what does not. Interventionist – or *Dirigiste* – policies had largely failed. The neoliberal position offered a plausible explanation for why this was so and a consistent set of policies to improve the situation.

From the beginning, however, there has been considerable questioning of this faith in market outcomes, not least because the policy prescriptions set out above have also not always led to the predicted positive outcomes. All of these perspectives question the assumption that free markets tend to optimal outcomes and that crises, volatility and seeming irrationality are anomalies in the financial system.

(f) Financial fragility, uncertainty and asymmetric information.

In an analysis of the nature of business cycles and financial crises, Kindleberger (1978) distinguished between upswings and downturns, with the former characterised by behaviour resembling a 'mania' and the latter by behaviour resembling a 'panic'. The mania stage is triggered by what Kindleberger calls a 'displacement', which is an exogenous event that produces a change in the perception of economic prospects – the dotcom boom is a clear recent example of this.

The demand for credit increases and the resultant rise in bank loans fuels the expansion. Asset prices rise, further enhancing the feeling of increased wealth and encouraging ever more borrowing. Investors switch out of cash, so as to 'get on the bandwagon', fuelling the rise in asset prices and the feelings of mania. The bubble expands, sucking in more and more investors.

At this stage Kindleberger distinguishes between 'insiders' and 'outsiders': the insiders, who are aware of the situation, sell out at the top of the market to the outsiders attracted by the mania to get in on the act – the dotcom boom of the late 1990s comes to mind. The bubble can only continue to expand if outsiders (buyers) outnumber insiders (sellers). At some point a period of 'distress' emerges where the nature of the bubble is recognised and the influx of outsiders ceases. An uneasy period ensues until some trigger sets off a panic as investors rush to withdraw their funds. Investors have a strong incentive to be first in the queue to withdraw their funds since all know that not every investor will be able to liquidate without loss, not unlike a bank run. This process is described by Kindleberger as a 'fallacy of composition', wherein individual investors acting in a rational way – attempting to withdraw their funds before a crash – ensure that the opposite occurs.

Keynes (1936) viewed the future as inevitably uncertain, so that contemporary fundamentals cannot be viewed as a reliable guide to future fundamentals – in such an uncertain world those in Kindleberger's 'mania' stage therefore cannot see that the 'panic' stage will later occur. From the perspective of inevitable future uncertainty there is no way to accurately determine, objectively, the 'true' value of an asset in today's market as, in the case of equities for example, that value is discounted future profits, and the level of these profits cannot be known. This is particularly the case when the exogenous 'displacement' – such as using new techniques to determine the 'value' of dotcom companies which perhaps have no revenues – changes the framework within which valuation occurs.

Davidson (1998) argues that Keynes's position sets him in opposition to the 'ergodic axiom' that Lucas and Sargent (1981) see as essential for developing economics as an empirically based science, and which underpins the EMH. Davidson goes on to define an ergodic system as one where 'today's objective probabilities calculated from an observed data set provide statistically reliable information about the conditional probability function that will govern future outcomes' (p. 2). In practice this implies that 'agents analyse past and present market data in forming rational expectations as a basis for making utility maximising decisions'(p. 2). The product of agents making decisions in this way is an objectively obtainable 'fundamental price' that the market can converge on. However, from Keynes's position of inevitable uncertainty, current data can never provide such a reliable guide to the future. Consequently, financial markets are not an ergodic, but a non-ergodic system.

Arthur *et al.* (1996) point out that the EMH assumes identical (homogeneous) investors who share rational expectations of an asset's future price. All new information is therefore instantly discounted into the current market price. In such a system, no possibility of speculative profit exists and booms and crashes, for example, reflect changes in an asset's value. However, Arthur *et al.* doubt the reality of homogeneous agents of this form. They argue that available market information such as past prices, dividends, other indicators or even rumours, 'are merely qualitative information plus data sequences, and there may be many different, perfectly defensible statistical ways, based on different assumptions and different error criteria to use them to predict future dividends' (p. 5).

For the authors, the consequence of this is that there is no 'objectively laid-down expectational model that different agents can coordinate upon, so there is no objective means for one agent to know other agents' expectations of future dividends.' Given this, deductive reasoning is impossible, and agents – now heterogeneous – must resort to the forming and testing of plausible hypotheses: that is, inductive reasoning.

In this world, with no agreed 'true' value for prices to converge upon, fashions and fads become important, and heterogeneous agents try out and either retain or discard expectational models of future market outcomes, depending on their success or failure.

A very important strand of theory that emerged in the 1980s was that of 'asymmetric information', which owed much to the work of Joseph Stiglitz, who won the Nobel Prize for Economics for his work in this area.[6] The asymmetric information problem identifies the fact that lenders and borrowers do not have access to equal information as to the credit-worthiness of a potential borrower. Asymmetric information is considered a particular problem in financial markets, which as we have seen are concerned with uncertain future events.

Mishkin (1996) draws on the pioneering work of Stiglitz and identifies two key problems of asymmetric information that afflict the financial system. The first is 'adverse selection': in debt and equity markets, lenders have no way of distinguishing good borrowers from bad. Therefore, the price that they are prepared to pay, rather than being a reflection of the genuine risks involved, represents the average quality of firms in the market. In consequence, high-quality firms may be unwilling to issue securities as the average price is not a fair reflection of their worth. Conversely, low-quality firms will be eager to issue securities at a price that inflates their true worth. The result of this, for Mishkin, is that credit markets are not efficient since many projects with positive potential are not undertaken.

The second problem of asymmetric information is one of 'moral hazard'. Here, the borrower has an incentive to engage in high-risk strategies since, if they come off, the borrower wins but, if they fail, the lender shoulders the burden. The consequence is that some lenders will not make loans and lending therefore remains at sub-optimal levels.

For Mishkin, these problems explain the significance of banks in the financial system, as banks are seen as less subject to asymmetric information problems than securities markets, due to their relationships with customers and knowledge of local markets. This situation is amplified in the developing world where securities markets are less well developed and, consequently, banks play an even greater role. However, whilst mitigating some problems of asymmetric information, Mishkin argues that banks have an incentive to take on excessive risk, which is essentially a moral hazard problem: if the risks come off, the bank wins but, if they fail, the depositors lose out.

(g) The return of psychology and behavioural finance

The foundation stone of orthodox financial theory is the assumption of rational, utility-maximising agents. Whilst this framework effectively banishes psychology from the study of economic behaviour, this is a relatively recent trend. Early classical economists such as Marshall, Fisher and, particularly, Keynes recognised the importance of psychology and analysed the nature of economic decision-making in this context. However, the psychological content of mainstream economics began to diminish in the 1940/50s as new quantitative techniques were brought to bear in support of the rationality hypothesis.

During the 1970s something of a revolution took place as the residue of psychological content was replaced by assumptions of strict rationality. Building on the work of Muth (1961), Lucas (1988) and others developed the rational expectations framework that enabled economists to incorporate the rationality assumption fully into macroeconomic models. In some ways this represents a sub-set of the larger trend of resurgence in the faith in the power of markets to deliver optimal outcomes, which was underpinned by the notion of rational, utility-maximising individuals.

Whilst the impact of psychology on mainstream economics was waning, however, something of a counter-revolution was occurring from an offshoot of mainstream psychology. Early pioneers in what would become behavioural economics were Amos Tversky and Daniel Kahneman, whose article 'Judgement under Uncertainty: Heuristics and Biases' appeared in a 1974 edition of *Science*.

Tversky and Kahneman demonstrated that actual behaviour systematically violates the precepts of rational, optimising behaviour. Crucially, they also showed that these 'anomalies' could be predicted. The fact that the 'anomalies' described are systematic and therefore predictable is important because supporters of the market efficiency position argue that deviations from rational behaviour are random and uncorrelated: consequently, this is just 'white noise' that effectively cancels itself out, and therefore cannot move markets away from the equilibrium implied by rational behaviour.

In Tversky and Kahneman (1974), however, it is argued that, in practice, individuals often do not make decisions in this way, but rely on a limited number of 'heuristic principals' that serve to simplify complex probability judgements. Usually these 'short-cut' decision making tools work fairly well – that is, they approximate to rational economic behaviour – however, they can also result in systematic errors of judgement. The work of Tversky and Kahneman provides the foundation for the school of thought known as 'behavioural finance'. From this perspective, markets are not always driven by rational, utility-maximising individuals, but often by people employing psychological short-cuts in their decision-making. Consequently, many of the 'anomalies' we see in the workings of markets are not anomalies at all, but the consequence of this consistent and predictable behaviour.

Concluding comments

All of these schools of thought question the foundations of the efficient market hypothesis – though in different ways – and suggest either individual (psychological) or structural reasons why market behaviour may deviate systematically from that predicted by neo-classical or neo-liberal theory. Under these frameworks, volatility, 'boom and busts' and financial crises are not anomalies that will be eventually eliminated by the efficient functioning of markets, but an inherent feature of the financial system.

However, it is important to remember that just as markets can and do fail, government intervention is no panacea. The observation of market failure suggests that, in theory, government interventions could produce superior welfare outcomes (Stiglitz, 1994). However, theory and practice are not the same thing. In the post-war era of the Keynesian consensus, the faith in the power of the state to produce optimal outcomes was analogous to today's faith in the power of markets. Historical experience is clear in this regard, however: just as we can observe market failure, we can also point to numerous examples of 'government failure'. It is hard for governments to intervene successfully in the economic and financial systems – some would say impossible.

This book does not take such a pessimistic view on the role governments can play in helping finance national economic development, but neither does it ignore the fact that such interventions must be carefully weighed on a cost-benefit basis, planned and executed to have any chance of achieving their objectives – and even then they may fail. Despite the problems that have been described, the market is the most powerful developmental tool we have: it is not perfect and can never be so, but is still capable of lifting billions out of poverty. In this regard, pragmatism and clear thinking are invariably more effective than blind adherence to any particular dogma.

When considering problems and issues in development finance, it is extremely important to bear these debates, disputes and disagreements in mind. There is rarely total consensus on any issue and often there is no consensus at all. We do not know as much as some would have you believe, but neither do we know nothing at all. Wherever possible, issues should be taken on a case-by-case basis. The evidence must be carefully assessed in the light of the particular circumstances and policy formulated on that basis. No school of thought is totally correct, with the result that their policy recommendations will not be totally correct in every circumstance either. It is therefore essential to combine judgement with evidence and strong local knowledge to find the right solution for the issues that you face as we navigate the world of development finance.

2 Finance, poverty, development and growth

Introduction

We saw in Chapter 1 that perspectives on the nature of the financial system – how it functions, what it can and cannot do, and what interventions are or are not needed for it to perform these functions – have varied considerably, both historically and in modern times. The forces shaping these perspectives have been twofold. First, real-world events have both shaped the priorities of researchers, and set parameters of what seemed possible and what did not. Secondly, broad schools of thought have emerged within this real-world context, driven by both theoretical developments and, in some instances, by the ideological stances held by their protagonists.

These schools of thought have – to a greater or lesser extent – attempted to demonstrate the veracity of their viewpoints through empirically testing the predictions which have flowed from their theories. However, the uncertainty described in the previous chapter in the context of the financial systems has been no less evident in this process. Karl Popper taught us long ago that it is not possible to prove a theory, only to disprove one. That is to say, I can argue that all swans are white, but we can never know for sure that this is correct, as the appearance of one black swan will immediately disprove the hypothesis, but the non-appearance of such a creature does not prove that it will never appear.

So it is with financial research. Rather than known certainties, what we have in reality is increasing (or decreasing) weights of evidence in favour of some theories, which may or may not be applicable in all circumstances, or may be contingent on particular times and conditions.

As we set out to explore the relationship between finance, poverty and development it is important to always bear these caveats in mind. Too often, policy-makers in developing countries have been encouraged – and in some cases obliged – to implement specific policies on the basis that policy X will inevitably result in outcome Y. Rarely, if ever, has such confidence been justified by the evidence. What is needed is greater humility on the part of those proffering such advice, coupled with a more nuanced understanding of how the particular economic, social, cultural and geographical circumstances of each country will shape policy outcomes.

Recent years have seen some progress in these areas, but much remains to be done. We are all impatient for progress, but impatience does not justify the implementation of simplistic 'one-size-fits-all' policies, not least because the implementation of such policies is highly unlikely to produce the progress we all seek. Clearly, therefore, we do not know everything, and this should be acknowledged. However, neither do we know nothing. In this chapter we will explore the progress that theoretical and empirical research has made in furthering our understanding of this fundamental question: what is the relationship between finance, poverty and growth?

The commonly held viewpoint on this question can broadly be put as follows: economic growth is the best means of reducing – and ultimately eliminating – poverty in developing countries, and the development of an efficient and effective financial system is a key driver of economic growth. This is – or certainly should be – the driving force behind efforts to develop the financial sector in developing countries.

As with the caveats given above, it is therefore of great importance to always bear in mind as you read this book that neither financial sector development, or even economic growth, are ends in themselves. Rather, the real goal is the elimination of poverty in developing countries, and, ultimately, the establishment of high standards of living – or, more broadly, high quality of life – for the citizens of these countries.

2.1 Why is growth important?

The focus on spurring growth of much of economic policy does not, as pointed out above, mean that growth is an end in itself. It is a means to an end, and should therefore be judged on how effectively it is able to achieve these ends: the reduction of poverty levels and the improvement in living standards across the economy.

Clearly, however, economic growth is not the only means of reducing poverty. One obvious alternative would be to redistribute resources within an economy, with the 'surplus' wealth or income of the better off being transferred to the poor directly. Particularly in very unequal societies – as many developing countries undoubtedly are – this would certainly have the effect of reducing levels of poverty. Such an approach has become very unfashionable in modern times but in principle, at least, there is no reason why it could not be done, particularly in middle-income countries with relatively large quantities of wealth and income concentrated in the hands of relatively few citizens.

The relative merits of growth or redistribution as policy aims is beyond the scope of this book, however. The issue is raised to make the point that there is nothing 'natural' or 'unnatural' about either approach: redistribution is currently frowned upon in many quarters, and there are perhaps good reasons for this. However, it was not always so, not least in today's developed countries. Growth, in contrast, is almost[1] universally seen as the only viable solution to endemic poverty in the developing world, but equally this may not always be so in the future. There are few, if any, 'iron laws' in this regard.

The options available to policy-makers should not be limited to those currently in vogue. Rather, the full spectrum is – or certainly should be – available as options, with each being judged on its merits in the particular circumstances of each country at a given point in time.

Having said all that, it is undoubtedly the case that today growth is seen as the key instrument for poverty alleviation. In the next section we will unpack this a little, and seek answers to the following questions:

1   Does growth always reduce poverty?
2   Are some forms of growth more 'pro-poor' than others?
3   Should policy be aimed at maximising general growth, or maximising pro-poor growth, and is there a trade-off between these two objectives?

2.2 Growth and poverty reduction: theory and evidence

An often cited study from 2000 by the World Bank[2] – 'Growth is good for the poor' – argues that, in general, the answer to the first question is yes. Using a sample of ninety-two countries from 1960 to 2000, the authors find that when average income rises, the average incomes of the poorest fifth of society rise proportionately. Why?

Empirically, the share of income accruing to the poorest fifth (bottom quintile) does not vary systematically with average income. The authors find that this holds across all regions, periods, income levels and growth rates.

More recently, one of the authors of this report, Kraay (2004), estimates that, in the short-run, 70% of variations in changes in poverty levels between countries can be explained by general income growth, and that this figure rises to 97% over the medium to long term. These are certainly impressive figures.

It is interesting to note how the first study was eagerly seized upon by a certain section of opinion in the international financial institutions (IFIs), particularly in the World Bank, but also within the International Monetary Fund (IMF). For some, this research, and its subsequent extensions, lends support to the view that efforts to proactively target the poor – so that growth would be 'pro-poor' – were often counterproductive, and could even adversely affect general growth rates, thus ultimately having a negative effect on poverty reduction.

However, as with many of the issues that we shall cover in this book, it is not quite as simple as that. It is perhaps human nature that we seize upon evidence that seems to support our pre-existing perspectives. However, when influential global development agencies have a dominant 'institutional perspective', there is a danger that this can skew policy recommendations, not least because the type of research undertaken or commissioned by such agencies is also influenced by these institutional perspectives.

Here we shall take as balanced a view as possible of the evidence, but it would be naïve to think that this author is immune to these influences. As with the IFI policy community, I too have pre-existing perspectives, which the reader may discern without too much difficulty. Let us be open about this, however, whilst striving for as much balance as can realistically be achieved.

To return to the issue at hand, before we can assess the evidence on general growth vs. 'pro-poor growth', we must first define our terms. The first of these is straightforward enough and can be measured as changes in per capita GDP. What of the second though?

2.2.1 What is pro-poor growth?

On one level, growth that is pro-poor can be defined as that which results in a significant increase in the incomes of the poor. Indeed, this is broadly the official definition adopted by the United Nations, for example. However, while no one would disagree with this definition, it does not take us very far. Specifically, the debate turns on what we mean by 'significant'.

Lopez (2005) identifies two strands of the literature, which answer this question in very different ways. In simple terms, the first of these strands focuses on the impact of growth on poverty with regard to the outcomes for inequality within societies, whilst the second focuses on changes in 'head-count' poverty rates, regardless of any changes in inequality.

(a) Poverty and inequality

Within this strand of the literature, growth is seen as pro-poor if it at least proportionately benefits the poor. That is, if average incomes rise by 5%, but the incomes of the poor rise by 3%, this is not seen as pro-poor growth.

White and Anderson (2000) propose two categorisations of pro-poor growth within this framework. The first suggests that growth is pro-poor if the incomes of the poor rise by more than the average growth in incomes – if average incomes rise by 3%, but the incomes of the poor rise by 5%, we have pro-poor growth. This definition therefore sees pro-poor growth as reducing the *relative* inequality within societies.

The second, more radical, definition defines pro-poor growth as that which reduces *absolute* inequality. Here, for growth to be pro-poor, the share of total income growth which goes to the poor must be equal to or greater than their share of the population. Thus, if the poor constitute 60% of the population, then they must receive at least 60% of the proceeds of economic growth for us to be able to describe this as pro-poor growth.

(b) 'Headcount' poverty

The second approach takes a far less exacting approach to defining what is 'significant' in terms of the growth of the incomes of the poor relative to general income growth. Ravallion and Chen (2004), for example, simply argue that growth is pro-poor if it raises the incomes of the poor, regardless of any effects on inequality.

(c) Pros and cons

Lopez (2005) describes what he sees as the advantages and disadvantages of both approaches. For those focusing on inequality, growth defined as pro-poor could actually result in less poverty reduction than that not defined in this way. For example, if growth in general incomes is 2%, but the incomes of the poor rise by 3%, we have pro-poor growth. However, if general income growth is at 6%, but the incomes of the poor rise by only 4% this is not pro-poor growth, despite the fact that poverty has been reduced in the second example more than in the first.

Also, for Lopez, from a policy perspective, holding to the more stringent versions of this definition in particular could lead to a disproportionate focus on reducing inequality, perhaps at the expense of growth. However, to remember our earlier caveats, this is to risk confusing ends and means, if taken to the extreme. That is, the *purpose* of growth is to reduce poverty, it is not an end in itself. If poverty can be reduced, regardless of the impact on growth, this achieves the same ends.

Where this runs into difficulties, however, is that one can divide up national income on a more equal basis and therefore reduce poverty, but the ultimate impact will obviously depend on the size of the 'cake' – i.e. national income – that is to be divided. In many developing countries, particularly the least developed countries (LDCs), the 'cake' is simply not big enough, regardless of how it is divided. Consequently, while levels of inequality are obviously extremely important, so is general growth of national income.

However, a balance must clearly be struck, since a strict adherence to the definition proposed by Ravallion and Chen (op. cit.) can lead to some perverse examples of growth that is pro-poor. For example, as pointed out by Lopez (op. cit.) such an approach would define a situation where average incomes rise by 6%, but the incomes of the poor rise by 0.1% as pro-poor.

As is often the case therefore, there needs to be a sensible balance struck between growth in average incomes relative to growth in the incomes of the poor. Below we consider the evidence on where this balance should be struck.

2.2.2 Inequality, growth and poverty reduction

At the beginning of section 2.2, we saw that Kraay (2004) estimates that the variation in changes in poverty levels between different countries, over the short term, can be largely (70%) explained by differences in general rates of income growth. Furthermore, the same study estimates that the explanatory power of general income growth rises to 97% over the medium to long term.

For some, this is the end of the matter. However, as we shall see, the answers one gets depend very much on the question that is asked, and the methodologies employed to answer it, particularly the level of aggregation. For example, rather than examining variations in changes in poverty levels between countries, Ravallion (2004) focuses on the 'growth elasticity of poverty', which can be defined as the percentage change in poverty associated with a 1% growth rate (Lopez, 2005).

Where Kraay (2004) essentially says that poverty will be best addressed by maximising general income growth, Ravallion (op. cit.) demonstrates that this is a specific not a general case. In particular, the outcome in terms of poverty reduction of increasing aggregate income will be strongly determined by the initial level of inequality in society. Specifically, the lower the level of inequality to begin with, the greater the impact of general growth on poverty levels – i.e. the higher the growth elasticity of poverty. In this regard, Ravallion estimates that a 1% general growth rate will produce 4.3% growth in the incomes of the poor in very equal countries, but for countries with very high levels of inequality the same level of growth results in the incomes of the poor rising by just 0.6%.

Clearly, therefore, the particular circumstances of individual countries will have a strong impact upon policy outcomes. As stressed in the introduction, policy X (i.e. maximising general growth) will not always result in outcome Y (i.e. maximum poverty reduction).

Lopez and Servén (2004) employ a different methodology, but arrive at a similar conclusion to Ravallion (op. cit.); namely, that high levels of inequality are an obstacle to poverty reduction. However, they also find that poverty itself represents a similar obstacle to poverty reduction.

Lopez (2005: 7) summarises the policy implications of these findings as follows:

> . . . these findings would justify poverty reduction strategies with a pro-growth bias in low income and low inequality countries and policy packages that adequately balance growth and inequality objectives in richer and more unequal countries.

We have explored some recent research into the impact of growth on poverty, and seen how levels of inequality in a society within a society can influence this relationship. In Box 2.1 below we consider how these issues relate to a fast-growing economy with high levels of poverty: India.

Box 2.1 Growth and poverty in India

As we can see from the figure below, in recent times India has exhibited high and sustained rates of economic growth, averaging almost 7% per year from the early 1990s to 2004. However, as we can also see, absolute poverty remains endemic: in 1993 85% of the population lived on less than US$2 per day; by 2004 after a decade of high rates of growth, this had fallen a little, but remained very high at more than 80% of the population.

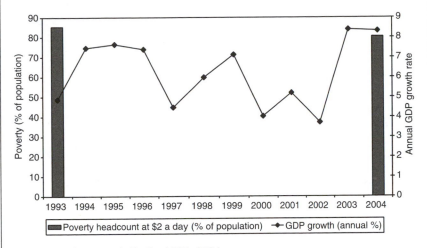

Growth and poverty in India, 1993–2004.

Furthermore, even this relatively small reduction in poverty has been very unevenly distributed throughout the different regions of the country, with much of the difference appearing to relate to 'initial conditions' in terms of land ownership and human capital:

1   States that have had more land reform tended to have had more rapid poverty reduction even though they have (if anything) had slower agricultural growth (Besley and Burgess, 2000).
2   States with more labour regulation have tended to have slower growth in manufacturing (Besley and Burgess, 2000).
3   States with more rapid bank branch expansion into unbanked areas have experienced greater poverty reduction (Burgess and Pande, 2005).
4   States with systems of land revenue collection that remained in indigenous hands have tended to experience better public goods provision (Banerjee and Iyer, 2002).
5   States with more rural industrialisation have reduced poverty more rapidly (Foster and Rosenzweig, 2003).
6   States with more female literacy have done better in reducing poverty (Ravallion and Datt, 2002).

Thus while growth may be a necessary condition for poverty reduction, it is far from being sufficient. The IMF estimates that India will have to generate at least 100 million jobs over the next decade simply to stop unemployment from rising. If there is to be an equitable distribution of the proceeds of growth, however, it is clear that the sources of the current imbalance in this regard that are described above will also need to be seriously addressed.

However, the relationship between growth and inequality has itself long been a subject of research and (sometimes fierce) debate. In the next section some key issues in this regard are considered.

2.2.3 Growth and inequality: some history, theory and practice

(a) From growth to inequality

The linkages between growth and inequality have a long tradition, which in modern times can be traced to the work of Simon Kuznets. Kuznets received the Nobel Prize in 1971 for his groundbreaking, empirically based work on the process of economic development and growth. His key insights in this respect live on in the form of the famous 'Kuznets curve'.

Box 2.2 Simon Kuznets

Simon Kuznets (1901–1985) was an American empirical economist who was a founding father of the field of econometrics. Today Kuznets is best known for his empirical work on the impact of economic growth on income distributions, which is described below. Although Kuznets received the Nobel Prize in 1971 for his work on the empirics of growth, he was also influential in the economics of public accounts, the empirical analysis of Keynes' Absolute Income Hypothesis, which he found did not hold over the longer term, thus opening the door for Milton Friedman's Permanent Income Hypothesis, which sought to explain the relationship between income and savings rates.

Kuznets's empirical work used cross-sectional analysis of countries at differing levels of development, where the relationship between per capita income and inequality was assessed. Kuznets (1955) found that in the early stages of growth income inequality tends to widen, before levelling off once income reaches a certain level and then falling as incomes continue to rise.

For Kuznets, this relationship could be explained by the process of development itself, notably the shift from agricultural to industrial production. He argued that in the early stages of growth, where much economic activity is based on agricultural production, the movement of people from the land to the urban centres would lead to a widening of inequality levels. This process was driven by the fact that the potential for productivity increases in industrial production in urban areas was greater than in the agricultural sector, so that urban (industrial) workers' wages grew much more rapidly than rural incomes. As urbanisation progresses inequality continues to increase, peaking when half of the workforce have moved into the industrial sector, and then declining as industrialisation continues and more and more workers are drawn into the higher-paid sectors.

Kuznets's work was extremely influential, leading many to argue that growing inequality in developing countries was a 'natural' part of the process of development, which would be inevitably reversed as incomes continued to rise. If this position is accepted, then there is no point in attempting to address high levels of inequality in developing countries. Indeed, if these efforts serve to slow the rate of growth, they may be seen as counterproductive, as they merely postpone the point at which the high point of the Kuznets curve is reached and inequality begins to fall.

The universal applicability of the Kuznets curve is now widely questioned. From a methodological point of view, Kuznets based his empirical work on cross-sectional analysis of different countries (at different levels of development) at the same point in time. Critics have argued that a time-series analysis of the development of individual countries would have been a more appropriate approach to take. In particular, at the time Kuznets undertook his work, many of the countries he used to produce the middle-income part of his curve were in Latin America, which is a region characterised – then as now – by high levels of inequality. Consequently, rather than being an 'iron law' of development, which is applicable to all countries, the 'relationship' described in the Kuznets curve may represent the unique circumstances of particular countries at one given point in time, and be allowed by the fact that, at the time, many middle-income countries happened to be in Latin America.

The status of the theory has also been adversely affected by the development experience of many countries in East and Southeast Asia, where growth has been associated with very low levels of inequality, the pattern of which in no way resembles that depicted in the Kuznets Curve.

However, the fact that the proposition has had such a powerful impact upon policy-makers historically again highlights the dangers of assuming that 'iron laws' of development exist, and that therefore the same policy approaches (or the absence of them) will result in the same outcomes.

This point is highlighted by more recent empirical work into the impact of growth on inequality, summarised in Lopez (2005). Research undertaken over the last two decades, using a variety of methodologies and case-studies, has all concluded that there is no consistent, predictable relationship from growth to inequality. That is, there is no tendency for growth to result in either an increase or a decrease in levels of inequality.[3] Either effect *may* occur, but this is due to the particular circumstances of the countries concerned, not an inherent feature of the process of economic growth and development.

(b) From inequality to growth: 1

We have seen that levels of inequality can have a strong impact upon the effectiveness of economic growth in reducing poverty levels: the growth elasticity of poverty. Other strands of research have also examined the question of how inequality may, in turn, impact upon levels of economic growth.

Box 2.3 Nicholas Kaldor

Nicholas Kaldor (1908–1986) was a Hungarian-born economist who, after studying in Berlin, spent his academic and policy-focused life in the UK, most prominently at the University of Cambridge. As well as his work on inequality and growth, Kaldor's work on inefficiency led to a more useable modification of standard Pareto efficiency forms. For a change to be Pareto efficient, it must be that someone is made better off, with no one becoming worse off. Kaldor-Hicks efficiency, in contrast, can arise where a change does lead to some people being worse off – which is far more likely to happen in practice – but that those better off could, in theory, compensate the losers and still remain better off themselves. This approach has been very influential in the policy sphere, forming the basis for much cost-benefit analysis work to judge whether particular policies should be undertaken. As well as his academic work, Kaldor was an advisor to post-war Labour governments and was instrumental in early work to move from direct to indirect taxation – i.e. VAT.

At the same time as Kuznets was developing his work on growth and inequality, his contemporary, Nicholas Kaldor, was formulating a theory that, at least in some regards, can be seen as complementary. Kaldor (1956) argued that relatively high levels of inequality are associated with higher levels of growth. The 'Kaldor hypothesis' states that because wealthy people have a higher propensity to save – as much of their income is surplus to the requirements of satisfying basic needs – unequal societies where income is concentrated in relatively few hands will have higher savings rates than more equal societies, which is translated into higher investment rates and faster growth.

It is not difficult to see how the Kaldor hypothesis could be combined with the Kuznets curve, with the result not only that would there be no point in aiming to reduce inequality as countries develop, but that growth could be accelerated if inequality was actively encouraged. Furthermore, faster growth would hasten the point at which the Kuznets curve turned down, thus reducing inequality more quickly than would otherwise be the case. In short, the best (and fastest) way to reduce inequality in the long term would be to increase inequality in the short term.

As well as the Kaldor hypothesis, there are other theoretical arguments to support the view that inequality is a spur to growth (Lopez, 2005). First, many of the investments needed to accelerate growth are large and not readily divided. Consequently, in developing countries where access to capital markets is often difficult, the concentration of wealth and income in relatively few hands makes investments of this form feasible, resulting in a higher level of growth than would be the case in more equal societies. Secondly, Mirrlees (1971) argues that equal societies with relatively uniform wage structures do not provide the correct incentives for individuals to excel and innovate, thus also resulting in lower levels of growth than would otherwise be the case.

Empirically, the evidence is largely inconclusive on this subject. Some studies[4] find that inequality is supportive of growth, others find the opposite, whilst yet others find no link at all.[5] What seems to determine the outcome of these empirical studies is largely the econometric methods – as well as the data – which are employed. This is not to say that the researchers pick their methods in the hope of finding the result which they hope to see, but the results in this area are far from robust to the methods used, suggesting that interpretation based on the results – particularly in the policy sphere – should be treated with great caution. What we can say, however, is that there is no convincing body of evidence to support the claim that more unequal societies grow faster.

(c) From inequality to growth: 2

Another strand of the literature has proposed that, contrary to the arguments and evidence presented above, *low* levels of inequality are supportive of growth. Lopez (2005) identifies three different arguments to support this position. Galor and Zeira (1993) argue that the 'credit constraints' associated with high levels of inequality restrain growth. In particular, the authors see the key driver of growth as being levels of investment in human capital. However, in highly unequal societies, the poor lack the resources – and the means of acquiring them – to make investments in the education of their children. Consequently, highly unequal societies are likely to grow slower than more even income and wealth distributions, as the number of families that are able to invest sufficiently in the human capital (i.e. education) of their children is considerably less.

Aghion *et al.* (1999) make an argument also based on human capital. In this framework, however, individual investments in human capital face diminishing returns, with the result that focusing the ability to make these investments in relatively few hands – as in very unequal societies – produces a society where investment in human capital has a lower marginal rate of return than would be the case in a more equal society.

Alesina and Rodrik (1994) develop a 'political economy' argument, which is based on three premises (Lopez, op. cit.). First, the authors argue that redistribution restrains growth by limiting capital accumulation. Second, as taxes are generally proportional to income but government expenditure is – at least in principle – the same for all citizens, individuals will favour tax and spending frameworks that are inversely related to income. Third, the authors propose that the tax rate chosen by the government is that favoured by the median voter. Taken together, these premises suggest that in a highly unequal society, with a large proportion of the population on very low incomes, the median voter will favour high tax and spend policies. Implementation of this redistributive framework by the government will then restrain growth.

Alesina and Perotti (1996) take a sociopolitical approach, which argues that high levels of inequality encourage antisocial behaviour such as crime, which is a strong disincentive to investment, not least as it increases uncertainty about the future outcomes from the investment.

It is interesting to note that the policy implications of these approaches are very different. For Alesina and Rodrik (op. cit.), it is redistribution that reduces growth, whereas from both the sociopolitical and credit constraint positions, inequality itself imposes a more direct restraint on growth, which would be mitigated by redistributive policies. On this point, the empirical evidence[6] is more supportive of the second position: that redistribution may have a positive effect upon growth.

As with the evidence given in the previous section, the rest of the empirical work on this issue is inconclusive. As we saw, some studies would contradict the theoretical positions given above, whilst others demonstrate no link. Some, such as Alesina and Rodrik (1994) and Perotti (1996), however, find that inequality is negatively associated with growth. As with research suggesting the opposite, we should treat this finding with caution, and conclude that there is no 'iron law' of development here: growth may be fast or slow in both equal and unequal societies; clearly other factors exert greater influence, which brings us to research into the policy implications in this area.

2.2.4 Policy impacts

There is an extensive and somewhat contradictory body of work – based on cross-country regressions – which examines the impact of different variables on levels of inequality during the growth process. The results are summarised in Table 2.1. below.

As can be seen, there is little agreement in these studies. Where there is some consensus is that:

- Better education (particularly at primary and secondary levels) is associated with lower levels of inequality.
- Better infrastructure and the rule of law *may* be associated with lower levels of inequality.

Table 2.1 Findings of cross-country regressions on impact of different variables on inequality

Study	Education	Trade openness	Rule of law	FSD*	Inflation	Infrastructure quality	Size of govt.	IMF/WB Structural adjustment
Barro (2000)	—**	+	–	na	na	na	na	na
Calderon/Servén (2003)	–	na	na	+	na	–	na	na
Dollar/Kraay (2003)	na	–	–	+	+	na	+	na
Li/Zhou (1998)	—	na	na	–	+	na	–	na
Lundberg/Squire (2003)	—	+	na	na	+	na	na	na
Kraay (2004)	0	0	0	0	0	0	0	0
Lopez (2004)	—	+	na	+	+	–	+	na
Easterly (2001)	na	na	na	na	na	na	na	+

Source: Lopez 2005.

* Financial sector development. ** Barro (2000) finds that primary and secondary education is associated with lower inequality, but university education is associated with higher levels of inequality.

- Higher levels of inflation are associated with higher levels of inequality.
- Structural adjustment programmes *may* be associated with higher levels of inequality.[7]

For the rest, the studies provide contradictory evidence. In some, an increase in the variable increases inequality, in others it reduces it. Though far from conclusive, the weight of evidence of these studies suggests that:

- Openness to trade *may* increase inequality.
- Financial sector development *may* increase inequality.
- 'Big government' *may* increase inequality.
- Effective implementation of the rule of law *may* reduce inequality.

Other researchers have undertaken country-level case studies to investigate the same issues, largely based on household survey data.[8] However, despite the limited consensus reached in the cross-country studies above, these country-level studies find that, even here, we cannot be sure that 'policy X will result in outcome Y'. Rather, even in terms of the variables seen as reducing inequality – macro stability, good infrastructure, etc. – the actual policy outcomes of reforms in this area do not necessarily produce the same result as is found in the aggregate data. As ever, the individual circumstances of the country have a greater effect on policy outcomes than does the specific policy employed (Lopez, 2005).

Where there is some agreement in these country studies, however, is that initial conditions are very important. It would seem – as is intuitively likely – that the potential of the poor to take advantage of the opportunities presented by growth has a strong influence on the subsequent trends in inequality. However, the factors that determine this potential – be they levels of education, land distribution or infrastructure – do not have equal importance in all countries.

We can therefore say that (a) growth of any type is generally good for the poor, and (b) certain forms of growth disproportionately benefit the poor. This is known as 'pro-poor' growth, and there remains considerable debate as to whether the aim should be to maximise general growth or to maximise pro-poor growth. For example, Dollar and Kraay (2001) find that much of what is considered to be specifically pro-poor forms of growth has little if any impact on poverty levels over and above that achieved through general growth.

2.2.5 Summary of linkages between growth, poverty and inequality

As was stressed at the outset of this chapter: while we do not know everything, we do know some things. The research that has been discussed has amply illustrated these points, particularly the first one perhaps. That is to say, much of the work in this area is contradictory, and there are few areas of consensus.

However, we can say the following:

- Growth will generally lead to a reduction in poverty.
- The magnitude of this impact – the growth elasticity of poverty – will depend strongly on initial levels of inequality, as well as on the general potential for the poor to take advantage of the opportunities presented by growth.
- Pro-poor growth can be defined in a number of ways. For some, any growth that raises the incomes of the poor can be defined as pro-poor. For others, the poor must disproportionately benefit from the proceeds of growth for it to be described as pro-poor.
- Some studies find that inequality is supportive of growth, while others find the opposite, and yet others find no relationship. There does not appear to be a stable relationship that holds for all countries at all times.
- The previously widely held view that growth will widen inequality in its early stages is no longer accepted. Recent studies all find there to be no stable relationship in this regard.
- Some factors are associated with widening inequality during the growth process: particularly, high inflation and *possibly* structural adjustment programmes, openness to trade and financial sector development.
- Some factors are associated with decreasing inequality during the growth process: particularly, good education and possibly good infrastructure and the rule of law.

Therefore, while we know that growth reduces poverty, we don't know by how much. The growth elasticity of poverty at the country level (and within the country) will be determined by a complex array of factors, including initial conditions and subsequent policy directions. What we do know, however, is that we need the growth in the first place for these secondary factors to have any relevance.

Accordingly, the next section explores what we know about the foundations and drivers of growth. This will be followed by a final section linking this research and evidence to the main topic of this book: financial sector development and how this is related to growth and, ultimately, poverty reduction in developing countries.

2.3 Growth theory: what we know and what we don't

The concept of economic growth has been with us for many centuries, but for much of this period little in the way of pure theorising was done on the subject. Prior to the European enlightenment, it was widely thought that growth was a matter of exploiting resources to one's own advantage – i.e. buying or acquiring them cheaply and processing the raw materials to add value, before selling the end product at a profit. Notions of the benefits of open competition were to come much later, and for a long period growth was broadly seen as being at the expense of another party; either those deprived of the raw material or those sold the expensive final product. That is, growth was, at least in part, a zero sum game, where to 'beggar your neighbour' was the surest route to success.

This 'mercantilist' approach was to be turned on its head, however, by the work of first Adam Smith, and then David Ricardo. Smith (1776) argued that growth was a product of increasing productivity, which in turn was the result of the division of labour and the increased specialisation – and thus higher productivity – that this process produced. Furthermore, not only did the division of labour increase productivity in the production of goods (and services), it also allowed a surplus to be generated (i.e. beyond the immediate needs of the individual producer) that could be profitably traded with other producers specialising in the production of other goods.

Ricardo (1817) developed a rigorous, and in some ways pessimistic, but in other ways prescient, theory of growth. Ricardo was concerned that the 'law of diminishing returns' would eventually lead to the end of growth and a 'steady state' economy. However, this logical end to his economic system could be avoided by increasing technical progress and/or international trade. For Ricardo, the second of these was the most important, and his famous theory of 'comparative advantage' encapsulated his powerful insight that trade was far from a zero sum game. On the contrary, Ricardo showed that free trade was of benefit to all parties. Differing levels of productivity of the factors of production – land, labour and capital – between countries ensured that if each country specialised in the production of goods in which it had a comparative advantage, total output would be maximised and mutually beneficial trade could be established.

Thus, for both Smith and Ricardo, specialisation and the division of labour leads to increasing productivity and growth – though for Ricardo this is subject to diminishing returns – and trade both within and between countries enables the benefits of this specialisation to be diffused throughout society, raising output, welfare and growth.

Modern growth theory[9] is, in large part, an extension of the work of these originators of classical economics. The following sections will sketch out the main developments that occurred in growth theory in the twentieth century, before linking this to recent findings on the relationship between financial sector development and growth, and concluding with a summary of what we know about the relationship between financial sector development and growth.

2.3.1 The Harrod-Domar growth model and its long-term developmental impact

The Harrod-Domar model (HDM) was developed independently by R. F. Harrod and E. D. Domar in the l930s, and was the dominant growth model in development economics until the late 1950s. Furthermore, as we shall see, aspects of the HDM have retained their importance even to the present day, despite the fact that the model itself is now widely discredited.

The fundamental prediction of the HDM is that national growth rates are directly proportional to the level of investment in the economy. The model makes a number of important assumptions to arrive at this prediction:

- Production results from the combination of labour and capital, which are in fixed proportions – i.e. more capital cannot be substituted for labour.
- There is no constraint on the supply of labour (particularly in developing countries with abundant supplies of workers, not least those moving from rural to urban areas).
- Physical capital is constrained (particularly in developing countries, which tend to have low savings rates and therefore low rates of investment in physical capital).
- The productivity of capital (the 'capital-output ratio') is fixed. Consequently, there are 'constant returns to scale'.
- More physical capital is therefore the only means to generate growth, and net investment leads to more capital accumulation, which generates higher output and income.
- Ultimately, higher income allows higher levels of saving, which feeds back into higher investment.

Technically, the HDM is very straightforward. The growth rate of GDP can be written as:

$$G(Y) = \Delta Y/Y$$

Where:
  Y = GDP.

To estimate the growth rate [G(Y)] the first step is to estimate the 'incremental capital-output ratio' (ICOR), which measures the productivity of capital. That is, how much additional output is achieved by employing one additional unit of capital?

$$ICOR = \Delta K/\Delta Y$$

Where:
  K = capital stock.

A high ICOR value implies that large increases in the capital stock are needed to produce small increases in output. Or, put another way, that the marginal productivity of capital is low.

As described in the HDM assumptions above, physical capital is taken to be the only constraint on increased production, so that investment (I) equates with the change in the stock of capital:

$$I = \Delta K$$

However, investment in the HDM is equal to national savings (S), which in turn is equal to the savings rate (S^r) multiplied by national income (Y):

$$I = S = S^r * Y$$

Therefore:

$$ICOR = S^r * Y / \Delta Y$$

Rearranging the terms gives:

$$G(Y) = \Delta Y / Y = S^r / ICOR$$

Therefore, as we can see, the rate of growth of the economy is simply the savings rate (and therefore the rate of investment) divided by the ICOR (the measure of the productiveness of the capital that these savings and investment produce). In basic terms, a country with a savings rate of 20% and an ICOR of 4 would be expected to grow at a rate of 5% per year.

A key implication of the HDM is that, in order to kick-start growth, countries with low savings rates should borrow to invest in physical capital, which will trigger a virtuous circle of growth, rising incomes, higher savings, higher investment in physical capital and, therefore, further increases in growth rates.

In the immediate post-war period, development economists began to look in earnest at means of reducing poverty in the developing world, with their preferred mechanism being to raise rates of economic growth. The HDM assumption that there was no constraint on the supply of labour looked eminently plausible at this time, where underemployment was the norm. Furthermore, as Easterly (1997) points out, the rapid industrialisation of the Soviet Union had been driven by forced savings and investment in physical capital, seeming to confirm the validity of the HDM.[10]

Taking the lead from Sir Arthur Lewis (1955), it was assumed that, to achieve meaningful growth (i.e. real per capita growth where GDP growth is greater than population growth by a significant margin) investment in the economy, the rate of investment would have to rise to somewhere around 12% of GDP. Assuming an ICOR of 4 – which was long the general assumption – this would result in growth of 3% per year.

However, if the savings rate (and therefore the investment rate) of the economy was just 4%, then growth would be 1%: below the rate of population growth and therefore producing falling per capita incomes. The difference between the 12% investment rate needed and the 4% actual savings and investment rate was termed the 'financing gap'. And it is here that we find the birth of the system of international aid (now termed 'official development assistance' [ODA]).

It was assumed that there was no prospect of developing countries being able to mobilise sufficient domestic resources to reach the 12% investment rate, which led to the conclusion that external resources from industrialised countries could fill this financing gap, until a self-reinforcing process of faster growth, higher incomes, higher savings rates and more domestically financed investment could be established. Aid, from the outset, was therefore seen as a transitional mechanism to 'kick-start' the process leading to this virtuous circle.

The notion that at some point growth would become self-reinforcing relies on Rostow's (1960) formulation in *The Stages of Economic Growth*. Rostow argued that the key stage was one of 'take-off' where growth became self-sustaining, and the key variable determining when 'take-off' would be reached was the level of investment in the economy approaching 10% of GDP (Easterly, op. cit.).

From a political economy perspective, it is important to remember – though hard to imagine today – that in the post-war era, many economists feared that capitalist economies would be unable to match the growth rates of the communist Soviet Union, not least because of its ability to marshal high levels of domestic savings and employ them as investments in physical capital on a mass scale. Politically, therefore, those such as Rostow who argued for high levels of aid to developing countries were able to play on fears that these countries would turn to communism rather than capitalism. As we shall see in later chapters – particularly regarding the birth of the regional development banks – many aspects of 'development' at this time were as much, if not more, a result of the need to prevent poor countries turning to communism, as they were the result of any particular altruism.

However, the arguments, whatever they were, worked. In the US, Kennedy increased the aid budget substantially, and by the presidency of Lyndon Johnson, US aid had reached its historic high of 0.6% of GDP (Easterly, op. cit.).

Box 2.4 Aid, East Asia and the Cold War

Aid is sometimes referred to as a form of 'soft power', as opposed to 'hard' military power. This is certainly not a new phenomenon, however. After the Second World War, the United States became increasingly alarmed at the rise of communism, as one country after another appeared to fall under its sway. As well as concerns over the ideological appeal of communism, a key factor was its then economic success, which was exemplified by the growth and technical advances of the Soviet Union.

The Cold War was perhaps hottest in East and South East Asia, the locations of both the Korean and Vietnam Wars. The US with its regional ally Japan saw it as essential to create successful capitalist economies in the region, to act as a bulwark, and overseas aid was a key component of this. As can be seen from the figure, aid flows to South Korea in the 1960s were huge, contributing more than 70% of the cost of total fixed investments in the early 1960s – this compares with a figure closer to 5% for low- and middle-income countries as a group.

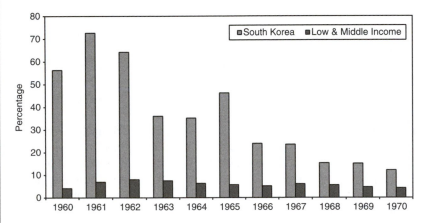

Aid as a proportion of total capital investment, 1960–1970.

Furthermore, this intervention was not restricted to South Korea, nor just to aid, as Benedict Anderson (1998) points out:

> In every important country of South-East Asia, with the exception of Indonesia, there were major, sustained Communist insurrections, and Indonesia, in the early Sixties, had the largest legal Communist party in the world outside the socialist bloc. In all these states, except Malaysia, which was still a colony, the Americans intervened politically, economically, militarily and culturally on a massive scale. The notorious domino theory was invented specifically for South-East Asia. To shore up the line of teetering dominos, Washington made every effort to create loyal, capitalistically prosperous, authoritarian and anti-Communist regimes – typically, but not invariably, dominated by the military. Each disaster only encouraged Washington to put more muscle and money behind its remaining political allies. No world region received more aid.

Furthermore, the export-led growth strategy employed in East and Southeast Asia could not have worked if the major export markets (particularly the US) had not been prepared to grant access to their markets, without insisting on reciprocal access to the Asian markets. This willingness to subordinate immediate economic interests to the strategic goal of creating capitalist 'paragons' in Asia was clearly an important factor in determining their success.

As we have seen, the 'financing gap' approach based on the HDM was supposed to be a time-limited injection of funds for investment to boost growth and achieve 'take-off'. Consequently, there was little thought put into the problems of the debt burden that developing countries were taking on, as it was assumed that growth in the future would be more than sufficient to cover this.

In practice, however, growth rates in much of the developing world did not respond as predicted to the influx of external financing, leading to the worst of all worlds: sluggish or even negative growth in per capita incomes, coupled with rising levels of indebtedness. The demise of the HDM as the pre-eminent growth model was therefore a result of the policies based on it to achieve their objectives. The model was seen to have failed.

Despite this, however, development economists – particularly those at the World Bank – continued to base their estimates of required external financing needed in developing countries on the 'financing gap' described above. Despite the growing complexity of the Bank's models – culminating in the Revised Minimum Standard Model (RMSM) – the financing gap was effectively calculated in exactly the same way as above (Easterly, op. cit.) To the best of my knowledge, the RMSM remains in use today, despite the manifest failings of the growth model from which it is derived.

Although it was ultimately to founder on practical grounds – i.e. it didn't work – the HDM had long been superseded on theoretical grounds. The seminal contribution in this regard was the neo-classical growth model (NCM), developed in the 1950s by Robert Solow.

Box 2.5 Robert Solow

The American economist Robert Solow was born in 1924 and is principally known as the founding father of neo-classical growth theory, which is discussed below. Solow developed his early interests in statistics and probability while studying under Leontief at Harvard, but his interests moved more towards macroeconomics when he joined MIT in 1949. During the next half century Solow worked – often in conjunction with Paul Samuelson – on a range of subjects, including capital theory and the famous Philips curve, which sought to describe the statistical relationship between the rates of unemployment and inflation as a trade-off where unemployment above a certain threshold leads to increased rates of inflation.

2.3.2 Solow's neo-classical growth model

An important assumption in the HDM is that capital and labour are employed in fixed proportions (more capital cannot be substituted for labour) and that the capital-output ratio (i.e. the quantity of output resulting from the employment of a given quantity of capital) is fixed. That is, there are 'constant returns to capital'.

In the 1950s Robert Solow adapted this model by relaxing these unrealistic assumptions of fixed ratios of capital-labour and capital-output. In Solow's model it is possible to vary the proportions of capital and labour employed, and, crucially, he assumed diminishing returns to capital (not constant returns as in the HDM).

Therefore, as each unit of capital is added, the marginal increase in output falls. Ultimately, the increase in output will fall to the extent that the economy's growth rate will equal the rate of growth of the population. If population growth is zero, economic growth will therefore also be zero.

In the Solow model, the production function can be written as follows:

$$Y = A*F(K,H,E*L)$$

Where:
- Y   = income/output
- A   = technological progress
- F   = a function of
- K   = capital
- H   = human capital
- E   = productivity of labour
- L   = labour force.

And the evolution of the capital stock is determined by:

$$\Delta K = S^r*F(K,H,E*L) - dK$$

Where:
- d   = depreciation rate.

As can be seen from the equations above, Solow's model was able to avoid reaching this 'end-state' by incorporating technological progress (A). Thus, in the absence of technological progress, output (growth) is a function of physical and human capital accumulation – which inevitably face diminishing – and the size of the population, or labour force (L). However, Solow allows technological advances to raise the productivity of capital – the capital output ratio – therefore enabling growth to be maintained at a level above the rate of population growth.

As is clear from the first equation, however, Solow assumed that techno-logical progress was exogenous to the model. That is to say, technological progress was viewed as something that is not the result of internal economic forces in society (i.e. endogenous), but is an external input.

The Solow model is therefore able to explain the aspects of growth which result from increases in the stock of physical and human capital and the labour force, but not that resulting from technological change. This unexplained portion was termed the 'Solow residual' and was an increasing source of dissatisfaction with Solow's model amongst economists. This is not surpris-ing, as estimates suggested that the share of growth accounted for by the Solow residual was not small. Quite the opposite. Economists increasingly came to see technical change as the key determinant of divergent growth rates between countries, and were understandably dissatisfied with a growth model that was unable to explain the determinants of this progress.

It is interesting to note that both the HDM and the NCM predicted that, under the right circumstances, higher growth in developing countries would enable them to catch up with the industrialised economies. In the HDM this would be achieved by raising investment rates sufficiently to achieve 'take-off' growth. In the NCM, in contrast, developing countries can inherently grow quicker as they start from a lower position, so that the process of diminishing returns to capital takes longer to kick in.

From a development perspective, the replacement of the HDM with the Solow model brought things to something of a dead-end, however. Whereas growth could be 'created' in the HDM through investment in physical capital, the NCM had very little to say about how growth could be increased. Indeed, as growth was largely viewed as a product of technological progress, which was exogenously determined, policy-makers could do little more than sit and wait for this 'manna from heaven' to fall into their laps.

Unsurprisingly, given that neither the HDM or the NCM could adequately explain the divergent growth experiences of developed and developing coun-tries, the focus shifted to developing models that *were* able to do this. The key aim, in all of this, was to discover how to make technological change inherent – or endogenous – to the growth process.

2.3.3 Endogenous growth models and new growth theory

Pritchett (2006) explains how the impasse reached in growth theory by the early 1980s coincided with the findings of the state-of-the-art macroeconomic models of the time, which suggested that policy-makers could do nothing to influence the rate of technical progress in the economy.

The immediate appeal of the approach that was to be termed New Growth Theory (NGT) was therefore that it opened up the possibility that the drivers of growth were endogenous to the economy, and could indeed be influenced by policy. Given this, it is unsurprising that national policy-makers and policy advisors in the international financial institutions seized upon this growing body of literature.

Although NGT can be said to have emerged in its modern form in the mid- to late 1980s, there were some earlier attempts to endogenise the drivers of growth. For example, Arrow (1962) stressed the key role played by knowledge in the generation and maintenance of growth, and argued that 'learning by doing' was a key part of this process. Despite the fact that, with very few exceptions, Arrow's work remained outside the mainstream of growth theory, the emphasis he placed upon knowledge as the key driver of growth was later to be picked up and developed by the new growth theorists.

The fathers of NGT are widely recognised to be Romer (1986) and Lucas (1988). Both assumed that, at the firm level, productivity – and therefore growth – is a function of the level of knowledge. This knowledge is assumed to have two sources. First, there is that which is generated within the firm as the result of research and development (R&D). Second, this firm-level knowledge invariably spills over to the wider economy adding to the existing stock of knowledge, which all other firms may draw upon.

The presence of these 'spillover effects' makes technological change integral to the growth process, and allows the possibility of increasing returns to scale – as opposed to the constant returns in the HDM, and the decreasing returns in the NCM.

Thus, unlike its predecessors, NGT was able to incorporate technological progress into the model. The increasing returns to scale that NGT predicts is therefore the result of research and development, innovation by firms, and spillovers to the wider economy leading to yet more R&D, innovation and so on by other firms.

Lucas (1988) reaches the same conclusions as Romer, but emphasised the importance of human capital accumulation as a driver of growth. Like Romer (1986), however, he argued that investment in R&D and the development of human capital would be suboptimal in market economies, as the private benefits to the investing firms are less than the public benefits to society at large.

Therefore, from the outset, NGT raised the possibility that policy-makers could affect the rate of technological progress by investing in R&D and making the knowledge freely available, but also by investing in human capital development.

Grossman and Helpman (1991) used an NGT approach to explain divergent rates of growth internationally, which are shown below for the developing regions from 1960 to 2005.

As can be seen, the divergence in performance in terms of growth is very wide between regions (as well as being highly volatile within them). Grossman and Helpman (op. cit.) hypothesised that the regional divergence could be explained if Ricardian comparative advantage is viewed as dynamic, rather than static. That is, some types of commercial activity have greater scope for productivity improvements than others. Consequently, a country that specialised in such an activity, and invested heavily in R&D in this area, could

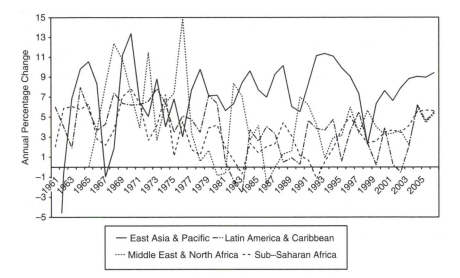

Figure 2.1. Regional GDP growth rates, 1960–2006.

see its comparative advantage increase over time, and would grow faster by capitalising on the greater scope for productivity improvements within its specialist sectors.

As was highlighted above, policy advisors within the IFIs seized upon this new research, and began building in aspects of NGT into structural adjustment programmes from the late 1980s. However, as Pritchett (2006) points out, it soon became clear that the approach was entirely unsuitable for developing countries in many ways. NGT was, at its heart, focused upon changing the 'technological frontier' over the very long term. However, this was 'not particularly useful for developing countries, whose primary interest was in restoring short-term economic growth and accelerating technological catch-up by adapting known innovations' (Prichett, op. cit.).

However, the real effect of NGT from a development (and development finance) perspective was that it unlocked the door for researchers to explore other endogenous features of economies that could be positively (or negatively) associated with growth. Researchers hoped to isolate the drivers of growth, which could be directly addressed to boost growth and reduce poverty in the developing world.

The next section will review these efforts, particularly in relation to the financial sector.

2.4 From new growth theory to financial sector development

Given these developments in growth theory, a whole new direction of research opened up in the 1990s. Pritchett (2006) describes how researchers – particularly in the World Bank – began to run numerous cross-country regressions with growth as the dependent variable (on the left-hand side of the equation) and endogenous factors on the right hand side of the equation, as the explanatory variables.

As we shall see, this work has produced some clear results. However, Pritchett (op. cit.) urges caution in the interpretation of these results. First, regressions of this form may be able to establish the existence of a negative relationship between growth and, say, corruption, but specific policies do not flow directly from this. Second, as with all cross-country studies of this type, the idiosyncratic characteristics of each country may, to some extent, cancel each other out, so that the aggregated results do not hold at the country level for many individual countries. Third, the regressions may establish a long-term relationship – even a causal one – but this says nothing about where the 'turning points' in the process are, or how they can be triggered. That is, sound institutions are positively correlated with higher growth rates over a long period (up to thirty years), but this does not tell policy-makers what specific reforms could be implemented in the short term to lead to an acceleration of growth.

Fourth, and perhaps most importantly, the results of this work have largely failed to explain the divergent growth experience of the developing regions in the 1990s. On the negative side, the decade was characterised by a series of severe financial crises, which had a devastating impact upon growth rates. These could neither be predicted nor explained by this body of work. On the positive side, a number of countries – notably China, India and Vietnam – performed very well in terms of growth, but again this could not be explained by the results of the regressions that have been described.

Therefore, as has been stressed throughout this chapter, it is clear that cross-country regressions of the kind detailed below can offer some insight into those endogenous features of the economy that may encourage (or discourage) growth. However, there will be countries that have all the 'right elements' in this sense, yet do not see accelerating growth, and others where seemingly few of the 'necessary' preconditions for growth are in place, yet growth does accelerate. As ever, policies cannot be implemented on one-size-fits-all basis, but need to be tailored for the different circumstances of each country.

With these caveats in mind, the final section of this chapter considers what we can say about the relationship between the elements of developing countries' financial systems and the rate of economic growth of these economies.

2.4.1 Finance and growth

Although this section focuses on the relationship between financial sector development (FSD) and growth, it is worth noting that, for many observers, *the* key variable in determining the divergent rates of growth that developing countries have seen is the quality of their institutions. The conclusion that 'institutions rule' was reached by Rodrik, Subramanian and Trebbi (2004), who demonstrated that the primary long-term determinant of a country's level of income was the quality of its institutions. Clearly, it is difficult to judge institutional quality in this sense, and the term 'institution' can also be defined either narrowly or broadly, but for the authors, it is these internal features of an economy – rather than their geographical location or integration in the world economy, for example – that determine long-term growth rates.

In addition to the political, legal and administrative framework, a country's financial infrastructure and institutions have also been associated with long-term growth. Although the idea that the financial system is a key driver of growth has, as we have seen, only come to receive attention relatively recently, it is by no means a new concept.

At the beginning of the twentieth century, Joseph Schumpeter[11] stressed the important role played by the banking system in allocating savings towards the most productive use, and thereby improving productivity and thus economic growth rates.

Box 2.6 Joseph Schumpeter

Joseph Alois Schumpeter (1883–1950) was an Austrian-born economist and political scientist, who is widely regarded as being one of the most influential political economists of the twentieth century. Schumpeter coined the phrase 'creative destruction' to describe the processes of capitalist development and was particularly influential with regard to the theory of business cycles. Schumpeter was critical of the approach taken by mainstream neo-classical economists, seeing it as too abstracted and idealised to be capable of capturing reality. Indeed, Schumpeter pointed out that 'equilibrium' in the standard 'Walrasian' sense is inherently static and so has nothing to say about economic growth and development. For Schumpeter, it is the entrepreneur who drives economic progress: although many will fail, some will succeed (i.e. creative destruction, where old methods and practices are continually replaced by new methods). Thus capitalist growth is maintained. However, Schumpeter also argued – like Marx – that capitalism contained the seeds of its own demise. Ultimately, the development of an educated middle class and an intellectual elite would lead – in a democracy – to the implementation of policies inimical to the entrepreneur. Though not a socialist on principled grounds, Schumpeter predicted that some form of socialism was therefore the destination of modern capitalism.

In the 1950s, Arthur Lewis[12] argued that the relationship between economic growth and financial development ran in both directions. That is, an increasingly sophisticated financial sector developed as the economy grew (growth caused financial sector development), and itself acted as a spur to further economic growth (financial sector development caused economic growth). This causality question remains a key issue, as we shall see below.

In the late 1960s Raymond Goldsmith[13] also emphasised the connection between the real and financial sectors, arguing that financial markets encourage growth through efficiently allocating resources through time.

What has more recent research to say on the process through which FSD may spur growth, however? In this regard, two channels are generally identified:

1   through its impact on capital accumulation, both human and physical;
2   through its impact on the rate of technological progress.

Both of these channels may facilitate growth through the intermediation of savings and their allocation to productive use within the economy, through investment in physical capital, education or training on the one hand, or through research and development on the other.

The key actors in this process are third-party financial intermediaries. Levine (1997) identifies five key functions of these institutions that enable them to perform this role:

1   the mobilisation of savings;
2   facilitating the management of risk;
3   obtaining and filtering information on investment opportunities. (i.e. *ex ante* monitoring);
4   monitoring the use of funds (i.e. *ex post* monitoring);
5   facilitating the exchange of goods and services.

As well as these features, financial sector development may also be a spur to economic growth through its impact on transaction costs, which increases the economic viability of many productive ventures. That is, the higher the transaction costs involved in a commercial venture then the higher the rate of return needed to make the venture viable. As transaction costs fall, therefore, ventures that were previously not viable, in this sense, increasingly become so.

Considerable empirical research has shown a strong correlation between FSD and economic growth. However, until fairly recently it has not been clear which direction this causality flows in. That is, as countries grow richer does this cause their financial sector to develop? Or, does the development of the financial sector itself cause countries to grow richer (i.e. economic growth to increase)?

The World Bank has undertaken extensive research into this issue since the early 1990s, largely in the form of the cross-country regressions described above. The results suggest strongly that FSD does indeed cause growth rates to rise – though this does not mean that economic growth does not also cause financial sector development as a positive feedback.

The size of the banking sector and size and liquidity of the capital markets are both strongly correlated with growth in GDP and can be shown to 'cause' this growth.[14] These findings support earlier work by King and Levine (1993), which looked at whether the degree of financial depth[15] that existed in the 1960s could predict the level of economic growth, capital accumulation and productivity advances over the following thirty years. The authors find that this is indeed the case, and that the correlation between the level of initial financial depth and the later level of national income is highly significant.

For example, financial depth in Bolivia in 1960 was 10% of GDP, compared to a developing country average of 23% at this time. The study finds that if Bolivia had exhibited this average level of financial depth in 1960, the country would have grown 0.4% faster per year, resulting in a GDP 13% higher than was actually the case in 1990.

Calderon and Liu (2003) study the period 1960–1994 for 109 countries and also find a strong causal link. However, while their study suggests the direction of causality runs both ways, financial sector development has a stronger effect on growth than does growth on financial development, particularly in developing countries. Indeed, the authors find that causality in this direction accounts for 84% of the total relationship, against 57% in industrialised economies over a ten-year period.[16]

Although this work is very much ongoing, the evidence gathered to date strongly suggests that financial sector development has a real impact on economic growth rates, as modern growth theory predicts. Furthermore, this impact appears to be significantly greater in developing than developed economies.

What is the evidence on financial sector development on poverty reduction, though?

2.4.2 *Financial sector development and poverty reduction*

Both theory and empirical evidence suggest that financial sector development can reduce poverty via two separate channels:

1   indirectly, through its positive impact on economic growth rates, which in general terms causes a reduction in poverty levels, though, as we have seen, the extent of this impact may vary widely;
2   directly, through providing financial services to the poor.

On this second point, the UK's Department for International Development (DFID) has the following to say:

> By enabling the poor to draw down accumulated savings and/or borrow to invest in income-enhancing assets (including human assets, e.g.

through health and education) and start micro-enterprises, wider access to financial services generates employment, increases incomes and reduces poverty . . . By enabling the poor to save in a secure place, the provision of bank accounts (or other savings facilities) and insurance allows the poor to establish a buffer against shocks, thus reducing vulnerability and minimising the need for other coping strategies such as asset sales that may damage long-term income prospects.[17]

In addition to these positive impacts that financial sector development can have on poverty levels, it is important to stress that the opposite is also true. Just as the provision of financial services to the poor can directly reduce poverty, the absence of these services is an important component in perpetuating high levels of poverty.

At the macro level there is also the issue of financial crises in developing countries. It is undoubtedly the case that any financial system – no matter how well developed and sophisticated – could fall victim to such a crisis under certain conditions. However, it is equally true that the robustness and level of development of the financial system also plays a key role in preventing (or facilitating) the onset of such crises. Furthermore, the extent of financial sector development will also strongly affect the transmission, depth and duration of any crisis should it occur.

This is an extremely important point, as demonstrated by evidence that currency and banking crises have reduced the average income of developing countries by 25% in the last quarter of the twentieth century (Eichengreen, 2004).

Finally, research by Jalilian and Kirkpatrick (2002) which attempts to quantify the impact on poverty levels of financial sector development finds that each positive unit change in financial sector development increases the growth prospects of the poor in developing countries by 0.4%.

Concluding remarks

In this chapter we have explored the relationship between economic growth, financial sector development and poverty reduction. Our end point has been the impact of financial sector development on levels of poverty, and our starting point was the relationship between economic growth and poverty.

As you progress through this book this theme will be stressed at each stage: the 'end' that we are trying to achieve is poverty reduction – and ultimately elimination – in developing countries, coupled with high and rising living standards and a good quality of life.

We have seen that growth – to a greater or lesser extent, depending upon many individual features of developing countries – is generally associated with reductions in poverty levels. We have also seen that financial sector development is positively associated with higher rates of growth, and therefore ultimately lower levels of poverty. Furthermore, we have seen that financial sector development can directly improve the lives of the poor by providing access to financial services. This much we know.

However, the chapter has also contained many caveats about the sometimes shaky foundations of this 'knowledge', and stressed the importance of avoiding simplistic, one-size-fits-all policy recommendations in the developing world.

What we know provides a guide to what can be done. However, there are – and surely will be again – countries that have prospered by taking an unorthodox route, and all too many that have tried diligently to implement orthodox policies, only to see growth fail to take off as predicted.

With this in mind, and with our end goal clearly defined, we are ready to take the next step in exploring the world of development finance.

3 Financial repression, liberalisation and growth

Introduction

In the previous chapter we examined the relationship between economic growth, financial sector development and poverty reduction. We saw that the relationships between these factors are far from straightforward: *in general*, economic growth will reduce poverty – though the strength of this relationship will vary significantly – and, *in general*, financial sector development (FSD) will lead to higher rates of economic growth, though again the strength of this relationship will differ markedly from country to country.

We also explored some of the theoretical foundations of these relationships and saw that FSD can affect growth – and hence poverty reduction – via a number of direct and indirect channels. Fundamentally, however, the rationale has not changed significantly since the work of Joseph Schumpeter at the beginning of the last century: a well-developed financial sector mobilises and intermediates surplus capital (i.e. savings) and allocates this capital to its most productive uses within the economy. The result? Higher productivity and higher rates of economic growth.

For Eatwell (1997), these effects are derived from a combination of two theoretical positions. The first of these is the 'fundamental theorem of welfare economics', which states that competitive markets produce 'Pareto optimal equlibria'. The second is the efficient market hypothesis that was introduced in Chapter 1, and which states that financial markets use information efficiently and allocate resources optimally. We also saw, however, that the efficient market hypothesis, at least in its strong form, is certainly not universally accepted, either theoretically or empirically. Furthermore, while it can be demonstrated that competitive markets are Pareto optimal in a theoretical sense, the 'perfection' of the competition required to produce this result is not a phenomenon that is seen in the real world.

However, if we put these caveats to one side for now – though we return to both in this chapter and later in the book – it is clearly the case that, even in theory, the financial system can only perform this role if prices accurately reflect underlying economic fundamentals, thereby allowing optimal allocations to be made on the basis of accurate price signals. As we saw in Chapter

1, however, the tenets of the 'efficient market hypothesis' have been regularly challenged, not least by those who point to the evidence of market movements and their relationship – or lack of it – with underlying economic fundamentals.

Box 3.1 Irrational exuberance

The phrase 'irrational exuberance' first entered the lexicon in December 1996, when it was used by the then Chairman of the Federal Reserve, Alan Greenspan, at a speech to the American Enterprise Institute. Greenspan posed the question of how was it possible to know whether asset prices had been driven up to unjustifiable levels by a period of irrational exuberance?

Theoretically of course, this should not happen. Friedman's 'rational arbitrageurs' would step in to sell overvalued assets or buy undervalued assets, thus ensuring the prices remained at or near their equilibrium 'fair value'. In practice, however, the facts suggest otherwise: as Robert Schiller has pointed out, fundamentals do not change to anything like the same extent as do the asset prices that are supposed to reflect them. Although the immediate aftermath of Greenspan's comments saw stock markets fall sharply round the world, they were soon to recover – notwithstanding the Asian crisis of 1997/8.

Indeed, this was the time when the 'dotcom' bubble began to really get under way, which would appear to represent the greatest example of irrational exuberance we have seen in recent times. However, as was discussed in Chapter 1, this is certainly not a new phenomenon: from the 'tulipmania' of the seventeenth century (where the price of tulip bulbs rose by twenty times in a month, culminating in the sale of one bulb for nearly US$80,000 in today's money) to the South Sea Bubble in the eighteenth century (where Isaac Newton lost £20,000 and commented that, 'I can calculate the motions of heavenly bodies, but not the madness of people').

The psychology of such episodes is fascinating and suggests that we are not always the rational calculating machines that orthodox economic theory would suggest. As was discussed in Chapter 1, researchers in cognitive psychology and behavioural finance have shown that, in reality, people use simple rules of thumb when making their decisions – that an upward price trend will continue, for example – rather than carefully weighing the evidence. In normal times, this approximates to basing decisions on changes in underlying fundamentals, but once a 'mania' gets going it is both difficult to stop and, as history teaches us, very difficult indeed to avoid the temptation to get on the bandwagon.

For proponents of financial liberalisation, the key 'price' was the level of interest rates. In the early 1970s two researchers independently stressed that, in many countries, prices and particularly interest rates were certainly not set in this way. Many financial variables were not determined by the interplay of open markets, but were directly controlled by the state. Furthermore, credit was not allocated to its most productive use – in the sense that capital flowed to projects with the highest rate of return on a straight commercial basis – but was again directly controlled by governments who channelled it to favoured sectors.

Robert McKinnon and Edward Shaw argued that this *financial repression* was directly responsible for economic growth being lower than would otherwise have been the case, for it prevented the financial sector being able to perform the role described above. The McKinnon-Shaw hypothesis (MSH)[1] has proven to be hugely influential since the 1970s. In many ways the MSH, and the policy implications that flow from it, can be seen as the framework within which the entire process of financial sector development has occurred over the past three decades. Indeed, for some, the liberalising policy reforms that flow from the MSH *are* financial sector development.

Consequently, this chapter will first illustrate the context in which the MSH emerged, before analysing the policy reforms that have been implemented in the light of it. The final piece of this jigsaw is then to assess the extent to which these reforms have achieved the results that were predicted, and then to tease out the implications for the future of development finance in this regard.

3.1 Financial repression

By 'financial repression', we mean the replacement of market mechanisms by direct government intervention in the determining of the level of financial variables and the allocation of credit at prices determined by the state. Despite the fact that the term was first coined in the 1970s, practices of this kind were certainly not new. Indeed, in many ways the opposite is the case. Today's orthodoxy, where financial systems and markets increasingly operate without direct government intervention – at least in the Anglo-Saxon economies – is the novel approach. Historically, with the exception of limited periods of relative liberalisation, financial repression in one form or another was the norm.

Despite the historical prevalence of a variety of forms of state control over the financial system, systemic financial repression as we understand it today is a phenomenon that developed in the second half of the twentieth century. Furthermore, there was nothing random about this: the rise of systematic and widespread financial repression, where it was just as much the norm as are liberalised financial systems today, was a direct response to the circumstances of the first half of the twentieth century.

As discussed in Chapter 1, the Wall Street Crash and ensuing Great

Depression shook people's faith in the ability of unfettered markets to produce optimal outcomes. For many at the time and since, these events were important contributing factors in the genesis of the Second World War. Furthermore, the war years amply demonstrated that command economies could function efficiently and that the state could direct the economy in such a way that desirable goals – such as stability and employment – were achieved. It was these powerful trends that swept Roosevelt's 'New Deal' government to power in the 1930s, and saw Clement Atlee's Labour Party elected with a landslide in 1945.

This faith in the power of the state was also enhanced by the economic and technological achievements of the Soviet Union. Hard as it is to believe today, the 1950s and 1960s was a time when many argued that the centrally controlled communist economies would inevitably grow faster than the laissez-faire capitalist economies of the West. In this context, it was not surprising that free markets were seen as unpredictable, sub-optimal and potentially dangerous. The job of the state was therefore to control and guide the economy so that these negative effects could be avoided, and positive outcomes – which the markets left to themselves could not ensure – were produced.

The immediate post-war years saw the establishment of a system of international fixed exchange rates pegged to the US dollar, which would be policed by the newly established International Monetary Fund (IMF). International capital flows were tightly restricted, and domestically many governments intervened extensively in the economic and financial systems with the aim of maximising growth and, particularly, achieving and maintaining full employment.

For Caprio *et al.* (2001) the increasing popularity of financial repression was also related to the rise of nationalism and populism in the post-Second World War era, which was itself related to the anti-colonial movements in many developing countries. For example, restrictions on the entry of foreign financial institutions were seen as protecting the nascent domestic banking sector, while control over the allocation of credit enabled governments to ensure financing for national firms. It should also be remembered from Chapter 1 that this era saw the rise of the structuralist school of thought, which fundamentally stressed the importance of national self-determination, and the dangers of developing countries being trapped in a situation of dependence vis-à-vis the industrialised economies.

Another feature of the time was the general view that social objectives were more likely to be met if the financial system was not entirely driven by the commercial pursuit of profit. For example, caps on interest rates were often seen as a means of redistributing income, while the (often direct ownership and) control of credit institutions by government facilitated the supply of long-term, developmentally focused financing, which a commercially driven financial sector was thought unlikely to provide. This period therefore saw the birth of many public development financial institutions (ibid.).

By the 1970s, financial repression of the kind identified by McKinnon and Shaw was deeply entrenched in virtually every country. Williamson and Mahar (1998) identify six key elements of financial repression:

1   interest rates controlled by government;
2   credit controls in place;
3   barriers to entry to the financial sector in place;
4   government control of banking operations;
5   government ownership of banks;
6   international capital flows restricted.

According to this definition, financial repression was almost universal amongst developing economies in the early 1970s, as detailed in Table 3.1 below. Furthermore, while there were liberalised aspects of the financial sectors of developed economies, there was also substantial financial repression. It is somewhat surprising to note that only Germany was liberalised, or largely so, in each of the six categories given above.

As discussed above, the process of financial repression was derived – at least in principle – from a more or less coherent view of the purposes and limitations of the financial sector to achieve the objectives of government. Furthermore, many of the features of repression are strongly interrelated. For example, a cap on interest rates may preclude the efficient allocation of resources by the financial system. As a result, government intervention – and ownership – in the banking sector to drive policy and direct credit would be necessary to some degree anyway. Moreover, artificially restraining interest rates in an environment when not all countries do the same – or at least not at the same level – provides large incentives for capital flight. In the absence of controls on the outflow of capital, domestic economic actors would be likely to move their financial resources to other jurisdictions where a higher rate of interest is paid. Finally, stringent barriers to entry in the domestic financial sector are imperative if such a system is to work, since the government must retain control over all participants in the financial system if its policies are not to be undermined by competing institutions, particularly foreign-owned institutions over which they may have far less leverage.

Williamson and Mahar (1998) contrast the situation in 1973 with that of 1996. By the later period developed countries are almost entirely liberalised, with remaining restrictions being 'vestigial'. However, the change in developing countries was even more dramatic, particularly given the fact that repression was almost universal in the earlier period. In East Asia and Latin America, directed credit programmes had been largely eliminated and interest rate controls entirely removed. At this time, barriers to entry of foreign financial institutions remained in place in many countries, but since 1996 have been greatly lowered.[2]

Similarly, the share of national banking assets controlled by the state had fallen substantially by 1996, largely due to the privatisation of state banks.

Table 3.1 Extent of financial repression, 1973

Country	Credit controls	Interest rates	Entry barriers	Govt. reg. of operations	Privatised bank sector	International capital flows
United States	B:L/ S&L:R	LL	PR	L	L	LL
Canada	L	L	PR	L	L	L
Japan	R	PR	R	R	LL	R
Britain	LL	B:LL	B:LL	L	L	PR
France	PR	R	D:PR	—	PR	R
Germany	LL	L	L	—	LL	L
Italy	R	LL	PR	—	R	PR
Australia	B:R	B:R	R	—	R	R
New Zealand	R	R	R	—	PR	R
Hong Kong	L	LL	B:R/ NBFI:LL	L	L	L
Indonesia	B:R	B:R	R	R	R	LL
Korea	R	R	R	R	R	R
Malaysia	R	R	R	LL	LL	LL
Philippines	R	R	R	PR	PR	PR
Singapore	L	L	B:R/ NBFI:LL	L	L	LL
Taiwan	R	R	R	R	R	R
Thailand	R	R	R	—	PR	R
Argentina	R	R	R	—	PR	R
Brazil	R	R	R	—	PR	R
Chile	R	R	R	R	R	R
Colombia	R	R	R	—	LL	R
Mexico	R	R	R	—	LL	LL
Peru	R	R	R	—	R	R
Venezuela	R	R	R.	—	PR	PR
Egypt	R	R	FB:R	R	R	R
Israel	R	PR	R	LL	LL	R
Morocco	R	R	R	—	PR	PR
S. Africa	R	R	R	—	L	LL
Turkey	R	R	R	—	PR	R
Bangladesh	R	R	R	R	R	R
India	R	R	R	R	R	R
Nepal	R	R	R	R	R	R
Pakistan	R	R	R	R	R	R
Sri Lanka	R	R	R	R	R	R

Source: Williamson and Mahar, 1998.

(R) = repressed; (PR) = partially repressed; (L) = liberalised; (LL) = largely liberalised; (B) = banks; (NBFI) = non-bank financial institutions; (S&L) = savings and loan institutions; (F) = foreign; (D) = domestic.

For example, in the early 1970s, the Chilean and Mexican states controlled 100% of banking assets, but by the mid-1990s the figure had fallen to 14% and 18% respectively. The region where state control of the banking sector remained highest was South Asia, where 87% of India's banking sector was still state-controlled by the mid-1990s. However, even in South Asia the trend was downwards, and in all regions this process has continued since the late 1990s, and looks likely to continue to do so. Indeed, the prospect of this policy being reversed looks all but impossible in much of the developing world. Box 3.2 discusses this with respect to the former communist states of central and eastern Europe.

Box 3.2 Bank privatisations in the transition economies

By definition, the demise of communism left all the countries of the Soviet Union with entirely state-owned banking systems. The change in this situation has been dramatic since then, though more so in some countries than in others.

Number of state-owned banks

Region	1992	1995	2001
C. & E. Europe	117	111	41
CIS	73	92	43
Baltic states	11	7	3

Source: World Bank, 2003.

As we can see from the table, the privatisation of state banks has been most rapid in Central and Eastern Europe and the Baltic states and less so in the CIS countries. The World Bank is very complimentary of the progress made in the Baltic states in particular, and critical of the lack of it elsewhere, particularly the CIS. Although the removal of the state from the banking system is likely to lead to increased efficiency of the sector, there are other consequences, however.

In particular, the privatisation of banks has been very attractive to large, foreign-owned banking groups, which have steadily increased their presence in many countries in the regions considered here. By 2002, for example, 99% of Estonia's banking system was foreign-owned, with the comparable figures for the Czech Republic, Lithuania and Poland being 90%, 78.2% and 69%.

It is very likely that some foreign involvement in domestic banking systems will have positive effects, but this is not the same as having virtually the entire banking system owned by foreign banks. Regardless of the national sovereignty issues this raises, a foreign-owned banking system will be – at least in part – driven by factors not relevant to the country concerned. The history of the travails of many international banks in 2008 in the wake of the US subprime crisis, and the consequent squeeze on credit that this entails, is a very good case in point.

By way of contrast, 8.8% of the Russian banking system was foreign-owned in 2002, which is widely considered to be too low. The figure for the United States, at 19%, also offers an interesting contrast with that in some Eastern European and Baltic states.

When we consider restrictions on free capital movements, no developed countries have retained controls and with a limited number of exceptions – again focused in the South Asian region – capital accounts have been largely liberalised in most emerging market economies, with restrictions also being significantly reduced throughout the developing world.

It is clear, therefore, that virtually every country in the world has embarked – to a greater or lesser extent – on a process of financial sector liberalisation since the 1970s. Many have completely liberalised their financial sectors across all the six categories described above, while others have gone a long way in this direction. In virtually every country, however, the liberalising trend is clear.

As we shall see later in the book, some of the pressure to liberalise has been external, not least from the Bretton Woods institutions. However, it is equally true to say that even where countries have been pushed in this direction, the pushing has often been at an 'open door'. That is to say, financial repression had become increasingly associated with economic costs in many countries: liberalisation was therefore seen as a means of potentially reversing these negative effects. For Caprio *et al.* (2001), the costs associated with repression are described as follows:

1 Countries with high levels of financial repression experienced deteriorating economic performance in terms of growth.
2 Repressed financial systems saw the quality of lending in the economy decline – since this was based on non-commercial criteria – resulting in widespread bank insolvencies.
3 The goals of redistribution associated with repression and described above were not met. Rather, it was the wealthy elites in repressed economies that were able to capture the 'rents' resulting from financial repression.
4 Negative real interest rates resulted in significant capital flight and an increased dependence on external sources of capital.
5 Low real interest rates led to the excessive use of capital-intensive production techniques.
6 Credit was often directed to support inefficient state enterprises, and this process reduced or eliminated the incentives for market actors to select viable economic projects *ex ante*, and to monitor the progress of investments *ex post*.
7 All of the above contributed to deteriorating fiscal balances, a higher tendency to borrow and/or print money, leading to increasing risk of external crises in many developing countries, a number of which came to fruition.

As well as these negative effects of financial repression, advocates of liberalisation predicted that significant benefits would result. What were these benefits?

3.2 Predicted benefits of financial liberalisation

For McKinnon and Shaw, most of the negative impacts of financial repression flowed from the imposition of artificially low interest rates. For both authors capping interest rates at very low or even negative levels in real terms – i.e. after taking inflation into account – has a number of negative effects.

First, artificially low rates of interest result in national savings rates being lower than would otherwise be the case. Second, as a result, the funds available for intermediation through the banking system for investment purposes is lower than is optimal. Third, very low rates of interest make low-yielding investment opportunities more viable than would be the case with market rates, leading to an inefficient misallocation of resources.

With regard to capital account liberalisation – which increasingly became an integral part of the liberalisation 'package' from the 1980s on – the predictions relate to the efficient allocation of resources at the global level, and the positive impact this would have on both global growth and growth rates within individual countries. That is, if all countries operate with no restrictions on inflows and outflows of capital, global financial resources will flow to those countries where investment opportunities offer the highest rate of return. As a result, global productivity – and thus growth – will be increased to the benefit of all. For each individual country, access to international capital flows enables it to finance a greater quantity of productive investments than is possible using purely domestic resources, with similar effects to those described for the global level. Furthermore, local investors are able to take advantage of diversified international investment opportunities in addition to those available domestically, thus raising returns while simultaneously lowering risk.

To summarise, the predictions of financial liberalisation were therefore:

1   a rise in real interest rates;
2   a concomitant rise in savings rates;
3   an increase in financial intermediation – i.e. financial 'deepening';
4   a reallocation of financial resources, both domestically where capital is redirected to its more productive use, and internationally where the same process occurs. In the latter case, the assumption is that capital would flow from relatively low-yielding developed economies to developing countries with a greater potential for growth – i.e. to produce a more efficient allocation of financial resources at the global level;
5   ultimately, higher levels of investment and growth, both domestically and globally, with associated reduction in levels of poverty within developing countries.

The next section will take each of these predictions in turn, and assess whether they were borne out in practice.

3.3 Financial liberalisation: from theory to practice

3.3.1 Liberalisation and interest rates

Unsurprisingly, given that financial liberalisation was largely proposed to remove artificial ceilings on interest rates, countries that have undergone a process of liberalisation saw real interest rates rise significantly.

However, in many cases interest rates did not move to modestly positive levels, but rather rose sharply to very high levels, often remaining there for some time. Figure 3.1 below illustrates this process with regard to Turkey. As we can see, real interest rates were negative in Turkey throughout the 1970s, reaching more than 100% in 1980. Following liberalisation in the early 1980s, however, nominal rates rose sharply taking real rates into strongly positive territory for the first time in a decade.

While it is broadly accepted that negative real rates of interest did have many negative effects as described by McKinnon and Shaw, this does not mean that very high rates of interest lead to positive outcomes. Below we consider the impact of interest rates on, first, the rate of saving and, second, investment rates.

3.3.2 Liberalisation and savings rates

Intuitively, it seems obvious that higher rates of interest paid on deposits will elicit higher rates of savings. However, one flaw in this prediction of the MSH that was highlighted quite early was the fact that it assumed all individuals

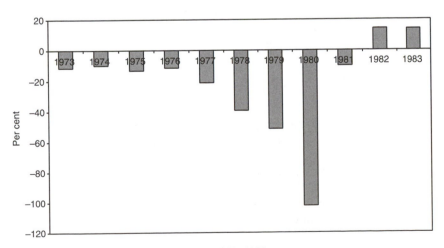

Figure 3.1 Real interest rates in Turkey, 1973–1983.

have equal access to credit markets. Campbell and Mankiw (1990) suggest that, in reality, some individuals will match this description, while others may have no access and therefore have no ability to smooth consumption over time by saving and borrowing.

Furthermore, for those at or near subsistence incomes, saving is not a viable option regardless of the rate of interest, which suggests that for the poorest developing countries, where a significant proportion of the population may be close to subsistence incomes, savings rates will be relatively insensitive to changes in interest rates.

Although a huge literature has developed to examine the link between real interest rates and savings, the question remains relatively ambiguous, with studies often producing contradictory results. For example, Fry (1978, 1980, 1995) finds that in a sample of fourteen Asian developing countries, higher real interest rates are positively associated with higher national savings rates, though the strength of the relationship is weak and not robust to changes in time periods or countries. However, the direction of causality is far from clear even in this limited relationship, with other studies suggesting that high regional savings rates were caused by factors other than movements in real interest rates. The contradictory and inconclusive nature of many studies in this area led to more nuanced work which examined the relationship for different levels of interest rate and in different time periods. Reynoso (1989) finds that savings increase rapidly as real interest rates move from extremely negative to slightly less than zero, but the strength of this relationship tails off as rates become positive, and then turns negative as real interest rates rise further (Williamson and Mahar, 1998).

Surprisingly, however, a considerable number of studies suggest that increases in the real rate of interest lead to a *fall* in the savings rate, rather than an increase. These effects are found most clearly in countries at higher levels of development, with the results suggesting that where interest rates are liberalised in a context of wider financial sector development, the greater financial options available may lead to a lowering of savings rates. For example, Chapple (1991) finds that individual and corporate savings rates declined in New Zealand following financial liberalisation, and Bayoumi (1993) finds a similar effect for the UK following financial deregulation in the 1980s.

Many other studies find little or no link between real interest rates and savings in developing countries, particularly the poorest, which is most likely related to low aggregate incomes and the 'subsistence income' effect described above.

To the extent that this evidence tells us anything, it is that:

1   modestly positive real interest rates in middle-income developing countries may be optimal for maximising savings rates;
2   both very negative and high real rates are associated with lower savings rates in the same group of countries;

3   for the poorest developing countries, there is little if any relationship between interest rates and the level of national savings; and

4   higher real interest rates – in the context of broader financial deregulation/liberalisation – are associated with lower rates of saving in high-income economies.

As we saw in Section 3.3.1, however, financial liberalisation in developing countries has often been associated with sharp increases in real interest rates. The evidence on the link between interest rates and investment rates suggests that very high interest rates have a negative relationship with rates of investment.

For example, Greene and Villanueva (1991) examine twenty-three developing countries from 1975 to 1987 and find that real interest rates are negatively correlated with investment. Demetriades and Devereux (1992) find similar results for sixty-three countries from 1961 to 1990, while Gelb (1989) finds a positive – though very weak – relationship between real interest rates and investment (Williamson and Mahar, op. cit.).

It is perhaps not surprising that high real rates of interest are associated with lower rates of investment, though the similar relationship between interest rates and savings rates in developed countries is less intuitively obvious. What is clear, however, is that the optimal outcome – mildly positive real interest rates – has not tended to follow financial liberalisation. Rather, we have tended to see very high real interest rates in most liberalising economies, particularly the less developed ones.

3.3.3 Liberalisation and financial depth

A number of different measures of financial depth have been proposed in the literature. In general terms, these measures focus on ratios of broad monetary aggregates to the size of the economy, which provide a snapshot of the importance of the financial sector.

The most straightforward of these measures – variants of which are the most commonly used indicators – is the money/GDP ratio, which measures the level of 'monetisation' in the economy. Studies may use either 'narrow money' (M1) or 'broad money' (M2/M3).[3] The rationale for using the broad money measures is that although narrow money – i.e. notes and coins in circulation – should increase at the same rate as the growth of the economy, broad money should increase at a faster rate in the presence of financial deepening; that is, as financial intermediation increases and credit is allocated to the private sector with greater magnitude. With a limited number of exceptions, most studies confirm that this is in fact what has occurred: financial depth has tended to increase following liberalisation.

In their panel of thirty-four developed and developing countries, Williamson and Mahar's (1998) findings on financial depth are summarised in Table 3.2 below. As we can see, financial depth increased in all developed

Table 3.2 Liberalisation and financial depth:
M2/GDP ratios, 1980–1996

Country	*Before liberalisation*	*After liberalisation*
United States	60	70
Canada	52	59
Japan	84	113
UK	37	46*
France	70	65
Australia	36	61
New Zealand	25	37
Indonesia	16	39
Korea	33	41
Malaysia	42	85
Philippines	28	46
Singapore	58	83
Thailand	54	74
Argentina	14	19
Brazil	12	40
Chile	9	34
Venezuela	31	23
Turkey	14	24
India	42	46
Pakistan	39	42

Source: Williamson and Mahar, 1998.

* UK's definition of M2 changed in 1987. Under
new formulation depth ratio increased from 81% in
1987 to 109% in 1996

countries following liberalisation, with the exception of France. For developing countries, financial depth increased substantially or moderately in most of the countries considered. However, the Philippines, Turkey and Venezuela all saw financial depth fall after liberalisation.

3.3.4 Liberalisation and the efficient allocation of (domestic) financial resources

As we have seen, one of the key arguments in favour of financial liberalisation was that it would lead to a more efficient allocation of resources, which in turn would increase the rate of growth. Whereas in repressed economies credit was often directed towards inefficient state enterprises, a liberalised financial system would see finance allocated on a straight commercial basis, with the financing of only the most productive ventures raising levels of productivity and growth throughout the economy. Thus, financial sector development need not increase the *quantity* of investment to have a positive impact upon growth, but may also do so through raising the average *quality* of investment.

We saw in Chapter 2 that it is this aspect of financial sector development that, for many commentators, explains the econometrically demonstrated link between financial sector development (FSD) and economic growth. This perspective has been supported in theoretical work where models are developed which explain the positive impact upon growth of FSD in terms of greater allocative efficiency.[4] In this regard, Gregorio and Guidotti (1992) estimate that three-quarters of the correlation between financial intermediation and growth can be explained by a more efficient pattern of credit allocation (Williamson and Mahar, 1998).

What has been the real-world experience at the country level, however? A number of country level case studies have been generally supportive of the view that financial liberalisation results in a more efficient allocation of investment. In the case of Ecuador, for example, Jaramillo *et al.* (1992) find that after liberalisation there was a greater supply of credit to more technologically efficient firms. Studies of Indonesia find a similar shifting of credit after liberalisation, which again tended to favour more technologically efficient firms.[5] In Korea, Atiyas (1992) finds that liberalisation led to a greater access to credit by smaller firms, who may have been disadvantaged in the previous repressed regime, where credit was focused on the large conglomerates, or *chaebols*. Similarly, improvements in the allocation of credit are found in studies of Mexico (Gelos, 1997), Argentina (Morisset, 1993) and Turkey (Pehlivan, 1996).[6]

For multi-country studies similarly supportive results are found. Chari and Henry (2002) examine the impact of liberalisation at the firm level in Jordan, Korea, Malaysia and Thailand, and find that in each case the average firm saw an increase in James Tobin's q[7] as well as an increase in the level of investment after liberalisation. The results are supported in an IMF study of the same countries by Abiad, Oomes and Ueda (2004). Finally, Galindo, Schiantarelli and Weiss (2007) report robust evidence that liberalisation in twelve developing countries resulted in an increase in the efficiency with which investment funds are allocated, particularly that the correlation between the supply of credit and the economic fundamentals of borrowing firms is higher after liberalisation.

3.3.5 Liberalisation and the efficient allocation of (international) financial resources

We have seen that, in line with the predictions of advocates of financial liberalisation, the process has been associated with a more efficient allocation of financial resources at the domestic level. However, it was also predicted that liberalisation of capital accounts would see a similar reallocation of global investment funds. In particular, there would be a shift in the allocation of global capital from the developed countries towards developing and emerging economies that have greater potential for growth.

Figure 3.2 shows net private capital flows to all developing and emerging economies from the early 1990s to 2006. As can be seen, there is certainly no

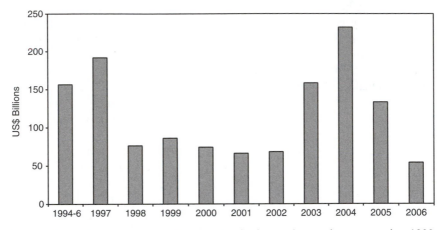

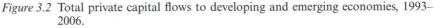

Figure 3.2 Total private capital flows to developing and emerging economies, 1993–2006.

Source: IMF WEO.

secular trend of increasing flows, as might be expected in the aftermath of an era of extensive financial liberalisation.

Rather, what we see are cyclical 'booms', where capital flows increase significantly, followed by lengthy 'busts', where the predictions of an increasing flow of capital from the developed to the developing world are turned on their head, and capital begins to flow from the developing world to the developed world.

Figure 3.3 looks at the same period broken down by type of capital flow and focusing on portfolio flows (i.e. equities and bonds) and international bank lending. Foreign direct investment (FDI), which was large (averaging a little

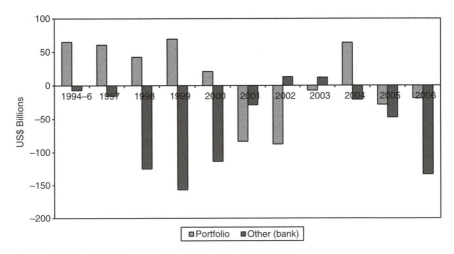

Figure 3.3 Portfolio flows and bank lending, 1993–2006.

under US$200 billion per year) and remarkably stable throughout the period is excluded. We are interested in determining whether international investors and bankers have increasingly sought out financial investment opportunities in the wake of liberalisation and so we concern ourselves with arm's-length financial flows rather than FDI, which responds to different drivers.

As we can see, once FDI is removed, the direction of financial flows since 1993 is largely from developing to developed countries. Clearly, the data is strongly affected by the Asian crisis of 1997–1998, with the negative banking flows in particular reflecting these events. However, in many ways this is the exception that proves the rule: one aspect of financial liberalisation that was not predicted – not by its advocates anyway – was the sharp increase in financial crises that has occurred.

Before considering issues of capital account liberalisation in more depth, the next section gives a broad outline of the impact that liberalisation has had upon the incidence of financial crises.

3.3.6 *Liberalisation and financial crises*

In 1985, Carlos Diaz-Alejandro argued that financial liberalisation would inevitably lead to an increased risk of financial crises in developing countries.[8] The evidence suggests that, on balance, he was right. Willamson & Mahar (1998) find that of the thirty-four countries they consider which underwent a liberalisation process, all experienced some form of systemic financial crisis between 1980 and 1997.

However, crises in only twenty-one of these countries followed directly after the liberalisation process, and while not all of these were necessarily directly caused by financial liberalisation it seems very likely that a substantial proportion certainly was.

When weighing up the benefits and costs of financial liberalisation – particularly of the capital account – it is essential to take the increased likelihood of crises into account. Too often policy-makers have received advice on financial liberalisation that has focused largely on the potential rewards, skirting over potential drawbacks. This practice has become less widespread since the Asian financial crisis of the late 1990s however, where the dangers in this regard were made all too clear. The subject of financial crises will be dealt with comprehensively later in this book, but now is an opportune time to sketch out the consequences of such events.

Research by Griffith–Jones and Gottschalk (2004) estimates the impact of crises on emerging markets output. Examining data for eight countries that have suffered serious financial crises, the authors conclude that their combined loss of output following a crisis totalled US$1.25 trillion. This foregone output corresponds to 65% of the combined GDP of Latin America and the Caribbean, and 54% of that for the East Asia and Pacific region. Effects of this magnitude clearly impact upon poverty levels in the countries concerned: in Indonesia, for example, poverty levels rose from 7–8% of the population in 1997 to 18–20% in 1998 (Suryahadi *et al.*, 2000) as a result of the Asian financial crisis. Looking at the last quarter of the twentieth century, Eichengreen (2004) estimates that currency and banking crises have reduced the incomes of developing countries by approximately 25%.

It should be noted, however, that although the risk of a crisis increases significantly after liberalisation, it is not inevitable. As we shall see, the risk in this regard is strongly related to the strength of regulation and supervision of the financial system, which suggests that liberalisation should proceed only after such reforms have been undertaken. These issues of sequencing of liberalisation will be discussed more fully in the following sections of this chapter.

Before this, however, the next section explores the issues surrounding capital account liberalisation in more depth.

3.3.7 Capital account liberalisation and growth

Many of the reforms instigated throughout the process of financial liberalisation are relatively uncontentious. For example, it is widely accepted that allowing the private sector to allocate scarce investment resources according to the relative merits – i.e. the prospective rate of return – of competing investment projects will result in a more efficient outcome than if this function is performed by government, assuming that the private sector is equipped to perform this role. Having said that, as we shall see later in this chapter, this consensus does not hold in all circumstances: recent advances in both theory and practice suggest that there are many situations where the market mechanism is likely to fail to deliver optimal outcomes, justifying targeted government intervention.[9]

When we come to capital account liberalisation, however, any consensus evaporates. Until relatively recently the debate has been largely polarised, with supporters of capital account liberalisation advocating its implementation in all circumstances, while, at the other extreme, opponents have argued that it is a mistaken and damaging reform in all circumstances. As with much in economics, positions taken on this debate are often more ideological than pragmatic, with perspectives being shaped as much theologically as empirically. To the extent that this is the case, opinions are not readily changed, regardless of the weight of evidence.

Before attempting to separate some light from the great quantity of heat that this process has produced by weighing the evidence on both sides, we need to first establish the context in which this debate has arisen.

(a) Capital account liberalisation: the theoretical benefits

Despite the fact that capital account liberalisation has increasingly been seen as a pillar of orthodox economic theory, there is little in the way of unequivocal evidence to support it. The case in favour has generally been something of an offshoot of better-established policy reform proposals, notably those in favour of free trade. That is to say, the theoretical support for free trade is a central tenet of economic theory, where the fundamental principles of comparative advantage mean that removing barriers to trade is widely viewed as a win-win policy: even if only one country unilaterally removes trade restrictions, the aggregate benefits to the country as a whole should still outweigh the costs, though there would certainly be losers as well as gainers in different parts of the country and sectors of the economy.

Given the central place this perspective holds in the field of economics, there has been a tendency to equate the case for capital account liberalisation with that for current account liberalisation: if all benefit from the free movement of goods and services, surely the same is true for the free movement of capital?

Intuitively, the case is straightforward: just as the allocation of capital within the domestic economy according to the strictures of commercial logic leads to a more efficient allocation of funds, the same should hold internationally. Domestically, the process should raise productivity and growth, by focusing scarce investment resources on those ventures that will yield the highest rate of return. Internationally, global capital should similarly seek out the most productive ventures, thus raising productivity at the global level and boosting global growth.

However, as Eichengreen and Leblang (2003) point out, this argument only holds in a 'first-best' world, and it should certainly not be assumed that the real world we inhabit fits this category. In particular, the predictions of advocates of capital account liberalisation are likely to be undermined in the presence of weaknesses in the domestic financial system, which may be amplified by an open capital account, and/or weaknesses in the international financial system that prevent the smooth and rational flow of capital described in stylised fashion above, but rather increase the likelihood of financial crises.

If it is the case that capital account liberalisation will only be positive with well-developed domestic financial sectors, and similarly well-developed, orderly international financial markets, what does empirical work tell us about the impact in practice? In particular, remembering the guiding principle of this book, has capital account liberalisation been associated with higher rates of growth in developed, developing and emerging economies?

(b) Capital account liberalisation: what is the evidence?

Modern empirical work to explore the link between capital account liberalisation and growth began in earnest in the early 1990s, and early results were not encouraging for advocates of reform.

Alesina *et al.* (1994) examined twenty developed countries for the forty years preceding 1990 to assess the relationship between capital account liberalisation (CAL) and growth, and found insignificantly small effects. The study was extended to sixty-one countries in Grilli and Milesi-Ferretti (1995), with similarly negative results. Rodrik (1998) also found no relationship with a larger set of countries, and Bordo and Eichengreen (1998) found no relationship between CAL and growth (Eichengreen and Leblang, op. cit.).

The first study to find a positive relationship was Quinn (1997). In this research, the author took a more nuanced approach to capital account openness, developing a scale to represent its degree, and testing for correlation between both the level of capital account openness and the rate of change in this regard. As with the previous studies, the author found no link between the extent of openness, but did find a significant relationship between the changes in openness and growth.

Edwards (2001) suggested that the results may have been compromised as growth itself may lead to CAL, so it is to be expected that changes in the degree of CAL will be correlated with growth. Correcting for this, the author still finds a positive correlation, but in this study the effect is restricted to high-income countries.

This finding is contradicted, however, in Edison *et al.* (2002) who see the link between CAL and growth as being higher in emerging than in developed markets. The contradictory nature of all this is perhaps confirmed by the fact that Arteta, Eichengreen and Wyplosz (2001) present results that question the robustness of studies purporting to demonstrate any link between CAL and growth (Eichengreen and Leblang, op. cit.).

It therefore seems clear that, even if there is a causal relationship between CAL and growth – and that must be seriously doubted – it is far from clear. However, as we have seen, the link between CAL and the incidence of financial crises *is* well-established. Certainly in countries without the experience of dealing with volatile, short-term capital flows (i.e. all countries with a restricted capital account), the link between removing restrictions on flows and the build-up of the potential for crisis is pronounced. Box 3.3 discusses this with respect to Thailand's experience prior to the Asian crisis of 1997/8.

Box 3.3   Capital controls, asset bubbles and crisis in Thailand

In the early 1990s Thailand lifted its remaining restrictions on capital inflows, not least because of the rationale for this move put forward by the International Financial Institutions. Furthermore, in 1993 the Bangkok International Banking Facilities (BIBF) were established, which permitted local and foreign banks based in Thailand to borrow in foreign currencies from abroad. At the same time, real interest rates were higher in Thailand than in many other comparable countries and the Thai baht was firmly pegged to the US dollar. Given the new possibility of borrowing abroad at relatively low rates of interest and lending in Thailand at higher rates – particularly as exchange rate risk was covered by the US dollar currency peg – this seemed to be a straightforward bit of arbitrage. The profits available could also be further increased if the foreign borrowing was very short-term but domestic lending was longer-term, given the difference in interest rates attached to the maturity of loans. 'Spreads' between US and Thai interests (i.e. the profit margin) was as high as 6–7% at some stages. Again, this was fine, just so long as the foreign creditors remained willing to roll-over the short-term loans. However, as early as 1995, half of Thailand's total US$80 billion of external debt was denominated in short-term loans.

The question then was where to allocate the inflows in the Thai economy? Given the huge increase in flows following capital account liberalisation, opportunities were not easy to come by. One sector, however, that seemed to promise high returns was Thailand's property sector, particularly that located in Bangkok. Just as with the South Sea bubble and 'tulipmania' described in a previous box, the seemingly inexorable rise in property prices must have appeared as if it would go on forever.

The old forces of supply and demand cannot be kept at bay indefinitely though. By the end of 1996 it is estimated that US$20 billion of commercial and residential property remained unsold in Bangkok. As is so often the case 'mania' turned to 'panic' and 'investors' started to demand their money back, refusing to roll-over loans. The breaking of the peg with the dollar was the final straw, with once affordable loans rocketing in value as the baht fell precipitously against the dollar. The rest, as they say, is history, but as recently as 2003, there were 350,000 residential properties standing empty in Bangkok.

Eichengreen and Leblang (2003) also highlight another strand of the literature, which finds a positive, quantitative relationship between capital controls and financial crises.[10] At first sight, this seems to contradict evidence linking liberalisation to financial crises. However, it is suggested[11] that the existence of capital controls may send a negative signal to the markets about the country's ability or willingness to pursue 'market-friendly' policies, thereby raising the likelihood of a financial crisis.

One of the few studies to examine the impact of CAL via both channels – i.e. through its positive impact upon growth due to a more efficient allocation of investment and through its negative impact due to a greater probability of a financial crisis – is Eichengreen and Leblang (2001).

The authors consider the link between growth rates and capital controls for twenty countries[12] from 1889 to 1997, using non-overlapping five-year periods of analysis. The results for the whole period see a positive and statistically significant link between the presence of capital controls and rates of growth; that is, countries with fully liberalised capital accounts are associated with lower rates of growth than those which retained some elements of controls. It should be noted, however, that the countries analysed are largely today's developed countries, which, given the fact that the time period considered begins in 1889, is not surprising. Despite this developed-country focus, the study remains a valuable examination of the long-term relationship between capital account openness and economic growth. The actual experience of the countries considered therefore offers important lessons to policy-makers in developing countries today.

After examining the whole 117-year period the authors break it down into smaller sections and find that the results are heavily influenced by specific periods of time in the last century. In particular, the positive relationship between capital controls and growth is strongly affected by the 1925–1935 period, and the 1993–1997 period. That is, countries that had capital controls in place at the time of the Wall Street Crash (and Great Depression) and in the years preceding the Asian financial crisis of the late 1990s, fared better in terms of growth than those that did not.

This is not, of course, surprising. Just as China and India emerged relatively unscathed from the Asian crisis – and have continued to grow strongly ever since – countries that were insulated behind capital controls in the 1920s would have experienced similar benefits, or at least avoided the worst costs.

In contrast, the authors find that in periods of calm in the international financial system, the presence of capital controls is negatively associated with growth, due to the impact on the efficiency of capital allocation described above.

After all of this, do we have an answer to the question: is capital account liberalisation good for growth? The answer: it depends. In a world of ordered, stable and rationally directed international finance, the answer may be yes. However, in a world of volatile international finance characterised by booms and busts, herd behaviour and predatory financial speculators, the answer will almost certainly be no.

From a policy-making perspective, it would therefore seem very unwise – at the very least – to unilaterally remove the option of imposing capital controls during periods of market turbulence, when failure to do so would result in damage to the country's prospects for growth and poverty reduction. This is particularly the case because, as we have seen, the Eichengreen and Leblang (op. cit.) study focused largely on the experience of developed countries. It is likely that, given the greater vulnerability to movements in the international financial markets that developing countries experience relative to the developed economies, the *costs* of maintaining no restrictions on capital movements in times of financial market turbulence will be considerably higher for developing countries.

One reason why the empirical evidence on this subject is so often contradictory and confusing is that the ultimate result of capital account liberalisation will depend on the interaction of numerous factors, many of which are inevitably country-specific. Thus what worked for country A may not work for country B, even if external circumstances are very similar. In contrast, what worked for country C may also work for country D, even if external circumstances are very different.

3.3.8 Financial liberalisation and growth

We have examined the evidence of the relationship between the different components of financial liberalisation and economic growth. What about the total package, however? It is easy to get bogged down in the minutiae of the specifics of reform, and even easier to focus on the mechanics of particular quantitative research techniques. What we always need to remember, however, is that financial liberalisation was ultimately undertaken for a simple reason: to boost rates of economic growth and thus reduce rates of poverty.

Figure 3.4 details growth rates since 1960 for high-, middle- and low-income economies. As can be seen, there is certainly no evidence of a secular rise in growth rates following the process of financial liberalisation. Rather, what we see is extreme volatility throughout – for high- and middle-income countries, however, the most stable period of relatively high growth is at the beginning of this period, from 1960 to the mid-1970s.

To recap, financial liberalisation was intended to raise levels of investment and growth. In this regard, Eatwell (1997) compares the 1960–1971 period before liberalisation with the 1979–1990 period of rapid liberalisation. Rather than showing the expected benefits of increased investment and growth rates the opposite has been the case for the G7, the OECD and, with the exception of parts of East and Southeast Asia, all developing countries. It should be noted, however, that Eatwell's analysis preceded the onset of the Asian financial crisis, so that, looking back from 2008, no region has performed as advocates of financial liberalisation had predicted.

Clearly, within these aggregate figures, some individual countries have fared better, with others doing worse, and much of this can be explained by the individual conditions in each country. However, despite the importance

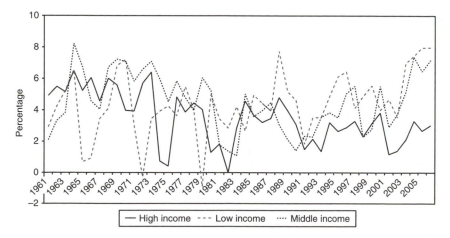

Figure 3.4 GDP growth rates: high-, middle- and low-income countries, 1960–2006.

Source: World Bank WDI.

of each country's individual circumstances in shaping outcomes, there are certain preconditions to capital account liberalisation – and more generally an accepted sequencing of financial liberalisation – which are widely accepted. The next section considers the extent to which liberalising countries have followed this consensus. Failure to have done so, of course, is one explanation of why financial liberalisation has largely failed to fulfil its predictions. To what extent has this been the case?

3.4 Financial liberalisation: sequencing issues

The importance of correctly sequencing the process of financial liberalisation was brought to light by the experience of pioneer liberalisers in Latin America in the 1970s. Both Argentina and Chile liberalised rapidly by removing controls over interest rates and privatising and injecting competition into the banking sector. However, this process was undertaken at a time of severe macroeconomic instability and before an appropriately robust framework of financial regulation and supervision was in place. The capital account was also liberalised in the same environment. In the early 1980s, both countries experienced significant economic turbulence and crises (Williamson and Mahar, 1998).

Almost immediately, economists focused in on the sequencing of reforms as the key issue, and a consensus began to develop as the appropriate sequencing in this respect (ibid.):

1   stabilise the macroeconomic environment;
2   remove restrictions on international trade;
3   develop robust and effective framework of financial regulation and prudential supervision;
4   remove controls over interest rates;
5   eliminate credit controls;
6   remove barriers to competition;
7   liberalise capital account.

When we compare the approach taken in Argentina and Chile in the 1970s to this ideal sequence, it is perhaps not surprising that these two countries ran into difficulties. However, it is very easy to be wise after the event, and it should be remembered that this 'consensus' only emerged *after* these two countries had gone through the first stage of liberalisation.

On reflection, however, it does seem intuitively obvious that countries attempting to liberalise their financial sectors are more likely to succeed if they do so in an environment of at least relative macroeconomic stability. Similarly, it must be sensible to develop an effective framework of regulation and supervision of the financial sector *before* it is freed from government control. Finally, it is clearly logical for capital account liberalisation to be the last piece of the jigsaw, since if it were the first, inflows would be likely to be misdirected to unproductive parts of the economy – as was the case under financial repression. Furthermore, channelling such inflows through an unreformed, and possibly insolvent, banking sector, with little experience of intermediating funds on a commercial basis, is clearly a recipe for disaster.

At the time, however, when financial repression had largely failed, and liberalisation was hailed as the only course for the future by the IMF and by the high proportion of government economists trained in neo-classical economics in developed country universities, it would be surprising if the sequencing was perfect.

Williamson and Mahar (1998) demonstrate that this was indeed the case for the majority of liberalising countries from the 1970s onwards. For example, while Chile, New Zealand, Peru and Turkey combined financial liberalisation with a broader package of measures aimed at macroeconomic stability, Argentina, Brazil, Egypt, Mexico and Venezuela began to liberalise during periods of high instability and before any stabilisation measures had been introduced. Also, half of the countries entered the liberalisation process with a long track record of government fiscal deficits at more than 5% of GDP.

The literature also suggests that trade reform is an important precondition for financial liberalisation, as it enables capital to flow to genuinely efficient and productive firms, and not just to ostensibly profitable, but inefficient firms, sheltering behind trade barriers. In this regard, the majority of developed countries did indeed introduce trade reforms ahead of financial liberalisation, as did Korea, Mexico, Sri Lanka and Thailand. For the remainder, many countries introduced trade reforms simultaneously with financial liberalisation, while a smaller number – Australia, Colombia, Indonesia, Malaysia and South Africa – embarked upon the process of financial liberalisation before restrictions on imports were lifted. With regard to the privatisation of the banking sector, the record is mixed, though few countries followed the literature and embarked on this process *before* financial liberalisation. Rather, the removal of the state from the banking sector generally occurred at or around the same time as financial liberalisation (ibid.).

The next stage of our ideal sequence sees a robust framework of financial regulation and supervision[13] put in place before financial liberalisation. Here, the record suggests that most countries did not view this as a particularly important component of the reforms. For developing countries, only Israel, Morocco and Peru tightened up the prudential supervision of banks ahead of financial liberalisation, while a number of countries attempted to perform both tasks simultaneously. The bulk of countries, however, only seriously attempted to improve the regulatory and supervisory framework some years after financial liberalisation had begun (ibid.).

We have seen that, although these reforms should ideally precede the liberalisation of interest rates, this was generally not the case. However, the one area where the ideal sequence given above was generally followed was in leaving the liberalisation of the capital account till last. For Williamson and Mahar (op. cit.) this was the only aspect of the 'conventional wisdom' regarding the sequencing of financial liberalisation that was followed by the majority of formerly repressed countries in their sample.

Furthermore, not only did the majority of countries leave capital account liberalisation (CAL) until the other reforms had been implemented, most also only did so when (most of) the preconditions for successful CAL were in place.

For Williamson (1993) preconditions for the liberalisation of capital inflows are:

1   trade liberalisation at least two years previously;
2   a fiscal deficit below 5% of GDP for three years previously;
3   domestic financial liberalisation two years previously;
4   opening of banking sector to domestic and foreign competition two years previously;
5   government ownership of banking sector reduced to less than 40% two years previously;
6   a robust system of prudential regulation and supervision in place.

For Williamson and Mahar (op. cit.), while most of these preconditions were in place, the fourth and sixth preconditions were less often met. That is, many countries opened their economies to unrestricted capital inflows – including short-term flows – before the domestic banking system had been exposed to competitive forces and before a robust system of prudential regulation and supervision was in place.

When we consider the broader process of financial liberalisation in developing countries, it is therefore clear that many of the preconditions now considered to be essential were not in place in many countries before the process began. In particular, the importance of exposing the domestic banking sector to competition, and to having an effective regulatory and supervisory framework in place before liberalisation, was clearly not given enough weight. It is interesting to note, of course, that these two features of the banking system perform the same task in many ways: both 'discipline' the banking sector. If we accept that, in general terms, banks have a tendency to take on excessive risk then mechanisms must be put in place to prevent this.

As has been stressed, however, it is important to avoid the danger of being wise after the event. These sequencing issues may seem rather obvious now – particularly in the light of the Asian financial crisis of the late 1990s – but in the 1980s and early 1990s there was far less talk of the importance of such matters. Indeed, as the IMF's own Independent Evaluation Office (IEO) reported in 2005, the Fund was often a 'cheerleader' for capital account liberalisation and tended to emphasise the positive consequences that could result and to place far less – if any – emphasis on the potentially negative implications. However, the report also argues that the Fund did not 'insist' upon CAL, but rather supported forces within governments that were intent on this course of action. The importance of Western-trained neo-classical economists rising to positions of influence within the policy-making bodies of many developing countries should not be underestimated here, as is discussed in Box 3.4.

Box 3.4 Neo-liberal economists and the promotion of capital account liberalisation

Chwieroth (2007) provides a fascinating study of the role of neo-liberal economists in the process of capital account liberalisation in developing countries. Using a sample of 1,500 high-ranking economists (finance ministers) and central bank governors in emerging market economies, Chwieroth tests quantitatively for the relationship between a neo-liberal perspective (which he associates with academic training at universities with a strong neo-classical tradition, predominantly in the US) and the probability of capital account liberalisation being implemented as a policy measure.

In the first stage of the study, Chwieroth tests to see whether the appointment of a neo-liberal finance minister or central bank governor is itself a 'random' event. Interestingly, he finds that such appointments are correlated with the need to establish international economic policy credibility, but only in the case of finance ministers. In the second stage of the research, Chwieroth (p. 456) controls for the factors that may have influenced the original appointment of the finance minister and finds strong evidence that:

> Even when the possibility of nonrandom selection is taken into account, the coefficient measuring the influence of a neoliberal policymaking team is signed as expected and significant. This finding strongly suggests that neoliberal economists matter for policy choices independent of the processes leading to their appointment.

The very unusual approach taken in this study suggests strongly that capital account liberalisation is not simply foisted onto reluctant governments by idealogues from the IMF, for example. Rather the inculcation and diffusion of economic ideas – particularly when taken as the only feasible or 'credible' option – through the conduit of shared academic experience is a strong force in shaping policy outcomes.

Many 'mistakes' were thus made in the process of liberalisation. However, as stressed above, this is unsurprising in many ways, as liberalisation itself may have been seen as something of a panacea to other ills, and perhaps promoted as such by those with the ear of developing country policy-makers who in turn may have been sympathetic to such views given their own academic backgrounds.

Before bringing this chapter to a close by considering what lessons should be imparted to countries being urged to liberalise today, the next section considers one final question: even if all of the 'mistakes' described above could be avoided, is full-scale financial liberalisation the best course to take for all countries and in all circumstances?

3.5   Financial liberalisation vs. financial repression: is the contest over then?

3.5.1   *The external sector*

Proponents of financial liberalisation rapidly extended their reform proposals from the domestic to the external sector. In this regard, Stiglitz *et al.* (2006) give the following rationale, which they dispute, for this move:

1   Free markets are inherently superior to restricted markets, and this is just as much the case for capital flows as it is for trade.
2   Developing countries are generally capital-poor, so the flow of capital from developed countries – in search of higher marginal returns – will enable more productive investments to be undertaken with beneficial effects on growth and thus poverty levels.
3   Liberalising the capital account is stabilising, since countries are able to access a broader range of sources of capital – i.e. a domestic downturn leading to a scarcity of internal financial resources can be offset by accessing external sources of funds.
4   CAL is also good for domestic investors as it enables them to broaden their investment portfolios beyond the local market, thus improving the risk/return trade-off through portfolio diversification.
5   Open capital accounts increase the likelihood of 'responsible' policies being followed as, through 'market discipline', countries that do so will be rewarded, and those that do not will be 'punished'.

The authors argue strongly that these arguments are ill-founded – at best they refer to particular rather than general cases – and that the problems that have accompanied financial liberalisation are not all the result of inappropriate sequencing. Rather they are the predictable consequences of certain key features of the financial system that proponents of across-the-board liberalisation ignore:

1   Fundamentally, they are out of touch with developments in modern economic theory, which question the notion that market solutions are always optimal. In particular:

(a) Market failure is pervasive in all markets, and particularly so in financial markets (Stiglitz, 1994).

(b) Given this, government intervention can often be – at least in principle – welfare-enhancing.

2   CAL does not necessarily lead to higher growth by attracting funds that can be used for investment purposes. It is just as likely to do the opposite, and lead to widespread capital flight from the country.

3   Even if CAL did attract short-term capital flows there is no evidence that flows of this kind will lead to higher growth through the funding of investment. Experience suggests that they are more likely to be used to boost consumption and lead to asset price bubbles in non-traded sectors such as the property market in pre-1997 Thailand.

4   External capital flows are not stabilising, as argued by proponents of CAL, but are the exact opposite. External capital flows to developing countries are highly procyclical, thereby tending to amplify pre-existing booms, leading to overheating and financial crises, and the exacerbation and lengthening of economic contractions.

5   As well as short-term volatility, external capital flows also exhibit medium-term waves of volatility, often driven by bouts of 'irrational exuberance' about the wonders of investing in developing countries, followed by equally irrational pessimism about the prospects of such markets.

6   The fact that capital flows are driven by short-term factors means that they cannot provide the market discipline that proponents suggest, although they certainly do restrict policy autonomy. Indeed, capital flows to developing countries can rise as economic fundamentals are deteriorating and vice versa. For most investors, the focus is on maximising short-term profits in markets that are liquid enough to allow for a rapid exit at the first sign of trouble. Furthermore, the 'punishment' doled out by international investors is often not directed at those most deserving of it, but is more likely to impact upon countries striving to implement orthodox policy reforms, since these are the countries that had attracted capital inflows in the first place.

For Stiglitz *et al.* (2006) the core argument against the wholesale liberalisation of the capital account is that it almost always increases instability and risk, but does not necessarily increase growth. Furthermore, this is more the result of the nature of the international financial system than of shortcomings in the countries that are recipients of capital flows. This suggests that, however well sequenced and adroitly managed, full capital account liberalisation may still result in damaging consequences. In particular, while short-term capital inflows may temporarily buoy up the economy in a superficial sense – such as raising asset prices and thus producing the sense of increasing wealth – they also greatly increase the potential for crisis. The negative effects of rapid capital outflows, however, are an unalloyed disaster for developing countries.

Moreover, when we consider the impact upon levels of poverty, it is clear that increasing instability within these countries will hit the poor and vulnerable first and hardest: those with the most precarious jobs will be the first to lose them in an economic downturn; in the absence of a social security safety net provided by the state, there is no mechanism to support affected families and facilitate a transition to other employment; and, with little or no savings or access to financial products such as insurance, the cumulative results can be catastrophic for individuals and their families.

When we weigh the evidence on the benefits of external financial liberalisation it is clear that to blindly follow the path of liberalisation may not be the best option. Indeed, if after carefully weighing the likely costs and benefits in their own particular case, countries do choose to liberalise then the process must be carefully sequenced and managed, and the option of retaining controls over some kinds of inflows – particularly short-term flows – should be seriously considered. As with much else in this book, there is no one answer that is suitable for all countries in all circumstances: Singapore is not China.

In this regard it is interesting to note the change of position taken on capital account liberalisation by the IMF. As recently as September 1997 the Fund was seeking to alter its Articles of Agreement to include a mandate to promote capital account liberalisation. The timing, to say the least, was not ideal. By 2003, however, the IMF took a far more cautious line on CAL, very much stressing the importance of getting the preconditions and sequencing right before the process should be undertaken.

Although caution would appear to be called for when considering liberalisation of the external sector, it has been suggested that, in the domestic sphere there is more consensus. Even here, however, there are dissenting voices, which have grown stronger in recent years. What are the issues in this regard?

3.5.2 The domestic sector

While it is the case that liberalised domestic financial systems can be far more effective than repressed systems, the majority of the evidence in this regard relates to developed economies. As pointed out above, it is certainly true that, within developing countries, very different historical, cultural, institutional and geographical characteristics mean that liberalising reforms will lead to very different outcomes. However, it is also the case that important differences between developed and developing economies, in the aggregate, mean that what is appropriate in the developed world may not be so in developing countries. In this regard, the far greater importance of the banking sector in developing countries – where capital markets are generally underdeveloped – is a key distinction. The approach to this sector is therefore of fundamental importance.

For Honohan and Stiglitz (2001) financial regulatory regimes, particularly the prudential supervision of banks, in developing countries are increasingly modelled on forms prevalent in developed countries. In particular, the authors note the trend towards minimalist, arm's-length prudential regulation, which relies on the assessment and approval of the risk control procedures of financial intermediaries and the imposition of small amounts of risk-adjusted 'accounting capital' to influence behaviour, and they characterise this trend as: 'dangerously complacent for developing countries' (ibid.: 31).

For the authors, the problems with such an approach are that:

1 It fails to take account of how imperfectly bank capital is measured in many developing countries, as well as the fact that senior management have an incentive to obfuscate in this regard, so as to minimise the quantity of capital needed to be set aside for regulatory purposes.
2 It overrates the accuracy with which the risk associated with the allocation of this capital – i.e. the risk-weighted capital – is measured. For example, the underestimation of risks encourages banks to raise their exposure to this 'underpriced risk'.
3 It overemphasises the accounting measures of capital at the expense of the more important interaction of capital and banks' franchise value.
4 More generally, principal–agent problems[14] are endemic in the financial systems in developing countries, which prevents the incentives of key actors becoming aligned and distorts the real-world impact of policy changes.

The result of these features is that the supervisory approach is too often one of box-ticking, rather than a more meaningful attempt to promote the stability of the financial sector. In part this is an inevitable consequence of the limited supervisory expertise in many countries – coupled with inadequate resourcing of this key sector – but the result is often that the tendency of banks to take on excessive risk is not constrained to the extent that it should be. Given the greater importance of banking in the developing world, the result of these shortcomings is often severe in terms of the incidence of banking crises, as well as the more general effectiveness of the banking sector in performing its vital intermediation role in the economy.

Honohan and Stiglitz (op. cit.) thus argue for a process of 'robust financial restraint' rather than full-scale financial liberalisation, of which more will be said when we deal with issues of financial regulation in subsequent chapters.

With regard to the desirability of some level of financial restraint, Caprio *et al.* (2001) make more general points about the shortcomings of the market mechanism. In particular, the authors argue that:

1 Free markets do not always produce a socially efficient allocation of credit within the economy.

2   Asymmetric information[15] is pervasive in all markets, but a particular feature of financial markets. The result is often credit rationing[16] with interest rates remaining at below market-clearing levels;[17] and therefore
3   Government intervention in the financial sector can lead to superior outcomes.

Caprio *et al.* (2001) thus argue that liberalisation may not produce optimal outcomes, no matter how well designed and sequenced. The authors accept, of course, that government intervention in the financial system is also no panacea: the outcome of the widespread use of financial repression is ample testimony to this fact. However, they do argue – and the evidence would suggest that they are right – that well-designed, targeted, and time-limited interventions in the allocation of credit and dispersal of risk throughout the economy can lead to superior outcomes in certain circumstances.

For the authors, an effective directed credit scheme would have the following characteristics:

1   It would be of small size relative to total credit within the economy.
2   Subsidies associated with the programme would be relatively small.
3   The responsibility for selecting specific investment opportunities (within set parameters) and for the monitoring of borrowers would be left to the banking sector.
4   Crucially, any such scheme should incorporate a 'sunset provision', whereby it would be wound up after a specified time period had elapsed.

Caprio *et al.* (op. cit.) argue that the approach taken in Japan met all of these criteria except for the last one: the relative size of the directed credit programme undertaken by the Japanese Development Bank continued to expand in the 1970s, although its effectiveness had largely been exhausted. Despite this shortcoming, the programme in Japan is widely seen as being effective, at least during its early years.

The effectiveness of the East Asian 'developmental state' model, where credit was directed towards key sectors and 'national champions', has been much debated. Those arguing for more proactive government involvement in the development process point to the success of many East Asian economies which appeared to have followed this path, often contrasting their success with the lack of progress in countries that had taken a more laissez-faire approach. Others argue, somewhat implausibly it must be said, that the region's success was due to its openness and outward orientation, particularly to the focus on export-led growth, and that the economies of the region thrived *in spite of* – not because of – their directed credit schemes.

With regard to the influence of financial repression in the region, Stiglitz and Uy (1996) argue that 'repression' in East Asia worked, and its success was based on the fact that it differed from that in other developing regions in six key ways:

1   There was a willingness to change credit policies rapidly in the event of failure.
2   More directed credit was channelled through the private sector than through government schemes.
3   Performance criteria were used to guide directed programmes.
4   The use of direct subsidies was strictly limited.
5   The proportion of directed credit allowed in the system was restricted.
6   There was strong and effective monitoring of the performance of recipients of directed credit.

The success of the East Asian region's economies suggests strongly that full-scale financial liberalisation is not the only – or perhaps even the best – means of spurring growth and development, particularly during the early stages of the process. Furthermore, it seems probable that the features of the directed credit schemes described by Stiglitz and Uy above did play a role in generating this success.

What does this cumulative evidence offer policy-makers today, when considering the merits or otherwise of financial liberalisation versus financial repression?

Some policy implications and concluding remarks

We have seen in this chapter that both governments and markets can and do fail. The financial repression of the post-war era was largely a rational response to the *market failure* that had preceded it in the 1920s and 1930s. Furthermore, the demise of financial repression was itself inevitable in the context of widespread *government failure* to limit, target and manage the process properly.

Where 'repression' worked it was time-limited, strictly focused and restricted and rationally planned with the incentives of key actors largely aligned. Where it did not, in contrast, it became a self-defeating and self-reinforcing source of rent-seeking and economic stagnation.

Liberalisation 'shock-therapy' has clearly failed, as evidenced by the example of Russia after the collapse of the Soviet Union – placing blind faith in market mechanisms to achieve optimal outcomes regardless of the historical and institutional context is a recipe for disaster.

As ever, therefore, we must seek a middle way that takes account of a country's level of development and its institutional context. For example, it is unlikely that full-scale liberalisation will be appropriate in the poorest developing countries, where market failure is endemic, regardless of how well it is sequenced and paced. As Caprio *et al.* (2001) argue, the more prevalent are market failures, the stronger the case for government intervention in the financial system.

As countries develop and domestic market failures are addressed, scope for increasing the pace of financial liberalisation would seem justified, though again the particular characteristics of each country – not dogma dressed up as technical and impartial advice – should be the key determinant. Ultimately, a liberalised domestic financial sector is the most appropriate destination of middle-income developing countries, though, as we have seen, it may well require governments to influence the allocation of credit in the economy if this stage is to be reached.

When we turn to the external sector, however, matters are less clear cut. A strong case can be made that capital account liberalisation is good for high-income developed countries – though the opposite case could also be made. It is very difficult to construct a compelling case that the same is true for developing countries, particularly if we rely on empirical rather than theoretical evidence. Over the long term, there may be some benefits in terms of the efficiency with which capital is allocated, but this only holds in periods when the international financial markets are stable and the domestic financial system is robust. Conversely, openness to international capital movements in times of financial turmoil is clearly negative, regardless of how soundly a country has structured its domestic financial system.

To conclude, early stages of development seem to call for focused government intervention in the domestic financial system. As market failures are addressed and countries develop, domestic liberalisation becomes more beneficial – it is crucial that the government's role is strictly limited in terms of both time and size relative to the private sector in this transition period. There is a strong case for the poorest developing countries to open their economies to FDI flows, but no case for them to do so for short-term capital flows. This case only becomes relevant at much higher levels of income, and even then the evidence suggests that policy-makers should retain the option of imposing capital controls as circumstances demand.

4 The domestic financial system

An overview

Introduction

Thus far, we have considered the key functions and institutions of the financial sector in Chapter 1, examined the relationship between financial sector development, economic growth and poverty reduction in Chapter 2, and assessed issues of financial repression and liberalisation in Chapter 3.

Throughout it has been stressed that the individual circumstances of each country exert a powerful influence on policy outcomes, such that there are few if any examples of policies that are universally applicable in the same form. In the same vein, it is also the case that there is no single, ideal 'end-state' for financial sector development – a variety of financial sector structures can and do function well, just as a similar variety of systems do not.

Furthermore, whilst there are important differences between financial systems in developed and developing countries, which we shall come to shortly, there are also major differences between the types of system that have emerged within countries at similar levels of development. For example, Japan and Germany are often described as having 'bank-based systems', as banks play the key role in mobilising savings, allocating capital, monitoring the decision-making of corporate managers, and providing risk management instruments. In contrast, the USA, for example, is more often described as a 'market-based system', as the capital markets share these functions with the banking sector in a more balanced manner.[1]

These differences are highlighted in Table 4.1. The table illustrates the greater relative importance of banking in Japan and Germany – where bank deposits are 121% and 97% of GDP respectively – compared to the situation in the USA, which sees bank deposits at 59% of GDP. In contrast, stock market capitalisation is 135% of GDP in the USA, but just 75% and 43% respectively in Japan and Germany.

As well as these statistical manifestations, a key difference in approach is the nature of financial relationships: in Japan and Germany, for example, banks are more likely to forge long-term relationships with corporate borrowers, where considerations beyond the immediate state of the company's balance sheet – such as the long-term prospects of the company

Table 4.1 'Bank-based' and 'market-based' financial
systems, 2005

Country	Bank deposits/GDP	Stock market capitalisation/GDP
Japan	1.21	0.75
Germany	0.97	0.43
USA	0.59	1.35

Source: World Bank Financial Structure Dataset, 2006.

concerned – are more likely to influence a bank's decision-making. In the US system, however, the relationship between lenders and borrowers is generally more arm's-length in nature – as exemplified by the greater importance of impersonal capital markets, but also the dominant forms of banking – such that decisions are more likely, on average, to be taken purely on the basis of the financial risk and return characteristics of each transaction.

As with much else in finance, each of these systems reflects a particular view of the way that the financial system works, and can be made to work better. For example, 'relationship-banking' of the kind common in Japan and Germany can prevent a company's short-term liquidity crisis becoming an avoidable solvency crisis, giving borrowers the breathing space needed to develop their business to its full potential. Furthermore, such relationships can be a highly effective way of mitigating problems of asymmetric information for lenders: a long-term financial relationship enables trust between the parties to develop, reducing the need for expensive *ex post* monitoring of loans, for example.[2] However, with advantages usually come disadvantages, and the very closeness of the relationships that can develop in systems of this kind increases the likelihood of issues such as corruption and rent-seeking coming to the fore.

In arm's-length systems, in contrast, one would expect corruption of this form to be less of a problem on average. Moreover, the fact that each transaction is assessed on its individual merits should increase the chance that investment funds – at least at that particular point in time – are allocated efficiently to the most productive investments available within the economy. The disadvantages of such systems are an inherent short termism such that projects that take a long time to come to fruition may not be undertaken, despite the fact that they might be highly productive over the longer term. Also, while all banking systems mitigate asymmetric information to some extent, this is less the case in arm's-length systems than in those based upon relationship-banking.

4.1 Financial structure: key differences between developed and developing countries

For developing countries, most financial systems would be characterised as bank-based rather than market-based, though this is not universally so. More generally, financial systems are mostly smaller in developing countries, with less activity – and less efficiency – in terms of banking, non-bank financial institutions and capital markets.

These differences are illustrated in Table 4.2. As we can see, the scale of the financial sector in high-income countries, relative to GDP, is vastly greater than is the case in low-income countries. For example, while total bank deposits equate to 22% of GDP in low-income countries, the figure for high-income countries is 95%. As a result, while high-income country banks provide credit at a level almost equal to national GDP, the respective figure for low-income countries is just 15%.

When we consider capital markets we see a similar disparity. Average stock market capitalisation represents 12% of GDP in low-income countries, but 99% in high-income countries, while the figures for private bond market capitalisation to GDP are 1% and 45% respectively. For public bond market capitalisation the difference is less marked, which reflects the central role that the domestic financial system often plays in financing government activity in developing countries. Despite this, the ratio remains higher in high-income countries than is the case in their low-income counterparts.

The only component of the financial system that is relatively larger in low-income countries – in Table 4.2 – is the ratio of central bank assets to GDP,

Table 4.2 Average financial structures of high-income vs. low-income countries, 2005*

Variables	Low income	High income
Central bank assets / GDP	0.10	0.03
Bank assets / GDP	0.19	1.14
Other financial institutions assets / GDP	0.08	0.54
Private credit by banks / GDP	0.15	1.08
Bank deposits / GDP	0.22	0.95
Bank overhead costs / total assets	0.07	0.03
Net interest margin[a]	0.08	0.02
Bank concentration[b]	0.83	0.76
Stock market capitalisation / GDP	0.12	0.99
Stock market turnover ratio[c]	0.64	0.80
Private bond market capitalisation / GDP	0.01	0.45
Public bond market capitalisation / GDP	0.33	0.47

Source: World Bank Financial Structure Dataset, 2006.

* Sample of 55 high-income and 55 low-income countries.
a: Banks' net interest revenue as a share of interest-bearing assets (0.08 = 8%).
b: Assets of three largest banks as a share of assets of all commercial banks.
c: Ratio of the value of total shares traded to average real market capitalisation.

which in turn is a reflection of the more dominant role that the public sector has played, and continues to play, in these economies. Although we saw in the previous chapter that the process of financial liberalisation has swept away many of the structures associated with financial repression, the far greater importance of central banks in the financial systems of low-income countries clearly illustrates that this process is far from complete.

The three other shaded rows in the table also represent variables where the ratios are higher for low-income countries. In broad terms these measure the inefficiency of the financial sector: bank overheads amount to 7% of total assets in low-income countries, compared to 3% in high-income countries, while the figures for banks' net interest margin are 8% and 2% respectively.

For bank concentration, the situation is broadly similar in the two categories, where the three largest banks account for a little over 80% of commercial banking assets in low-income countries, and a little under this figure in high-income countries.

In combination, these statistics suggests that, although one would expect the relative size and efficiency of the financial sector to move towards levels seen in high-income countries as countries become wealthier, there is no clear trend in terms of bank concentration: the tendency is for a small group of banks to dominate regardless of the level of national wealth.

Another key difference between developing and (most) developed countries' banking systems is the extent of foreign ownership. Particularly in the last decade, there has been an increasing trend towards foreign banks from developed countries buying up banking assets in the developing world. In part this is supply-led – the reduction or removal of restrictions on foreign ownership as a component of financial liberalisation has made foreign ownership possible where this was previously not the case. The realisation of this potential, however, has been demand-driven – developed country banks have increasingly wished to 'cross the border' and conduct their business from within the country using local currency.

Much of the impetus here relates to the exchange rate risks associated with lending in international currencies. As we shall see in later chapters, a country with a large quantity of foreign-denominated debt faces extreme difficulties if the value of this debt increases following a currency crisis. Indeed, it may be that the presence of such a debt burden can itself precipitate the onset of such a crisis.

Furthermore, as well as increasing 'demand' for domestic banking assets in developing countries, financial crises can also directly affect the 'supply'. As illustrated in Table 4.3, one effect of the Asian crisis was to accelerate the trend towards foreign ownership in all emerging regions. The process was made possible in Asia – where before the crisis foreign ownership of the domestic banking system was largely prohibited – as the conditions attached to IMF rescue packages obliged countries to remove these restrictions. Foreign banking groups were thus able to avoid currency risk by lending

Table 4.3 Foreign bank ownership in emerging markets before and after the Asian crisis

	Foreign control (a) December 1994	Foreign control (a) December 1999	Foreign control (b) December 1999
Central Europe	7.8%	52.3%	56.9%
Latin America	7.5%	25.0%	25.5%
Asia	1.6%	6.0%	13.2%

Source: IMF, 2000.

(a) Where foreigners own more than 50% of total equity.
(b) Where foreigners own more than 20% of total equity.

in local currency through their newly acquired domestic banking assets, the attractiveness of which was further enhanced by the fact that the crisis had left these assets extremely undervalued.[3]

However, while the logic behind these trends from both a supply and demand perspective is understandable, the fact that a large proportion of a country's domestic banking system may be foreign-owned raises important issues, which will be covered in subsequent chapters in depth.

It should be remembered, however, that there is no point in having a large and efficient financial sector simply for its own sake. Efforts to move towards these ends are stimulated by the belief that improvements will bring meaningful benefits in terms of both economic growth and, ultimately, poverty alleviation. What is the evidence in this respect?

As we can see from Table 4.4 there is a clear positive correlation between the size of the financial sector – both in terms of banking and stock markets – and GDP per capita. Furthermore, there is a clear negative correlation between the inefficiency of the financial sector and GDP per capita, as well as between the relative size of the public sector in the financial system and GDP per capita.

Table 4.4 Correlations of financial sector development and GDP per capita

Measure of financial sector development	Correlation
Liquid liabilities/GDP	0.465
Bank assets/GDP	0.663
Claims of banks on private sector/GDP	0.639
Central bank assets/GDP	−0.442
Overhead costs	−0.353
Bank net interest margin	−0.443
Public share in total bank assets	−0.462
Stock market capitalisation/GDP	0.282
Turnover ratio	0.409

Source: Demirgüç-Kunt and Levine, 1999.

As we have seen, in terms of positive correlations, all of these indicators are significantly higher in richer than in poorer groups of countries, and have a tendency to rise as economies become more developed. Similarly, the efficiency of the financial system is higher in richer countries and correlated with higher GDP per capita levels.

However, although stock markets also tend to become larger, more efficient and more important to the economy as incomes rise, this does not lead to a uniform outcome, particularly as different measures are often used to measure the degree of stock market development. There are some countries that show up as well developed by all measures (Australia, Great Britain, Hong Kong, Malaysia, the Netherlands, Singapore, Sweden, Switzerland, Thailand, and the United States, for example). Other markets – such as Chile and South Africa – are large but relatively illiquid, whilst others – such as Korea and Germany – have stock markets that are relatively small but are also quite active and liquid.

When we look at non-bank financial institutions (NBFIs), the same pattern emerges. Insurance companies, pension funds, mutual funds and other NBFIs are all larger as a share of GDP in richer countries. They are therefore not just larger in absolute terms, but also more important relative to other components of the financial sector, particularly banks and development banks.

It is therefore clear that the different components of financial sector development are strongly associated with higher levels of GDP per capita. Furthermore, as we saw in Chapter 2, this relationship is, at least in part, a causal one: growth may lead to financial sector development, but financial sector development does itself lead to growth.

4.1.1 The formal vs. the informal sector

As well as the specific structural differences between developed and developing countries described above, a key distinction between economic systems in general and the financial sector in particular is the relative sizes of the 'formal' and 'informal' sectors.

As discussed later in this chapter, the tax take (as a percentage of GDP) in developing countries is generally much lower than that in developed countries. Although there are numerous reasons for this – and therefore numerous remedies proposed – a key factor is the size of the (untaxed) informal sector. In this regard, it is estimated that within developing countries informal firms account for around 30% of total production and between 50% and 75% of jobs in the non-agricultural labour force.[4] That is, in many developing countries, the informal sector's importance is comparable to that of the formal sector.

Table 4.5 gives comparative estimates of the total size of the informal sector in developed countries compared to three developing regions, and makes this importance abundantly clear. Clearly, therefore, no national

Table 4.5 Informal sector as percentage of GNP

Developed countries	12%
Africa	44%
Latin America	39%
Asia	35%

Source: Gerxhani, 2004.

development strategy can afford to ignore a sector which is equivalent to between a third and one half of total GNP. The issues in this regard will be explored fully in the following chapter on reform of the domestic system.

A corollary to the size of the informal sector is the extent of financial exclusion in developing countries. That is, to a far greater extent than is the case in developed countries, a high proportion of the population of many developed countries have no contact with and no access to the formal financial system.

Table 4.6 highlights the lack of access to formal finance starkly: in none of the countries, regions or cities considered does more than 50% of the population have a bank account, whereas in the USA 91% of people have bank accounts. For many this is a clear example of market failure: it must be the case that a large proportion of those excluded from the financial sector could effectively use its services. Furthermore, any country that excludes more than 50% of its population from the formal financial system cannot be optimally employing its human resources. Consequently, economic growth *must* be lower than would be the case if the financially excluded could be drawn into the formal financial system.

Although those working in the informal sector – as well as small-scale entrepreneurs – certainly do require financial services, these differ in certain key ways to those offered by the mainstream financial sector. In particular, the sums involved may be very small and the potential borrowers widely disbursed with no 'credit history' and little or no collateral. Given the cost of setting up bank branches, the relatively high fixed costs of monitoring

Table 4.6 Proportion of the population with bank accounts

Botswana	47%
Brazil (urban)	43%
Colombia (Bogota)	39%
Djibouti	24.8%
Lesotho	17%
Mexico City	21.3%
Namibia	28.4%
South Africa	31.7%
Swaziland	35.3%
Tanzania	6.4%

Source: Emerging Market Economics, 2005.

small-scale loans (i.e. it costs much the same to monitor a loan for £100,000 as for one for £100), and the very low returns earned on small-scale savings, most formal financial institutions have simply not attempted to access this potential market.

For many, the solution to this problem is microfinance. In its modern form, microfinance emerged from the work of the Grameen Bank in Bangladesh, though there have been historical versions as long ago as seventeenth-century Ireland and eighteenth-century Germany.[5] Today, there are a number of differing forms, but microfinance institutions generally provide small loans to the poor, with minimal bureaucracy and often require little or no collateral. The great attention that has been paid to microfinance from the development community and some mainstream economists has been the result of microfinance schemes' seeming ability to reach the financially excluded *and* to achieve very high repayment rates. This latter point is attributed to many factors, but particularly to the focus on 'group lending' (where if one member of the group defaults the remainder become liable for their debt) and the associated *ex ante* and *ex post* peer group monitoring that this involves.

By getting borrowers themselves to screen their fellow borrowers and to monitor repayments, microfinance institutions have been able to alter the nature of the financial calculus described above; if the costs of monitoring small loans is dramatically reduced, the economic viability of making such loans is greatly increased.

From small beginnings in the 1970s, these successes led to the replication of the original microfinance model, and to its development into other forms. By 2002 it was estimated that more than 10,000 microfinance institutions had been established, reaching more than 30 million people. However, demand for microfinance was estimated at between 400 and 500 million, leading the United Nations to designate 2005 as the 'Year of Microcredit' in an effort to expand its reach significantly.

For supporters the microfinance revolution has the potential to effectively eliminate poverty in developing countries. For others, however, the obstacles that prevented the formal financial sector targeting the poor and excluded in the first place will place inevitable limits on what can be achieved in terms of poverty reduction.

To summarise, observable features of financial structure and development are as follows:

- As per capita incomes rise, the role of the state in the financial system tends to fall.
- As per capita incomes rise, the size and efficiency of the private financial sector tends to rise.
- As per capita incomes rise, stock market *activity* tends to rise relative to the activity of the banking sector and to that of NBFIs.
- As per capita incomes rise, stock markets tend to become more efficient relative to banks.

- As per capita incomes rise, financial systems *tend* to become more market-based, though this is not universally the case (e.g. Germany and Japan) and care must be taken in interpreting the data in this regard. For example, Germany and Ecuador are both classified as bank-based systems – due to the relative size of banks vs. capital markets – but in Ecuador banks are not as well developed as German banks, and therefore less able to efficiently perform their key functions. In the same way, the United States and the Philippines are both classified as market-based systems, but the markets in the Philippines are clearly not as effective at providing financial services as those in the US.
- The informal economy in developing countries can be almost 50% of the size of total GNP, but tends to diminish in relative importance as national income rises.
- Financial exclusion is a major issue in many developing countries: at the extreme more than 93% of the population of Tanzania was without a bank account in 2005.
- For some, the 'microfinance revolution' has the potential both to effectively eliminate poverty, and to provide a bridge between the informal and formal sectors. For others, its growth is inherently self-limiting.

We have examined the key structural differences between financial systems in developed and developing countries, as well as considering the different patterns of financial sector development within these two groups of countries. Furthermore, we have seen how economic growth exerts a strong influence over the nature of financial sector development (as well as the relative size of the informal sector), and it has been suggested that, at least in part, the causality in this regard may run both ways.

The next section considers factors other than a country's level of development that impact the structure of the financial system and the pathway of financial sector development. As we shall see, these factors have much explanatory power when we survey the very different financial systems that countries at similar levels of income have developed.

4.2 Other key influences on the structure of the financial system

4.2.1 Macroeconomic stability

Countries with a historical tradition of macroeconomic instability – particularly of high rates of inflation – are more likely to have underdeveloped financial systems. The reasons for this are relatively intuitive, in that high rates of inflation undermine confidence in money itself as a store of value, discourage the development of financial intermediation in the formal financial system, and encourage the acquisition of real rather than financial assets.[6]

Without confidence in the system there can be no financial sector development: macroeconomic stability is thus central to this task.

4.2.2 Legal framework/origins

It has become increasingly recognised in recent years that the nature of a country's legal framework is a major influence upon the development of its financial system. Furthermore, in many developing countries, the legal framework itself is often a product of the country's colonial legacy. In the early 1970s, Robert Mundell argued[7] that Anglophone countries in sub-Saharan Africa were likely to have better-developed financial sectors than their Francophone counterparts in the region. In more recent years, empirical evidence has suggested that this is indeed the case, with countries whose legal framework is based on English common law also tending to be more market-based than those based on French civil law.[8]

The explanation often given[9] is that English common law stresses the importance of protecting shareholder and creditor rights, which is positive for financial sector development in general, and capital market development in particular. Conversely, French civil law places less stress on these rights, and more on the power of the state, with the result that former French colonies tend to have less-developed financial systems, often dominated by a limited number of banks. Moreover, given the emphasis on the discretionary power of the state, contract enforcement in the French tradition is often less strictly adhered to, which again has a negative impact upon financial sector development and may lead to higher levels of corruption.

4.2.3 Geography and climate

An alternative viewpoint to that focusing on the impact of legal traditions, but which also stresses the importance of the colonial era, proposes that the low quality of institutions in many former colonies – and the consequent obstacles to financial sector development – is more the result of climate and the prevalence of disease.[10] That is, in countries where the climate was unsuited to European colonists, who were highly vulnerable to local diseases, there was less emphasis placed on long-term institution building. Rather, the focus was on the short-term exploitation of natural resources – not least human beings – driven by the desire to extract as much profit from the colony in as short a time as possible, rather than the taking of a long-term view of its economic and political development.

It is likely that both of these factors had some influence on subsequent financial sector development. However, the fact that financial sectors tend to be more developed in Anglophone than in Francophone sub-Saharan Africa, despite the same climatic conditions, suggests that, even if the climatic factors did retard institution building, this was less the case in countries where the English legal tradition was imposed.

4.2.4 Regulation

We saw in the previous chapter that the existence of a robust system of financial regulation and supervision is now recognised as a crucial pre-requisite for the liberalisation of the financial system, and the absence of one is strongly associated with the development of financial crises. More generally, however, the existence (or more often the lack of it) of particular forms of regulation has a strong impact upon the nature of financial sector develop-ment. These impacts emerge through a number of channels. For example:

(a) Countries with strong accounting standards are less likely to have under-developed financial systems, which are more likely to be market-based.
(b) Countries that restrict the rights of banks to engage in non-banking financial services are more likely to have underdeveloped financial systems.
(c) Countries with deposit insurance systems are less likely to have market-based financial systems.

In many ways, issues of regulation are similar to those relating to the legal framework, of which the regulatory system can perhaps be seen as a subset. Consistently applied and enforced regulations enhance stability and spread confidence: both vital for financial sector development and, ultimately, economic growth.[11]

However, as was also pointed out in the previous chapter,[12] it is unlikely to be optimal to simply import arm's-length developed country forms of regulation into the very different environment of many developing countries. In the following chapter on the reform of the domestic system, we will explore the implications of this in some depth.

4.2.5 Contractual savings institutions

Contractual savings institutions such as pension funds and insurance com-panies are vital for developing and sustaining the financial system in developed markets. For example, 84% of the shares on the London Stock Exchange are held by institutions of this type. What role can these institutions play?

First, given the nature of their liabilities (i.e. generally very long-term) they may seek investments of a similar maturity so that their assets and liabilities are matched. Consequently, they tend to have strong demand for shares and long-term bonds. This provides a source of longer-term investment funds, which has a positive impact on capital market development and, ultimately, economic growth in the longer term. When these factors are combined with the scale of these institutions, this also affords them the opportunity to exert significant leverage over corporate behaviour, which again may have a posi-tive impact upon growth.[13]

Contractual savings institutions remain relatively small in developing countries, and many reforms have been proposed to alter this situation. We will be examining these issues in the next chapter, in the context of domestic reform, but to lay the foundation for this, it is important to stress the potential importance of contractual savings institutions at this stage.

4.2.6 Private ownership

When considering issues of the growth of contractual savings institutions and the development of capital markets the subject of private ownership is clearly pivotal.

While the growth of contractual savings institutions will raise the demand for equities in developing countries, there obviously needs to be sufficient supply to meet this demand. In this regard private ownership is clearly fundamental, and the privatisation of previously state-owned enterprises that we have seen in recent decades has certainly boosted this supply.

Figure 4.1 above depicts regional and total privatisations from 1988 to 2003, which grew steadily through the 1990s reaching a peak in 1997 and declining thereafter. Over this period, almost eight thousand separate privatisations were carried out, generating more than US$400 billion in revenues for developing country governments.

Table 4.7 relates these revenues to regional and total GDP over the period. As we can see, privatisations amounted to a little over 0.5% of total developing country GDP, but there were considerable disparities between the regions. Latin America and Eastern Europe were the regions that, relative to GDP, saw the highest level of privatisations with 0.78% and 0.62% respectively. In contrast, South Asia and sub-Saharan Africa saw the least, with 0.19% and 0.22% respectively.

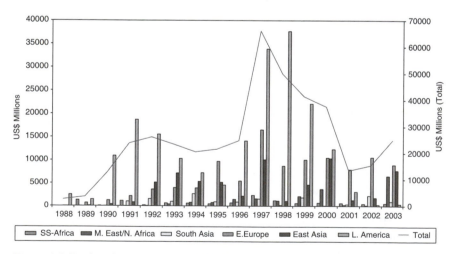

Figure 4.1 Regional privatisations, 1988–2003.

Source: World Bank Privatization Database and author's own calculations.

Table 4.7 Regional privatisations as percentage
of GDP, 1988–2003

Region	% of GDP
Sub-Saharan Africa	0.2190
Middle East & North Africa	0.3351
South Asia	0.1914
Eastern & Central Europe	0.6186
East Asia	0.3076
Latin America & Caribbean	0.7773
Total	**0.5016**

Source: World Bank Privatization Database, World
Development Indicators and author's own
calculations.

These figures do not allow us to consider the pattern of privatisations –
both in terms of sectors and over time – as well as issues of political economy
that relate to the process and its effects. Box 4.1 discusses these issues with
respect to Latin America, where recent reversals of support for economic
liberalisation make this a particularly pertinent subject.

Box 4.1 Privatisation and backlash in Latin America

Privatisation has been an important feature of economic reforms in
Latin America. As we have seen, privatisations equalled 0.78% of the
region's GDP from 1988 to 2003, with the total level of privatisations
peaking at US$37.7 billion in 1998. The main sectors targeted for pri-
vatisation are shown in the figure below, weighted according to their
overall value over the period.

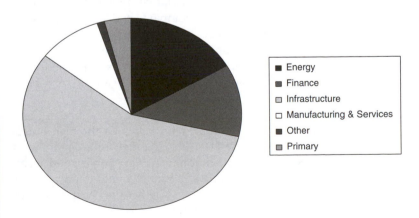

Legend:
- Energy
- Finance
- Infrastructure
- Manufacturing & Services
- Other
- Primary

Sectoral breakdown on privatisations in Latin America, 1988–2003.

As we can see, by far the largest sector is infrastructure, which includes public utilities such as electricity, gas and water, as well as transport and telecommunications. In terms of the relative size of the privatisations (to GDP) the countries of Latin America were the most 'enthusiastic' privatisers of state assets, particularly in the late 1980s and 1990s. However, much of this was driven through by right-of-centre governments and was also often integral to IMF/World Bank structural adjustment programmes.

More recent years have seen the return to power of left-of-centre governments throughout Latin America, often coming to power on a wave of popular support – or popular discontent with the free market policies implemented by their predecessors. By 2005 privatisations had almost ground to a halt in the region. In part, of course, this is related to the fact that there may be little left to privatise. However, it is also the case that – if anything – the process has now gone into reverse: the epicentres of this are in Venezuela, Bolivia and Ecuador.

The Venezuelan President Hugo Chavez came to power on a wave of populist sentiment, promising to take back the country's 'national assets'. Chavez has indeed taken greater control – in one form of another, often stopping well short of full nationalisation – of the country's oil and gas assets. On his re-election in 2007 he promised to extend this to the national telephone company and the power sector. Rafael Correa in Ecuador has been equally unilateral, dictating terms of the country's external debt, renegotiating oil contracts and talking of a twenty-first century socialism. In Bolivia, Evo Morales has perhaps gone furthest of all, seizing control over state gas reserves, and sending in troops to enforce the order. Furthermore these trends are not restricted to 'strategic sectors' such as oil and gas.

In 2005, Bolivia also cancelled the contract of the privatised water provider Aguas del Illimani, a subsidiary of the $53 billion French company Suez. The move was highly popular with the people, not least because of the high charges that the company had introduced. Furthermore, this widespread dissatisfaction with the record of privatised utilities can be seen in many Latin American countries, where there is increasing resentment at escalating costs and, more subtly, the feeling that profits should not be made through the provision of such basic services.

It will be very interesting to see how this process develops in Latin America and beyond, but we do appear to have seen the high water-mark of privatisations pass. The view that 'market forces' are always and everywhere superior has been undermined. The 'public good' element of many essential services has resurfaced. The vital importance of strong regulation of monopoly providers – whether they be in private or public hands – has never been more relevant.

It should also be noted that this process of the divesting of state assets through privatisation raises major regulatory issues, since the now private industries – often in a natural monopoly position – are no longer directly controlled by the state, but must be regulated in the public interest. As with many of the more descriptive elements of this chapter, these issues will be considered in Chapter 5 when we consider reform of the domestic financial system in developing countries.

To summarise the key points thus far:

- Financial sector development is associated with economic growth.
- Macroeconomic stability is an essential prerequisite for financial sector development.
- Countries with an English common law tradition, strong protection for shareholder rights, good accounting standards, low levels of corruption and no explicit deposit insurance tend to be more market-based.
- Countries with a French civil law tradition tend to have underdeveloped financial systems and be more bank-based.
- Effective regulatory regimes are crucial for financial sector development.
- Contractual savings institutions are important for developing key aspects of the financial system, notably stock and bond markets.
- Private ownership is crucial in ensuring that there is a sufficient supply of local equities to meet this demand.
- The privatisation of state enterprises has an important role to play in this regard, but the process raises serious political and regulatory issues.

We have seen that different countries at different levels of development and with different legal traditions are likely to have different forms of financial sector development, and the relative size and efficiency of the different aspects of their financial system will also vary significantly.

What lessons does this hold for developing countries wishing to develop particular aspects of their financial sectors?

4.3 Banks, stock markets, bond markets and economic growth

4.3.1 Banks

The important role that banks can play in facilitating economic growth has long been known. Both Walter Bagehot in the nineteenth century, and Joseph Schumpeter at the start of the twentieth have stressed the importance of banks in channelling surplus finance to productive investments, and this is clearly a fundamentally important function in any successful economy.

In his seminal paper[14] on the foundations of economic growth, the economic historian Alexander Gerschenkron argued that, particularly at an early stage of development, countries could not rely on arm's-length capital markets to provide the long-term investment finance needed to kick-start growth. For this, large banks were an essential prerequisite.

More recently, Boyd and Prescott (1986) have developed models where banks lower the aggregate cost of obtaining and processing information below what would occur via capital markets alone, where each investor must acquire information individually.

The role of banks in reducing the asymmetric information problems inherent in financial transactions has already been discussed in this chapter, but as research into information theory has developed, this vital role has come to be seen as increasingly important.

As highlighted in previous chapters, King and Levine (1993) show empirically how these combined effects lead to a more efficient allocation of resources and therefore to higher economic growth. Levine and Zervos (1998) also test the proposition that banking development is positively associated with growth empirically, and find robust evidence that this is indeed the case.

4.3.2 Stock markets

Levine and Zervos (op. cit.) also test empirically for the relationship between growth and stock market development, and find that, as with banks, stock market development is also positively associated with economic growth. Why should this be, however?

A key function of stock markets is to provide liquidity. Thus investors can buy or sell shares whenever they choose to do so. For Levine (1991) and Bencivenga *et al.* (1995), this positively affects growth, as liquid markets enable longer-term investments to occur more easily than would otherwise be the case. The rationale for this is that investors will only be prepared to commit funds to long-term projects if there is sufficient liquidity, so that they know they can withdraw this funding at any point.[15]

For Hicks (1969) this attribute of stock markets was a key factor in the start of the industrial revolution in Britain in the eighteenth century. For Hicks, the necessary technological innovations had been made some time before the start of the industrial revolution, and it was only with the development of deep and liquid stock markets that sustainable long-term financing became available and the industrial revolution began.

Another explanation for the link between stock market development and growth is that a large, integrated stock market enables investors to diversify their portfolios fully.[16] As a result, they are prepared to invest in higher risk assets than would be the case if their portfolio were not balanced with other less risky, and uncorrelated assets. This enables more risky projects to be undertaken than would otherwise be the case, leading to higher growth on average over the longer term.

However, other theoretical work on the role of stock markets has suggested that stock market development may be negative for growth. The liquidity that stock markets introduce into the financial system may also have the effect of reducing incentives for investors to monitor corporate behaviour, as they know they can withdraw their funds at any point. For Shleifer and Vishny (1986) this can adversely affect corporate governance, leading to a less efficient allocation of resources and therefore lower growth. Another perspective in this respect is that the development of stock markets may adversely affect savings rates, as savers may prefer to seek higher investment returns on the stock market.

From an empirical perspective, the evidence on this theoretical debate currently suggests that (a) stock markets are positively associated with economic growth, capital accumulation and productivity growth, and (b) stock market development does not adversely affect savings rates (Levine and Zervos, 1998).

However, it is also the case that stock market development may only become a positive impetus to higher growth after a certain level of economic development has been achieved. In particular, many of the positive features described above – such as the ability of investors to fully diversify their portfolios through the stock market – are dependent on there being a sufficiently developed and diverse industrial structure to the underlying economy. In less developed countries this may not be so, suggesting that overly focusing on establishing the structures of a stock market in poorer countries may be the wrong priority.

Box 4.2 considers these issues in this regard with respect to the experience of stock market development in sub-Saharan Africa in the 1990s.

Box 4.2 Stock market development in sub-Saharan Africa

The oldest stock market in sub-Saharan Africa was established in South Africa in 1887. For more than half a century that was it, until Zimbabwe established an exchange in 1946. The next to follow suit was Kenya in 1954, followed by Nigeria (1961) and Côte d'Ivoire (1976). There was then a hiatus in the process of developing stock exchanges, until a wave of exchanges were established in the late 1980s and early 1990s as shown in the table below.

Stock markets in sub-Saharan Africa

Country	Companies	Market capitalisation (US$mn)		Turnover (US$mn)
		1990	1996	
South Africa (1887)	626	137,540	241,571	27,202
Zimbabwe (1946)	64	2,395	2,635	255
Kenya (1954)	56	453	1,846	67
Nigeria (1961)	183	1,372	3,560	72
Côte d'Ivoire (1976)	31	549	914	19
Botswana (1989)	12	na	326	31

Ghana (1989)	21	na	1,492	17
Namibia (1992)	12	na	472	38
Swaziland (1990)	6	17	1,642	8
Mauritius (1989)	40	268	1,676	78
Malawi (1996)	na	na	na	na
Zambia (1994)	5	na	229	3

Source: Kenny and Moss, 1998.

In this chapter we have considered the theoretical and empirical arguments in favour of stock exchanges as an important component of financial sector development – as well as more general economic development. It was arguments of this form no doubt that were put to policy-makers in the latest group of countries in sub-Saharan Africa to establish exchanges.

As can be seen from the table above, with the exception of South Africa, stock markets in the region remain very small indeed, both in absolute terms as well as relative to the size of their economies – for example, market capitalisation in Nigeria in 1996 was 8% of GDP, compared to more than 100% in other developing regions. Also, with the exception of South Africa again, the exchanges tend to be concentrated in a narrow range of sectors that are most important to the countries concerned. Furthermore, excluding South Africa, turnover is very low relative to that seen in other regions: in 1995 none of these markets had a turnover greater than 10% of market cap (compared with more than 200% in Turkey and more than 100% in China at the same time) and eight of the twelve most illiquid stock markets in the world were in sub-Saharan Africa.

This small size, high concentration and low liquidity has – unsurprisingly – produced high levels of volatility, with national exchanges gaining or losing more than 100% of their value in any one year not being uncommon.

However, as the table above shows, there was considerable growth in some newly founded exchanges in the years immediately after their launch and – given their small size – this growth has continued since the mid-1990s.

Sub-Saharan African exchanges remain characterised by the factors described above, however: in 2007 the top performing exchange was Zimbabwe's Mining Index, which rose 160% on the back of booming global commodity prices. This highlights the fragile nature of the exchanges – massive ups or downs driven by international factors which may not have any relationship with the real economies in question. Market turmoil – including suspension of trading – in early 2008 as the impact of the US subprime crisis is felt highlights this point well.

As long as the exchanges remain small, concentrated and illiquid this will continue to be the case. There has been considerable debate about the creation of regional exchanges in sub-Saharan Africa to overcome the problems described above, and create a situation where the benefits identified with stock market development can materialise. For the positives to outweigh the negatives, this would seem a very promising option.

4.3.3 Bond markets

Although numerous studies purport to investigate the role of capital markets in spurring economic growth, in reality the overwhelming bulk of this work has focused on stock rather than bond markets. In part this is understandable, since the importance of bond markets in most developing countries is very low, as illustrated in the table below for some Asian economies in 1996.

Despite this relative lack of academic interest in the subject, policy-makers have increasingly stressed the importance of developing broad and deep local bond markets in developing countries. This has been particularly notable in recent years in Asia, where the perception has developed that the lack of such markets made the region vulnerable to the financial crises of 1997 and 1998.

Why do equity markets seem to develop more readily than bond markets, though? In many ways this is related to the nature of the two instruments. An equity share affords the investor a proportional stake in the future of the company, where the 'upside' is essentially unlimited. In contrast, the return on a bond is limited to the interest, while the downside is that the principal may not be paid – there may be a default. If there are concerns about the

Table 4.8 Banks, stock markets and corporate bond markets in emerging Asia

Country	Domestic credit by banking sector		Stock market capitalisation		Domestic corporate debt securities	
	Amount (% GDP)	Change (% GDP)	Total (%GDP)	Equity raised (% GCF*)	Outstanding (% GDP)	Net issues (% GCF)
Hong Kong	162.4	70.8	244.8	na	0.6	0.0
Indonesia	55.4	31.9	34.8	8.0	na	na
Korea	65.7	29.5	33.5	4.0	17.4	10.9
Malaysia	93.1	43.9	269.2	14.0	23.3	18.9
Philippines	49.0	68.5	84.8	8.0	0.0	0.0
Singapore	97.3	36.1	161.6	na	2.7	18.9
Taiwan	142.2	35.8	84.7	na	na	na
Thailand	100.0	31.3	65.8	6.0	3.9	1.*
Average	**95.64**	**43.48**	**122.4**	**8.0**	**8.0**	**5.3**

Source: Herring and Chatusripitak, 2000.

* = Gross fixed capital formation.

possibility of default, it will be difficult to develop a local bond market, particularly where the legal framework establishing and enforcing a bondholder's rights in the event of a default are not clearly set out.

Given all this, issuers of bonds may not credibly be able to offer a high enough rate of interest to compensate investors for the perceived risks. In contrast, while equity investors also hold significant downside risks, their incentives and those of the company's management are usually more aligned – both tend to profit from a rise in the share price. Consequently, a well-developed stock market may result in investors being happy to purchase shares in a company, when they would not be prepared to hold the same company's corporate bonds. The incentives facing the issuers and holders of bonds are clearly not well aligned (Herring and Chatusripitak, 2000).

Despite these problems, there are clear advantages in developing a local corporate bond market, not least of which is the fact that important information is contained in the market-determined interest rates attached to corporate bonds. This has important implications for the efficiency and structure of the other aspects of the financial system, and will be covered in more detail in Chapter 5.

To summarise, while there is little academic evidence to link bond market development to economic growth, and corporate bond markets are extremely limited in most developing countries, the development of a deep and broad corporate bond market is an important component of a country's financial sector development, particularly at later stages of development.

Having considered structural issues in financial sector development, and the linkages between the components of the financial sector and growth, the next section focuses on the crucial role played by governments in the domestic financial system.

4.4 The role of the government in the domestic economy and financial system

From an economic perspective, a number of key governmental functions are commonly identified. If the market mechanism always worked perfectly, circumstances where governments could beneficially intervene in the economy would, in theory, be non-existent. However, even the strongest champions of free markets accept that the market will not always function in this way: three clear circumstances where government intervention may be warranted are commonly proposed:

(a) The provision of 'public goods' and prevention of 'public bads'

From the earliest days of economic thinking, a key role of the state has been seen as the production of 'public goods'. A public good is one that, even if consumed by one person, can still be consumed by others. Furthermore, it is not possible to prevent other people consuming it, or at least not in any practicable sense. Consequently, such a good will not be provided by the private sector, since they cannot control its consumption and thereby profit from its use.

For example, if the state did not provide street lighting, you might decide to invest in a system of lighting for your street. However, there would be no way to prevent other residents from benefiting from this – from 'free riding' on the back of your investment, despite the fact that they had not contributed to it.

As well as public goods of this form, there are also 'public bads' – pollution, for example. Just as the private sector has no incentive to provide public goods, they have little or no incentive to prevent public bads.

This captures the idea of 'externalities', where the cost or benefit to society differs from the private cost or benefit in ways that cannot be captured by the price mechanism. The idea of externalities was formalised in the work of the economist Arthur Pigou in the first half of the twentieth century. Pigou was concerned with how economics could be used to enhance public welfare, and argued that the presence of externalities prevented the market producing many welfare-enhancing goods. For example, Pigou argued that the planting of trees by a private individual brought benefits to his neighbours for which the planter was not compensated – they were able to free-ride on his efforts. As a result, there would be fewer trees planted than was desirable from society's perspective. Similarly, a company that pollutes a river may be able to escape the economic consequences of its action, but the cost to society may be large. Again, there will be an 'overproduction' of such social bads as those responsible do not bear the economic consequences of their actions.

To address these issues, governments therefore have an accepted role in the provision of public goods, and, increasingly, in the prevention of public bads. No other party can perform this function.

(b) Correcting (or compensating for) market failures

If the market mechanism were always perfect the result would be a Pareto efficient competitive equilibrium, where it would be impossible to allocate resources more efficiently – for one person to be made better off without another being made worse off. However, where markets do not operate in this manner, government may be able to improve outcomes through intervention. Formally, this is a situation of 'market failure' where the first fundamental theorem of welfare economic[17] does not hold.

Market failures may occur in many situations. For example, a lack of competition, the presence of externalities as discussed above, or – as has been increasingly stressed – the impact of asymmetric information, may all lead to market failures. This latter point came to the fore in the 1970s and 1980s,[18] where it was demonstrated that the pervasive nature of asymmetric information inevitably implied that market failure was not a rare anomaly, but rather was commonplace in many market situations. Having said that, the degree to which the existence of market failure is accepted, and the extent to which it is seen as possible for governments to improve on the situation is very much a matter of perspective.

Stiglitz (1989a) famously argues that the extent of market failure was such that government intervention could be welfare-enhancing in many situations and was therefore often justified. Others have argued that, while this may be correct in principle, in practice government policy rarely achieves its stated outcomes: 'government failure' is therefore the other side of the coin to market failure.

Those who look for market failure tend to find it. Those who look for market efficiency (or at least potential efficiency) also tend to find it. Similarly, examples of government failure are not difficult to find, but supporters of government intervention can also point to significant successes.

On balance, therefore, it is certainly the case that markets can and do fail, and that this occurs more frequently than is often supposed. Furthermore, in many of these situations, government intervention has the *potential* to produce superior outcomes. However, to err is certainly human, and this fact is compounded by strong pressures on government which often have the effect of distorting policy, even if correctly conceived in the first place.

The acceptance of the fact that markets do not *automatically* lead to optimal outcomes is demonstrated by the pervasive use of regulation by governments of all hues, even those with the strongest free-market traditions. As we have seen, in the financial sphere, if liberalisation proceeds before a robust and effective system of prudential regulation and supervision is in place the result is very often a serious financial crisis. That is, if left to their own devices, the activities of financial actors do not necessarily produce positive outcomes from the perspective of society: they need to be firmly steered in this direction through regulation and supervision.

In the more general economic sphere, competition is often viewed as the guarantor of efficient and positive outcomes. However, many of the privatisations described above have turned public monopolies into private monopolies. Economic theory teaches that monopolists will tend to exploit their position to the detriment of society at large. Again, therefore, the government has a vital role to play in effectively regulating these newly privatised industries.

(c) Redistribution

Although, as we have seen, competitive market equilibriums result in Pareto efficient outcomes, this says nothing about the equity of these outcomes. In this regard, the role of redistributing income and wealth has also long been a key function of government. Consequently, despite its erosion in many countries, most developed nations retain a progressive taxation system to at least some extent. Under these systems the rich pay proportionally more of their income in tax, allowing resources to be redistributed to poorer sections of society.

As we shall see below, progressive taxation systems of this form are far less common in developing countries, although the greater levels of inequality in these countries – particularly in Latin America – suggest that redistribution is, if anything, a more urgent task in these societies.

These three categories describe the broad areas within which governments operate, but what does this mean in practice?

4.4.1 Implement fiscal policy

In order to do almost anything a government needs resources. By far the most important source of government revenue is the tax system, and two distinct different forms of taxation can be identified.

(a) Direct taxes

Direct taxes are, as the name suggests, levied directly on income or wealth and are applied to both individuals and corporations.

The two major forms of direct taxation are, first, *personal income tax*, which is levied on personal income regardless of its source. Income tax may be levied in a uniform (or 'global') system where everyone's income – regardless of source – is subject to a single tax rate or, alternatively, taxes may be set at different rates depending on the individual's level of income. The first of these finds its modern expression in the increasingly popular 'flat tax', whereas the latter is associated with 'progressive taxation' where the rate levied on income rises as you move up the income scale. With progressive taxation, higher earners pay a proportionally larger slice of their income in taxes. Income tax may also be applied as a differentiated (or 'schedular') system, where each source of income is subject to a specific rate of tax.

The second main form of direct taxation is *corporation tax*. As with personal income tax, corporation tax could, in principle, be levied in a 'global' or 'schedular' manner, though in practice a flat rate is usually applied to all profits, regardless of source.

Having said that, governments can and do use the corporate tax system to encourage growth in particular industries, and may also apply a lower rate of tax to smaller companies so as to spur the development of the small-and-medium-enterprises (SME) sector.

In addition to personal and corporate income taxes, many countries implement a levy to fund national services such as social security and healthcare. In theory, such schemes are not officially taxes at all, as individuals contribute to national schemes from which they can later draw down benefits – such as pensions, for example. In the UK, this is termed National Insurance, and the corresponding scheme in the USA is known as the Payroll Tax. Despite the fact that such schemes are not officially taxes, they have gradually increased so that, in some cases, their impact on the individual is greater than that of direct personal taxation.

(b) Indirect taxes

Indirect taxes are most commonly applied to the sales of goods and services – such as VAT in the UK, for example. Indirect taxes derive their name from the fact that, although they are collected from the seller of a good or service, they are passed on to the ultimate consumer in the form of higher prices.

As well as sales taxes such as VAT, other forms of indirect taxation are, first, excise duties, where the intention is not to raise revenue *per se*, but rather to influence the pattern of consumption, by discouraging the consumption of certain goods – tobacco, for example.

A third form of indirect taxation is trade taxes, which may be levied on either imports or exports – overwhelmingly they have been applied to imports in practice. As we shall see, in many developing countries, import taxes have been and remain an important source of government revenue. As with direct taxation, import taxes may be uniformly applied to all imports or may be differentiated if the desire is to protect a particular sector from international competition.

Having considered the various forms of taxation that could, in principle, be levied, Table 4.9 below details the sources of government tax revenue in practice for different categories of country and region.

Perhaps the most striking feature of Table 4.9 is the disparity between the total tax take as a proportion of GDP between developed and developing countries. For the former the average figure for 1990 to 2002 is 27.6% of GDP, while the corresponding figure for developing countries is just 12.6%. Clearly, therefore, the scope for public expenditure in developing countries – relative to the size of the economy – is far less. Indeed, it is less than half of what is possible in the developed world.

When we consider the different sources of tax revenue, we see that developed countries obtain roughly a third of their total tax take from each

Table 4.9 Sources of government tax revenues as percentage of GDP, 1990–2002 averages

Category	Direct taxes	Payroll taxes	Sales taxes	Trade taxes	Total
Developed countries	9.9	8.9	8.7	0.1	27.6
Developing countries	4.3	0.1	5.2	3.0	12.6
Region	*Direct taxes*	*Payroll taxes*	*Sales taxes*	*Trade taxes*	
Africa	4.6	0.0	5.2	5.0	14.8
Asia & Oceania	4.8	0.0	4.0	2.6	11.4
Latin America & Caribbean	3.4	1.1	5.6	2.1	12.2

Source: United Nations Online Network in Public Administration and Finance (UNPAN).

of direct, payroll and sales taxes and a negligible quantity from trade taxes. In contrast, almost a quarter of developing countries' tax take was derived from trade taxes with 34% and 41% being obtained from direct taxes and sales taxes respectively.

The regional snapshot highlights the fact that trade taxes are a particularly important source of revenue in Africa – amounting to 5% of GDP – and that the direct tax take is particularly low in Latin America and the Caribbean.

The second aspect of fiscal policy is obviously government expenditure. What are the key issues and trends in this respect? Although, as we have seen, government tax revenues in developing countries are, on average, less than half that of developed countries, this pattern is not mirrored when we consider expenditure.

Table 4.10 highlights the fact that, although developed country governments receive only 12.6% of GDP as tax revenues, their expenditure is almost double this at more than 24% of GDP. Governments clearly have other sources of revenue beyond taxation – as demonstrated by the fact that developed countries' expenditure is also considerably higher than their total tax revenue. However, in relative terms the additional expenditure in developing countries is far greater than that seen in the developed economies, which reflects the impact of external borrowing on the one hand, and 'official development assistance' (i.e. aid) on the other. These issues will be explored in depth in Chapter 6 when we consider the external sector, but it is worth highlighting the importance of these external sources of finance to many developing countries at this stage.

Table 4.11 reveals some interesting facts about the pattern of public expenditure – as well as its scale relative to GDP – in developed and developing countries. For the developed economies, the largest expenditure item by far is 'other social services', which refers to social safety nets such as unemployment benefits, as well as pensions and other direct transfers by the state. For developed countries, expenditure of this form amounts to 42% of

Table 4.10 Government expenditure as percentage of GDP, 1996–2002

Category	Median level
Developed countries	36.8
Developing countries	24.1
Region	*Median level*
Africa	28.6
Latin America & Caribbean	21.0
Asia & Oceania	23.6

Source: United Nations Online Network in Public Administration and Finance (UNPAN).

Table 4.11 Government expenditure as percentage of total expenditure and GDP,*
1990–2002 average

	Category		Region		
	Developed	Developing	Africa	Asia	Latin America
Administration and public order	11.2 (2.1)	13.7 (3.4)	15.4 (3.9)	12.8 (3.5)	13.3 (2.8)
Defence	5.3 (1.8)	10.6 (2.7)	10.3 (2.4)	14.7 (4.3)	5.9 (1.1)
Education	7.8 (2.9)	15.9 (4.1)	16.1 (4.6)	15.1 (4.1)	16.7 (3.6)
Health	10.9 (3.8)	7.6 (2.0)	6.1 (1.8)	6.3 (1.8)	10.6 (2.3)
Other social services	42.0 (14.9)	14.5 (3.9)	10.1 (3.2)	12.3 (3.8)	21.3 (4.7)
Economic services	9.9 (3.5)	18.6 (4.5)	18.1 (4.8)	21.3 (5.3)	15.7 (3.3)
Interest payments	9.8 (3.4)	11.6 (3.0)	13.4 (3.7)	9.4 (2.4)	12.8 (3.0)
Other expenditure	7.9 (2.6)	7.4 (1.7)	10.4 (2.5)	8.1 (1.9)	3.7 (0.7)

Source: United Nations Online Network in Public Administration and Finance (UNPAN).

* Figures in parentheses equal expenditure as proportion of GDP.

total government expenditure, and almost 15% of GDP – the corresponding figure for developing countries is just 14.2% of total spending, and 3.9% of GDP.

More generally, another important difference is that spending is quite evenly spread in developing countries, with no single category accounting for more than a fifth of total expenditure. The largest single category is 'economic services', which relates to government spending on agriculture, energy, all forms of industry (including research and development), transport and communication. On average developing countries devote 18.6% of total spending to these areas, compared to 9.9% for developed countries.

This higher relative spending reflects the fact that, on average, governments in developing countries have been and remain more directly involved in their economies than is generally the case in developed countries. However, the data presented here are averages for 1990–2002, a period that, as we have seen, witnessed more than eight thousand privatisations in developing countries. Clearly, therefore, the difference between developed and developing countries in this respect has narrowed, though it is certainly the case that a significant distinction remains.

Figure 4.2 highlights spending patterns on the key areas of defence, education and health, comparing developed countries as a group with Africa, Asia and Latin America. Again some interesting and rather surprising features emerge. First, spending on education as a proportion of total expenditure is considerably higher in each of the developing regions than is the average case in developed countries – indeed, as Table 4.11 makes clear, this is true even if one looks at education spending as a proportion of GDP. Secondly, relative spending on defence is also higher in each of the developing regions than is

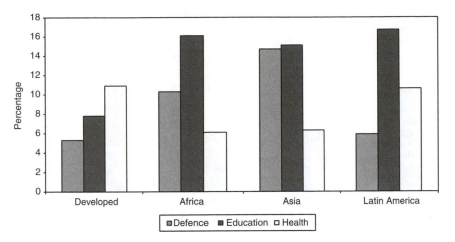

Figure 4.2 Pattern of government expenditure on selected categories, 1990–2002 (% of total expenditure).

Source: United Nations Online Network in Public Administration and Finance (UNPAN).

the average case in developed countries – the difference in Latin America is slight, but that for Africa and, particularly Asia is far more pronounced, with both committing a substantially higher proportion of their GDP to defence spending.

Thirdly, relative health expenditure in developed countries is above that seen in all the developing regions – again, the difference with Latin America is slight in terms of total expenditure, but not so with respect to GDP. On average developed countries commit almost double the proportion of GDP to health expenditure compared with developing countries as a group, and more than double the amount committed in Africa and Asia.

A final, quite surprising, aspect of the comparative patterns of public spending to emerge from this analysis is that expenditure on debt interest payments is quite similar across all the categories. For developed countries as a whole the figures are 9.8% of expenditure, or 3.4% of GDP, while the corresponding figures for developing countries are 11.6% and 3%. Regionally, Africa devotes the highest proportion of total expenditure to interest payments at 13.4%, but even here this amounts to 3.7% of GDP, a similar level to that seen in developed countries.

4.4.2 Macroeconomic policy and macroeconomic stability

In every aspect of development finance that we have considered thus far, the importance of macroeconomic stability has been stressed. Indeed, if the government is to achieve its principal long-term objective of raising growth rates, it is widely accepted that achieving macroeconomic stability is an essential prerequisite. What are the issues and what is the record in this regard, however?

The three principal instruments used to conduct macroeconomic policy are fiscal policy, monetary policy and exchange rate policy. In the previous section we examined government revenue raising and expenditure but, from a stability perspective, the crucial issue is the overall fiscal balance. That is to say, a government that consistently spends more revenue than it obtains runs an overall fiscal deficit, which must ultimately undermine macroeconomic stability – not least through the temptation to print money to finance the deficit.

Table 4.3 illustrates the recent record in this respect, comparing central government fiscal balances between developed and developing countries on the one hand, and between the developing regions on the other. As we can see, the aggregate picture for developing countries – while still in deficit in 2006 – has shown a steady improvement from the late 1990s. In contrast, the trend for aggregate balances in developed countries has gone in the other direction, with the situation in 2006 being considerably worse than was the case in 1998 – though an improvement on the low point of 2003.

From a regional perspective, all have seen an improvement over the period, with Eastern and Central Europe showing the least progress and Africa showing the most. Indeed, of all the categories and regions considered, it is only Africa that ends the period with a central government fiscal surplus.

Turning to monetary policy, the key to stability is control of the rate of inflation. Various approaches to this have been adopted over recent decades, which have been more or less successful. From the late 1970s and early 1980s, the monetarist prescription of controlling the money supply as a means of

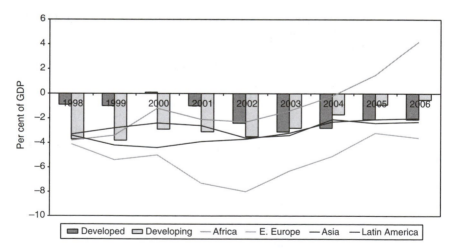

Figure 4.3 Central government fiscal balances, 1998–2006.

Source: IMF WEO.

holding down inflation was even less successful in developing countries than it was in the developed world, and has generally been abandoned.

More recently, the trend – particularly, though not exclusively in developed countries – has been for central banks to be given independence in setting interest rates, and charged with targeting the rate of inflation itself, often in a symmetrical fashion. This approach is well demonstrated by the UK, where following the election of the Labour Government in 1997, the Bank of England's Monetary Policy Committee (MPC) was granted independence in the setting of interest rates, with a mandate to hit a particular inflation target set by the UK Treasury. At the time of writing (2008) this target is 2.5% and it is symmetrical in the sense that the job is not to keep inflation below this level, but to aim precisely to hit it. Therefore, just as when inflation is too high, the MPC should raise interest rates to reduce it, if it is persistently below this level the onus is on the Committee to reduce interest rates and raise inflation to this level. The rationale behind this policy is to prevent an excessive focus on squeezing inflation out of the system from adversely affecting growth rates, a policy that the US Federal Reserve has long followed through its dual mandate of controlling inflation and maximising growth and employment.

Although these issues will be discussed in more detail in the context of reform in developing countries in the next chapter, it is useful to consider what the record has been with respect to inflation in recent years.

Figure 4.4 illustrates the fact that, as with fiscal balances, developing countries as a group have seen a steady improvement in their inflation record since the late 1990s, although at the end of the period inflation remained above that seen in the developed economies.

That said, an aggregate figure of 5.2% is a remarkable achievement when seen in its historical context. From 1988 to 1997, for example, the average rate

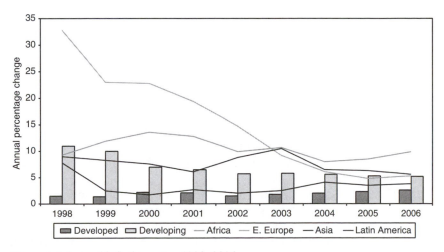

Figure 4.4 Annual inflation rates, 1998–2006.

Source: IMF WEO.

of inflation in developing countries stood at 53.5%, compared to a developed country average of 3.4% over the same period.

From a regional perspective, all the developing regions considered saw inflation fall over the period, with Africa seeing the least progress in this respect and Eastern and Central Europe seeing a huge fall from more than 30% to less than 5%. Clearly, therefore, both in the aggregate and for each developing region, macroeconomic stability – in terms of fiscal balances and inflation rates – has improved significantly over the past decade.

The situation with regard to exchange rates is more complex, and is strongly related to events in the developed economies. As we know, the 1970s saw the collapse of the system of fixed exchange rates established at Bretton Woods in the 1940s. Subsequently, freely floating or managed floating rates in the developed world exhibited far greater volatility than had previously been the case. Policy issues with respect to exchange rates – i.e. to float or not to float – will be examined in detail in subsequent chapters, but it should be noted that more than half of all developing countries have continued to peg their currencies to those of the developed world – usually the US dollar. Higher volatility in developed country exchange rates has therefore been transmitted directly to the developing countries whose currencies have been pegged, which has had significant implications for international trade and domestic financial policy.

Regionally, by 2002 more than 70% of Latin American economies maintained a fixed exchange rate peg, with slightly less than 70% of African economies doing likewise. For developing Asia, the figure was slightly less than 50%, down from a high of 90% in 1996, prior to the Asian crisis (IMF, 2003). As we shall see in later chapters, a key impact – from a policy perspective – of the Asian crisis was to call into question the faith in pegged exchange rates, which for many observers gave speculators a one-way bet against the currencies concerned and played a major role in the onset of the crisis, as well as its depth and duration.

4.4.3 Economic and financial regulation

An important determinant of macroeconomic and financial stability is the effectiveness of government regulation. We have seen in repeated studies and in repeated contexts that effective financial regulation and supervision is essential for developing a strong financial sector, and for ensuring that the financial system is able to have the positive effect on economic growth that theory predicts.

Historically, most governments have attempted to regulate and supervise indirectly, through appointing specific institutions to perform these functions within particular areas of activity. That is, these functions have been divided, so that different institutions have responsibility for regulating and supervising different components of the financial system: the banking industry, securities markets and the insurance sector.

As we have seen, of all the components of the financial system in developing countries, by far the most important is the banking system. Table 4.12 below gives some selected information on the most important structural differences in the regulation and supervision of the banking system between developed and developing countries.

The first section of Table 4.12 deals with the regulation of bank activities. In terms of levels of restriction, the higher the number the greater the restriction, with 4 representing the maximum level of restriction. As we can see, it is clearly the case that developing countries – on average – impose considerably higher restrictions on the non-banking activities that banks can engage in than do the developed economies. This trend is confirmed by the fact that restrictiveness decreases as one moves from low- to middle- to high-income countries. It is also noteworthy that, regardless of the level of development, all countries impose stricter restrictions upon banks engaging in real estate than in the other two categories of activity.

The second section considers restrictions on banks owning non-financial institutions and vice versa. Although restrictions are somewhat higher in developing than in developed countries, the difference is not great, but both categories of countries place fewer restrictions on non-financial firms owning banks than vice versa.

Turning to restrictions on the entry and participation of foreign banks in the domestic market, we see that, despite the fact that considerable liberalisation has occurred, developing countries on average retain stronger controls in this respect.

For measures of the capital banks are required to hold, all show greater stringency in developed than in developing countries, though interestingly restrictions on the total bank capital that can be held by a single owner are stronger in the developing world.

Again, it is interesting to note that the official power granted to banking supervisors is similar for both developed and developing countries, though, as has been stressed before, it is not the extent of official powers that is often crucial, but rather the degree to which they are enforced in practice.

When we consider overall supervisory resources, we see the developing countries have a far greater number – more than 3 to 1 – of supervisors per bank, with supervisory hours spent at banks also being correspondingly higher. The other variables in this section are slightly in the favour of the developed countries, with the exception of supervisory independence, where the advantage enjoyed by the developed countries is significantly more pronounced.

Finally, private monitoring of the banking system tends to increase as one moves from developing to developed countries, but the stringency of accounting disclosure requirements is broadly the same in both categories.

In Chapter 5 we will consider the relative importance of these differences in regulatory and supervisory approaches, particularly with regard to differences between the developing regions. Also, in terms of general trends, an

Table 4.12 Banking regulation and supervision: developed vs. developing countries, 2001

Variable	Developed countries	Developing countries
Bank Activity Regulatory Variables		
a) Securities activities[1]	1.37	2.04
b) Insurance activities[2]	2.22	2.90
c) Real estate activities[3]	2.40	3.19
Mixing Banking/Commerce Regulatory Variables		
a) Bank ownership of non-financial firms[4]	2.22	2.53
b) Non-financial firms' ownership of banks[5]	1.77	2.13
Competition Regulatory Variables		
a) Limitations of foreign banks' ownership of domestic banks[6]	0.08	0.31
b) Limitations of foreign bank entry[7]	0.04	0.17
c) Entry into banking requirements[8]	7.19	7.38
Capital Regulatory Variables		
a) Overall capital stringency[9]	4.19	3.20
b) Initial capital stringency[10]	1.85	1.46
c) Capital regulatory index[11]	6.08	4.65
d) Maximum capital % by single owner[12]	88.70	59.49
Official Supervisory Action Variables		
a) Official supervisory power[13]	11.08	11.11
i) Prompt corrective action[14]	1.19	2.27
ii) Restructuring power[15]	2.50	2.60
iii) Declaring insolvency power[16]	1.27	1.62
b) Supervisory forbearance discretion[17]	1.96	1.49
c) Loan classification stringency[18]	280.3	408.05
d) Provisioning stringency[19]	33.7	133.4
e) Liquidity/diversification index[20]	2.04	1.90
Official Supervisory Resource Variables		
a) Supervisors per bank[21]	0.94	3.13
b) Bank supervisor years per bank[22]	10.96	31.79
c) Supervisor tenure[23]	8.57	7.14
d) Onsite examination frequency[24]	1.70	1.49
e) Likelihood supervisor moves into banking[25]	1.92	1.79
f) Independence of supervisory authority[26]	2.19	1.55
Private Monitoring Variables		
a) Certified audit required[27]	0.96	0.92
b) % of 10 largest banks rated by international rating agency[28]	68.50	44.69
c) Accounting disclosure and director liability[29]	2.54	2.66
f) Private monitoring index[30]	6.85	6.66

Source: Barth, Caprio, Levine and Ross, 2001.

* The variables from Table 4.10 are described on p. 121. Following the description the figures in parentheses are first, the minimum possible value and, second, the maximum possible value.

Variable	Developed countries	Developing countries

1. The ability of banks to engage in the business of securities underwriting, brokering, dealing, and all aspects of the mutual fund industry. (1.0–4.0)
2. The ability of banks to engage in insurance underwriting and selling. (1.0–4.0)
3. The ability of banks to engage in real estate investment, development, and management. (1.0–4.0)
4. The ability of non-financial firms to own and control banks. (1.0–4.0)
5. The ability of banks to own and control non-financial firms. (1.0–4.0)
6. Whether there are any limitations placed on the ownership of domestic banks by foreign banks. (0.0–1.0)
7. Whether there are any limitations placed on the ability of foreign banks to enter the domestic banking industry. (0.0–1.0)
8. Whether there are specific legal submissions required to obtain a licence to operate as a bank. (2.0–8.0)
9. Whether there are explicit regulatory requirements regarding the amount of capital that a bank must have relative to various guidelines. (1.0–6.0)
10. Whether the source of funds counted as regulatory capital can include assets other than cash or government securities and borrowed funds as well as whether the sources are verified by the regulatory or supervisory authorities. (0.0–3.0)
11. The sum of the previous two measures of capital stringency. (1.0–9.0)
12. The maximum allowable percentage ownership of a bank's capital by a single owner. (2–100)
13. Whether the supervisory authorities have the authority to take specific actions to prevent and correct problems. (3.0–16.0)
14. Whether a law establishes pre-determined levels of bank solvency deterioration which forces automatic enforcement actions such as intervention. (0.0–6.0)
15. Whether the supervisory authorities have the power to restructure and reorganize a troubled bank. (0.0–3.0)
16. Whether the supervisory authorities have the power to declare a deeply troubled bank insolvent. (0.0–2.0)
17. The extent to which, even when authorised, supervisory authorities may engage in forbearance when confronted with violations of laws or regulations or with other imprudent behaviour on the part of banks. (0.0–4.0)
18. The degree to which loans in arrears must be classified as sub-standard, doubtful, or loss. (31–2,520)
19. The degree to which a bank must provision as a loan is classified first as sub-standard, then as doubtful, and lastly as loss. (0.0–205.)
20. The degree to which banks are encouraged or restricted with respect to liquidity as well as asset and geographical diversification. (0.0–3.0)
21. The number of professional bank supervisors per bank. (0–18)
22. The total number of years for all professional bank supervisors per bank. (0.09–270)
23. The average years of tenure of professional bank supervisors. (1.0–25.0)
24. The frequency of onsite examinations conducted in large and medium-size banks, 1 = annual, 2 = every 2 years. (0.5–5.0)
25. The fraction of supervisors employed by the banking industry subsequent to retirement. (0.0–3.0)
26. The degree to which the supervisory authority is independent. (1.0–3.0)
27. Whether an external audit is required of the financial statements of a bank and, if so, by a licensed or certified auditor. (0.0–1.0)
28. The percentage of the top 10 banks that are rated by international credit rating agencies. (0–100)
29. Whether the income statement includes accrued or unpaid interest or principal on non-performing loans and whether banks are required to produce consolidated financial statements. (1.0–3.0)
30. A composite measure of total private monitoring. (2.0–11.0)

important point to note is that recent years have seen something of a move away from segregated regulatory bodies with responsibility for particular sectors, towards single, unified regulators with responsibility for the financial system in its entirety (Luna-Martinez and Rose, 2003). Again, the rationale and implications of these moves will be assessed in the context of financial sector reform in the following chapter.

4.4.4 Reducing poverty through boosting growth

All the different roles that government can play in the financial system and wider economy are – or certainly should be – geared towards the end of increasing living standards and reducing poverty levels within their societies. As we have seen throughout this book, it is broadly accepted that the best means of doing this is through raising economic growth rates and ensuring that the proceeds of this growth are distributed equitably throughout society.

The approach taken here, of course, depends on what you consider the key drivers of growth to be: if the unfettered market is the best producer of growth in the long run, then the government should avoid direct intervention in the economy other than to set the framework within which the market mechanism can function. Alternatively, if you think that market failure is common and inherent, and that markets have no automatic tendency towards producing optimal outcomes, then it is necessary for the government to intervene far more in the economy for growth to be maximised.

Although, as we have seen, both theory and empirical evidence can offer a general guide in these areas, what is best for each individual country may often be influenced more by its particular features than by the faithful implementation of the policy recommendations of one school of thought rather than another. That is, active intervention can be highly successful, as best demonstrated by the success of the East Asian developmental states. Similarly, however, active intervention can also be disastrous if poorly designed or implemented. On the other hand, while markets have a vital role to play, assuming that the market mechanism by itself will always produce optimal outcomes is a recipe for disaster: institutions are not something to be added at a later stage, but a fundamental prerequisite for successful liberalisation. Similarly, sequencing and pace are vital. The varying records of developed countries and regions over recent decades are an undeniable testament to these facts.

In Chapter 2 we looked at headline GDP growth rates in the context of the relationship between financial sector development and growth, and noted the wide divergence between the developing regions. However, what actually matters of course is not GDP growth *per se*, but changes in per capita GDP: if GDP increases by 2% per year, but population growth is 4% per year, then average incomes decline by 2%.

As we can see from Figure 4.5, the record in this regard has been mixed to say the least, with very high levels of volatility exhibited. Furthermore, per

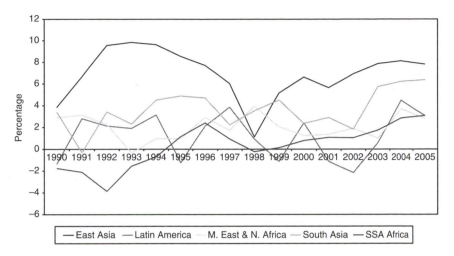

Figure 4.5 Annual percentage changes in GDP per capita, 1990–2005.

Source: World Bank WDI.

capita incomes have actually fallen at some points and in some regions, while many years are characterised by very low rates of growth.

Figure 4.6 illustrates the cumulative effects of these differential rates of growth in each of the regions, comparing the situation in 1990 with that in 2005. As we can see, in absolute terms Latin America and the Caribbean has by far the highest per capita GDP with an average income of more than US$4,000 per annum – though as we saw in the analysis of regional inequality, this income is concentrated in relatively few hands. In contrast, sub-Saharan

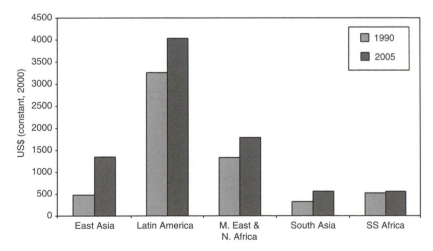

Figure 4.6 Regional per capita GDP rates, 1990 vs. 2005.

Source: World Bank WDI.

Africa has the lowest rate of per capita GDP, with an average of just US$560 per annum being earned.

These absolute levels are clearly of fundamental importance, but of equal weight is the progress being made – the direction of travel. When we examine the percentage change in per capita GDPs over the period, we see that the East Asian region has made remarkable progress, with the level of per capita GDP increasing by more than 180% between 1990 and 2005. The second largest increase has been in South Asia, which despite starting the period with the lowest per capita GDP level in absolute terms, saw it rise by 71.5% by 2005. The Middle East and North Africa, together, and Latin America also saw reasonable increases, though at 34% and 23% respectively these were less impressive, especially if one considers that this equates to average annual rises in per capita incomes of 2.2% and 1.6%.

However, it is sub-Saharan Africa that ends the period with both the lowest per capita GDP in absolute terms and the least progress in the preceding fifteen years. From 1990 to 2005 per capita incomes in the region grew by just 6.6%, or 0.4% per year on average. If average per capita incomes were to continue to grow at this rate, it would take the region almost 450 years just to reach the level of average incomes seen in Latin America in 2005, and 885 years to reach the level of per capita incomes enjoyed in today's high-income countries.

The successful experience of some developing regions in terms of raising per capita incomes strongly suggests that such poor outcomes are far from inevitable, and the proven link between financial sector development and growth implies that this sector has a crucial part to play. In the next chapter we will examine reforms that might further these goals, drawing on what we have learned from both theory and practice.

5 Reforming the domestic financial system

Options and issues

Introduction

In previous chapters we have seen that financial sector development has a strong influence on growth rates, which in turn are likely to result in reductions in poverty levels. We have also seen that there is not one single financial sector model that produces these outcomes: financial systems may facilitate sustained economic growth and development whether they are predominantly 'bank-based' (as in Germany and Japan) or 'market-based' (as in the UK and USA). Similarly, while either of these frameworks can produce these outcomes, it is equally true that neither is guaranteed to do so. Success, it seems, is not a matter of following a particular dogma.

To recap, the key functions of the financial system are:

1   to mobilise savings;
2   to transfer risks through time;
3   to obtain information on alternative investment opportunities;
4   to efficiently allocate capital to its most productive use;
5   to monitor the use of capital once allocated.

Historically, many of these functions have been undertaken by governments in developing countries, which, given the historical scepticism about the ability of free markets to produce optimal outcomes, was perhaps understandable. As we saw in Chapter 3, however, the results of controlling interest rates, directing credit and over-regulating the financial system were mixed at best: whilst there have been some noticeable success stories of the 'developmental state', particularly in East Asia, there are many more examples of failure.

These failures led to strong calls for the market mechanism to be placed at the heart of the financial system, and for an end to financial repression from the 1970s onwards. Financial liberalisation has been undertaken, to some extent, in virtually every developing and developed country since that time. However, as with the earlier developmental state approach, the results have been mixed. Examples of success sit alongside many cases where liberalisation has not achieved the predicted results.

This, in turn, has led to an increasing realisation that it is not liberalisation as such – just as it was not 'repression' as such – which inevitably leads to positive outcomes in terms of growth and poverty reduction. Rather, it is how the process is done in practice that counts. In this regard, the role of policy and institutions has become central to the debate on reform.

The World Bank (2001: ix) puts the issues as follows:

> At its best, finance works quietly in the background; but when things go wrong, financial sector failures are painfully visible. Both success and failure have their origins largely in the policy environment. Policy needs to create and sustain the institutional infrastructure – in such areas as information, law, and regulation – that is essential to the smooth functioning of financial contracts. Above all, policymakers need to work with the market to help align private incentives with public interest. As the ever-diminishing cost of communications and information technology leads to greater integration of global financial markets, policymakers face new challenges in ensuring this alignment. Governments must be prepared to recast their policies to take advantage of the opportunities resulting from global integration, and also to guard against the associated risks.

5.1 Reform of macroeconomic management

Whilst there are often disagreements on the best way to develop the different components of the financial system (or even whether to develop some of them at all), there is broad agreement that macroeconomic stability is an essential prerequisite for financial sector development – and economic growth and development more generally.

The three key areas of macroeconomic management are monetary policy, fiscal policy and exchange rate policy. Below we consider reform issues in each of these areas.

5.1.1 Monetary policy and the exchange rate

The purpose of monetary policy is to manage the level of prices in the economy and to encourage (or discourage) economic expansion (through an 'accommodating' or 'loose' monetary stance) or economic slow-down (through a 'tight' monetary stance). The primary tools of monetary policy are interest rates, which may be raised or lowered either directly (through the rate at which financial institutions can access central market funds) or indirectly (through 'open market operations', where the central bank issues or buys government debt, thereby altering the supply of money in the economy and so influencing the 'price' of money – i.e. the interest rate).

As indicated above, the national central bank is usually the institution charged with conducting monetary policy, but the nature of each bank's relationship with the political system has changed considerably, both over time within countries and at each point in time between countries.

As we shall see, the ability of countries to operate an independent monetary policy is dependent upon a number of factors, with perhaps the most important being exchange rate policy. In simple terms, a fully autonomous monetary policy is incompatible with a fixed exchange rate policy. One of the basic tasks of monetary policy is to alter the supply of money in the economy in response to domestic economic conditions, so that economic booms would require higher interest rates and a squeeze on the money supply and vice versa. However, in order to maintain an exchange rate peg, the central bank – or other competent authority – must intervene continually in the foreign exchange market, and the buying or selling of foreign exchange directly affects the size of money supply in the domestic economy. For example, to prevent an appreciation of its currency the central bank may buy foreign exchange (and sell its own currency) thereby increasing the money supply. The opposite condition holds when the central bank wishes to prevent a depreciation of its currency. Consequently, under a fixed exchange rate regime, the activities of the central bank with respect to the money supply are no longer governed solely by concerns over the domestic economy, but are primarily driven by the need to maintain a certain exchange rate.

This trade-off between policy objectives has been termed the 'impossible trinity'. The impossible trinity states that it is not possible to have a fixed exchange rate, an independent monetary policy and free movement of capital, and is formally based on the Mundell-Fleming model developed in the 1960s by Robert Mundell[1] and Marcus Fleming.

Despite these disadvantages, many developing countries have maintained a fixed exchange rate since the collapse of the Bretton Woods system in the early 1970s. In contrast, the trend among developed countries has been increasingly towards floating exchange rate regimes, with the exception being full monetary union, as introduced in the 1990s in European Union with the launch of the euro.

As we saw in the previous chapter, by 2002 70% of Latin American economies still maintained a fixed exchange rate peg, with slightly less than 70% of African economies doing likewise. For developing Asia, the figure was slightly less than half, which was significantly down from the high of 90% in 1996, prior to the Asian crisis (IMF, 2003).

For developing countries, the advantages of fixed exchange rates have long been rather compelling. Particularly in countries with a poor record on controlling inflation, a credible fixed exchange rate will, over the long term, cause the rate of inflation to converge with that in the country to which the currency is pegged. Thus the 'outsourcing' of monetary policy may be desirable if it leads to better outcomes regarding inflation. Secondly, maintaining a fixed exchange rate – particularly if the currency is fixed with respect to a country's main trading partner – is beneficial for the stability of international trade and ensures that the exchange rate does not become uncompetitive through appreciation.

It should be pointed out, however, that this is very much a best case scenario. If a fixed exchange rate is accompanied by fiscal and monetary laxity leading to high rates of inflation, the real exchange rate will progressively rise, leading ultimately to uncompetitive exports and a deteriorating balance of payments position. In such a situation, speculative pressure on the exchange rate is likely to build as speculators observe foreign exchange reserves – and so the means of maintaining the currency peg – used to finance the growing trade deficit.[2]

Under a fixed exchange rate regime, it is therefore the exchange rate that provides the 'anchor' for prices (and price expectations). Developed countries, in contrast, have tended to allow their exchange rates to float, and have looked elsewhere for price 'anchors'. As we saw in Chapter 4, the 1980s was the high-water mark of monetarism, where monetary policy was geared towards directly controlling the money supply (the 'intermediate target') with the aim of controlling inflation (the ultimate target). However, in practice this proved far more difficult than it had seemed in theory.

By the end of the 1980s, very few countries still directly targeted the money supply, with increasing numbers preferring to target prices directly. Since then more and more developed countries have adopted inflation targeting as the principal form of monetary policy and the central anchor for price expectations. An important part of this trend has been the credibility (or lack of it) of the central bank's commitment to hit its inflation target.

Inflationary expectations have powerful effects upon the outcome of monetary policy, with the result that policy has become increasingly geared towards managing these expectations. If a central bank has a known inflation target of, say, 2%, but it is widely believed that it lacks the will or means to achieve this target, then pay claims, for example, will factor in the assumption that inflation will be higher than the target. Higher pay settlements can then lead to the outcome that inflation is higher than 2%, as the cost of meeting the higher wages is passed on in the form of higher prices: the so called 'cost-push' form of inflation. Similarly, higher wages may increase the level of aggregate demand in the economy, again encouraging inflation: 'demand-pull' inflation.

A key determinant of the credibility of the central bank in this respect is the extent to which its decisions are politically influenced. So, for example, a needed increase in interest rates may be delayed prior to an election for political reasons, leading to the need for a sharper increase in rates after the election. Theoretically, these factors have been well-documented in the 'time inconsistency' literature,[3] which is built upon the observation that the 'pain' of monetary policy is immediate (i.e. higher interest rates) but the benefits may take years to materialise. The political cycle is therefore far more concerned to avoid inflicting 'pain' on the electorate (for which the politician may be punished by being voted out of office) than to taking the necessary steps to maintain monetary stability (for which the politician may obtain no benefit at all, as the time-scale is too long and the politician may already be out of office by the time positive effects can be seen).

Increasingly, the solution has been to make central banks independent and give them complete control over monetary policy. Where inflation targeting is used – as in the UK and Eurozone, for example – the central bank is thus given a target for inflation and is charged with implementing monetary policy to achieve this target.

While some developing countries have adopted a system of inflation targeting, the majority have not. The divergence of policy choices of developed and developing countries with regard to monetary and exchange rate policy is interesting, and suggests some underlying structural differences between the different types of economy.

Bird (2004) lists a number of preconditions that are needed if inflation targeting is to be effective:

1   Inflation forecasting needs to be accurate and well-developed.
2   The central bank must be independent, or effectively autonomous in practice.
3   The monetary authorities have to be free of pressure to finance the fiscal deficit. That is, there must be no 'fiscal dominance'.

However, as Bird points out, the majority of developing countries do not display these characteristics. First, inflation is generally both higher and more volatile in developing countries. Combined with the relative lack of forecasting skill and experience, this tends to undermine the first condition. Second, while many developing countries today have central banks that are officially independent, in practice there is often significant political control. Finally, in historical terms, persistent fiscal deficits have been a bigger problem in developing countries, which often also lack the broad and deep government bond markets used to finance deficit in most developed countries. Consequently, pressure on the monetary authorities to print money to finance fiscal deficits has generally been high.

The lack of well-developed government debt markets has a further impact, however. As well as restricting the government's access to funds, it also severely affects the implementation of monetary policy, particularly with regard to inflation targeting.

Masson (2006: 100) describes four channels through which monetary policy is transmitted:

(i)   Direct interest rate effects, which influence investment decisions and the choice between consuming now and consuming later.
(ii) Indirect effects via other asset prices, such as prices of bonds, equities and real estate, which will influence spending through balance sheet and cash flow effects.

(iii) Exchange rate effects, which will change relative prices of domestic and foreign goods, influencing net imports, and also the value of foreign currency denominated assets, with resulting balance sheet effects.
(iv) Credit availability effects, which may include credit rationing if there are binding ceilings on interest rates.

As we have seen in previous chapters, however, people in developing countries tend to be less sensitive to changes in interest rates than are those in developed countries. Similarly, if they exist at all, capital markets are generally less developed, reducing the impact of this indirect transmission channel. The prevalence of informal credit systems and the increasing importance of microfinance institutions in providing credit in developing countries also reduces the extent to which monetary policy is transmitted through the economy, as does the prevalence of a large informal economy and/or the presence of foreign-funded corporations. Also, the financial system in general, and the banking system in particular, may be relatively uncompetitive in many developing countries, reducing the responsiveness of deposit and lending rates to monetary policy (Masson, op. cit.).

All of these factors will tend to make the effects of monetary policy more uncertain in developing countries, and the practice of inflation targeting thus less attractive as an option. It should also be remembered that, despite the widespread financial liberalisation that we have seen in developing countries, many governments retain at least some control over interest rates, and may have different rates for different sectors to encourage preferred industries. In these circumstances – as with that of a fixed exchange rate in a different way – monetary policy is, at least partially, subordinate to broader policy objectives.

Obviously, the third channel described by Masson – the exchange rate – will only be relevant in a situation of flexible exchange rates, or at least exchange rates with a minimum degree of flexibility. However, as we have seen, many developing countries exhibit a marked 'fear of floating'. Levy-Yeyati and Sturzenegger (2002) also demonstrate that many countries that claim to have a floating exchange rate regime actually manage their exchange rate quite closely, so that the distinction between *de jure* floating and fixed rates is often not as great as one would suspect.

As we shall see in more detail in later chapters, a key issue when deciding on an exchange rate regime – both *de jure* and *de facto* – is the danger of a speculative attack on the currency. The Asian financial crises of the late 1990s highlighted the dangers of fixed exchange rates vividly, and as we have seen, the number of Asian economies that maintain a fixed exchange rate has fallen significantly. However, we have also seen that the number of truly floating exchange rates in the developing world is very low.

It would seem, therefore, that many countries exhibit both a 'fear of floating' and a 'fear of fixing', with regard to the exchange rate. In many ways this middle ground is the opposite to the well-known 'corner solutions' for exchange rates that gained much popularity after the Asian crisis. The basic argument is simple: 'fixed' exchange rates are only viable over the longer term if the fix is 'hard' and essentially irrevocable. If this is not so, speculators will come to see the currency as a one-way bet and launch an attack on the peg. A hard peg, in contrast, is by definition stable.

Under a currency board, for example, the monetary authorities forsake the power to issue fiat money, and instead guarantee that all domestic currency is supported – one for one – by foreign exchange held by the central bank. Money can therefore only be created as these reserves rise. Whilst bringing stability and credibility to policy, currency boards also have disadvantages, not least the giving up of any autonomy in monetary policy. Some of these issues are detailed in Box 5.1, which describes Argentina's experience with the currency board system.

Box 5.1 Argentina's Currency Board

From the early 1970s Argentina experienced sustained periods of very high inflation, as well as episodes of hyperinflation. Between 1970 and 1988 inflation averaged more than 200% per year (right hand scale on figure), while growth (left hand scale) averaged 1.5%, and was strongly negative for sustained periods. In 1989 inflation rose to more than 3,000%, falling back to a little under 2,500% in 1990. Something clearly had to be done . . .

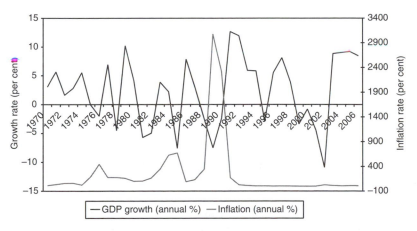

Inflation and growth in Argentina, 1970–2006.

Source: World Bank WDI.

Despite repeated efforts to reduce inflation the Argentine authorities could not succeed in establishing the necessary credibility, not least because of its history of money supply expansion to finance the government's persistent fiscal deficits. After the resignation of then President Alfonsin in 1989, the new President, Carlos Menem initially sought to rein in inflation using traditional measures: as we can see from the figure, these did not succeed.

Then in 1991 the government introduced a raft of liberalising economic reforms in conjunction with the establishment of a currency board, under which the peso was directly exchangeable on a one-to-one basis with the US dollar – i.e. all Argentine currency was backed by equivalent US dollars held by the Currency Board. As we can see, the effects on the inflation rate were immediate and profound: inflation fell from 2,300% in 1991 to 171% in 1992 and to 10.6% in 1993. By 1997 inflation was just 0.15%. We can also see that the impact on growth was very positive: other than the impact of the 'tequila crisis' in the mid-1990s, growth was high and positive throughout the decade.

The increased openness to international trade also had negative effects: unemployment doubled in the 1990s as domestic firms struggled to compete with foreign importers, and wage rates were similarly depressed, particularly amongst low-skilled workers. A further problem was generated as Argentina's external debt grew sharply, as there were no other options available to the government to finance its deficits – both fiscal and, increasingly, on the current account. The debt was primarily denominated in US dollars.

As the value of the dollar rose in international markets in the second half of the 1990s, Argentinian exports became less and less competitive, putting pressure on the current account and increasing the external borrowing needed to finance. Again, something had to give . . .

In 2001, Argentina announced a suspension of its international debt payments, repealed the convertibility law and restricted bank withdrawals. Initially there was an attempt to keep the dollar peg (after a devaluation) but the peso was soon allowed to float. But it sank.

The collapse in the currency's value hugely increased the value of Argentina's debt. However, the authorities stood firm in negotiations with creditors, eventually agreeing a restructuring in 2005 where creditors would receive about 25% of the debt's value.

Lessons: currency boards are extremely effective in establishing credibility and reducing inflation (though perhaps less so after Argentina's experience) but longer-term use creates major economic difficulties, particularly if the currency is pegged to just one currency rather than a basket weighted to reflect the country's major trading partners.

The other 'corner' is a pure float, but as we have seen, developing countries have generally been reluctant to pursue this option. In part this is a fear of volatility, but it is also related to the fact that many developing countries have external debt denominated in foreign currency, the value of which is directly related to the exchange rate. As the Asian economies found in the late 1990s, a sharp fall in the value of the currency results in a sharp increase in external debt obligations.

A final option, which strongly affects both monetary and exchange rate policy, is full currency union, where member countries fix their exchange rates permanently against each other, centralise monetary policy and issue a common currency. The obvious example is the Eurozone in the European Union, which despite some difficulties has functioned reasonably well.

The idea of currency unions also has its origins in the work of Robert Mundell. Mundell (1961) developed the idea of the 'optimum currency area' (OCA) which underpinned the birth of the euro, but has also been proposed as an alternative option for developing regions or groups of countries.

For example, Berg *et al.* (2002) propose Latin America as a potential OCA, while Sakakibara (2002) does the same for Southeast Asia. While these areas may fulfil OCA conditions such as a high proportion of intra-regional trade, an important difference with the European Union is that much of the success of the euro has been based on the international credibility of the Eurozone's central banks, particularly the strong anti-inflation reputation of the Bundesbank. As we have seen, credibility is fundamental to the effective operation of monetary policy, which might be seen as an obstacle to the launch of other regional currencies in developing regions. Clearly this is something of a chicken and egg issue, since credibility can only be gained in practice, but the absence of credibility may preclude the possibility of acquiring such experience.

Whichever option for monetary and exchange rate policy is preferred, however, there is one common feature. None of them are likely to succeed unless fiscal policy is well managed: persistent fiscal deficits undermine any monetary regime in the end. The next section therefore considers issues of reform in the area of fiscal policy.

5.1.2 Fiscal policy

Fundamentally, macroeconomic stability – and effective monetary policy implementation – is only achievable in an environment where the government's fiscal position is under control. Consequently, fiscal reform has largely focused on measures to reduce fiscal deficits. That said, from a theoretical perspective, fiscal reform potentially goes far beyond this narrow remit. Tanzi (2004) sketches the theory of fiscal policy, tracing it back to the work of Jan Tinbergen, who was awarded the Nobel Prize for his work in this area. In simple terms, the aim of (all) policy is assumed to be to maximise social welfare, which is measured by a variety of economic indicators – growth, employment, inflation, etc. – and a variety of social indicators – life expectancy, crime rates, and so on.

Aware of the relative importance of these indicators on society's welfare function, policy-makers use particular instruments (or 'handles') to influence these indicators and thus affect societal welfare. However, not all instruments are equally effective in terms of their impact on these indicators, so policy-makers aim to select only those that are 'efficient' in that they produce a relatively large ultimate effect. From the perspective of fiscal policy, such instruments (or handles) refer to different forms of taxation and different forms of expenditure.

For Tanzi (op. cit.) the theory of fiscal policy rests on a number of assumptions:

1   The existence of a centralised government, with a unitary budget and the power to both analyse options objectively and rationally and to implement policy effectively on the basis of this analysis.
2   Government officials take decisions purely on the basis of the public interest – i.e. they are 'disinterested'.
3   Legal changes required to impact upon particular instruments are transparent and understood equally and fully by all parties.
4   The executive branch of government must have – as far as is possible in a democracy – control over the processes needed to alter laws/instruments.

Tanzi goes on to point out, however, that this is a normative theory – i.e. it describes the way the world could/should be rather than how it is – that was devised in a developed country context in the 1950s and 1960s. Consequently, it may not accord with circumstances on the ground, particularly in developing countries, and especially where the assumptions listed above do not hold.

For example, the 'public choice' school of thought[4] rejects this theory of fiscal policy as unrealistic, particularly with regard to the 'altruism' that is assumed on the part of policy-makers. From a public choice perspective, politicians are no better than anyone else – and may in fact be worse – which suggests that their choices will be shaped by their own incentive system, with positive welfare outcomes only occurring where these happen to coincide with those of the wider society.

From another perspective, the 'positive theory of fiscal policy', as the name suggests, takes a more positive view of what fiscal policy can achieve, and focuses on the institutional frameworks that influence outcomes in this respect.[5]

The positive theory approach is not incompatible with Tinbergen's classical theory of fiscal policy, but assumes that it is dependent upon the existence of an appropriate institutional framework. In contrast, the public choice approach is largely at odds with the classical approach, assuming that policy-makers are inherently self-interested rather than altruistic.

In practice, of course, these rather abstruse debates have had only a limited relevance for most developing countries, which have not had the luxury of designing and implementing a coherent set of reforms aimed at producing an optimal fiscal system. Rather, reforms undertaken in the 1980s were more often of a short-term nature as part of macroeconomic stabilisation and structural adjustment programmes, where the overriding focus was on reducing fiscal deficits.

That said, following the initial stabilisation of the fiscal situation, a more considered approach was then adopted in many countries, where (often tentative) attempts were made to move towards a more 'optimal' system, i.e. one that maximises social welfare. In this, economic theory of optimal fiscal systems played an important role.

For Coady (1997) an optimal fiscal system should incorporate both efficiency (i.e. the minimisation of distortions) and equity (i.e. distributional) considerations. Coady stresses the importance of analysing both the revenue raising (tax) and expenditure aspects of fiscal policy simultaneously: if distributional objectives can be largely achieved using government spending, then tax policy can focus on achieving the government's efficiency objectives.

For tax policy, Coady argues that theory points towards the levying of indirect taxes on final consumption, rather than on production inputs, as is commonly the case in developing countries. From an efficiency perspective, this is seen as less distortionary, and has become a central plank of policy advice to developing countries, particularly from the Bretton Woods institutions (BWIs) where the introduction of sales taxes such as VAT has often been a component of structural adjustment programmes. One example of this is described in Box 5.2, which gives details of the structural adjustment-related tax reform programme that has taken place in Ethiopia since the early 1990s.

Box 5.2 Tax reform in Ethiopia

In 1991, the Marxist 'Derg' regime was forcibly ousted from power by the Ethiopian People's Revolutionary Democratic Front (EPRDF), ushering in a new era of economic policy in Ethiopia. In combination with the Bretton Woods institutions (BWIs), the EPRDF embarked upon an extensive period of reform, designed to transform the economy from a socialist, command-economy model to a free-market based system. Tax reform was one part of this.

Prior to 1991, tax policy in Ethiopia was geared towards (a) revenue generation, and (b) reducing inequality. Consequently, marginal income tax rates were very high – 89% for the highest earners – which, it was argued, created little incentive to work beyond a certain level, as well as strong incentives to avoid taxes (Fantahun, 2002).

The reforms were designed to broaden the tax base (and particularly to reduce the reliance on distorting trade taxes) and to incentivise wealth creation.

The top rate of income tax was therefore reduced from 85% to 40%, and corporation tax to 35%. In the external sector, export taxes were eliminated (except on coffee), and import tariffs reduced from a maximum of 240% to a top rate of 40%, and the number of tariff bands reduced significantly (Fantahun, 2002). Furthermore, a sales tax was introduced with a top rate of 15%.

Ethiopian government tax revenue as a % of GDP, 1991–2000

	1991/2	*92/3*	*93/4*	*94/5*	*95/6*	*96/7*	*97/8*	*98/9*	*99/00*
Direct taxes	3.19	2.76	3.34	3.87	4.62	4.59	4.15	4.15	4.50
Domestic indirect taxes	2.57	2.79	2.94	2.79	3.05	3.11	2.62	2.49	2.78
Foreign trade taxes	2.02	2.71	4.58	4.79	4.78	5.22	4.93	4.91	5.17
Total tax revenue	7.78	8.26	10.86	11.45	12.45	12.92	11.70	11.54	12.45
Non-tax revenue	2.84	4.52	3.04	6.00	5.59	6.09	6.88	8.83	7.03
Total govt. revenue	**10.62**	**12.79**	**13.9**	**17.45**	**18.04**	**19.01**	**18.58**	**20.38**	**19.48**

Source: Ministry of Finance and Economic Development (MOFED).

The table above gives details of the impact of these reforms. As we can see, total tax revenue rose relatively steadily over the period, from less than 8% of GDP in 1991 to almost 12.5% by 2000. Furthermore, we can see that the contribution of direct taxation also increased, though at a slower rate. This suggests that the lowering of top tax rates and streamlining/broadening of the tax base was, at least to some extent, successful in raising revenues. However, this effect is seen more strongly with regard to trade taxes, which rose from 2% of GDP in 1991 to more than 5% by 2000 – clearly the goal of reducing dependence on trade taxes was not a success, though this did occur at the same time as export taxes were being eliminated and import tariffs progressively reduced: the increase therefore reflects a lower level of evasion and, particularly, a significant rise in overall imports as a result of the accompanying reductions on restrictions in this area.

Although tax revenues therefore increased significantly, the 12.45% of 2000 remained very low by international standards, and low in comparison with other sub-Saharan African countries. There was therefore need for further reform in the tax field. The second period of tax reform was developed as part of the Enhanced Structural Adjustment Programme agreed with the IMF in 1996 and envisaged an increase in government tax revenue to around 15% of GDP by 2003. However, its major component – the introduction of VAT to replace the existing sales tax – was not implemented until 2003.

Intriguingly the IMF did not undertake a Poverty and Social Impact

Assessment (PSIA) of the effects of the VAT introduction until after it was implemented – PSIAs are supposed to be done before policies are introduced – but when it did the conclusion was that the VAT was mildly 'progressive'. However, this assessment – which was marginal in any event – was conducted in an 'abstract' way – i.e. progressiveness was not considered relative to the sales tax it replaced. If this comparison was made, however, the IMF found that the introduction of VAT had a negative impact on the poorest 40% of Ethiopians, and that this impact was largest for the very poorest groups.

Lessons: (1) although all developing countries would like to broaden the tax base and move away from a reliance on trade taxes this is not as easy as it sounds, not least because collecting trade taxes is much more straightforward than collecting other forms of tax: 'optimal' is not the same as 'practical'. (2) If the poverty impacts of possible tax reforms are to be taken into account, the necessary studies should take place *before* the tax is actually implemented.

Furthermore, in an 'optimal system', import taxes – which as we have seen remain an important revenue raising instrument in many developing countries – should be structured so as to correspond with the taxation of domestic goods, again so as to minimise distortions and therefore maximise efficiency considerations. Moreover, while it may not be practical or desirable to levy indirect taxes at a uniform rate across the economy, it is important that differences are not overly large, so as to avoid severe distortions within the economy.

For Coady (op. cit.) a coherent process of fiscal reform must take account of how the various distortions within the economy interact with each other, which in turn will provide guidance on how reforms should be paced and sequenced. However, Patel (1997) argues that, in terms of the sustainability of reforms, a 'big bang' may be more effective than a gradual, piecemeal approach. This is because any genuine process of reform will inevitably see powerful vested interest groups lose out. These 'insiders' have strong incentives to derail reforms, which is more easily achieved if the reform process is a gradual affair, carried out over a lengthy period of time.

The effectiveness of any reform process will also be strongly affected by the level of administrative capacity in the country concerned. The key aspects in this regard are:

1   the quality, training and scale of staffing;
2   the conditions of work;
3   management powers to discipline employees if necessary;
4   coordination, planning and accounting skills.

The importance of undertaking administrative reforms in conjunction with fiscal reforms has often been underestimated in practice, as was the case with the sequencing of financial liberalisation, for example. This has led to very mixed results.

How effective have reforms been in practice, however?

(a) Increasing tax revenues

In practice increasing revenues from tax has proved extremely difficult to achieve, not least because of the large numbers of complicated taxes, tax evasion, poorly trained tax collectors with limited resources, and so on.

As we can see from Figure 5.1, the 1990s saw central government tax revenues fall in all developing regions, at the same time as developed countries saw revenues increase. Furthermore, as well as this divergent trend, the overall level of tax revenue in developing countries remains well below that seen in the developed world, and this difference is most marked for the least developed countries.

Therefore, while some countries have been able to reduce fiscal deficits from increased tax takes, this is certainly not the norm: the bulk of the reductions have resulted from cuts in expenditure.

(b) Cutting expenditure

In terms of expenditure, the (theoretical) consensus has been to recommend that current spending be cut rather than capital expenditure.[6] However, as with the raising of taxes, this is not as straightforward as it may first appear. Therefore, while total expenditure has fallen in all developing (and developed)

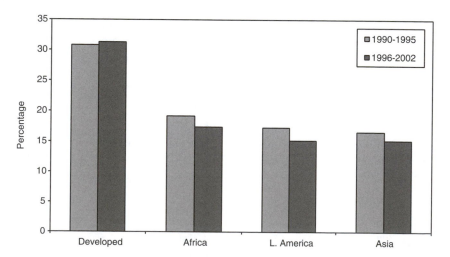

Figure 5.1 Regional tax revenues as percentage of GDP, 1990–1995 vs. 1996–2002.

Source: UNPAN.

regions as shown in Figure 5.2, the cuts have largely been made in current expenditure. Why is this?

It is often extremely difficult to cut current expenditure due to exogenous factors such as the high burden of interest payments, over which the government may have little control. Politically, the greater traditional role of the state in the economy in many developing countries also creates significant obstacles: transfers to state owned enterprises may be politically difficult to reduce, not least because of the employment-supporting nature of many such transfers. The state may (quite rightly) weigh the benefits of reform against the political unrest that such measures could produce, and decide that the 'optimum' outcomes predicted by theory may, in practice, be far from optimal.

As a consequence of these difficulties, the bulk of reductions in expenditure have come as a result of cuts in the capital budget. In the case of 'prestige projects' and the support of inefficient state enterprises, for example, this is a good thing. However, there have also been cuts in areas such as infrastructure investment and social services – i.e. the provision of public goods such as health and education.

(c) Outcomes for the fiscal balance

As can be seen from Table 5.1 below, developing countries have been remarkably successful in reducing fiscal deficits over the past two decades. Indeed, by 2005, the average deficit in the developing world was lower than in developed countries. However, an important question to ask is: at what cost had this fiscal restraint been bought?

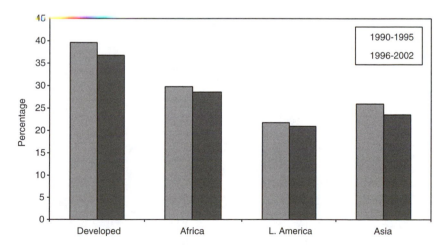

Figure 5.2 Regional government expenditure as percentage of GDP, 1990–1995 vs. 1996–2002.

Source: UNPAN.

Table 5.1 Central government fiscal balances (% of GDP)

	1992	1993	1994	1995	1996	1997	1998	1999	2000	2001	2002	2003	2004	2005
Developing countries	−3.0	−3.2	−2.7	−2.4	−2.6	−4.0	−3.8	−4.0	−3.0	−3.3	−3.5	−2.9	−1.7	−1.1
Africa	−6.8	−7.3	−5.1	−3.8	−2.9	−3.9	−3.8	−3.5	−1.3	−2.1	−2.5	−1.9	−0.2	−0.6
Sub-Sahara	−8.1	−7.9	−5.7	−4.0	−3.6	−3.6	−3.7	−3.8	−2.4	−2.5	−2.7	−2.5	−0.8	−0.3
Asia	−2.9	−2.9	−2.5	−2.4	−2.1	−2.6	−3.8	−4.5	−4.7	−4.2	−4.0	−3.5	−2.6	−2.7
M. East						−1.6	−5.2	−1.8	−4.3	−0.5	−2.2	−0.1	−1.6	−6.8
W. Hemisphere	−0.4	−0.2	−0.9	−1.9	−1.8	−1.6	−3.4	−2.9	−2.4	−2.6	−3.1	−3.1	−1.5	−2.1
Advanced economies	−4.1	−4.4	−3.7	−3.3	−2.7	−1.5	−1.1	−1.1	−0.2	−1.0	−2.4	−3.0	−2.8	−2.6

Source: IMF WEO.

Recent years have seen the emphasis change considerably in this area. For example, the focus on achieving the Millennium Development Goals (MDGs) in recent years has highlighted the fact that low levels of expenditure in areas such as health and education are simply not compatible with the achievement of the MDGs. In United Nations (2005) for example, it is convincingly argued that the argument should be turned on its head. Rather than aiming for and achieving a particular fiscal balance, regardless of the cost, governments in developing countries should estimate the health and education budgets that would be required to meet the MDGs. To the extent that these spending levels cannot be met by domestic resources, the gap should be filled by increased and targeted foreign aid.

Clearly, it remains of vital importance for developing countries to maximise the tax take from the domestic economy, however. The next section looks in more detail at the issues and obstacles in this regard.

5.2 Tax reform

The first question when considering tax reform in developing countries is: why is it necessary? As we have seen, the key problem in this regard is the relatively low tax take (as a proportion of GDP) that most developing countries experience. Clearly, raising the tax take is fundamental if governments wish to both achieve their development objectives, whilst simultaneously holding down fiscal deficits.

Secondly, tax systems in developing countries are often regressive in nature, which results in a disproportionate tax burden falling on the poor. Finally, poorly designed tax systems may cause severe distortions in the economy, leading to lower growth than could otherwise be achieved.

5.2.1 Designing a tax system in theory and practice

As we have seen, tax revenues tend to rise as national income rises – although there are exceptions to this rule, the overall relationship is relatively stable and has been confirmed in numerous studies.[7] As well as the overall level of taxes, countries also display considerable difference in terms of tax structure, and again these differences can, in broad terms, be related to levels of national income. So, for example, trade taxes are generally of higher importance for low-income countries, particularly small, relatively open economies. However, despite their low/middle-income status, most transition economies do not rely heavily on trade taxes (Bird and Zolt, 2003).

In similarly general terms, the importance of both direct taxes on income (personal and corporate) and consumption taxes (such as VAT) also increases as countries' national income rises. However, as pointed out above, broad-based VAT has become increasingly important in countries at all levels of development, so that by the year 2000, 70% of the world's population lived in one of the 123 countries that had implemented some form of VAT (Ebrill *et al.*, 2001).

In the preceding section we discussed issues of theory surrounding fiscal policy, and it should come as no surprise that tax itself has a relatively well-developed theoretical base. Whilst avoiding delving too deeply into the minutiae of these issues, the following sub-sections consider what the objectives of tax policy should be in principle, drawing on the typology developed in Bird and Zolt (2003).

(a) Revenue raising

Clearly, the primary aim of taxation is to raise revenue to enable the government to spend on its priorities without generating a fiscal deficit, with all the negative consequences that this entails.

In a neutral system, tax revenues would increase at the same pace as economic growth, but the exact relationship between these two variables is determined by the 'elasticity of tax yield'. The 'elasticity of tax yield' is therefore the change in tax revenue associated with a given change in GDP. For example, if a 1% change in GDP results in a 1.5% change in tax collected, the tax system is considered 'elastic'. Conversely a tax take that change by 0.75% following a 1% in GDP would be described as 'inelastic'. As well as the design of particular taxes, elasticity will also be affected by the efficiency of tax collection and the level of tax evasion in the economy.

The elasticity of any one tax – and the elasticity of the tax system is simply the sum of the individual elasticities – is also affected by the following factors:

- Elasticity increases during economic booms and declines during economic contractions.[8]
- Commodity/natural resource taxes display considerable volatility, which is a function of the cyclicality of global commodity prices.
- Personal income tax – elasticity is the result of the progressivity of the rate structure and the level of exemptions relative to average incomes.
- Consumption tax – elasticity increases as the proportion of fast-growing goods and services that are covered by the tax increases, and if the tax is levied as a percentage of the retail price paid rather than on the number of items purchased.
- Property tax – elasticity rises with the frequency of value assessments (Bird and Zolt, 2003).

While elasticity refers to the GDP-driven change in tax revenues without any change in tax structure, 'buoyancy' describes the responsiveness of revenues to a change in GDP *and* a change in tax structure.

In principle, tax revenues should rise at the same level as revenue requirements, which should therefore be factored into tax design at an early stage through calibrating the elasticities of different taxes, estimating GDP growth and designing a system that will deliver the revenues needed to meet expenditure estimates. In practice, however, many developing countries have struggled to ensure that revenues rise in this orderly manner, and so have resorted to regular short-term measures to boost tax revenues and so fill funding gaps. But tax policy should be designed with the long term very much in mind, and short-term 'fixes' of this kind have rarely succeeded in addressing the underlying cause of the revenue/expenditure mismatch (ibid.).

An important point to stress is that countries with a diverse range of taxes in place will benefit from lower revenue volatility than will countries that rely on a narrower range of taxes. Given that developing countries are more likely to be in the latter group it is unsurprising that tax revenue volatility is considerably higher than is the case in developed countries. This makes matching revenues and expenditure intrinsically more difficult, which both complicates fiscal policy considerably, and makes the case for broadening and rationalising the tax system.

(b) Efficiency issues

The first point to make with regard to efficiency is that taxes can produce economic costs, and an efficient system is designed to minimise these effects. For example:

- On average in developed countries, taxes cost around 1% of revenue raised to collect. The figure in developing countries is often higher, however, which represents a 'deadweight' economic cost to society. For example, Mann (2002) estimates that tax collection in Guatemala costs 2.5% of revenues
- The 'compliance cost' of a tax system refers to the cost of meeting tax obligations over and above the financial cost of the tax itself. This may relate to administrative or accounting/auditing requirements and, in general terms, 'compliance cost' is inversely related to 'administrative costs'. That is to say, the more that taxpayers have to do to fulfil their tax obligations the less the tax authorities are required to do. A good example of this relationship is the declining administrative costs but higher compliance costs of the UK's move to personal assessment of income tax.[9]
- All taxes are 'distortionary' to some extent, but some are more distortionary than others. Taxes alter financial incentives and so influence behaviour, and tax design must be carefully conducted to minimise the distortionary effects on behaviour. For example, tax on rental profits in Ethiopia in the early 1990s was 75%. As a result, little rental property was provided, and what there was tended to be outside the formal sector so as to avoid this tax.

These factors have led to tax policy advice to developing country governments that has resulted in:

- Introducing broad-based VAT – VAT is non-distortionary if implemented at a uniform rate across all goods and services (which is rarely, if ever, the case); the compliance costs – though high at the outset in terms of the 'fixed' costs of compliance – are relatively low on an ongoing basis; and the same holds true for collection costs.
- Simplifying import tariffs and reducing tariff levels – the main argument here is that trade taxes are highly distortionary, impose costs on consumers (i.e. more expensive imports) and encourage an inefficient allocation of resources, particularly with relation to the 'infant' industries who may be the intended beneficiaries.
- Tax rates should be kept as low as possible, to minimise the distortionary effects of changing relative prices.
- The tax base should be as broad as possible with as low a number of different tax bands/categories/sectors and thus rates as possible, again to minimise distortions in the economy.[10]
- 'Competitive' (i.e. low) tax systems are also important in attracting international investment in a world of mobile international capital. The tax system should thus be designed to be attractive to international investors.

These features, while theoretically plausible in a broad sense, are problematic in practice in many developing countries:

- VAT requires familiarity with – and practical application of – modern accounting and auditing practices. It is likely that the development of these features may be an attraction of the introduction of VAT, but logistical problems are likely to be high unless the logistical infrastructure is put in place prior to implementation.[11]
- VAT is also a largely regressive tax.
- One reason why trade taxes remain important in developing countries is that they are considerably easier to collect than most other taxes. Furthermore, the distortionary nature of selective import tariffs is entirely deliberate – in many ways, the 'distortion' is the point of the tax in the first place, so it is strange that the practice is criticised on these grounds.
- Reducing tax rates from extreme levels which clearly provide a disincentive to economic activity is clearly a positive development. However, the danger lies in going too far the other way, where 'tax competition' drives down national tax rates to levels below that needed to fund expenditure commitments.
- This is compounded by the narrow tax base in most developing countries, where the relative importance of the (untaxed) informal sector directly constrains the growth of the (formal) tax base.

- There is also the point that 'non-distortionary' taxes – i.e. those levied at a low, uniform rate to avoid overly distorting economic incentives – are, in general terms, regressive in practice.
- Finally, using the tax system to attract FDI has gone far beyond reducing and rationalising corporate tax rates, with a variety of incentives such as tax holidays are offered as 'sweeteners'. In this area, changes have often been misguided, particularly with the over-generous tax holidays that characterise many export processing zones (EPZ), for example. The important issue to bear in mind is that countries offer incentives because of the benefit they expect to get from the investment. An important part of this is revenues, but overly generous incentive packages may result in the country losing rather than gaining, at least in the financial sense.

(c) Equity issues

Debates on fairness are central to any discussion on tax. However, what one person considers 'fair' another may not. Economists have tended to distinguish two forms of fairness, or equity with regard to tax. First, 'horizontal equity' means that those with equal ability to pay should pay equal amounts, irrespective of where they live, or what influence they may have. Secondly, 'vertical equity' means that those with different abilities to pay should pay different amounts in proportion to their abilities (i.e. progressive taxes). As we have seen, income taxes are generally progressive (though they need not be). VAT can be either progressive or regressive, depending on how they are implemented though, as argued above, a uniform, universally applied VAT will be regressive in its impact.

However, in practice these concepts have not been particularly useful in shaping debates over tax policy, as they leave too many issues undecided. That is, for horizontal equity 'those with equal ability to pay' can be defined in many different ways: it could refer to gross income, or to wealth, or to net income after commitments have been met, or to net income taking into account government expenditure patterns. Similarly, vertical equity says little about whether a tax system should be proportional (e.g. the flat tax) or progressive, and if the latter, how 'progressive' it should be (Bird and Zolt, 2003).

Ultimately, of course, these are political questions which should be settled in the context of the social contract between a government and its citizens. However, it should also be stressed that the seeming technicality (or even objectivity) of much theoretical work on tax should not distract from these basic facts. Despite the advice that they may receive from tax experts, governments have both the right and the responsibility to develop the tax structure which is suited to their own countries' circumstances, and not seek to implement an abstract, idealised model of best practice.

Economists with a concern for the equity of outcomes, but also with concerns over the economic impacts of the tax system, tend to argue that issues of equity are best addressed through government expenditure – i.e. in targeting spending on the poor – rather than through redistribution via the tax system. In part, this is because of the historical difficulty that developing countries have had in implementing progressive systems of income tax, but it also reflects a theoretical preference for the type of tax system described above.

(d) Administrative issues

An important issue in this regard is feasibility: there is no point having an elegant tax system designed with optimality in mind if the taxes cannot realistically be collected. As pointed out above, this is an important factor in many countries' decision to retain taxes on external trade. The different structure of developing country economies is also an important constraint:

> Tax design in developing countries is strongly influenced by economic structure. Many developing countries have a large traditional agricultural sector that is not easily taxed. Many transitional and developing countries have a significant informal (shadow) economy that also is largely outside the formal tax structure. The potentially reachable tax base thus constitutes a smaller portion of total economic activity than in developed countries.
>
> (ibid.: 24)

In addition to these structural constraints, Bird and Zolt (2003: 25) argue that three factors are essential to effective tax administration:

(i)   The political will to administer the tax system effectively.
(ii) A clear strategy for achieving this goal.
(iii) Adequate resources for the task.

'Political will' may be related to the 'time inconsistency' issue discussed with respect to monetary policy. That is, by definition, major tax reforms will see some groups suffer and others benefit. Furthermore, if a country is to follow the guidelines on tax policy considered above, the position of these affected groups within the society should not be relevant. Consequently, the economically and politically important are as likely to be adversely affected as anyone else. Indeed, they are likely to be more affected, as these are the groups who have been in the position to secure relative advantages for themselves. Tax reform will therefore harm these groups immediately, who may be in a position to damage the government politically, whereas the benefits that result from tax reform may take some years to emerge, after the political damage has been done.

For these reasons it has often been very difficult in practice for governments to implement major tax reform independently, which has led to a trend for such measures to be included as conditions in structural adjustment programmes, enabling the government to pin the blame on the Bretton Woods institutions if necessary.

For Tanzi (1987), regardless of a tax system's structure and its capacity to collect revenues, the system should:

(a) have a high 'concentration index', with most revenues coming from a small number of taxes;
(b) avoid the introduction of low-yielding taxes that unnecessarily complicate the system;
(c) have a low 'erosion index', keeping tax evasion to a minimum;
(d) have a low 'collection lag', where taxes are collected promptly;
(e) have a high 'objectivity index', where taxes accurately reflect the taxable base rather than relying on estimates;
(f) contain enforceable and widely accepted 'penalties' for those guilty of tax evasion;
(g) have a low 'cost of collection'.

From this brief discussion of tax policy issues, a number of points should also be made clear:

- There is no one tax system that is optimal for all countries.
- Theoretically 'optimal' systems may be decidedly sub-optimal in practice.
- The structure of developing country economies differs from the developed economies. It is therefore logical that tax systems should also differ.
- While issues of efficiency are important, they should not be used to override concerns over equity, which are at least as important to the long-term sustainability of the tax system and the 'social contract' between government and citizens.
- Many of the most 'efficient' taxes may also be the least progressive. Again, the trade-off should be taken fully into account.
- The feasibility of implementing any form of tax should be taken into consideration from the start of tax policy design.

We have seen that part of the reason for the low tax take in developing countries relates to tax evasion. What are the issues in this regard?

5.2.2 Tax evasion

The result of evasion is that the effective tax base is much smaller than the potential tax base, which has serious fiscal consequences for governments. In a developing country context, tax evasion may be facilitated by underdeveloped accounting frameworks and, as we have seen, administrative deficiencies in terms of tax identification and collection.

As we have seen, many developing countries continue to rely, to at least some extent, on trade taxes, not least as they are hard to evade. The main avenues of evasion that are used, however, are smuggling of goods and under-invoicing by importers (or exporters).

A third issue relates to the taxation of transnational corporations (TNCs), who may seek to evade tax in two ways:

1   TNCs may engage in 'transfer pricing' where their subsidiaries in developing countries 'buy' materials from the parent company and then 'sell' them back the finished products. In such an environment, it is possible to manipulate the prices paid in these flows so as to reduce the tax due. For example, the TNC may charge a high rate for the inputs to the subsidiary, but only pay a discounted sum for the end product, thus reducing the subsidiary's profit margin and therefore tax.
2   TNCs may vary where taxes are applied to them. They may choose a 'source' tax base, so that taxes are due in the territorial region where the taxable activity takes place. Alternatively, they may prefer a 'residence' tax base, where they are taxed on their worldwide income (regardless of source) in their home country.

Given the scale and complexity of the global operations of many TNCs, it is often difficult to completely avoid this problem, so that some TNCs may effectively pay very little tax on a global basis.

In recent years, efforts to combat tax evasion in developing countries have focused on the following areas:

(a)   lowering marginal income tax rates as overly high rates encourage evasion;
(b)   replacing reliance on trade taxes with broad-based taxes on domestic consumption;
(c)   improving official tax collection capacity and improving the public image of tax collecting agencies;
(d)   reducing time lags for payments and imposing tougher penalties for arrears;
(e)   negotiating international tax treaties and improving exchanges of information.

As we have seen, however, despite these policy reforms, there has been little progress in increasing the size of the effective tax base, particularly in the poorest developing countries. Clearly, much remains to be done.

5.2.3   Stability vs. growth?

As we saw in Chapter 4, macroeconomic stabilisation programmes in developing countries have, on one level, been remarkably successful: average inflation rates in the developing world have fallen precipitously from more than 50% in the 1980s to a little over 5% in 2006. Furthermore, as shown in Table 5.1, the situation with fiscal balances in developing countries has also shown considerable improvement.

The question that arises, however, is whether this 'stability' has been so successful that it has undermined the overriding objective of stimulating high and sustained rates of economic growth.

As we can see from Figure 5.3, the simple answer is that macro stability has, on aggregate, been associated with stable or rising rates of growth across the developing world. However, a very large proportion of this growth has been concentrated in particular regions, notably developing Asia and, particularly in recent years, in China and India.

The decline in inflation rates has been relatively uniform across developing regions. In contrast, as we can see from Figure 5.4, rates of growth have certainly not been. This strongly suggests that while macro stability may be a necessary (pre)condition for growth, it is far from being sufficient to generate growth in and of itself.

Montiel and Servén (2004) argue that while macro stability is important,

> ... the burden of jump-starting growth in developing countries has to fall primarily on pro-growth policies outside the macroeconomic arena. Such policies include, for example, the implementation of an open international trade regime, the adoption of national innovation policies, well-functioning factor markets and an investor friendly legal and regulatory environment. In some cases, those policies actually facilitate the adoption of reforms aimed at macroeconomic stability – e.g., disinflation or the correction of a real misalignment are easier and less costly to achieve with well functioning labor and financial markets. The key lesson is that policies of this type are mutually complementary with policies that focus

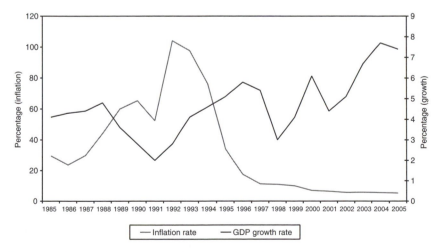

Figure 5.3 Developing world inflation vs. growth, 1985–2005.

Source: IMF WEO.

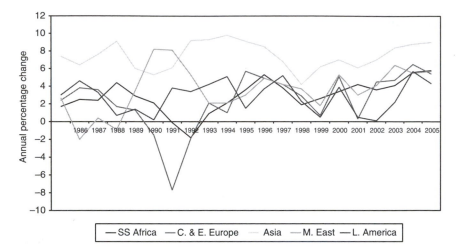

Figure 5.4 Regional growth rates, 1985–2005.

Source: IMF WEO.

on the creation and preservation of macroeconomic stability. An unstable macroeconomic environment tends to undermine the growth benefits of such policies. Nonetheless, what we have learned from the 1990s is that macro stability alone is not enough; policies outside the macroeconomic arena are themselves indispensable to harvest the fruits of macroeconomic stability in the form of sustained high rates of economic growth.

In the remaining sections of this chapter, we consider some of these issues.

5.3 Reform of the banking sector

We have seen how developing countries' financial systems tend to be dominated by the banking sector. Clearly, therefore, a well-functioning and efficient banking sector is a prerequisite for successful financial sector development (FSD). While countries may eventually come to be more 'market-based' systems, the role of banks will remain of crucial importance, just as is the case with the more market-based developed countries. What are the issues from a developing country perspective, however?

A number of key weaknesses with developing country banking systems can be identified:

1   As we saw in Chapter 4, banking systems in developing countries tend to be relatively highly concentrated – i.e. dominated by a few, large banks. This uncompetitive situation leads to high costs, in terms of margins and spreads (Knight, 1999).

2   This situation is compounded by the often-large degree of state owner-ship, which, in general terms, reduces the efficiency of the system, and by restrictions on foreign banks entering the domestic financial sector (ibid.).

3   This lack of integration with the international financial system may restrict banks' access to international finance, particularly longer-term financing on favourable terms.

4   Private sector banks are often owned and controlled by family and/or business groups, which engage in 'connected lending' – i.e. lending to other parts of the family or business empire – rather than basing decisions on purely commercial grounds. Lending on non-commercial terms is obviously likely to increase the quantity of non-performing-loans (NPLs) in the loan portfolios of the banking sector (World Bank, 2001).

5   Due to the general lack of capital market development, corporate bor-rowers in developing countries are often entirely reliant on the banking system for finance. This leads to a lack of risk-sharing (as provided by equity markets) and a dependence on debt-financing. The resulting highly leveraged borrower base raises the risk of the banking sector's loan portfolios, increasing the chances of systemic risk in the banking sectors spreading throughout the economy. As Keynes remarked: 'If you owe your bank a hundred pounds, you have a problem, but if you owe a million, it has.'

6   Higher information asymmetries, coupled with a lack of shareholder control due to weak equity markets, can result in little or no monitoring of banks to prevent excessive risk taking (Mishkin, 1991). There is an extensive literature on why banks may tend to take on excessive amounts of risk. In part this is a moral hazard issue: if the bank's 'bet' comes off it gains; if it does not come off, the depositors lose. This is likely to be exacerbated by the sense that banks in trouble will be rescued by the state due to their importance to the financial system.[12] In a more balanced financial system, the behaviour of banks will be monitored and restrained by large, institutional shareholders, for example.

7   Banks may also suffer from poor-quality human resources. The World Bank (1989) identifies the following specific problems that result from this problem:

- *Technical mismanagement* refers to a lack of technocratic banking skills, which is often a result of previously repressed financial sys-tems, where such skills were less needed. Thus lending may be sub-optimal due to: deficient internal controls, inadequate analysis of creditworthiness, political pressure or pressure from parent groups.

- *Cosmetic mismanagement* refers to the situation where banks attempt to hide or disguise losses. For example, to avoid alerting shareholders to problems, banks may keep dividend payments high despite losses, thus worsening an already difficult situation. Also various 'creative accounting' techniques may be employed.

- *Desperate mismanagement* refers to a situation where losses are too large to enable cosmetic mismanagement to be possible. In such a situation, bankers may 'gamble for survival' by lending to very risky projects at high rates of interest, or speculating on national or international capital or real estate markets.
- *Fraud* becomes more likely to occur in a context where the previous forms of mismanagement have taken place and failed to rescue the situation. In circumstances like this, where it is clear that the 'end' is coming for the bank, senior managers may be tempted to grant themselves loans that they will not have to repay, for example.

8   'Credit rationing' may be more of a problem in banking sectors in developing than in developed markets, though it is clearly an issue in both. Stiglitz and Weiss (1981) argue that banks cannot easily ascertain which borrowers have high probabilities of default due to problems of asymmetric information. In such an environment, if banks raise interest rates, they may simply encourage borrowers to switch to riskier projects, which if they succeed will allow the interest payments to be met (i.e. moral hazard effects). Furthermore, high interest rates may lead to 'adverse selection' where it is precisely those borrowers who do not intend to repay their loans who are willing to accept very high interest rates. Given that it is financially prohibitive to monitor these effects in practice, profit-maximising, rational banks will not raise interest rates to market clearing levels, but instead will 'ration credit', when faced with excess demand for loans. Moreover, some sectors may be entirely excluded on the grounds that monitoring their activities is particularly difficult – such as small farmers, for example.

9   Asymmetric information leading to credit rationing is one example of banks in developing countries (though also more broadly) behaving in ways contrary to what orthodox economic theory would suggest. Similarly, Honohan and Stiglitz (2001) argue that many of the modern risk management practices in the banking sector that international regulators use to inform their activities simply do not occur in many developing countries to any meaningful extent.

In this regard, the authors argue strongly against adopting a 'minimalist' approach to banking regulation and supervision, which is premised on the existence of a largely self-regulating system employing modern risk management practices. Regardless of one's view as to the effectiveness of such quantitative means of controlling risk in developed countries, it is clearly the case that their absence is likely to lead to banks taking on excessive risk in an environment of 'minimalist' regulation:

The conventional retreat into a minimalist regulatory strategy is dangerously complacent. For example, it neglects just how imperfectly bank capital is measured and the fact that bank management may have an incentive to increase the measurement difficulties. It over-rates the accuracy of the risk-adjustments, potentially encouraging banks to increase their assumption of under-priced risk. Finally, it over-emphasizes accounting measures of capital, neglecting the economically relevant aspects of franchise value.

(Honohan and Stiglitz 2001: 1)

The combination of these weaknesses in the domestic banking systems in developing countries leads to (a) suboptimal performance by banks in terms of their key functions within the financial system, and (b) a fragile system, prone to banking crises as banks take on excessive risk. These two outcomes are of course strongly related. A fragile banking system is one where many banks may be technically insolvent, which in turn may be a result of their failing to follow best practice in commercial banking.

From the perspective of regulation and supervision of the banking system, the key aim is therefore to ensure the solvency of banks. This focus on solvency was not always the core purpose of bank regulation and supervision, however. Before financial liberalisation, for example, the core function of regulators and supervisors was to ensure that banks were acting in accordance with government policy and directives regarding the setting of interest rates and the allocation of credit to the appropriate sectors. The transition to the focus on bank solvency has, perhaps not surprisingly, been a difficult process given the very different expertise required on the part of bank supervisors.

Based on formal calculations of insolvency,[13] whole banking systems in many developing countries may be insolvent, despite the fact that they are liquid.[14] It was concerns on the solvency of banking systems which led to the 1988 Basel Capital Accord.[15] The Accord established a minimum 'capital adequacy ratio' for banks, which stipulated that banks must hold a particular level of capital, measured as a percentage of risky assets. The figure was set at 8%, i.e. banks were (and are) required to hold 8% of risky assets as 'regulatory capital'. Therefore 8% is the capital adequacy ratio.

The impact of the Basel Accord has been dramatic. In 1988 many developing countries did not have capital requirements at all, and of those that did, many were well below the 8% level. Furthermore, it was often the case that no prudential supervision was undertaken to verify the figures reported by banks, so that banks had an incentive to 'massage' the figures by, for example, reducing levels of provisioning. By 1999, in contrast, only 7 out of 103 countries had capital ratios under 8%, with almost 30 countries having ratios greater than 10%. Interestingly, only one of these countries was an OECD member.

Despite the fact that it was originally devised with banks from developed markets in mind, by the end of the 1990s more than 93% of all countries (88% in emerging markets) claim to adjust capital ratios for risk in line with the guidelines set by the Basel Accord. Recent years have seen a fundamental restructuring of the Basel Capital Accord. 'Basel II', as it is known, was due to come on stream in 2007/8, and the implications of its introduction for developing economies are discussed in Box 5.3 below.

Box 5.3 Basel II and developing countries

Prior to 1988 banks were largely free to choose how much capital they should set aside to protect themselves from future losses. However, growing international competition in the banking sector saw the amount of risk capital held by banks progressively fall. Concerned about systemic risk to the banking system, regulators decided to act: the Basel Capital Accord of 1988 stipulated that banks should hold a minimum of 8% of capital, i.e. for every £100 that was lent, £8 should be set aside in case of default. This 8% figure did vary, according to whether the loan was short- or long-term, or was made to an OECD member country or not, but these distinctions were rather crude and, it was argued, led to distortions in the banking system.

The Basel Committee for Banking Supervision (BCBS) has since spent more than a decade developing and refining the long-awaited reform to the 1988 Accord. The headline objective is simple: to align the regulatory capital with the actual risks inherent in lending and other activities. Basel II has evolved through a number of incarnations, and in 2008 is in the process of fine-tuning prior to full-implementation.

Key features

- Countries can choose from a 'menu' of options ranging from the 'standardised approach' (which is broadly similar to the 1988 Accord with some refinements and extensions to better align capital with risk) to the 'Internal Ratings Based' (IRB) approaches.
- The IRB approaches, as the name suggests, enable banks to determine their own regulatory capital requirements, through an assessment of the risk inherent in any particular activity. Although the BCBS currently stipulates the modelling process through which this should be undertaken, the intention is to ultimately move to a situation where the banks use their own internal risk management models.

The table below gives some estimates of the differential impacts of these changes – though these are in terms of orders of magnitudes rather than precise estimates due to the evolving nature of the reforms. As we see, compared to the original 8% borrowers rated BBB or above will see lower capital requirements associated with their loans, while those

Estimated changes in capital requirements under Basel II

Borrower's credit rating	Probability of default (PD)	1988 Accord	Standard approach	IRB foundation
AAA	0.03	8	1.6	1.13
AA	0.03	8	1.6	1.13
A	0.03	8	4.0	1.13
BBB	0.20	8	8.0	3.61
BB	1.40	8	8.0	12.35
B	6.60	8	12.0	30.96
CCC	15.00	8	12.0	47.04

Source: Bank of England's Spring Quarterly Bulletin, 2001.

below this will see higher requirements. The first impact is therefore likely to be an increase in the cost of borrowing for lower-rated borrowers, who are disproportionately located in developing countries. Of course, this is to be welcomed to the extent that it accurately reflects risk. However, there are reasons to suggest this will not be the case, particularly as the Accord does not take into account the benefits of international diversification, which lower the risk of lending to developing countries in the context of an internationally diversified portfolio. Some other implications are:

- Increased 'procyclicality' of lending: as capital requirements vary with a bank's perception of risk, they will move with the business cycle, encouraging lending in boom times and discouraging it in bad times.
- Countries where large international banks dominate their banking system (as in many Eastern European and Baltic states) may see the supply of credit to lower (or unrated) borrowers decline and/or become more expensive, as banks using the IRB approach reassess the regulatory capital implications of lending.

Lesson: the BCBS has no formal representatives from developing countries, yet Basel II will certainly become a global standard; if developing countries are expected to implement international standards they should (a) be involved in their formulation, and (b) have this formulation take account of their own circumstances, and not just those in developed countries.

Whilst it is relatively straightforward to set headline figures for things such as capital adequacy ratios, as pointed out above, this in itself does not ensure that the banking sector is solvent in reality. Indeed, as Liliana Rojas-Suarez (2001) demonstrates, levels of regulatory capital held by banks in developing countries have had no relationship to actual riskiness. That is to say, the numerous banking crises that have occurred in developing countries since the advent of the Basel Accords could not have been predicted by observing holdings of regulatory capital, which also seem to have had no effect in restraining excessive risk-taking behaviour. As with the Honohan and Stiglitz (2001) argument discussed above, where international regulatory forms devised to be suitable for developed economies are simply transferred whole-sale to the very different financial systems in developing countries, the results are likely to be very different.

If banks cannot 'police themselves' the onus on strong regulation and supervision becomes all the stronger. However, as illustrated in Figure 5.5, there is considerable evidence that, in practice, supervision is less stringent in lower income countries. However, this should be contrasted with the fact that, in many instances as seen in Chapter 4, headline regulations are at least as stringent in developed countries as is the case in developed ones.

To determine the effectiveness of these regulations Barth *et al.* (2004) examine regulatory and supervisory practice in 107 countries to assess the relationship between specific practices and banking sector development and soundness. They try to answer seven specific questions:

1 Should banks be prevented from providing other financial services?

From an economic perspective, many have argued that banks should be pre-vented from doing so. In part this reflects their special status as deposit-taking institutions, and the systemic risks of bank failures, but is also the result of concerns about the level of power and influence that such integrated financial giants could yield.

The authors find that restricting banks in this regard has a negative effect on both bank stability and banking sector development.

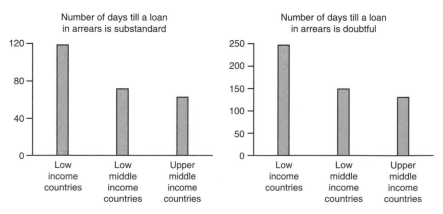

Figure 5.5 Comparative stringency of banking supervision.

Source: Barth, Caprio and Levine database.

2 Should entry into the banking system be controlled by barriers?

Again, it has been argued that the importance of the banking sector to the economy is such that the most vital task is to prevent weak or failing banks undermining the integrity of the financial system.

However, Barth *et al.* find no evidence that such restrictions are positively related to banking stability. Instead, they find some evidence that suggests that restricting the entry of foreign banks reduces stability. This is supportive of the view that restricting entry – and therefore competition – is likely to encourage corruption and a general decline in the efficiency of the system.

3 Do regulatory capital requirements enhance the stability of banks?

In this regard, the authors concur with Liliana Rojas-Suarez (op. cit.) and find little in the way of clear relationships in either direction. This leads them to caution on the widely held view that regulatory capital requirements are effective in preventing banks taking on excessive risks.

4 Do deposit insurance schemes enhance the stability of banks?

Here, quite the opposite is found. Deposit insurance, particularly generous schemes, are negatively associated with bank stability, which supports the view that strong regulation may not be sufficient to offset the moral hazard-producing effects of deposit insurance. More generally, the World Bank (2001) points out that to be successful, deposit insurance schemes require a minimum level of infrastructure, and should therefore not be attempted in the least developed countries: this would be likely to lead to excessive risk taking and increased fragility of the banking sector.

5 What is the relationship between different specific powers of regulators and supervisors and bank performance and stability?

Interestingly, very little evidence of any statistically significant kind emerged in this respect: 'Thus, measures of supervisory power, resources, independence, loan classification stringency, provisioning stringency, and others are not robustly associated with bank development, performance or stability' (Barth *et al.*, 2002: 245).

6 Does regulation that encourages private sector monitoring of banks enhance performance and stability?

Here, Barth *et al.* give an unequivocal yes. Furthermore, they suggest that regulation of this sort may be important in preventing financial crises from developing. Examples of private monitoring include:

- *Treatment of 'insiders'*: owners, directors and senior management work best with a sensible incentive structure. For owners, incentives should be based on franchise value and the threat of removal of the banking licence; for the board, penalties should exist for failing to disclose information; for managers, compensation should be performance-related, with no rewards for failure.
- *Ratings agencies* have the potential to play a key monitoring role of the behaviour of banks. However, it is not clear that their record stands up to scrutiny, as they have historically been very poor at predicting systemic failures.
- *Markets* such as creditors in corporate bond markets can send clear signals on bank performance through the trading of the bank's corporate debt in the secondary debt market.

7 Does government ownership of banks enhance performance and stability?

Here, the answer is an unequivocal no: 'There is no evidence, even in weak institutional settings, that government-owned banks are associated with positive outcomes' (Barth *et al.*, 2004: 245).

For the authors of the study, these findings suggest a number of key conclusions. First, regulation that forces the disclosure of information and encourages effective private sector monitoring of banks activities is likely to be most effective in producing both bank stability and development. And, second: '. . . these findings raise a cautionary flag regarding reform strategies that place excessive reliance on countries adhering to an extensive checklist of regulations and supervisory practices that involve direct, government oversight of and restrictions on banks.'

In short, the findings of this study suggest that 'market discipline' is by far and away the most effective means of supervising the activities of the banking sector, and many of the myriad banking regulations that have been introduced in developing countries in the past decade have had little or no positive effect on the robustness or development of the banking system.

However, this 'advice' should also be treated with some caution. As both Honohan and Stiglitz (op. cit.) and Liliana Rojas-Suarez (op. cit.) point out, many of the strongest pillars of market discipline – such as a corporate bond market where the price of banks' debt in the secondary market is both a barometer of their riskiness and an incentive to lower risk so as to improve borrowing terms – may simply not exist. Similarly, international ratings agencies have shown little interest in rating financial institutions in developing countries, particularly the poorer ones. In such circumstances, effective, direct supervision – or 'robust restraint' of the financial system – may be the best available alternative. Relying on market discipline where there is no such discipline to restrain the risk-taking impulses of banks would appear to be a recipe for disaster. However, if the onus is to be placed on regulation and supervision, then it is vital that it is effective.

The key point to make, therefore, is that it is not the existence of strong banking regulation that is the crucial determinant of developing a robust and effective banking sector. What matters most is that supervision is effective enough to enforce the regulations that exist.

In this regard, some basic requirements are that:

- Regulators and supervisors have sufficient skills and resources to perform their role and be relatively well remunerated.
- Regulatory and supervisory agencies should be free of political influence, with appointments made on merit.[16]
- The supervisory approach – while based on international standards such as the Basel Committee on Banking Supervision's (BCBS) *Core Principles of Banking Supervision* – should be tailored to the circumstances of each individual country.
- Regulations should be consistent and transparent and supervision conducted according to similar standards of consistency and transparency.

5.4 Capital market development

We have seen in previous chapters that capital market development – particularly stock market development – is positively correlated with higher rates of economic growth. It is therefore to be expected that a key aspect of reform in developing countries has focused on the development of broad and deep capital markets. In 2005, the World Bank described this process as follows:

> Many developing countries tried to deepen their securities markets by introducing major reforms, especially during the 1990s. They liberalized their financial systems, improved their investment climates (through macroeconomic stabilization and better business environments), developed new supervisory frameworks and institutions, and improved the basic infrastructure for capital market operations. Many countries also implemented comprehensive pension reforms and privatized state-owned enterprises, hoping to encourage capital market development. As reforms intensified, so did expectations regarding capital market development in developing countries. These high expectations, however, have not been met in many countries. After nearly two decades of reform, the state of capital markets in developing countries is quite mixed. The pace of growth, though rapid overall, has not been as dramatic as in developed nations. Some developing countries have experienced stagnation or even contraction of their securities markets, particularly for equity and domestic currency-denominated bonds.
>
> (De la Torre and Schmukler, 2005)

How can this lack of progress be explained, however? For the World Bank (op. cit.) it is difficult to explain this disappointing performance on the basis of economic fundamentals, since better fundamentals have been proven to foster both domestic stock market development and its internationalisation (i.e. the issuance and trading of securities abroad). However, these effects are not symmetrical. As economic fundamentals improve, stock issuance and trading abroad tend to rise relative to domestic activity, but this has not been followed by a 'crowding in' of domestic stock market activity as had been expected.

On the contrary, there has been a growing internationalisation of stock markets – i.e. the 'migration' of local companies' listing to major international exchanges such as New York and London. Specifically, firms that list overseas see the liquidity of their stocks on local exchanges decline. This has a ripple effect through the local market resulting in a general decline in liquidity for all local stocks, with the remaining liquidity being concentrated on those large companies that have already accessed the international capital markets.

Whilst this effect can be seen across the developing world, it is particularly pronounced in Latin America, as shown in Figure 5.6 below. As we can see, the value of stocks traded outside the region in 2000 was almost 125% of that traded within Latin America, up from 0.7% in 1990. The corresponding figures for 2000 in the G7 and East Asian economies was 3.4% and 4% respectively.

How are we to interpret this?

1   First, it may be that local stock market development will eventually occur and that patience is needed to wait for market forces to work their way through the system.

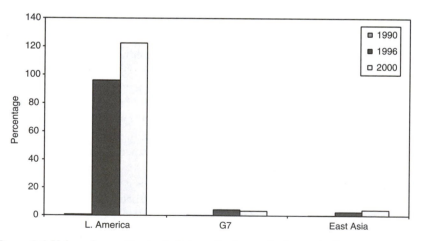

Figure 5.6 Value of securities traded abroad/value trade domestically.

Source: World Bank, 2005.

2   An alternative viewpoint is that countries which undertake the necessary reforms to develop local stock markets may, in fact, succeed in primarily increasing the internationalisation of the stocks of their major companies.

3   A third explanation is that sequencing has not been correct in many instances, and that regulatory and institutional reforms needed to precede full financial liberalisation to reap the benefits anticipated in terms of capital market development.

For the World Bank (2005) all of these explanations fail to take adequate account of certain basic factors – financial globalisation, liquidity, diversification and size – which have serious implications for the reform agenda.

Globalisation complicates capital market development of equity and bond markets in a number of different ways.

- In debt markets, globalisation magnifies the problems associated with weak currencies, with benefits (or costs) being allocated depending on how the local currency performs two functions: the role of a 'shock absorber' and the role of a reliable 'store of value'. There are very few currencies, even in developed markets, that perform both of these functions well. If the local currency does not hold the confidence of the domestic population, there is a tendency for financial contracts to be denominated in a foreign currency, usually US dollars, and/or for contracts to be of very short maturity. This in turn creates large foreign exposures in borrowers' balance sheets, leaving them vulnerable to large exchange rate fluctuations.

- In equity markets, globalisation does not create these balance sheet mismatches (in currency terms) for equity issuers, and does not therefore create systemic risk, regardless of the weakness of the local currency concerned. Furthermore, as we have seen, equity contracts are not subject to the risk of default as both upside and downside risks are shared by the purchaser and issuer of the equities. However, globalisation leading to the 'internationalisation' of equity markets as described above may create a serious policy dilemma: as soon as companies become large enough to issue equity in the deeper, more liquid stock markets in global financial centres, they have no incentive to issue equities in local stock markets (World Bank, 2005).

Liquidity, diversification, and size have similarly strong effects.

- From a liquidity perspective, there is something of a vicious circle in evidence: illiquid markets discourage new investors from entering, thus generating further illiquidity. This is a particularly important issue since most international asset management companies have high liquidity thresholds which must be passed before they will consider entering a new stock market. Most developing stock markets do not pass this threshold and are therefore not eligible for inclusion in the investment 'universe' of many asset management companies.

- As we have seen, a key function of stock markets is to enable investors to hold a diversified portfolio. However, the limited number of stocks on many developing exchanges, coupled with the concentration of the economy (and therefore available stocks) in a narrow range of economic sectors, greatly restricts the extent to which investors can obtain diversification benefits from investing in local exchanges.
- In many ways, these features are not just a matter of capital market development, which may be eventually overcome, but may also reflect the small size of many developing economies, which may place an ultimate limit on the liquidity and diversification that can ultimately be achieved.

What are the implications for the reform agenda, however? It may be that it is not practical – or desirable – for all of the developing countries that have attempted to develop their own capital markets to do so. Smaller developing countries may simply not be large enough to sustain such a market in the longer term.

In these circumstances, one solution is to look to establish regional markets, which would potentially have the liquidity and size to develop broad, deep and liquid capital markets. Such a process is of course fraught with difficulty, particularly from a political perspective. However, if these difficulties can be overcome, the benefits of regional capital markets could be significant.

5.5 Pension reform

We have seen in previous chapters that financial sector development is strongly influenced by the growth (or not) of contractual savings institutions. Also, in the previous section we discussed issues of capital market development. An important issue in this regard is that, whilst it may be possible for countries to develop stock markets, thereby providing a *supply* of equity assets, this is unlikely to be sustainable and fulfil its potential impact without a corresponding rise in the *demand* for these assets: the development of a deep and broad pension fund sector has become fundamental to these efforts.

When considering forms of national pension systems, there are a number of possible options:

1   Workers (and possibly their employers) could make contributions of a certain proportion of their salaries into state pension funds. The state pension fund would then provide payments to workers after their retirement, with the size of the pension being a proportion of the worker's final salary, modified by the number of years worked.

This model is called a 'pay-as-you-go' (PAYG) or 'unfunded' scheme and is based on the idea that today's workers provide the financing to fund pensions for today's retired, who in turn had supported the previous generation of retired people while they were working. On retirement, therefore, there are no savings built up to provide a pension. Rather, retiring workers have a claim on a collective fund. The pension that the retiree will receive may be fixed in relation to their previous salary, which is termed a 'defined benefit'.

2 The government could compel workers to buy individual pensions from private pension funds. Each worker would therefore accumulate his or her own fund, which would form the basis for the pension to be paid in retirement. The contribution rate (i.e. the percentage of salary) would be set by legislation, and could also include an employers' contribution. In this structure, payments would be in the form of an 'annuity', which is purchased from an insurance company. The annuity provides a fixed income stream for the period of retirement.

   This type of model is called a 'funded scheme', where workers accumulate a pot of money with a pension fund, the size of which depends upon the performance of the stock market in which the pension fund had invested the funds. It is also known as a 'defined *contribution* scheme' – as opposed to a defined *benefit* scheme – as it is the worker's contribution that is predetermined. The size of the resulting pension, however, depends on the size of the individual's fund on retirement, as well as market conditions when the annuity is purchased.

3 It is also possible to have a hybrid system, where a defined benefit scheme may be 'funded', or a defined contribution scheme may operate like a PAYG scheme as it only invests in a limited range of instruments, such as government bonds.

The great majority of developed and developing countries went for the PAYG option after the Second World War, with the remainder providing pensions direct from government revenues (i.e. option 1). By the 1980s, however, PAYG systems were facing difficulties. In particular, increasing life expectancy and falling birth rates altered the demographics of many countries, largely in the developed world but also in Latin America. As a result the 'old-age dependency ratio'[17] rose, placing additional financial burdens on today's workers, who had to fund the pensions of increasing numbers of retirees.

A rising old-age dependency ratio, if it continues, is ultimately unsustainable, and can be fiscally damaging in both the long and the short term if the government has to make up any deficit in the scheme. In order to make PAYG sustainable, however, the options available were for governments to cut pension benefits and/or raise workers' contribution rates. Both of these alternatives are likely to be politically unpopular.

5.5.1 Pension reform in practice

In 1981, Chile established the world's first funded pension scheme, starting a fashion which spread to other countries in Latin America, and also to European transition economies in the 1990s. Box 5.4 gives an overview of Chile's experience in this regard, and the issues it raises for other countries considering reform.

Box 5.4 Pension reform in Chile

In 1980 the Pinochet government in Chile took what was then an unprecedented step: faced with an increasingly unaffordable PAYG pension system with defined benefits, where the costs of payments far exceeded those of contributions, the government implemented a system of 'personal retirement accounts'. That is, a system of 'defined contributions' rather than defined benefits.

Members of the existing PAYG scheme were given the option of joining the new system and the majority chose to do so.

Rationale

- A fully 'funded' scheme such as that implemented in Chile is, by definition, affordable, since individual pensions are simply the annuity that each pension 'pot' can purchase in the market on any given day.
- By linking ultimate pensions to contributions, a strong incentive to work and increase income is created.
- By establishing a system of private pension funds to invest these 'individual accounts', a spur is given to the development of a domestic capital market, particularly if the pension funds are required to invest a significant proportion of their assets in the local equity market.

Outcomes

- Although defined contribution schemes based on this form are ultimately self-funding, the costs of transition are significant. PAYG schemes rely on the working generation paying the benefits of the current generation of retirees. If the former move into individual schemes, however, the government must pick up the shortfall: these averaged 7% of GDP in the first five years of the scheme and, although they have steadily fallen, have averaged around 4% of GDP per year since 1987. On current projections, the transition costs will not fall to zero until after 2030.
- There has indeed been a huge financial deepening in Chile since the

introduction of the new scheme, and much of this is attributable to the pension fund sector: in 1982 financial assets (M1-M7) to GDP was a little over 25% and pension fund assets were negligible; by 2005 the assets/GDP ratio had risen to more than 80% with the increase being almost entirely attributable to pension fund growth.

- The cumulative administrative costs of the scheme are such that, over a twenty-year period, fees and commissions account for 20% of the 'pot' available to purchase the annuity.
- By 2003, only 62% of those employed were regular contributors to the scheme, but the minimum requirement to receive the full benefits of the scheme is twenty years of full contributions. Consequently, many do not receive sufficient benefits on retirement to keep them above poverty levels.

Recent changes

- Individual schemes of this form are certainly beneficial for those of above average income and in steady work. However, for those on lower income and/or in sporadic work this is not the case.
- In 2007 Chile's President Bachelet introduced reforms into the scheme to replace the minimum pension guarantee (which was certainly inadequate) with a new national pension scheme, targeted at the bottom 60% of the income distribution and calibrated to ensure that all have the minimum income needed.

Lessons: individual schemes benefit some and harm others. Universal schemes do likewise, though the 'harm' is more in the sense of the relatively well off not being able to further increase their incomes in retirement. Any individual-based schemes will inevitably see some 'fall through the gaps' of the system, and this will generally be the poorest members of society. If the advantages of individual schemes are to be enjoyed, the system must be designed to address this inherent problem, and ideally from the start.

While all types of scheme have advantages and disadvantages, there is also a considerable fiscal cost of transition from PAYG to funded schemes. As Orszag and Stiglitz (1999) point out, there is nothing to be gained from comparing types of schemes as if they were to be implemented from scratch:

out of the 172 countries included in the 1997 edition of *Social Security Programs Throughout the World*, only 6 . . . lack an old age, disability and survivors program . . . for many countries initial choices have already been made. It is of little practical import at this point to re-examine these initial choices. A more fundamental objective is to examine potential reforms that would improve the future functioning of pension systems, taking into account the transition costs that would be embodied in any such shift.

(1999: 7)

For example:

1   The need to honour commitments to (a) current retirees, and (b) workers who stay with the PAYG system when they retire (i.e. older workers), despite the fact that the new generation of workers is no longer contributing to the PAYG system.
2   The need to compensate workers moving from the PAYG system for the value of their contributions to it, unless the PAYG system remains open and continues to operate alongside the new funded system.
3   Some governments also provide a minimum state pension for anyone in the system whose pension fund is insufficient to provide the minimum pension.

In Chile, for example, the fiscal cost of transition has been estimated at 5.7% of GDP from 1981 to 1996. Similarly, the cost of transition in Argentina is widely viewed as playing an important part in the crisis of 2001.

5.5.2   Key policy issues

1   For Barr (2000) the key issue for pension reform is 'output' (i.e. economic growth).

- If output is rising, a PAYG system can remain balanced despite the rise in the old-age dependency ratio, and funded schemes can deliver the expected benefits.
- If output is static, a PAYG system will become bankrupt unless major sacrifices are made by workers and/or pensioners, and a funded system will fail to deliver expected real benefits because nominal pensions will be eroded through goods and asset markets.
- If the average nominal wage is rising enough, there is no need to increase the contribution rate, as a sufficient increase in wages (and therefore contributions) should offset the increase in the number of pensioners.

2   The key to sustainable pension systems is therefore to calculate future obligations and to adjust the system if necessary by:

- increasing contribution rates of workers/employers;
- reducing pension benefits by (a) reducing payments and/or (b) raising the retirement age, which reduces the number of pensioners;[18]
- making the management of pensions more efficient;
- building up a contingency fund to meet any shortfall.

Therefore, while each type of pension system has advantages and disadvantages, a common feature is that all are likely to succeed in an environment of economic growth, just as all are likely to fail in an environment of stagnant or negative growth.

Policy advice has generally not reflected these nuances, however. Since the mid-1990s,[19] the World Bank in particular has argued in favour of a privately managed, mandatory defined contribution scheme, backed up by an unfunded public safety net and the option of making additional private contributions.

The momentum that this process has gained has, to some extent, given the impression that these are the only options that are available, but as Orszag and Stiglitz (1999: 2) point out, this reasoning is based on a number of myths about pension systems:

(a) Macroeconomic myths

- Myth 1: Individual accounts raise national saving.
- Myth 2: Rates of return are higher under individual accounts.
- Myth 3: Declining rates of return on PAYG systems reflect fundamental problems with these systems.
- Myth 4: Investment of public trust funds in equities has no macroeconomic effects.

(b) Microeconomic myths

- Myth 5: Labour market incentives are better under individual accounts.
- Myth 6: Defined benefit plans necessarily provide more of an incentive to retire early.
- Myth 7: Competition ensures low administrative costs under individual accounts.

(c) Political economy myths

- Myth 8: Corrupt and inefficient governments provide a rationale for individual accounts.
- Myth 9: Bailout politics are worse under public defined benefit plans.
- Myth 10: Investment of public trust funds is always squandered and mismanaged.

The authors demonstrate that none of these 'accepted wisdoms' is necessarily true, though each of them may be true in particular circumstances. They contend that a major problem is that critics of PAYG schemes often confuse the way these schemes have sometimes been implemented in practice with their 'inherent features'. Thus, while it is one thing to say that the PAYG system in country X has been badly implemented and managed, it is quite another to then extrapolate to the conclusion that PAYG systems are inherently flawed.

As with much else we have covered in this book, the success or failure of the reform agenda is likely to be determined by the vibrancy and growth of the economy, the choice of the policy package and the skill with which it is implemented and managed. Privately managed, defined contribution schemes do have advantages, but so do PAYG schemes. Supporters of the former generally point to the positive impact on equity market development, particularly where pension funds are obliged to invest in the domestic market. However, it is not just privately managed funds that can act as a spur to equity market development, as there is no reason why publicly managed funds could not do the same. Also, there is evidence to suggest that 'locking-in' pension funds to the local market is both negative for their returns – and therefore the pensions they can ultimately pay – and negative for the long-term development of the domestic equity market.[20]

What is clear is that the debate is – or certainly should be – more nuanced and country-specific than is currently the case. The 'World Bank approach' is not the only one, and those who would suggest otherwise are failing to give a complete picture of the range of policy options available.

Concluding remarks

In Chapter 4 we described the key features of the domestic financial system in developing countries, highlighting differences between developed and developing countries as well the considerable differences that exist within each of these categories.

It was argued that there is no one model that is applicable for all countries, and so no particular 'destination' towards which financial sector development is therefore heading. That said, it is clear that the financial systems in many developing (and developed) countries have deep-seated problems and are failing to perform the functions of the financial sector well. Reform is therefore essential, and this has been the subject of this chapter. Just as in Chapter 4, however, different reforms are both possible and advisable for countries in different circumstances.

One country may benefit more from autonomy over monetary policy, while another may benefit from a fixed exchange rate and an 'outsourced' monetary policy, for example. Similarly, while a stable fiscal position is essential, the pattern of tax and expenditure policies which lead to this is not fixed. High tax and spend countries can be just as fiscally stable as low tax and spend countries.

What is clear, however, is that stability does not equal development. It is perfectly possible to run a rigorous monetary and fiscal regime with low inflation and balanced budgets and for the economy to stagnate. Indeed, too 'tight' a stance is quite likely to lead to this outcome. The key point is that this is a necessary prerequisite for development, but it is far from being sufficient to ensure it.

As we have seen, genuine development requires far-reaching reforms – both macro and micro – across the economy and most of these relate to institutions, conceived in the broad sense as the 'rules of the game', which shape the behaviour of market actors and thus market outcomes.[21] Whether considering banking, capital market, tax or pension reform, it is this institutional context which is increasingly recognised as being the fundamental determinant of outcomes.

Just as this is true domestically, it is just as true for countries' engagement with the international financial system. As we shall see, the institutional context of this engagement determines whether countries are able to reap the (potentially large) benefits, or suffer the (equally large) costs of this engagement.

To consider these issues, the next chapter therefore turns to the external financial system.

6 The external financial system (I)

Characteristics and trends

Introduction

In the previous two chapters we examined the key features of the domestic financial system in developing countries and considered options for reform in this respect. As we enter the second half of this book, the attention shifts to the international financial system and how this interacts with, and impacts upon, these domestic systems.

Chapter 7 will analyse issues of debt and financial crisis, whilst Chapter 8 will consider the role of the multilateral financial institutions and reform of the 'international financial architecture'. In this introductory Chapter, however, we set the stage for these chapters, by providing an overview of key trends in external financing for development.

The chapter is divided into two parts: Sections 6.1 to 6.4 examine issues surrounding 'official development assistance' (or 'aid'), while Section 6.5 addresses the subject of private capital flows to developing countries.

6.1 Trends in official development assistance

The first question to ask is why we need official development assistance (ODA) at all. In its 2005 report focusing on development finance, the UN's Department for Economic and Social Affairs (DESA) answers the question as follows:

> The architects of the post-war international economic system had recognized the need for official financing to counteract the insufficiency of private capital flows and, since the 1960s, there has been an increasing perception of the need to support developing countries, an issue that became embedded in the politics of decolonization and the cold war. The surge of private financing to developing countries beginning in the 1970s and the end of the cold war generated an increasing realization that the era of official development financing had passed. However, the vagaries of private capital flows during the 1980s and, again, since the 1997 Asian crisis, in addition to the increasing marginalization of the poorest

countries from the world economy, have led to a renewed focus on the critical role of official development finance.

(UN, 2005: 109)

Indeed, the aim of directly transferring funds from developed to developing countries (i.e. redistributing wealth internationally) has been a central concern of the UN and its various bodies since 1950. In resolution 400 (V) of November 1950, the General Assembly of the United Nations noted that the domestic financial resources of the developing world, even in combination with private flows of capital (which were very small at that time in any event), were insufficient to act as a catalyst for the high and sustained rates of economic growth needed.[1]

In 1952, the General Assembly called on the Economic and Social Council to establish a capital fund, which would provide long-term low-interest loans and grants to developing countries and, in 1954, resolution 823 (IX) instructed the International Bank for Reconstruction and Development (i.e. the World Bank) to create the International Finance Corporation.

Recognising the need to augment the official flows emanating from the UN and its agencies, the World Council of Churches proposed in 1958 that developed countries commit themselves to earmarking 1% of GDP as aid for developing countries, a figure accepted by the UN as being compatible with its development goals, and which was confirmed at the inaugural meeting of the United Nations Committee on Trade and Development (UNCTAD) in 1964. Subsequently, the figure was reduced to 0.7% of GDP, on the assumption that the remaining 0.3% could be made up with private sector flows.

At the start of the 1960s, the proportion of GNP which OECD[2] member

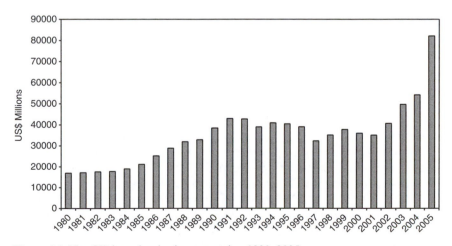

Figure 6.1 Net ODA to developing countries, 1980–2005.

Source: OECD DAC Database.

countries devoted to aid averaged 0.53%. Whilst the UN then called on developed countries to raise this figure substantially, however, the opposite actually occurred: from 1966 to 1969 the figure fell to 0.39%; by 1970–1973 the proportion of GNP devoted to ODA was lower still at 0.32%. By the early 1980s, the figure was broadly unchanged at 0.35%, but by the end of the 1990s it had fallen to an all-time low, so that the proportion of developed countries GNP devoted to ODA was only 0.21% (UN, 2005).

The Monterrey Consensus of 2002 sought to stop and reverse this decline, and called on all developed countries to set a specific target for reaching the 0.7% figure. A number of countries have now made this pledge, and ODA flows as a proportion of GNP have started to rise, albeit slowly.

The largest single source of ODA is the European Union, which contributes more than half of the global figure. A few EU countries have met the 0.7% target (Denmark, Luxembourg, the Netherlands, Norway and Sweden), whilst the remainder have now committed to reach the target by 2015. Traditionally, the Scandinavian countries have been both supportive (in terms of relative and absolute financing) and engaged (in terms of actively participating in, and sometime shaping, debates on international development from the donor perspective). Box 6.1 figures the history and record of the Swedish Development Agency (SIDA) in this regard.

Box 6.1 The Swedish International Development Authority (SIDA)

Sweden is one of the few countries in the world to have surpassed the UN target of 0.7% of GDP devoted to international development. Today, SIDA is one of the world's most prominent national development agencies, both in terms of the level of its interventions and its place at the centre of many debates surrounding issues of international development.

Origins

As was true of many European countries – and not only the colonial powers – Sweden's first experience of 'development' came through the work of its Christian missionaries in the nineteenth century. The first Swedish missionaries went to Ethiopia in 1860 seeking converts but also started schools and provided medical assistance. No formal bodies were established until the post-Second World War era. In 1952 the first governmental department was formed – the 'Central Committee for Swedish Cooperation'. Intervention was rather *ad hoc* at first, focusing on countries with which Sweden had historic links, and there was no central 'philosophy' guiding the work. This was to change after 1962, when a bill passed through the Swedish Parliament establishing that the goal of Sweden's development efforts should be to 'improve the living standards of poor people' – this remains intact today.

Evolution of development 'philosophy'

In 1965 the Swedish International Development Authority (SIDA) was established. Initially its programmes were focused on Ethiopia, India, Kenya, Pakistan, Tanzania and Tunisia, countries where there had been Swedish Christian missions and where the English-speaking nature of the former British colonies 'suited Sweden culturally'.

> During the 1970s, development assistance was the concept. The first development assistance was very much a question of building schools, hospitals, power plants and factories. At the same time there was a growing realisation that it was not simply a matter of transferring Western European models to other countries and cultures. The expression assistance on the recipient's terms started to be heard.
>
> (SIDA, 2008)

Although in the 1980s it was still common to talk of 'donor countries' and 'recipient countries', the 1990s saw a shift in SIDA – shared with some of the other development agencies – towards 'cooperation'. 'Development' was increasingly seen not as something which is done *to* a country, but something that is done *with* a country. This found an echo in the Bretton Woods Institutions' call for developing countries to have 'ownership' of structural adjustment programmes, for example, and is more broadly related to the growing realisation that 'the voices of the poor' needed to be central to the development discourse.

> In the 1990s, people started to speak about development cooperation and partner countries. These terms express equality, as well as a long-term perspective that is far from the development assistance perspective of the early years. In the increasingly globalised society we live in today, we have expanded the concept and now we talk about a policy for global development.
>
> (ibid.)

Policy

In 1978 the goal of raising living standards was augmented with four further objectives – economic growth; economic and social equality; economic and political independence; democratic development – and in 1980 the focus shifted towards rural development so as to target the poorest sections of developing countries. SIDA also progressively stepped up its work with NGOs and grassroots organisations in developing countries from this point on.

Along with the other major bilateral agencies SIDA was an active

participant in the structural adjustment reforms pushed by the IMF
and World Bank from the 1980s onwards.

Most recently, in 1998 SIDA introduced a further goal to its development cooperation to encourage the sustainable use of natural
resources and protection of the environment. Today SIDA has a staff
of 900, of whom 190 work in programmes or missions in the developing
world.

Figure 6.1 above shows the trend in overall ODA flows from 1980 to 2005.
As we can see, there was an upward trend from the mid-1980s, followed by
a decline in the 1990s and a return to a rising trend from 2002 onwards.
However, although rising, the level of total ODA in 2005 was US$82 billion,
which in real terms is only marginally higher than that which existed in
1990.

As shown in Figure 6.2, however, much of the recent growth in ODA
has been in the areas of debt relief, emergency aid and technical assistance.
'Other ODA' in the figure refers to those aid flows that are directed through
central governments' budgets – there has been no growth in this area. As
we have seen in previous chapters, however, administrative deficiencies
within government departments – not least due to poorly paid, trained and
motivated staff working in inappropriate surroundings – are a key drag on
the effectiveness of policy reforms in the financial sector, and therefore an
obstacle to spurring economic growth and poverty reduction. Funds for
technical cooperation obviously have a role to play here, but do nothing to
address large shortfalls in fiscal budgets, for example. Furthermore, whilst

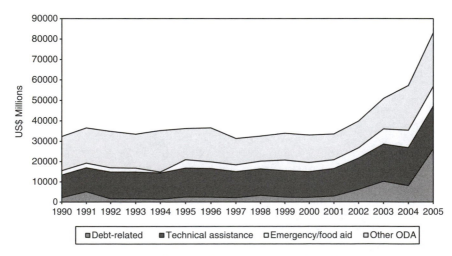

Figure 6.2 Composition of ODA to all developing countries, 1990–2005.

Source: OECD DAC Database.

debt relief is important it is not a source of additional revenues, and ODA targeted at disaster relief is, by definition, not developmental in nature.

As well as the type of ODA, and its overall scale, a third crucial issue is its destination. In 1990, at the UN Conference on the Least Developed Countries, developed countries agreed that, within the 0.7% ODA target, 0.15–0.20% would be earmarked specifically for the poorest countries. Whilst some countries have honoured this commitment, the actual proportion of ODA going to the poorest developing countries fell to around half this level in the 1990s.

As with total ODA flows, this trend has been partially offset since the Monterrey Consensus in 2002, as shown in Figure 6.3 below.

Despite this increase, however, it is clear from the figure above that the bulk of the increase in ODA has been in areas of debt relief, technical assistance and emergency support, as well as in peace-building initiatives. Again, it is not that these aspects of ODA are unimportant. Far from it, particularly in the poorest developing countries. However, it is equally true that direct assistance channelled through central government budgets has a crucial role to play, and that ODA of this form was only marginally higher in 2004 than had been the case in 1990.

Today, a vital reason why it is particularly important to (a) increase overall ODA flows, (b) increase the proportion of ODA to central government budgets, and (c) increase the proportion of ODA going to the poorest developing countries, is that governments throughout the developing world are striving to meet the UN's Millennium Development Goals by 2015. Without substantial progress on points (a), (b) and (c) it is now widely understood that this will simply not be possible.

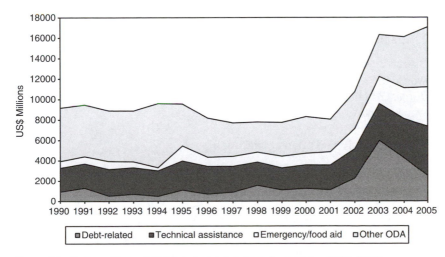

Figure 6.3 Composition of ODA to least developed countries, 1990–2005.

Source: OECD DAC Database.

In the next section we explore these issues in more detail.

6.2. The Millennium Development Goals

In late 2000 the United Nations published the Millennium Declaration. The document, which was ratified by 189 heads of state, expressed a commitment on behalf of its signatories to address critical global problems of poverty, disease and underdevelopment in a way compatible with environmental sustainability.

Following the Declaration, eight Millennium Development Goals (MDGs) were formulated, with explicit indicators established for each and a deadline of 2015 set for achievement of all eight goals. The eight MDGs are as follows:

1   Eradicate extreme poverty and hunger;
2   Achieve universal primary education;
3   Promote gender equality and empower women;
4   Reduce child mortality;
5   Improve maternal health;
6   Combat HIV/Aids, malaria and other diseases;
7   Ensure environmental sustainability;
8   Develop a global partnership for development.

The specific targets for each of these goals are described in Box 6.2 below.

Box 6.2 Millennium Development Goal (MDG) targets

1. Eradicate extreme poverty and hunger

Target 1: Halve, between 1990 and 2015, the proportion of people whose income is less than one US dollar a day.
Target 2: Halve, between 1990 and 2015, the proportion of people who suffer from hunger.

2. Achieve universal primary education

Target 3: Ensure that, by 2015, children everywhere, boys and girls alike, will be able to complete a full course of primary schooling.

3. Promote gender equality and empower women

Target 4: Eliminate gender disparity in primary and secondary education, preferably by 2005, and in all levels of education no later than 2015.

4. Reduce child mortality

Target 5: Reduce by two-thirds, between 1990 and 2015, the under-five mortality rate.

5. Improve maternal health

Target 6: Reduce by three-quarters, between 1990 and 2015, the maternal mortality ratio.

6. Combat HIV/Aids, malaria and other diseases

Target 7: Have halted by 2015 and begun to reverse the spread of HIV/AIDS.
Target 8: Have halted by 2015 and begun to reverse the incidence of malaria and other major diseases.

7. Ensure environmental sustainability

Target 9: Integrate the principles of sustainable development into country policies and programmes and reverse the loss of environmental resources.
Target 10: Halve, by 2015, the proportion of people without sustainable access to safe drinking water and sanitation.
Target 11: By 2020, to have achieved a significant improvement in the lives of at least 100 million slum dwellers.

8. Develop a global partnership for development

Target 12: Develop further an open, rule-based, predictable, non-discriminatory trading and financial system. Includes a commitment to good governance, development and poverty reduction, both nationally and internationally.
Target 13: Address the special needs of the least developed countries. Includes: tariff and quota-free access for least developed countries' exports; enhanced programme of debt relief for heavily indebted poor countries (HIPC) and cancellation of official bilateral debt; and more generous ODA for countries committed to poverty reduction.
Target 14: Address the special needs of landlocked developing countries and small island developing states (through the Programme of Action for the Sustainable Development of Small Island Developing States and the outcome of the twenty-second special session of the General Assembly).
Target 15: Deal comprehensively with the debt problems of developing countries through national and international measures in order to make debt sustainable in the long term.

Target 16: In cooperation with developing countries, develop and implement strategies for decent and productive work for youth.

Target 17: In cooperation with pharmaceutical companies, provide access to affordable essential drugs in developing countries.

Target 18: In cooperation with the private sector, make available the benefits of new technologies, especially information and communications.

Source: http://www.un.org/millenniumgoals/

6.2.1 Progress towards meeting the MDGs

The UN General Assembly met in September 2005 to review progress, which had been uneven at best, both in terms of the specific MDGs, and the pattern of geographical progress towards meeting them. In the summer of 2005, the UN Secretary-General, Kofi Annan, made these concerns explicit in the UN's progress report on the MDGs:

> If current trends persist, there is a risk that many of the poorest countries will not be able to meet many of them [MDGs]. Considering how far we have come, such a failure would mark a tragically missed opportunity . . . As I said in my March report: 'Let us be clear about the costs of missing this opportunity: millions of lives that could have been saved will be lost; many freedoms that could have been secured will be denied; and we shall inhabit a more dangerous and unstable world.

These concerns are backed up by the evidence, perhaps most comprehensively set out in the 2005 report, *Investing in Development: A Practical Plan to Achieve the Millennium Development Goals* (UN Millennium Project, 2005), which was drawn up by 265 of the world's leading development experts and – although positive in some regards – makes for sobering reading in others.

Table 6.1 details aggregate global progress on the key indicators. As can be seen, there has been positive change on every indicator, with the notable exception of HIV prevalence.

However, whilst this aggregate picture is broadly encouraging, it gives a very unrealistic picture of the reality on the ground at the regional and country level.

Table 6.1 shows that the proportion of people living in absolute poverty (measured as those living on less than $1.08 per day) had fallen from 28% to 21% between 1990 and 2002. However, as Figure 6.4 below demonstrates, these global aggregate figures give little sense of the prevalence of absolute poverty in each region: in 1992, the figure for sub-Saharan Africa was more than 45% of the population, whilst the corresponding figure for the Middle East and North Africa, was just 2%. Furthermore, the decline in the global

Table 6.1 Global progress on the MDGs

Indicator	1990	2002
GDP per capital (1995 US$)	1,071	1,299
Headcount poverty (%)	28	21
Undernourishment prevalence (%)	20	17
Under-five mortality (per 1,000 live births)	103	88
Life expectancy (years)	63	65
HIV prevalence (%)	0.5	1.6
Access to improved drinking water (%)	71	79
Access to improved sanitation (%)	34	49

Source: UN, 2005.

average over the period considered is almost entirely the result of large reductions in poverty levels in East Asia and South Asia, containing the billion-plus populations of China and India respectively.

In East Asia, the proportion of the population living in absolute poverty fell from 30% to 12% in 2002, and 9% in 2004, whilst South Asia saw a reduction of 12 percentage points, from 43% to 31% between 2002 and 2004. In contrast, Latin America and the Middle East regions saw only a very small improvement, and Eastern Europe and Central Asia saw a deterioration, albeit from a very low starting point. The most alarming region, however, is sub-Saharan Africa which, despite a reduction of 6 percentage points over the period, still saw 41% of the population living on less than US$1 per day by 2004.

Much of these regional differences can be explained by two factors: economic growth rates and levels of population growth. For example, while

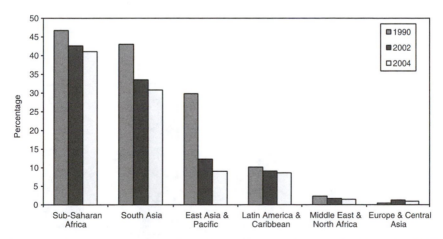

Figure 6.4 Proportion of regional populations living on less than US$1 per day, 1990 vs. 2002 vs. 2004.

Source: World Bank WDI.

India's growth record has been impressive in recent years, the country's population has also increased substantially. In contrast, China's relatively stable population growth has allowed its impressive economic growth rates to feed through into significantly higher per capita incomes. Sub-Saharan Africa has seen the worst of all worlds: low (even negative) economic growth combined with rapid population growth. Indeed, the situation in sub-Saharan Africa is such that, on current trends, few if any of the MDGs have a realistic chance of being met.

The fourth MDG relates to child mortality rates, with the target of reducing the rate by two-thirds by 2015. Figure 6.5 depicts progress in this regard between 1990 and 2005. At the beginning of this period, the average sub-Saharan African rate of under-5 mortality (per 1,000 children) was 184. That is, almost 20% of sub-Saharan African children died before they reached the age of 5. Since that time, the rate has fallen by around 5% every five years, so that fifteen years later in 2005 the figure was still more than 162 children per 1,000. If this trend were to continue, the target of reducing the figure by two-thirds would certainly not be achieved by 2015 – it would take another eighty-five years, until 2100, before this level was reached.

On current trends, only a very few targets – such as the aim of achieving universal primary education by 2015 – may be achieved in all regions, including sub-Saharan Africa. Others, however, such as the target of reversing deforestation under the seventh MDG which addresses environmental sustainability, are unlikely to be met in any region, as illustrated in Figure 6.6 below.

It was concerns of this kind that motivated the Make Poverty History campaign in 2005, and which contributed to the announcement of increased overseas development assistance (ODA) by the G8 in 2005. Responding to this pressure, and one hopes also recognising the crucial importance of

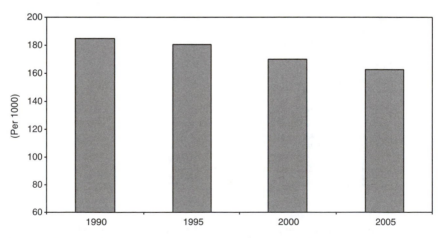

Figure 6.5 Sub-Saharan Africa: under-5 mortality rates, 1990–2005.

Source: World Bank WDI.

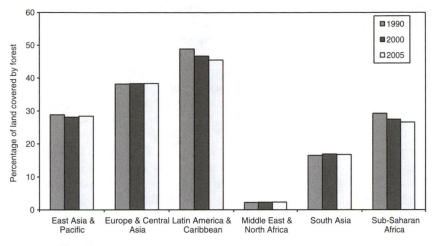

Figure 6.6 Regional progress on reversing deforestation

Source: World Bank WDI.

accelerating progress if the 2015 deadline is to be met, G8 leaders – meeting in Gleneagles in July 2005 – agreed to double aid to Africa from $25 billion per year to $50 billion by 2010, and to increase total ODA to $129 billion by the same year.

If fulfilled, these pledges have the potential to accelerate progress on meeting the MDGs. However, even with this additional funding, it is highly likely that many MDGs will not be met, particularly – though not exclusively – in sub-Saharan Africa.

Figure 6.7 below gives the most authoritative estimate of the total ODA

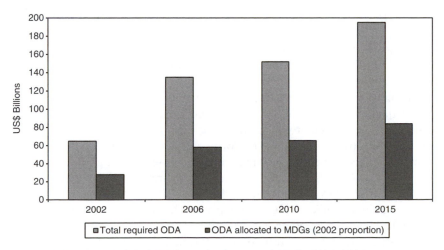

Figure 6.7 Estimated global ODA required to meet MDGs, 2002–2015.

Source: UN, 2005.

needed to meet the MDGs by 2015. As can be seen, in 2010, required ODA is more than $150bn, significantly above that promised at Gleneagles – indeed, the figure that was needed for 2006 was higher than that currently committed to for 2010. Furthermore, historically less than half of ODA has been spent in ways that would contribute towards meeting the MDGs, as depicted with the darker bars in Figure 6.7 and discussed above. If this trend were to continue, then MDG-dedicated-ODA, would be less than half that required, with clear implications for the world's ability to meet the development goals.

A final issue in this regard relates to the willingness (or ability) of donor governments to honour these pledges made in 2005. The G8 Summit had barely finished before a number of governments began talking of budget constraints and fiscal considerations affecting their ability to honour these pledges. Past experience suggests that it is highly likely that these pledges will become 'aspirations'.

By 2007, however, it appeared that the long-standing shortfall between ODA commitments and ODA disbursals was alive and well. The Africa Progress Panel, chaired by former UN Secretary-General Kofi Annan, reported that ODA to Africa from the G8 rose by US$1 billion between 2005 and 2007. However, the Gleneagles commitments specified an increase of US$12.5 billion by 2010. This suggests that the years from 2007 to 2010 will require a very large increase in ODA to Africa if the Gleneagles commitments are to be met. At the time of writing, there seems little prospect of this happening.[3]

However, a vital point to bear in mind is that, even in the unlikely event that the commitments were to be fully honoured, the world would still face a significant funding shortfall from that required to meet the MDGs.

6.3 ODA and growth

While it is widely accepted that appropriately targeted and utilised ODA flows are an essential component in the battle to meet the MDGs by 2015, particularly in the poorer developing countries, there is less agreement as to the impact of ODA on growth. Indeed, some commentators see it as having a potentially negative effect.[4]

For some (particularly the World Bank) the effectiveness of aid in general, but particularly its impact on growth and poverty reduction, is strongly related to the policy environment in the recipient countries. Countries with a record of effective and sustained reforms are also more likely to use ODA effectively.[5] This influential view has led to a certain 'herding' on the part of donors, so that 'successful' developing countries are more likely to see donors raising levels of ODA than less successful ones. The EU, for example, focuses the overwhelming bulk of its ODA on around thirty 'donor darlings', such as Tanzania, Uganda and Vietnam, while other countries – 'donor orphans' – receive little external assistance, despite the fact that they are often poorer countries.

In 2007, for example, a variety of donor organisations operated around 600 different health projects in Tanzania, often with little or no coordination between them. This 'herding' process is described in more detail in Box 6.3 below, in the context of the broader issue of the international distribution of ODA.

Box 6.3 The distribution of international ODA

As we have seen in this chapter, today's consensus priority of international development agencies is poverty alleviation – or elimination. This has been given added impetus by the focus on achieving the MDGs by 2015, particularly with respect to the halving of global poverty. Given this, one would expect international ODA to be stringently targeted on the world's poorest countries. It is also now broadly accepted that ODA is most effective in countries with 'good governance', but countries with a poor record in this area are also those most likely to have very high levels of absolute poverty. Finally, we have also seen that ODA is often influenced by 'strategic' considerations, as well as the commercial interests of donor countries. How do these seemingly conflicting forces play out in practice?

Extent to which ODA is focused on the poorest (–1) to the richest (+1) in 2001

Donor	*Population < \$1 per day*	*Whole population*
DAC (all)	0.133	−0.130
USA	0.322	0.059
Japan	0.213	−0.178
Germany	0.267	0.005
UK	−4.05	−0.543
France	0.289	0.029
Netherlands	−0.152	−0.306

Source: Baulch, 2003.

The figures given in the table above are the 'Suits index' for the largest bilateral donor groups. The index is a measure of progressiveness which ranges from −1 (where all aid is focused on the poorest country in the world) to +1 (where all aid is focused on the richest).

Here we see that the US is the most 'regressive' donor, giving a high proportion of its total ODA to middle-income countries such as Egypt, Morocco, Russia. Japan also disproportionately targets its ODA on relatively well-off countries, such as Peru and Thailand. France and Germany also give substantial aid to these middle-income countries, but this is balanced by a focus on small, very poor countries, particularly those in sub-Saharan Africa. The UK and the Netherlands score better in terms of 'progressivity' as much of their aid is targeted on small sub-Saharan countries. With regard to these patterns of aid flow, there is a linkage between a European donor's aid and the location of its former colonies, while the US appears more influenced by 'strategic' concerns (i.e. high aid flows to Israel and Iraq) and Japan by commercial, strategic and 'cultural' issues. As Baulch (op. cit.) points out, however, all the major donors give less significance to South Asia than one would expect, given that almost half of the world's total population of those living on less than $1 a day live in that region.

The well-known 'donor darling' phenomenon can also be seen in sub-Saharan Africa, where the majority of aid goes to a small group of countries (around ten). Much of this 'herding' by donors is related to issues of governance and logistics: put crudely if good governance and the ability to get things done are key drivers of development outcomes, then donors will get more 'bang for their buck' in countries with these characteristics.

There is an exception that many of the countries with the most pressing developmental needs do not have these features, however, and the trend has been to assume that international NGOs are more suited to making direct interventions on the ground in these circumstances.

Koch *et al.* (2007) find that, while NGOs do focus more on the very poorest countries than do the bilateral agencies, this is not as pronounced as is often assumed:

> The figures show that NGOs spend relatively more money in countries with moderately good governance than in those with bad governance. They prefer Costa Rica to Cuba, Ghana to Togo, and Georgia to Azerbaijan ... There is a definite tendency towards clustering. Honduras, Nicaragua, the Palestinian Territories and Zambia, for example, received more than 20 times more aid per capita from NGOs than, for example, the Central African Republic, Guinea and Yemen.

As with the official agencies, part of the explanation will relate to the simple practicality of getting into a country and getting things done. However, there also appears to be a 'path dependency' at work, where, having established a programme in one area, donors tend to move from these bases developing links with local partners as they go. Perhaps more worrying, however, is the fact that NGOs tend to be disproportionately represented in countries where their own national development agency has a strong presence. One factor here may be the increasingly large share of NGO funding that comes from their national development agencies: Koch *et al.* (op. cit.) find a strong correlation between the pattern of country funding from Dutch NGOs and the national development agency.

If all are competing over the 'darlings', however, who will focus on the very poorest?

The rationale for this position is that of ODA value for money: if aid is disproportionately targeted at those countries where it is most likely to be used effectively, the number of people lifted out of poverty will be maximised. However, others dispute the clear link between policy effectiveness, aid and economic growth, arguing that ODA is often used to offset the effects of economic shocks, and is therefore unlikely to be associated with higher rates of economic growth, at least in the shorter term.[6]

We have seen that much ODA is not of the kind that would be likely to spur economic growth. However, studies that focus on the link between forms of ODA that should be helpful in this regard – budget support, investments in infrastructure and aid for productive sectors, for example – do find a positive relationship between ODA and growth.[7] At present the issue has not been settled conclusively, though it would seem that donors at least are largely supportive of the World Bank view.

What is clear, therefore, is that ODA has not always been positively associated with economic growth and poverty reduction. However, it is equally clear that there is no inherent reason why it should not do so. Rather, as with much else we have covered in this book, it is the quantity, quality, targeting and effectiveness of ODA that matters – not just the headline figure – as well as the domestic institutional and policy frameworks through which the ODA is mediated. If ODA gets these aspects right, then ODA will positively affect growth. If they are not, the opposite may occur. What are the key issues in this regard?

In terms of its effectiveness – and therefore its ultimate impact on growth and poverty reduction – the stability and certainty of ODA flows is extremely important, both in terms of meeting the MDGs and of generating higher growth rates. The UN (2005: 113) puts the issue as follows:

> . . . aid flows tend to rise and fall with economic cycles in donor countries, with policy assessments of the recipient countries, and with a shift in donor policies. This uncertainty has a negative impact on public investment and thus on growth, as well as on the conduct of monetary and fiscal policy. Empirical work suggests that the volatility of aid flows exceeds that of other macroeconomic variables, such as GDP or fiscal revenue. Aid is significantly more volatile than fiscal revenue, and tends to be procyclical on average. When aid falls, it leads to costly fiscal adjustments in the form of increased taxation and spending cuts that reinforce the cyclical impact of declining aid flows. In this respect, the volatility in aid flows has a similar impact to volatility in commodity prices in countries that are dependent upon the exports of a single commodity.

Interestingly, there is little distinction between the volatility of ODA and that of private flows, which have very similar standard deviations.

This volatility can cause serious macroeconomic problems in developing

countries, particularly small ones with limited abilities to absorb surges in
ODA and an underdeveloped financial sector. For example, surges of inflow
can put upward pressure on exchange rates, reducing the competitiveness of
the export sector.[8]

It is therefore important for the inflow of ODA to be predictable and
smoothly managed if its positive effects are to be realised and potential negative impacts on growth rates caused by macroeconomic disturbances are to be
avoided. This is not just a matter of reducing the volatility of pledged ODA,
but also of its disbursement, as historically the relationship between the two
has varied considerably: in some periods and regions all pledged ODA is
disbursed; at other times far less ends up being disbursed.

For the UN (2005: 116):

> Aid conditionality is another source of volatility. This is due not only to
> the types of specific conditions required by donors, but also to the fre-
> quent requirement that aid recipients have the seal of approval of an
> International Monetary Fund (IMF) programme that is on track. When
> these programmes go off-track, the negative impact is intensified by the
> withdrawal of aid flows by donors.

The consensus today is that such conditionality is often counterproductive. If
a reform programme is not genuinely 'owned' by the country concerned there
is a substantially larger prospect of it not being fully implemented. The UK
has been at the forefront of moves to reduce or eliminate conditionality in
ODA flows, with the announcement in 2005 that UK ODA would no longer
be tied to specific policies.

The UK has also led moves to eliminate 'ties' from ODA flows, where aid is

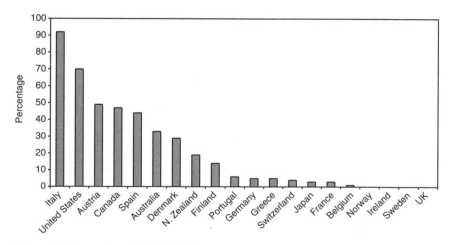

Figure 6.8 Proportion of 'tied' ODA, 2006.

Source: Action Aid, 2006.

provided on the condition that it is used to purchase goods and services from the donor countries. As can be seen from Figure 6.8, along with Sweden, Ireland and Norway, the UK is one of only four countries to have completely untied aid. At the other extreme, 92% of Italy is tied, while the corresponding figure for the US is 70%.

More generally, donors have been working to increase the effectiveness of their aid, with a focus on greater coordination of their policies, so that the total impact is greater than the sum of the constituent parts. For example, the Paris Declaration of Aid Effectiveness of 2005, where over 100 countries and donor agencies were represented, listed five key principles of aid effectiveness:[9]

(a) ownership of development strategies by partner countries;
(b) alignment of donor support with those strategies;
(c) harmonisation of donor actions;
(d) managing for results; and
(e) mutual accountability of donors and partners.

The Declaration also provided quantitative indicators to assess progress on each of these five areas, with the target of reaching them by 2010.

To summarise, it is clear that when it comes to aid, it is not only size that matters. Other key factors are:

- It is directed to the most appropriate sources.
- It is directed through central government budgets.
- It is stable both in terms of pledged and disbursed ODA.
- It is not conditional on the implementation of particular policies.
- It is part of a broader development programme, which is genuinely owned by the governments concerned.
- The activities of donors are coordinated to maximise the impact of ODA.

However, even if all these objectives were to be met and aid was 'perfectly' delivered, there would still be insufficient ODA to enable many developing countries and regions to meet the MDGs by 2015. Other sources of income are clearly needed, which has led attention to 'innovative sources of finance'.

6.4 Innovative sources of finance

The need for additional sources of external finance was explicitly stated in the Monterrey Consensus of 2002. Since then there has been much discussion on this issue, but only limited progress.

Initially, the greatest impetus had been in support of the International Finance Facility (IFF) – proposed by the UK's then Chancellor and future Prime Minister, Gordon Brown – wherein future ODA flows would be 'front-loaded' through the issue of bonds today by G8 members. The money raised would be used to meet the MDGs now, and the bonds paid through future ODA commitments of the countries concerned. Despite the efforts of the UK government, however, the IFF has not attracted the broad international support that was hoped for.

As an alternative – or as a 'first step' – a less ambitious facility was launched in 2005, where a smaller IFF would focus on immunisations. The IFFIm aims to raise an additional US$4 billion by 2015, to fund immunisations against the deadliest diseases in developing countries, and is supported by the UK, France, Spain, Italy and Sweden.

At around the same time UNITAID was launched under the auspices of the World Health Organisation (WHO), which again focuses on the health sphere, and provides financing for the purchase of drugs to combat HIV/AIDS, malaria and tuberculosis, with delivery undertaken by bodies such as the WHO, the Global Fund[10] and the Clinton Foundation.[11] As of 2007, the fund was supported by thirty-five countries, with much – but not all – of the financing being generated by a 'solidarity levy' on airline tickets, initiated by the French government. In 2007, UNITAID raised US$300 million to further these goals.

While these initiatives are certainly welcome, there have been many other options proposed. As illustrated in Figure 6.9 below, the UN (2005) considered various innovative sources of finance options, distinguishing between

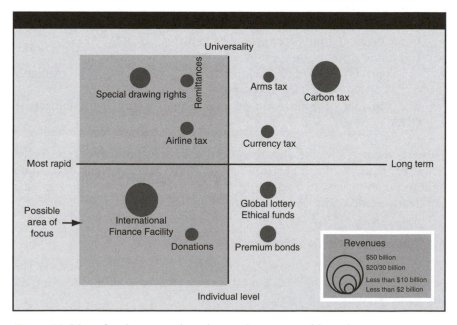

Figure 6.9 Map of main proposals on innovative sources of financing.

Source: UN, 2005.

the proposals in terms of the need for universal adoption, and the speed with which each could be implemented – thus identifying 'quick wins'. A full-scale IFF was the primary 'quick-win' identified. However, because the IFF initiative has progressed more slowly and with fewer partner countries than originally intended, and because of the more limited nature of the initiatives that have been implemented, it is necessary to look seriously at other possible sources of finance such as the currency transaction tax (CTT), for example. In all likelihood a number of innovative mechanisms will need to be employed to bridge the funding gap. Clearly, the need for universal adoption is a key drawback of any proposal – even if such agreement could be reached, it would inevitably take a long time to get there.

For the UN, the proposals in the bottom left quadrant of the figure are those that do not necessarily require universal adoption and therefore could be implemented relatively rapidly. As well as the IFF, this includes an increase in direct donations.

Others that could be rapidly implemented, but may require at least some degree of universality, are the proposal for the IMF to create additional funding by allocating special drawing rights (SDRs),[12] and an increased role for remittances – i.e. money sent from nationals working overseas back to their home country. The initiatives seen as taking longer to implement range from a global lottery and use of premium bonds to a number of global taxes, such as a carbon tax, an arms tax or a tax on global currency transactions.

In each instance, the size of the revenue available ranges from US$2 billion to US$50 billion, and is represented by the size of the circle. Thus the largest possible sources, as described by the UN, are the IFF and carbon tax, which have the potential to raise up to US$50 billion annually. However, as well as the funds ultimately obtainable for development purposes, other initiatives also have the potential to create other positive effects. For example, both a carbon and an airline tax can be argued for on environmental grounds, regardless of the money raised. Similarly, a currency transaction tax – or Tobin Tax – has long been advocated as a means of reducing the excessive volatility of global FX markets, by 'throwing sand in the wheels' of this system. James Tobin (1978) argued that a small tax on all currency transactions would reduce speculative trading and therefore would lower market volatility by bringing market prices more in line with underlying fundamentals, which drive the behaviour of longer-term – fundamentalist – investors.

Opponents cited Milton Friedman (1953), arguing that speculators act to stabilise markets through rational arbitrage. That is, when prices rise above their fundamental 'fair value', rational speculators will sell and drive prices back to their equilibrium level. Conversely, when speculators see prices below this equilibrium level, they will buy, thus bidding prices up. Reducing speculation would not therefore reduce price misalignments, but rather would enable them to persist for longer periods.

Those taking the opposite view,[13] however, argue that 'noise traders' do not tend to move the market towards fundamental equilibrium but, in fact, do the exact opposite. Consequently, a transaction tax that disproportionately targets such traders – such as the Tobin Tax – would, *ceteris paribus*, keep prices closer to their fundamental values by increasing the proportion of traders in the market who base their decisions on underlying fundamentals.

The evidence on this issue remains inconclusive. For example, Umlauf (1993) concludes that the imposition of a transaction tax increased the volatility of the Swedish stock market. Habermeier and Kirilenko (2001) report similar findings, where the imposition of a securities transactions tax increases volatility through a reduction in the volume of trading. Aliber *et al.* (2003) find evidence that transaction costs were positively related to volatility (and inversely related to volume) for four major global currencies between 1971 and 1999. In contrast, using a model-based approach, Wei and Kim (1997) find transaction taxes reducing volatility in the FX market, a result confirmed in a separate model developed by Westerhoff and Dieci (2004), which uses a behavioural finance approach to the issue.

Interest in the idea of the Tobin Tax grew substantially in the 1990s, largely due to the increased incidence of financial crises in general and currency crises in particular, and the hope that a Tobin Tax could reduce the likelihood of such events. However, this view was countered by the observation that, in many such events, speculators are betting on forcing a devaluation from a fixed exchange rate peg, where 'success' might see the currency devalued by 10% or 20%. In the face of potential profits of this magnitude, a small tax on trading is no disincentive.

This flaw in the original concept was addressed in Spahn (1996), where a two-tier structure was proposed. Under normal market conditions, a minimal (perhaps zero) 'transaction charge' would apply to all currency transactions. However, this charge would be augmented by an 'exchange surcharge', which would only come into effect when the exchange rate moved outside a predetermined range. In these circumstances, a very high rate of tax would apply to transactions in the affected currency, which would act as a severe disincentive to currency speculators, who would no longer be facing a 'one-way' bet. In effect, the Spahn proposal would short-circuit speculative attacks. Indeed, as Spahn argued, in practice the exchange surcharge might never be invoked, since speculators seeing the exchange rate approach the level at which it would become operational would adjust their behaviour to avoid being caught by the tax.[14]

This highlights a particularly relevant, but often overlooked point, regarding the Tobin Tax: it is rarely made clear that there is not one Tobin Tax, but two. The Spahn proposal is the most developed example of one of these. Here the aim is not to raise tax revenue, quite the opposite. Indeed, such a system could be said to have failed if it did raise substantial sums. To succeed, the short-circuit mechanism should be so effective that it prevents speculative attacks and currency crises, thereby raising little or no revenue. Consequently, such a framework is best suited to middle-income emerging and developing countries which wish to protect their economies from the highly damaging impacts of exchange rate volatility and financial crises.

The second form of Tobin Tax, however, is quite explicit in its tax-raising objectives. This approach is exemplified in Schmidt (2001), where the author demonstrates that, contrary to received wisdom, it is now entirely possible for countries to unilaterally impose a currency tax on their own currency's transactions.[15] Furthermore, although the revenues raised could be used for any purpose by the government concerned, it has been historically argued that these should be ring-fenced and used for international development objectives. This approach is therefore suited to developed countries seeking ways to increase aid volume for purposes such as meeting the MDGs.[16]

It is therefore only quite recently that the proposal has been altered to stress the potential to raise funds for development purposes. This distinction needs to be borne in mind when considering the merits of proposals for a 'Tobin Tax'.

We have seen how ODA flows have started to rise again, albeit from historically low levels. Perhaps the key driver in this regard has been the desire to meet the MDGs by 2015. Whilst some ODA can have a direct impact in this regard through expanding government budgets for health and education, for example, other aid flows may, if appropriately designed and executed, lead to higher rates of growth and therefore an indirect effect on poverty levels.

The 0.7% of GDP target remains a long way off in many instances, but it should be remembered that this was just the official component of the estimated 1% of developed countries' GDP needed to be redistributed to developing countries. The remaining 0.3%, it was assumed, would be made up of private sector flows, which would also facilitate higher rates of economic growth and poverty reduction. In the next section we consider these issues in some detail.

6.5 Overview of private sector flows

The UN (2005: 73) opens its discussion of private capital flows by restating the theoretical benefits that should accrue to developing countries as follows:

> Standard economic theory argues that international private capital flows will make a major contribution to development to the extent that they will flow from capital-abundant industrialized countries to capital-scarce developing countries, and help to smooth spending throughout the business cycle in capital-recipient countries.

However, the report goes on to argue that, in recent years, the reality of private flows to developing countries has contradicted this perspective in two ways. First, capital has not moved from developed to developing countries, but instead has tended to flow the other way.[17] Second, the volatility and reversibility of capital flows has itself contributed to financial crises in

developing countries, and has not served to 'smooth' domestic spending, but
has actually made it more volatile. Furthermore, private flows tend to be
concentrated in middle-income developing countries, so that the poorest
countries may get little or none of the predicted benefits in any event.

Before exploring these issues further, we shall examine the behaviour
of private flows, both to the developing world in total and to each of the
developing regions individually.

As can be seen from Figure 6.10 above, the total level of net private capital
flows to developing countries has shown considerable volatility since the early
1990s (though this certainly does not mean that the situation was one of
stability before that point). By 2003, total net flows were a little over US$175
billion, which is about 15% higher than the yearly average for the period
1993–1997 (the first bar on the figure). To put this in context, Figure 6.11
below compares the level of net private flows over this period, with the
corresponding level of GDP in developed countries.

In 2006, the figure fell to a little over 0.8% after having risen year-on-year
since the turn of the century. However, this should be contrasted with the
figures for 1999 and 2000, which at 0.2% or less of developed market GDP
was substantially below that envisaged by the UN as necessary for development purposes. Again, however, this should be contrasted with the 1993–1997
period, when at more than 0.6%, the level of net flows to developing countries
was more than double this figure.

What is the regional picture, however?

Figure 6.12 highlights the extremely uneven geographical distribution of
private capital flows. Perhaps most striking is the dominant role played by
developing Asia and Central and Eastern Europe in this respect: by 2004,
these two regions accounted for more than 85% of all capital flows to developing countries. Interestingly, the 1993–1997 period saw relative parity

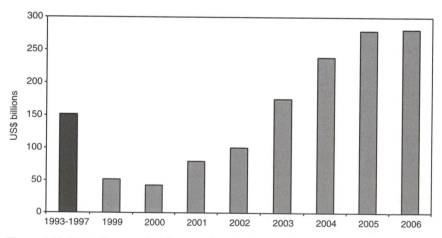

Figure 6.10 Net private capital flows to developing countries, 1993–2006.

Sources: UN (2005) for 1993–97 average; IMF WEO for 1999–2006.

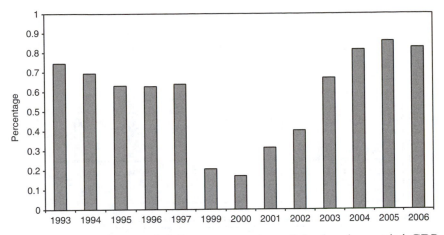

Figure 6.11 Net private capital flows as percentage of developed countries' GDP, 1993–2006.

Source: IMF WEO for 2007.

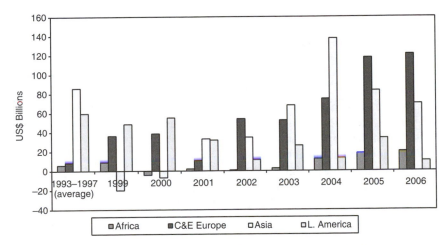

Figure 6.12 Net private capital flows to developing regions, 1993–2006.

Sources: UN (2005) for 1993–97 average; IMF WEO for 1999–2006.

between developing Asia and Latin America in terms of the total level of private inflows. Since that time, the total flows to Latin America have declined steadily, so that in 2006 they were just a sixth of the average level achieved from 1993 to 1997 and less than 5% of total private capital flows to developing countries.

For Asia, the impact of the Asian crisis can be seen in 1999 and 2000, with net flows being negative. After 2001, however, the recovery was dramatic, so that by 2004 the region received 60% more net private inflows than was the case immediately before the onset of the Asian crisis in 1997.

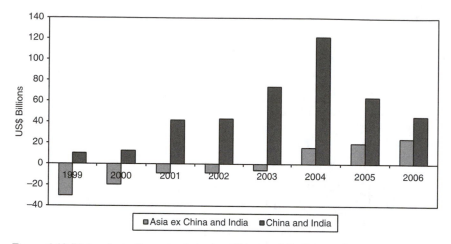

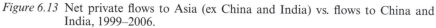

Figure 6.13 Net private flows to Asia (ex China and India) vs. flows to China and India, 1999–2006.

Source: IMF WEO.

The subsequent decline in flows to the region in 2005 and 2006 is explained in Figure 6.13 above, which disaggregates the flows to emerging Asia, separating out those going to China and India and those going to the rest of the region. As we can see, combined flows to these two economies dwarf those going elsewhere in Asia from 1999 onwards, and the decline in total Asian private inflows from 2005 is entirely the result of the decline in flows to China and India, which more than offset the modest increase in private capital flows to the rest of developing Asia.

What about the composition of inflows, however?

As is shown clearly in Figure 6.14, the volatility of total private sector flows is almost entirely a result of the volatility of (a) portfolio flows, and (b) bank lending. In contrast, FDI flows have shown remarkable stability over the period, even holding up well in the turbulent 1998–2002 period which contained the Asian and Russian crises.

In general terms, the composition of capital inflows for all developed countries is replicated in each developing region. In particular, the stability of FDI flows to each region, relative to other forms of capital inflow, is clearly observable. There are some interesting distinctions, though.

Figure 6.15 below illustrates the cumulative inflow for each type of capital for each region, from 1993 to 2004. In each case, the largest form of flow was FDI. However, both in terms of the absolute scale of FDI, and the relative importance of FDI over other types of inflow, the Asian and Latin American regions have clearly been the most important destinations for FDI in the developing world – though, as illustrated in Figure 6.12, the transition economies of Central and Eastern Europe have seen a sharp increase in capital inflows since 2004, and much of that has been in the form of FDI.

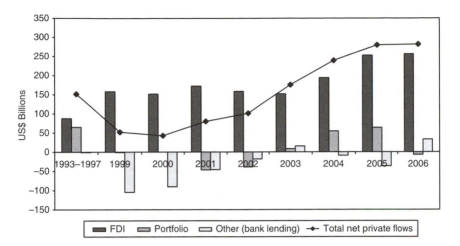

Figure 6.14 Composition of private capital flows to developing countries, 1993–2004.
Sources: UN (2005) for 1993–97 average; IMF WEO for 1999–2006.

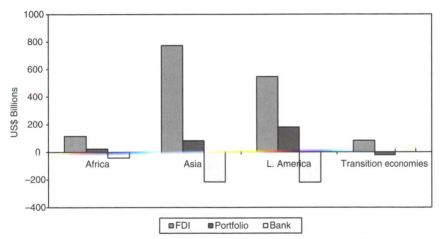

Figure 6.15 Cumulative capital inflows to developing regions, 1993–2004.
Sources: UN, 2005.

From 1993 to 2005, FDI flows to all developing regions totalled more than US$1,500 billion. In contrast, bank flows were strongly negative at –US$450 billion, while portfolio flows were positive at a little over US$250 billion. More than half the negative figure for bank lending was accounted for by the Asian region, reflecting the aftermath of the Asian financial crisis, though bank lending to Africa and Latin America was also negative over the period.

As we have seen, the increase in private capital flows has continued after 2004, reaching US$281 billion by 2006.

One interesting aspect of international financial flows in recent years relates to changes in the level and distribution of foreign exchange reserves. Over the past decade current account surpluses in some developing regions – most notably developing Asia, but also Japan – have grown enormously. This has led to a rapid build-up of foreign exchange reserves in these economies, which in turn have been invested in US Treasury bills.

Between 1999 and 2006, an astonishing US$2.75 trillion of foreign exchange reserves were accumulated by developing countries. Figure 6.16 below illustrates the regional distribution of this build up of reserves.

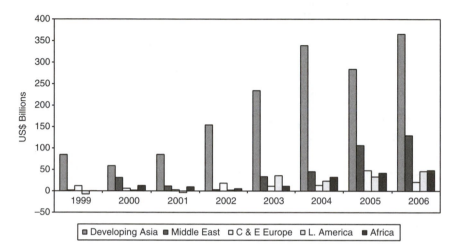

Figure 6.16 Regional reserve accumulation, 1999–2006.

Sources: IMF WEO.

As we can see, the overwhelming majority (67% of the cumulative total) of these reserves have been accumulated in the Asian region, although the Middle East region has also seen a substantial pick-up in reserve accumulation since 2002, reflecting the impact of rising oil revenues as the price of oil has risen. Recent years have seen considerable disagreements over the causes of this phenomenon, which has crystallised into a dispute between China and the United States. Box 6.4 describes the nature of this dispute.

Box 6.4 US and China's exchange rate dispute

More than a decade ago the Chinese authorities pegged the remninbi to the US dollar at a fixed rate. Since then China has experienced annual double-digit growth, driven in large part by a surging export sector, a high proportion of which goes to the US market.

By 2005 the United States' trade deficit with China had risen to around $200 billion. As we can see from the figure above, the US's overall trade deficit was almost 6.5% of GDP in the same year. That

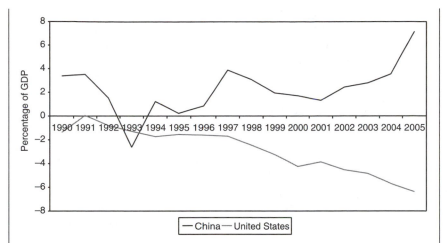

Current account balances in China and the United States, 1990–2005.

Source: World Bank WDI.

equates to around $780 billion, so that the deficit with China accounts for around one quarter of the entire US trade deficit.

Despite the fact that China alone cannot account for the scale of the US deficit, many US-based commentators have accused China of 'mercantilism' or using an undervalued currency to unfairly increase its share of global markets at the expense of other nations. The testimony of Professor Navarro of the University of California to the Subcommittee on Trade of the House Committee on Ways and Means in early 2007 is typical of this position:

> By practicing a highly evolved form of 18th century 'beggar thy neighbor' mercantilism, China is emerging as a 21st century economic superpower. While consumers around the world have benefited from the flood of cheap goods, China's broad portfolio of unfair trade practices has resulted in the loss of millions of jobs in countries ranging from the United States and Mexico to Brazil and Lesotho ... To maintain its undervalued currency – and thereby sell its exports cheap and keep foreign imports dear – China maintains a fixed currency peg between the U.S. dollar and the yuan. To maintain that peg, China must recycle large sums of its surplus U.S. dollars gained in the export trade back into the U.S. bond market. Through such activity, China has become the de facto 'central banker' of the U.S. with its net capital inflows roughly equal to that needed to finance the U.S. budget deficit.

The second point here is very interesting. While many have called on China to allow its currency to float – and have proposed various means of applying pressure, ranging from the WTO to bilateral trade sanctions to achieve this – if this were to result in China having much lower trade surpluses, then its tendency to invest these surpluses in US Treasury bills would no longer be available to fund the US deficit. What we appear to have, therefore, is a form of 'Faustian pact', where both China and the US benefit from the status quo, regardless of whether it is sustainable in the longer term.

As the US dollar continues to slide on global markets in 2008, it is likely that the huge US trade deficit will start to reduce. Furthermore, as China moves to a more flexible peg against a basket of its major trading partners it is likely to be less of a target of US ire. However, China's move to peg to a basket of currencies may simply be a reflection of its desire to remain competitive in *all* its major markets, rather than any conversion to the principle of free floating exchange rates determined by the market.

The UN (2005) includes these figures in its total net financial transfer estimates, the result of which is that they describe a huge transfer of private capital from developing to developed countries. Clearly, however, reserve build-up and transfer to US Treasury holdings by (largely Asian) economies is different to other types of capital flow.

The rationale for this course of action is twofold: first, as described in Box 6.4, investing in US financial assets prevents the US dollar from falling further than it otherwise would, which safeguards the competitive export position of East Asian economies, many of whom still attempt to peg their currencies to the dollar. Secondly, countries may be wary of a speculative attack on their currency precipitating a financial crisis. The massive build-up of reserves can therefore be seen as 'insurance' against this event – the existence of huge foreign exchange reserves may be sufficient to prevent such an attack, as speculators can see that the exchange rates can be defended with the reserves for a lengthy period.

That said, the situation of developing countries building up large foreign exchange reserves and depositing them in the US does indeed represent a financial transfer on an enormous scale. In effect, the countries of East Asia are lending the US money – at very low rates of interest – to enable the US to purchase their exports. In recent years, economists have developed a rule of thumb for the optimal level of foreign exchange reserves. The 'Greenspan-Guidotti-Fischer rule' holds that reserves should be sufficient to cover three months' worth of imports: today many developing countries – particularly in East Asia – have reserves far in excess of this level, suggesting strongly that the motivation for this build-up relates more to the strategic objectives described above than to any search for optimality.

While this may be in both parties' interests at the present time, it is a highly precarious, and ultimately unsustainable, global financial situation.

6.5.1 Private capital flows and economic growth

We have seen how there has been something of a boom in private capital flows to emerging markets in the past few years. However, there have been many such booms before, and we must assume there will be many more to come in the future.

An unfortunate fact in this regard is that booms are almost always followed by busts. This cyclicality of private flows to developing countries is particularly notable with portfolio and bank flows, which as we have seen, display far more volatility than does FDI. From a theoretical perspective, one would expect the transfer of global capital to developing countries (and therefore to its most productive global use) to result in higher growth in recipient countries, and thus higher global growth. For example, the 'debt-cycle' hypothesis states that external inflows raise total savings, which allows an increase in the rate of domestic investment and thus, ultimately, spurs faster economic growth. This in turn will allow the foreign debt accrued to be paid off comfortably from the proceeds of growth. While this is the theory, Ffrench-Davis and Reisen (1998) list five requirements for this to occur in practice:

1 External flows should be used for investment, rather than consumption purposes.
2 The investment should be efficient.
3 The inflows should be invested in tradable sectors so that a trade surplus is generated, enabling the foreign currency debt to be paid off.
4 Domestic savings should be aggressively mobilised.
5 The 'virtuous circle' requires those exporting capital (e.g. from developed countries) to do so in a stable and predicable manner.

Interestingly, these features are more likely to pertain to some types of capital flow rather than others. In particular, long-term FDI is inherently used for investment purposes, whereas portfolio flows in particular may result in appreciating exchange rates and asset prices bubbles, which are likely to raise consumption rather than investment. The same is also true of short-term bank lending used to support and perpetuate asset prices bubbles, as occurred in Thailand in the mid-1990s.

A crucial distinction between these flows is their stability, however. As we have seen, FDI flows have been remarkably consistent since the early 1990s, in sharp contrast to the volatility of other types of inflow.

The UN (2005) describes this volatility in the context of financial market uncertainty as follows:

> The basic reason for existence of these patterns is that finance deals with future information that, by its very nature, is not known in advance; therefore, opinions and expectations about the future rather than factual information dominate financial market decisions. This is compounded by

asymmetries of information that characterize financial markets. Owing to the non-existence or the large asymmetries of information, financial agents rely to a large extent on the 'information' provided by the actions of other market agents, leading to interdependence in their behaviour, that is to say, contagion and herding. At the macroeconomic level, the contagion of opinions and expectations about future macroeconomic conditions tends to generate alternating phases of euphoria and panic. At a microeconomic level, it can result in either permanent or cyclical rationing of lending to market agents that are perceived by the market as risky borrowers.

The problems of uncertainty and asymmetric information described here are also likely to be more prevalent in developing than developed economies, which at least partly explains the greater volatility we see in these markets. Furthermore, some commentators argue that these 'boom-bust' cycles have been exacerbated by the common use of certain modern, quantitative risk management techniques: investors receive the same information processed through the same systems, which encourages them to take the same allocation decisions, thus exacerbating tendencies to herd.[18]

When these 'surges' and 'droughts' are combined with the relatively small size of many developing economies in comparison with the scale of global capital flows, we can see how macroeconomic stability can be seriously undermined, with negative effects on growth and poverty reduction.

An important element in this regard is the inability of most developing countries to issue sovereign debt in their own currencies – the so-called 'original sin' problem.[19] While recent years have seen some progress in this area, with international investors increasingly willing to hold local currency debt, there remains a long way to go before the problem is resolved: in 2000 just 6% of local currency debt issued by developing countries was held by international investors; by 2005 this had risen to 12% – a significant increase certainly, but one that leaves 88% of debt held domestically (IMF, 2005a).

This is more of a problem in some developing regions than others. Clearly, the more developed a country is the more likely it is that investors will be willing to purchase sovereign debt in its own currency. Consequently, for the least developed countries, there is generally no option but to issue debt in foreign currencies.

Figure 6.17 below gives a regional picture of the proportion of outstanding debt denominated in US dollars from 1980 to 2005.

Perhaps the most striking aspect of this figure is its consistency: between around 40% and 60% of debt is denominated in dollars for all regions for most of the twenty-five-year period. Furthermore, if there is a discernible trend it is for this proportion to increase, particularly from 1990.

Figure 6.17 only covers US dollar-denominated debt, however. Historically, developing countries have issued debt in a variety of currencies, although the US dollar has been by far the most important. Since the launch of the euro

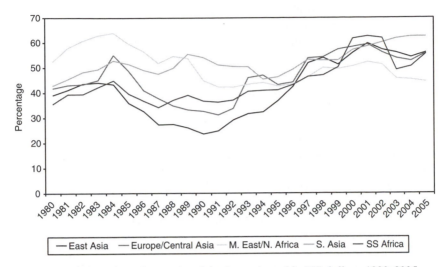

Figure 6.17 Proportion of sovereign debt denominated in US dollars, 1980–2005.

Source: World Bank GDF.

though, the dollar has had a serious competitor, and euro-denominated debt has become increasingly popular.

Table 6.2 gives a snapshot of the proportion of outstanding debt denominated in both dollars and euros for 2005. It is clear that in some regions – particularly the Middle East and Africa – the euro has grown rapidly in importance. In combination, we can see that the lowest proportion of dollar/euro-denominated debt is East Asia, but even here the figure is only slightly less than 65% of all outstanding debt. At the other extreme, in Europe and Central Asia almost 90% of debt is denominated in dollars or euros. Furthermore, as shown in Figure 6.17, despite the increasing acceptance of local currency-denominated debt, there is little sign of foreign currency debt decreasing in importance.

This accentuates problems of volatility by creating large and potentially damaging currency mismatches. For example, a developing country whose currency experiences a speculative attack, but where much of its external debt

Table 6.2 Proportion of external debt denominated in dollars and euros (%)

Region	USD	Euro	Total
East Asia	55.99	8.5	64.49
Europe/C. Asia	55.68	3.45	89.13
M. East & N. Africa	44.34	31.18	75.52
S. Asia	62.44	5.98	68.42
SS Africa	55.49	18.18	73.67

Source: World Bank GDF.

is denominated in US dollars, will see the burden of this debt (in US dollar terms) rise sharply if the domestic currency is devalued. This is also an important issue with bank loans denominated in international currencies rather than the local currency, of course. Portfolio equity flows do not face this problem, but the volatility of flows creates its own problems.

The common feature of these types of flow is their short-term (at least potentially) nature. That is, portfolio flows can be withdrawn at any time, and short-term bank lending, which is 'rolled-over' in good times, can be abruptly cut off. This creates huge uncertainty in recipient countries, with macro-economic indicators often being more influenced by volatile movements in external capital flows than by the needs of the domestic economy.

It is perhaps not surprising, therefore, that no clear evidence has been found to link openness to capital flows (i.e. integration in the global financial markets) with improved growth performance. A number of models have been developed[20] which demonstrate this link in theory, but empirical evidence to support these claims has yet to emerge. Indeed, there is some evidence that integration is positively associated with the volatility of growth rates, not their actual level (Prasad *et al.*, 2003).

In contrast, FDI flows are relatively stable and are therefore generally preferred to other types of capital flows by recipient countries. Furthermore, there is some evidence linking FDI inflows to higher rates of growth.[21] This preference is amplified by the fact that, as we shall cover in some detail in Chapter 7, FDI flows are also seen as bringing other benefits to recipient countries.

These generally include the following:

- knowledge transfer;
- technology transfer;
- management know-how;
- establishment of economic linkages with suppliers of goods and services in recipient countries, particularly the SME sector;
- earning of foreign exchange through exports;
- increased competitiveness of domestic companies that face a more competitive environment.

For all of these reasons, there is a recognised 'hierarchy' of capital flows. With FDI being the most preferred, followed by portfolio flows and bank lending, particularly short-term bank lending. What are needed are inflows that increase investment, not inflows that distort macroeconomic variables and increase consumption.

There would therefore appear to be four options for developing country policy-makers:

1   Remain closed to capital inflows.
2   Open fully to external capital flows and 'take your chances'.

3   Open selectively so that flows seen as most beneficial for investment and growth (e.g. FDI) are encouraged while those seen as damaging (e.g. short-term, speculative flows) are discouraged.
4   Attempt to reform the 'international financial architecture' to reduce the damaging volatility of particular types of capital flows.

Clearly these are not all mutually exclusive. Either option 2 or 3 could be combined with option 4, for example. However, as we shall see in later chapters, efforts to reform the international financial architecture in recent years have not been a great success, or at least not in the way that would address the problems described above.

Concluding remarks

In this chapter we have given a broad overview of key trends in external financial flows to developing countries. In the first part of the chapter issues surrounding official development assistance (i.e. aid) were discussed with particular reference to the drive to meet the Millennium Development Goals by 2105. As we saw, however, the external resources required to meet the goals in every country – and particularly in sub-Saharan Africa – are simply not sufficient: additional sources of aid are clearly needed even if all existing commitments are met, which does not seem particularly likely.

It might be hoped that the shortfall could be filled by private capital flows, but in reality much of the expenditure needed to meet the MDGs is not of the form that would attract private investors: the social 'return' of such investment may be very high indeed, but international investors are interested solely in financial returns, and it is difficult to see how MDG-related expenditure could provide this.

Furthermore, developing countries wishing to maximise the benefits obtainable from access to private capital flows should proceed with caution if they are to avoid the potentially severe negative impacts of such inflows. As we shall see in the next chapter, the cost of financial crises can be very high, and has the potential to set back development efforts significantly, if not terminally. On the other hand, access to appropriate levels of *developmentally beneficial* private capital flows have the potential to greatly accelerate the development process, but only if the negative aspects of private capital flows can be avoided. As we shall see, this is far from being an easy task.

7 The external financial system (II)

Debt and financial crises

Introduction

We saw in Chapter 6 that there has long been considered to exist a 'hierarchy' of private capital flows to developing countries. Historically, this has had FDI flows at the top of the hierarchy (i.e. the most preferred type of inflow), followed by bank lending, with portfolio flows at the bottom of the pile.

Before considering the issue of financial sector crises in developing countries, it is worth spending a little time considering the rationale for this viewpoint, which is strongly related to (a) the stability of flows, (b) the impact (beneficial vs. negative) of different types of inflow, (c) the maturity and 'reversibility' of inflows, and (d) the volatility of private flows more generally. Of course, each of these issues is itself clearly related to both the incidence and magnitude of crises, though understanding of the nature of these relationships has changed considerably over the past three decades, not least in response to the series of financial sector crises that have occurred in developing countries and regions over this period.

7.1 FDI = 'good flow'?

As we have seen, different types of private capital flows exhibit different characteristics in terms of scale, stability, volatility and reversibility. In this regard, FDI flows have shown considerable stability over recent years, particularly when compared to the more volatile nature of portfolio flows and bank lending as shown in Figure 7.1.

As well as the consistency displayed by FDI, it is also seen as bringing additional benefits to recipient countries. The combination of these factors has therefore made FDI the 'inflow of choice' for policy-makers in developing countries seeking to attract beneficial private capital flows.

The UN (2005: 82) puts the issue as follows: 'FDI is regarded as a potential catalyst for raising productivity in developing host countries through the transfer of technology and managerial know-how, and for facilitating access to international markets'. However, the same report goes on to argue that, although these benefits *may* occur, they are by no means certain, and the

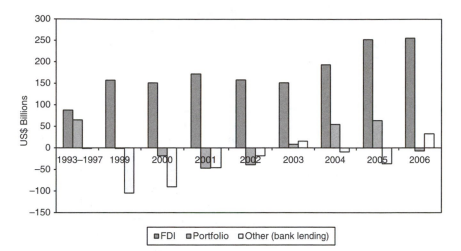

Figure 7.1 FDI vs. other capital flows, 1993–2006.

Source: UN (2005) and IMF WEO.

benefits that have accrued have been distributed very unevenly between, and within, developing countries.

Possible negative effects of FDI are given as follows:

- Limited linkages between domestic firms and international TNCs may greatly reduce or even eliminate these potential benefits.
- Trade deficits may be exacerbated through the need to import capital equipment, particularly if the FDI concerned focuses on meeting the needs of the domestic economy rather than exporting, and thus earning foreign exchange.
- Large FDI inflows from international TNCs may result in domestic companies being unable to compete, therefore stifling the development of a diverse and competitive domestic economy, and leaving domestic consumers little option but to deal with dominant (foreign-owned) companies.
- Finally, as a result of the perceived attractiveness of FDI, policy-makers in developing countries may agree to take on an excessive share of the investment risk in order to persuade the company to invest (ibid.).

In addition to these potentially negative effects, there is much debate on (a) the size of the benefits from FDI that will ultimately accrue, (b) the time this will take to happen (i.e. the 'lag'), and (c) the precise mechanisms through which the predicted benefits are transmitted to the domestic economy.

The key factor in this regard is the quantity of linkages that the TNC develops with the local economy in the course of its activities. An isolated TNC operating in a tax haven 'export processing zone' (EPZ) and importing most of its supplies from overseas will produce little in the way of linkages and therefore little in the way of additional benefits to the local economy. Box 7.1 below considers some of the issues in this respect, in relation to the experience of EPZs in sub-Saharan Africa.

Box 7.1 Export Processing Zones (EPZs)

The use of EPZs in developing countries became extremely popular in the 1980s and 1990s, not least because of the success of zones in some of the fast-growing Asian economies. EPZs are formally defined as being outside the customs jurisdiction of the country, so that firms located within them can purchase duty-free imported materials, which can then be processed for export to the international market. Clearly the main intention of having an EPZ is to boost exports and foreign exchange earnings – as well as the removal of import tariffs, exporters in EPZs also benefit from dedicated and concentrated infrastructure and favourable tax and regulatory treatment, particularly with regard to labour market restrictions.

In a review of trade promoting policies in sub-Saharan Africa, the World Bank (2003) assessed the success of EPZs in its ten sample countries: Benin, Burkina Faso, Cameroon, Côte d'Ivoire, Mali, Mauritius, Senegal, Tanzania, Uganda and Zimbabwe. Of these, only four had EPZs in place at the time of the study in the late 1990s. Furthermore, only one of these – Mauritius – was considered to have a 'functional' EPZ. The other three – Cameroon, Senegal and Zimbabwe – were all categorised as having 'dysfunctional' EPZs, which had no positive effects at all.

The Bank gives the following reasons for the 'failure' of the EPZs in Zimbabwe and Senegal (the success or otherwise of the EPZ in Cameroon remained questionable due to lack of data):

Zimbabwe

In Zimbabwe, the EPZ scheme granted duty-free status to imports of capital goods and inputs. According to the legislation, EPZ firms were obligated to pay statutory tariffs on capital and intermediate goods used to produce the output sold on the domestic market. In practice, however, only capital goods were imported duty-free as there were no fenced industrial sites in operation as the legislation required and there was a shortage of trained personnel in customs to monitor the proper utilization of inputs imported under this scheme. Firms thus applied for both tariff suspension and EPZ privileges in order to obtain waivers from import tariffs. The manner in which this EPZ scheme was implemented led to redundancy of benefits with the tariff suspension scheme and had no significant impact on exports.

Senegal

(i) Bureaucratic red tape delayed the application process for potential investors; (ii) government mandated labor market rigidities made the hiring and firing of workers difficult, which, along with the low educational level of workers, reduced labor productivity; (iii) investors were required to build or lease their own factories long term with the result that foreign direct investment was discouraged through imposition of increased business risks; and (iv) utility and transportation costs were high in the zone.

Mauritius in contrast

Special advantages granted to EPZ firms included an exemption from the corporate income tax on retained earnings for the first ten years and paid only reduced taxes from then until the 20th year of operations. EPZ firms could repatriate capital and profits freely and were eligible for preferential interest rates. The labor market was also effectively segmented with more favorable conditions applying to EPZ than domestic firms. EPZ firms had greater flexibility in discharging workers, and the conditions of overtime work were less rigid. Mauritius's lower legal minimum wage for female workers, disproportionate numbers of whom were employed in the garment and other export industries, also favored EPZ firms relative to import-competing domestic industry.

As a result of the success of its approach, exports from its EPZs accounted for 66% of total exports, and 10% of national GDP by the mid 1990s. The rationale in setting up an EPZ is compelling: export diversification, the earning of foreign currency, employment creation etc. However, the plethora of EPZs established by developing countries in the 1980s and 1990s greatly increased supply relative to demand. As a result, a 'buyers market' for international firms looking for a base from which to export was created. Of the three examples above, the failure of the EPZ in Zimbabwe seems to have been largely the result of the lack of resources and incompetence. The differences between Senegal and Mauritius are more telling, however. The latter was successful – at least in part – because of its 'favourable' labour market conditions and its low legal minimum wage for female workers. Similarly the extensive tax holidays must have helped its competitiveness relative to other EPZs. Senegal, in contrast, is criticised for bureaucracy and 'labour market rigidities'. A race to the bottom?

In recognition of this, many countries in the not-too-distant past insisted that TNCs operating in their economies sourced a proportion of their inputs from local suppliers as part of their licensing arrangements. However, 'trade-related-investment-measures' (TRIMS) were viewed – by developed countries – as violating WTO rules on impartial treatment of foreign and domestic businesses. As a result, a TRIMS agreement was negotiated in the Uruguay trade round, requiring WTO members to phase out these requirements on TNCs. More generally, this has also become 'less fashionable', not least because of the fierce competition to attract FDI on the part of developing countries.

As we have seen, however, this competition is largely driven by the perceived benefits that FDI can bring, yet if the measures needed to attract the investment serve to reduce or eliminate these benefits, then the rationale for the attractiveness of FDI is undermined. This point is supported by the findings of a study by the Asian Development Bank (ASDB, 2005), which reported that incentives (particularly financial incentives) to attract FDI were a very minor part of the factors that TNCs consider with regard to allocating investment internationally. Instead, the ASDB stressed the following factors as most important:

1   the existence of 'an enabling investment climate' in the recipient country, widely viewed as being crucial to TNC decision-making;[1]
2   levels of human resource development in the recipient country;
3   entrepreneurial capacity of the recipient country.

Consequently, there would appear to be considerable scope for developing countries to reduce the financial incentives that they offer to TNCs: they would most likely see better results by focusing on the areas listed above as important factors in decision-making. Furthermore, in principle at least, there may also be scope for countries to reintroduce 'investment policies' which insist on TNCs forging linkages and transferring technology, 'know-how' and R&D. The biggest obstacle here is clearly WTO regulations on neutral treatment of foreign and domestic entities, but, even if these could be overcome, such measures would only be effective if the country were attractive to TNC investors for other reasons. Furthermore, there is also a collective action issue to consider, which suggests that the reintroduction of TRIMS-style investment requirements may be particularly effective if a group of developing countries were to act in a coordinated manner.

Whilst there is broad agreement on the potential benefits of FDI, what is the evidence? Bosworth and Collins (1999) study the effect of capital inflows on domestic investment for fifty-eight developing countries during the period 1978–1995. The authors find that while each US$1 of inflow leads to a US$0.50 increase in domestic investment on average, the effects of different type of capital flow vary widely.

As shown in Figure 7.2 below, the impact of FDI flows on domestic

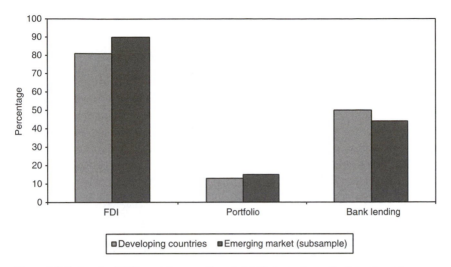

Figure 7.2 Impact of different forms of capital inflow on domestic investment.

Source: Bosworth and Collins, 1999.

investment in both developing and emerging markets is highly significant (i.e. up to 90% of inflows translate into higher domestic investment). In contrast, the impact of portfolio flows is very small (10–20%), whilst that for bank lending falls between these two extremes.

Despite this evidence, there have been increasing calls for policy-makers to be cautious about an over-reliance on FDI flows. For example, Hausmann and Fernández-Arias (2000) argue that, where FDI is a high proportion of total capital inflows, this may be a sign of a recipient country's weakness rather than its strength. This is demonstrated by the fact that FDI flows as a proportion of total inflows are negatively related to the credit quality (i.e. the 'riskiness') of the countries concerned. This relationship is shown in Figure 7.3 below.

In many ways this finding is not particularly surprising, since it says nothing about the level of total inflows. That is, very risky countries may receive little in the way of portfolio inflows, and limited international bank lending. In such an environment, any FDI will 'loom large' as a proportion of total inflows.

More generally, however, it is likely that more risky countries will have less well-developed capital markets and banking sectors, as well as possibly weaker regulatory structures and contract enforcement mechanisms. In this context, it is understandable that investors would want to keep direct control over their investments in the country: FDI is the best means of achieving this.

In order to achieve a balance of capital inflows – i.e. to be attractive to forms of capital inflow beyond FDI – it is therefore necessary for countries to develop the robustness and effectiveness of their financial sectors and legal frameworks. That is, to create the 'enabling environment' referred to above.

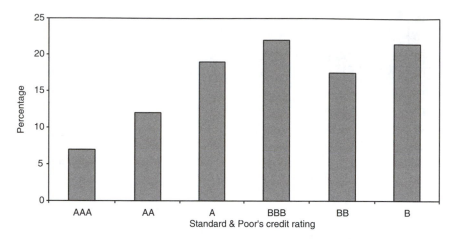

Figure 7.3 FDI's share of total capital inflows relative to credit rating.

Source: IMF (2001).

Another possibly negative impact of FDI concerns the circumstances under which it arrives. Particularly following the Asian crisis, there were concerns that many distressed firms and financial institutions in the region were being bought at 'fire-sale' prices, where foreign investors could take advantage of the troubled circumstances to acquire valuable assets at a fraction of their true worth. Krugman (1999) puts it as follows:

> .. loosely speaking, are foreign corporations taking over control of domestic enterprises because they have special competence, and can run them better, or simply because they have cash and the locals do not? . . . Does the firesale of domestic firms and their assets represent a burden to the afflicted countries, over and above the cost of the crisis itself?

A further potential issue is the actual increased investment that results from FDI. That is, TNCs may fund much of their FDI (a purchase of a domestic company, for example) through borrowing in the domestic market. They may then repatriate funds (raised domestically), therefore significantly reducing the net domestic investment effect.

Finally, there have been some concerns raised as to whether FDI is really as stable as it appears. The IMF (2001) puts the issue as follows:

> 'Though it is true that the machines are bolted down' and, hence, difficult to move out of the host country on short notice, financial transactions can sometimes accomplish a reversal of FDI. For instance, the foreign subsidiary can borrow against its collateral domestically and then lend the money back to the parent company. Likewise, because a significant

portion of FDI is intercompany debt, the parent company can quickly recall it.

A related aspect of FDI stability is the hedging activities of TNCs. Just as a developing country government may face a currency mismatch if it is forced to borrow in an international currency, so a TNC may face serious currency risk where its revenues and costs are not in the same currency. The primary means of reducing this risk is through hedging activity in the FX derivative market, where the treasury department of the corporation in question may enter in forward contracts or swaps, for example, or may purchase options to hedge itself against adverse currency movements. A very important consequence of this activity, however, is that if there is fear of a devaluation, it exacerbates downward pressure on the exchange rate, thus potentially precipitating the very currency movements that is being hedged against.

Ironically, it is in countries with a history of exchange rate volatility and currency crises that such practices are most needed, but these are also the very countries where large-scale hedging by TNCs could indeed precipitate a currency crisis.

Moguillansky (2002) provides a useful typology of corporates with differing risk exposure, and thus differing hedging requirements. Starting with the lowest risk exposure, these are:

1 *TNCs in the export sector* – Those corporates with the lowest risk exposure are commodity exporters and then assembly plant manufacturers. In these cases, the investment (FDI) is generally in non-local currencies, with revenue, interest payments and remittances in the same currency. This provides a natural hedge.

2 *Geographically diversified TNCs* – Companies where production is geared towards local markets, but have productive capacity diversified across a range of countries, have the next highest risk exposure. In this case, revenues are paid in local currencies but liabilities (loans) are generally in non-local currency. These companies therefore face significant transaction risk exposure in each market.[2] Bodnar and Gebhardt (1998) show that approximately 49% of US firms and 34% of German firms typically hedge this type of risk. However, Moguillansky (2002) finds that multinationals of this diversified type seldom hedge balance-sheet account or translation exposure – risk associated with the impact of currency movements on the value of assets and liabilities – as a devaluation in one country is likely to be offset by a revaluation in another.

3 *Geographically focused TNCs* – Firms that are focused on production for the local market in only one region or country do not have the 'hedging' benefits of diversification. Consequently, they are more likely to hedge balance-sheet exposure. For Moguillansky (2002) 'The exposure arises from the periodic need to report consolidated the world-wide operations of the group in one reporting currency'. In this situation, they will tend to

try and finance investments in the currency in question. In addition, they can employ derivatives to hedge translation[3] and transaction risk.

4   *TNCs in public services* – Those firms that have taken advantage of the privatisation programmes in developing countries (telecommunications, electricity, water etc.) face the highest currency risk exposure: their revenue is in local currency, but the projects typically require investments on a scale beyond that which the local financial system can fund. Thus hedging becomes essential.

To summarise, while there are undoubtedly benefits that are potentially obtainable from FDI, there is no certainty that they will materialise in reality. In particular, for the benefits to be maximised the following are necessary:

1   There must be genuine transfer of technology, know-how and R&D from the investing TNC to the domestic economy.
2   There must be genuine linkages formed between the TNC and local suppliers, thereby facilitating the development of a vibrant supply chain with multiplier effects through the economy.
3   If the FDI is of M&A form, the full value of the company should be paid.
4   The TNC should invest in training of local employees.
5   Funds repatriated from the domestic economy by the TNC should be kept as low as possible so as to not adversely affect domestic investment rates.
6   To maximise positive spillovers, TNCs should ideally operate in a competitive domestic environment where their presence has a positive impact on the competitiveness of domestic firms, and not use their superior economies of scale to eliminate domestic competition.
7   The TNC should make a significant contribution to domestic tax revenues.[4]
8   TNCs should either refrain from large-scale hedging activity, or manage it carefully in such a way as to avoid destabilising the exchange rate and provoking a currency crisis.

The difficulty of achieving these benefits is clear, however. Most FDI is concentrated in a relatively small number of middle-income developing countries. Indeed, in 2003, the top ten recipients of FDI amongst developing countries attracted almost 75% of all FDI flows. This suggests that efforts to attract FDI may prove difficult for countries outside this group, and this is likely to be a particular issue for the smallest, and poorest, developing countries. For example, it is estimated that the ratio of FDI to GDP in the top ten recipient countries was more than twice that in low-income countries in 2003, which highlights the fact that, although FDI may dominate in the poorest countries as a share of total inflows, this is largely the result of the absence of other forms of inflow, rather than the size of FDI itself (UN, 2005).

That said, there has been an increase in flows to the least developed countries in recent years, though this is from a very low level. In 1995, the share of developing country FDI going to the least developed countries was just 2%. By 2003 this had risen to 5% – still a woefully low figure, which is lower than ODA to these least developed countries in virtually every instance, and is concentrated in those LDCs with large reserves of natural resources, such as oil and gas.

Figure 7.4 illustrates this point with respect to sub-Saharan Africa. As we can see, from 1997 to 2002 the bulk of FDI (i.e. 60%) to the region went to just three countries: South Africa, Angola and Nigeria. In South Africa this was heavily focused in the extractive sectors, particularly gold and other minerals. In both Angola and Nigeria, FDI has gone almost exclusively to the oil sector.

Another relatively recent trend has been the increased proportion of FDI going into the service sector, particularly telecommunications, financial services and public utilities. In general, this is strongly associated with the wave of privatisations in these sectors since the early 1990s. This process is, of course, inherently limited, as much that could be privatised has already been, which suggests the pattern of FDI may change significantly in the coming years. These recent sectoral trends are shown in Figure 7.5 below.

To summarise, we have seen that FDI is considered to be the most attractive form of capital inflow. This is because (a) it is significantly less volatile (and reversible) than other types of flows, (b) it is associated with higher rates of domestic investment (positive for growth), and (c) it has the potential to bring major additional benefits to recipient economies. However, we have also seen that (a) FDI is concentrated in a few middle-income countries, (b) it may be more volatile than commonly supposed, (c) the estimated

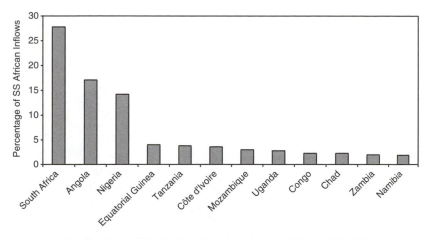

Figure 7.4 Distribution of FDI inflows in sub-Saharan Africa, 1997–2002.

Source: Obwona and Mutambi, 2004.

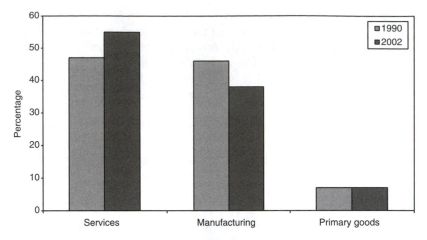

Figure 7.5 Proportion of inward FDI to different sectors, 1990 vs. 2002.

Source: UN, 2005.

impact on domestic investment rates may be lower than assumed, and (d) the predicted benefits of FDI do not automatically follow in every instance, but depend on the type of FDI and the linkages formed with the domestic economy.

Despite these caveats, FDI is clearly a beneficial form of capital inflow under certain circumstances, which accounts for its increased importance in terms of overall capital flows since the 1980s.

Figure 7.6 shows how FDI became increasingly important, almost entirely at the expense of bank lending, between 1978 and 1995. Before considering the even greater rise in the importance of portfolio flows, the next section

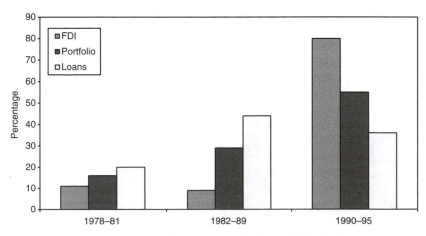

Figure 7.6 The changing composition of capital inflows, 1978–1995.

Source: IMF, 2001.

will consider the role of banks: long considered to be ranked second in the 'hierarchy' of capital flows described above.

7.2 Bank lending = 'quite good' flow?

Historically, bank lending has been considered to be more favourable than portfolio flows (but less so than FDI flows) because of its relative stability. However, this assumption has been widely questioned in recent years, not least because of the role played by short-term bank lending in the Asian crisis of 1997/8.

As can be seen from Figure 7.7 below, the proportion of short-term debt in total external debt holdings of the developing regions showed considerable variability from the late 1980s to 1997. In 1988, 20.4% of East Asia's external debt was short-term (i.e. less than one year maturity). Of this short-term debt, 13.6% was accounted for by commercial bank lending, with the remaining 6.8% comprised of short-term bond issuance. By 1996 (i.e. just before the onset of the Asian crisis) the proportion of short-term debt in the region had risen to 33.4%, with more than 29% of this being accounted for by commercial bank loans. That is, by 1996, almost a third of developing Asia's external debt was comprised of short-term loans from international banks.

Latin America shows a similar pattern of short-term debt build-up to Asia over the period. However, in Latin America this peaks in 1994 (i.e. just before the 'tequila' crisis in the region), and fell steadily thereafter. In contrast, Asia continued to build up short-term obligations through 1995 and 1996, when the process actually accelerated.

The situation was more mixed in Europe, and it is interesting to note that

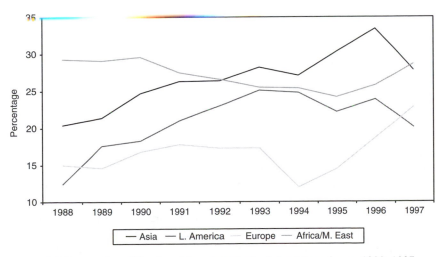

Figure 7.7 Proportion of foreign debt comprised of short-term loans, 1988–1997.

Source: Rodrik and Velasco, 1999.

only Africa and the Middle East, of the regions given above, had a lower proportion of short-term debt in 1997 than was the case in 1988.

As we shall discuss below, many commentators have pinpointed the cause of the Asian crisis in this area: the build-up of short-term debt. This situation raised the possibility of a liquidity (as opposed to a 'solvency') crisis, where borrowers become unwilling to roll-over short terms loans thereby triggering a default. There is a 'collective action' issue at work here, as banks may be unwilling to roll-over loans if they assume that other banks may also be unwilling, though each *would* be prepared to roll-over the loans if they *knew* that other banks would do so.

Much of this understanding of the danger of reliance on short-term bank lending is relatively new. As pointed out above, bank lending had long been considered to be comparatively stable. In such an environment, there was logic in developing country borrowers opting for short-term lending, for the simple reason that borrowing short-term is inherently cheaper than borrowing long-term.[5] And if the loans are simply rolled-over – as is common practice under normal conditions – the borrower is effectively obtaining very cheap long-term finance.

Despite the lower margins that they can earn, shifting towards shorter loan maturities in developing countries also made sense from the perspective of the lending banks. From their perspective, the volatility of developing and emerging economies made longer-term lending relatively unattractive. The banks assumed, wrongly as it turned out, that restricting maturities would enable them to get out of the situation quickly should problems emerge in the countries concerned. Clearly, however, this cannot be true for every bank – though it may be for individual banks. A consequence of all banks trying to close off their short-term loans at the same time, however, is to seriously worsen the economic difficulties that they are trying to remove themselves from. Individually rational but collectively irrational behaviour of this kind is known as a 'fallacy of composition', and is by no means uncommon within financial markets operating, inevitably, under conditions of uncertainty (Kindleberger, 1978).

Following the Asian crisis and its aftermath, net bank lending to all developing regions collapsed, and remained negative until 2002 – this reflected both an unwillingness to lend and an unwillingness to borrow on the part of developing countries, who had seen the consequences of doing so in Asia.

Since that point, some important changes can be observed in the pattern of bank lending. First, average loan maturities have lengthened. As can be seen from Figure 7.8 below, in June of 1997 the ratio of short-term to total international bank lending in developing countries was 56.5%, and the figure for Asia was 62%. By March 2000 the corresponding figures were down to 46.6% and 46.8%. Since that point, the ratio for all developing countries has remained relatively constant, averaging 46.6% to December 2006.

Following declines from the high of 1997, most other developing regions also follow this pattern, the exception – somewhat surprisingly – being the

Asia and Pacific region. Here, the low point for short-term lending came in March 2001, where the ratio fell to 44.5%. Since then, however, there has been a steady increase, so that by September 2005, the figure was again above 60%.

Secondly, there has been an increasing trend for international banks to 'cross the border', either by buying domestic banks in developing countries, or by establishing their own branches within the country. In both cases, the international banks have tried to fund their lending from domestic activities, therefore eliminating any currency mismatch risk from their perspective. Lending from international banks through domestic subsidiaries grew by almost 30% per year from 1998 to 2002 (ibid.).

Table 7.1 above shows this trend clearly. In 1996, emerging markets received $556.7 billion in cross-border bank lending and $97.8 billion from local subsidiaries of international banks. By 2002, however, the figures were $336.9 and $422.8 billion respectively. Lending through subsidiaries grew at around 30% a year over the period, while cross-border lending fell by around 6.5% per year. The pattern holds in all the emerging regions covered in this table.

Interestingly, it was North American and Japanese banks that pulled back from cross-border lending the most aggressively, while European banks increased their activities in this area, presumably hoping to gain market share as their international competitors withdrew.

The impact of this major shift in banks' approach to developing countries is not fully understood. Whilst there is some evidence that the entry of foreign banks raises the efficiency of the domestic banking sector,[6] others argue that foreign banks will 'cherry pick' the most attractive clients in developing

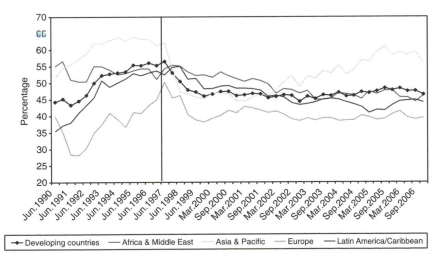

Figure 7.8 Proportion of international bank loans of less than one-year maturity, June 1990 to September 2006.

Source: BIS.

Table 7.1 Changing patterns of regional bank lending, 1996–2002

	Total lending 1996 (US$ bn.)	Average annual growth 1993–96 (%)	Total lending 2002	Average annual growth 1997–2002
East Asia				
Domestic banks	769.5	18.1	876.1	2.4
Local subsidiaries of foreign banks	29.8	15.4	84.9	21.2
Cross-border	282.2	29.0	130.3	−11.6
Latin America				
Domestic banks	563.7	17.3	484.8	−2.7
Local subsidiaries of foreign banks	58.5	28.6	241.7	31.2
Cross-border	199.9	6.2	166.1	−2.8
Eastern Europe				
Domestic banks	242.5	9.4	252.8	0.8
Local subsidiaries of foreign banks	9.6	80.5	96.3	48.5
Cross-border	74.7	1.6	70.4	−0.6
All emerging markets				
Domestic banks	1,575.7	12.7	1,613.7	0.4
Local subsidiaries of foreign banks	97.8	24.4	422.8	29.4
Cross-border	556.7	14.5	366.9	−6.5

Source: UN, 2005.

countries (particularly the larger ones), thereby crowding domestic banks out of this lucrative banking sector. More generally, there are concerns that a banking system dominated by the subsidiaries of large international banking groups will be less prepared to lend to the SME sector, preferring to focus on larger corporate clients. In this regard, Berger *et al.* (2000) find that in Argentina in the late 1990s small firms were less likely to receive funding from foreign banks than from (smaller) domestic banks. However, while Escudé *et al.* (2001) confirm that foreign banks in Argentina did indeed allocate a smaller proportion of their loan portfolio to the small-and-medium-enterprise (SME) sector, the sheer size of these banks meant that they accounted for more than half of all SME lending in the country.

In a detailed cross-country study, the World Bank[7] finds that foreign bank entry is positive in terms of access to credit in developing and emerging economies, and argues that it is not the nationality of the bank that influences its policies towards SMEs, but the size of the bank.

US-based studies[8] in the 1990s demonstrated that large, complex financial institutions are generally reluctant to lend to information-poor SMEs, and in developing countries this would also appear to be the case. The World Bank study of 2001 found that foreign banks behave very much like large domestic banks in this respect.

To summarise, the reversal of the trend towards ever-shorter maturities in international bank lending to developing countries since the Asian crisis is undoubtedly a positive development though, as we have seen, there has been a steady rise in the importance of short-term bank lending in the Asian region since 2001. Furthermore, the fact that international banks have increasingly 'crossed the border' into developing countries, by establishing subsidiaries and funding their activities in domestic currency, reduces currency risk for borrowers (who previously would have borrowed cross-border in an international currency such as the US dollar).

However, the decline in cross-border lending also reduces net inflows (i.e. additional external savings) to the economy and contributing to higher investment and therefore growth. By funding their activities domestically, international banks bring no additional capital, but do bring the possibility of other benefits such as increased efficiency of the banking system, greater competition, and so on. However, the evidence on this is currently inconclusive, and there remains a real risk that foreign banks could come to completely dominate the domestic banking system in some developing countries. As shown in Figure 7.9, foreign banks controlled almost 33% of all domestic banking assets in developing countries by 2002. The regions most dominated by foreign banks were sub-Saharan Africa and Latin America, with 45% and 30% of their banking system under foreign control. In contrast, the regions

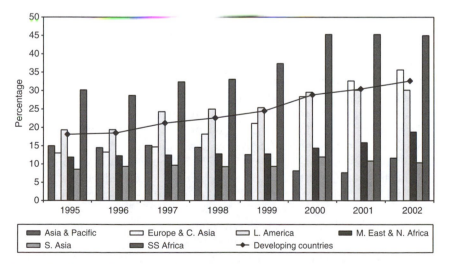

Figure 7.9 Foreign bank ownership in developing regions, 1995–2002.

Source: Cull and Peria, 2007.

with the least foreign banking presence were South Asia and Asia and Pacific, with 10.4% and 11.7% respectively.

> These regional averages, however, disguise some wide variations at the country level. For example, while the 2002 average for Eastern Europe & Central Asia stood at 35.7%, the figures for the Czech Republic, Estonia and Lithuania were 59%, 73% and 92% respectively.
>
> (Cull and Peria, op. cit.)

To recap, we have seen that FDI appears to (just about) warrant its place at the top of the 'hierarchy' of capital flows, while bank lending – particularly of a short-term nature – is clearly less beneficial than had been thought. Before considering how these types of capital flow come together in terms of crises in developing countries, we will briefly consider the role of portfolio flows – long seen as the 'worst' type of capital flow.

7.3 Portfolio flows = 'bad' flows?

We have seen that portfolio flows to emerging and developing countries have displayed consistently high levels of volatility over the past two decades, and that, of all three major types of capital flow, portfolio flows are associated with the least positive impact on domestic investment rates: whereas up to 90% of FDI – and 50% of bank flows – are translated directly into higher domestic investment rates, the figure for portfolio flows is between 10% and 20%.

However, portfolio flows have not just been volatile, they have also been very procyclical. That is to say, during an economic upturn, portfolio flows to emerging and developing economies tend to surge, but during a downturn the opposite occurs. Thus, rather than smoothing business cycles in developing countries, portfolio inflows and outflows tend to amplify them.

For example, as shown in Figure 7.10 below, the two-year period between the 'tequila crisis' and the Asian crisis of 1997 saw a sharp rise in net issuance of debt by developing countries. However, after the onset of the Asian crisis, net issuance fell rapidly towards zero, turning negative in 1998.

More recently there has been a significant reversal in this trend. Between 1998 and 2003, net issuance of debt from developing countries averaged less than $25 billion per year. In 2004, however, the figure was more than double this, and has continued to rise. By 2006, net issuance of debt had reached US$85 billion, which is the same as that reached in the previous high point of 1997.

Although overall debt flows to developing countries were, in aggregate, the same in 2006 as was the case in the mid-1990s, the pattern across the regions shows considerable differences. For example, prior to 1998, the largest issuing (or borrowing) region was Latin America, followed by Asia and then Europe. By 2006, in contrast, after 2000 the Latin American region sees net outflows

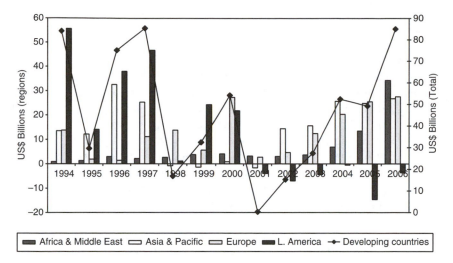

Figure 7.10 Net international debt issuance by developing countries, 1993–2007.

Source: BIS.

(or repayments) in every year. By 2006, the largest issuing region is the Middle East and North Africa, where US$35 billion of the total US$85 billion of debt was issued. The remainder is accounted for equally by the Asian and European regions, with Latin America again seeing net outflows.

The pattern of access – or the lack of it – to primary debt markets is related to the riskiness, or creditworthiness, of the borrowers. That is, lower-rated developing countries are more likely to lose access to international capital markets after some financial turmoil, and will take longer to regain that access than will higher-rated borrowers. However, even those higher-rated borrowers who manage to retain access to international debt markets have seen the risk premium attached to their issuances (i.e. the rate of interest demanded, or 'coupon' on the bond) rise significantly following periods of financial distress. This process is exacerbated by the procyclical nature of international ratings agencies, which tend to 'lag' the market by downgrading countries after problems have occurred, rather than before the event.[9]

In contrast, periods of 'boom' in emerging and developing markets have seen the interest rates at which countries can issue debt progressively squeezed, which unsurprisingly leads to 'booms' in debt issuance, as borrowers take advantage of benign economic conditions.

Whilst some of these pricing trends are related to events within emerging and developing markets, much of it is determined by circumstances in developed markets. Eichengreen and Mody (1998) find that only a small component of changing spreads can be explained by economic fundamentals in the country concerned, with the remainder largely the result of events in developed economies.

The UN (2005: 89) describes the nature of this relationship after 2002 as follows.

> Low international interest rates and increased investor search for yield was reflected in an increase in the appetite for risk. However, the negative impact of international factors on the emerging economies bond market was underscored again when expectations of larger-than-anticipated United States interest rate increases were raised in April 2004 and early 2005, resulting in abrupt and sharp reversals in the tightening of yield spreads of emerging market bonds. Although emerging market countries were able to weather the heightened volatility, these developments raise questions about the sustainability of the favourable external financing environment for developing countries.

Thus the procyclicality of portfolio debt flows to developing countries is strongly influenced by business cycles in developed countries, which are directly transmitted to developing countries by the availability and terms on which they can issue debt internationally.

These trends relate to the issuance of international debt (i.e. in international currencies such as the US dollar or the euro), which developing countries have traditionally had no option but to issue because of the unwillingness of international (and domestic) lenders to purchase debt denominated in local currencies. Since the end of the 1990s, however, as described in Chapter 6, there has been some increase in the quantity of local currency debt issued, which is to be welcomed, despite the fact that it remains largely at the margin.

From a developing country perspective, issuing debt in local currencies allows it to mobilise local savings, and prevents currency mismatches that can be important channels for increasing the impact of financial crises. However, even local debt has not been immune to the impact of economic developments in developed countries, as demonstrated by the sharp rise in local currency bond spreads (i.e. the rate of interest demanded in the secondary bond market) in 2003, which followed a sell-off of US Treasury bonds.

Portfolio equity flows have seen a similar cyclical pattern to that exhibited by debt flows in the last ten years – peaking before the Asian crisis and falling rapidly thereafter, before rising again from 2002 onwards. Figure 7.11 illustrates this trend from 2000 to 2006, where we see a net outflow in the first three years followed by a sharp and consistent year-on-year rise thereafter.

Regionally, we can see that equity flows to the developing world have been dominated by those to the East Asian region from 2002 onwards. Furthermore, if we delve a little deeper, we find that flows to East Asia are themselves dominated by equity flows to China, which account for 66.5% of all regional flows on average over this period. This pattern can be observed in other regions also: in South Asia, the overwhelming bulk of equity flows go to India, while equity flows to sub-Saharan Africa are almost entirely accounted for by those to South Africa.

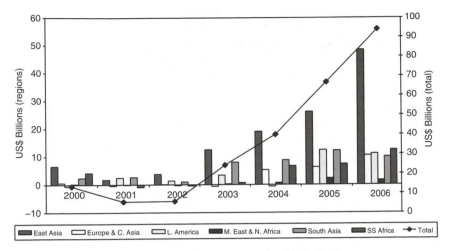

Figure 7.11 Net equity flows to developing countries, 2000–2006.

Source: World Bank WDI, 2007.

Just as debt flows and spreads are strongly influenced by events in developed markets, the same is true for equity flows. For example, the bursting of the dotcom bubble in 2000 triggered the end of a mini-boom in equity flows to developing countries, which often had only very tenuous connections with the hi-tech sector.[10]

The key points to establish are that portfolio flows to developing countries – be they debt or equity – are highly volatile, highly procyclical and strongly influenced by events in developed economies. Furthermore, as we have seen, these types of flow are often diverted into consumption, and are more likely to generate asset price bubbles and long-term investment.

To summarise, we have seen that there is a 'hierarchy' of capital flows to developing countries, which traditionally has seen FDI as the preferred form of flow, followed by bank lending and then portfolio flows. Whilst FDI remains at the peak of this hierarchy – and portfolio flows are still seen as bringing negative as well as (some) positive effects – the position of bank lending, particularly, short-term bank lending, has become more precarious. In large part this relates to the role of bank lending in the Asian crisis, which brings us to our next section.

This will consider banking and currency crises, and will be followed by a review of debt crises. The chapter will then conclude with an examination of (a) means of preventing crises, and (b) proposals on how they should be resolved if they do occur.

7.4 Financial crises and contagion

The world has seen banking crises in 69 countries since the late 1970s, and 87 currency crises since 1975. And the frequency of such crises has risen sharply over the last decade. After the recent series of meltdowns in Asia, Eastern Europe and Latin America, no observer can be surprised at the apparent instability of financial markets. The debate on the causes of these crashes will undoubtedly go on for a long time. Bad luck, in the form of exogenous shocks from abroad and from mother nature, and bad policy, in the shape of poor regulation and imprudent macro policies, doubtlessly carry some of the blame. But that cannot be the end of the story. The main message of this paper is that the potential for illiquidity was at the center of recent crises, and that short-term debt is a crucial ingredient of illiquidity. The empirical evidence is clear in that respect.

(Rodrik and Velasco, 1999: 22)

As this quote makes clear, the incidence of financial crises in developing countries has certainly increased markedly since the 1980s. However, as illustrated by Figure 7.12 below, this is by no means a new phenomenon, though it is certainly a growing one. This section will focus on, first, banking crises, and second, currency crises. This does not mean that crises in equity markets, for example, are unimportant, but their wider economic impact does not have the significance of banking and currency crises.

To recap some of the material covered in Chapter 1, the efficient market hypothesis states that market prices should fully and accurately reflect underlying economic fundamentals, and will therefore only change when these fundamentals change, either directly or in relation to other financial assets. However, if this were so, how are we to explain the fact that history is full of examples of speculative asset price bubbles – that inevitably burst, periodic bank runs and currency crises. It is difficult to argue that, in each case, the pre-crisis 'boom' accurately reflected fundamentals. Nor that the crisis was

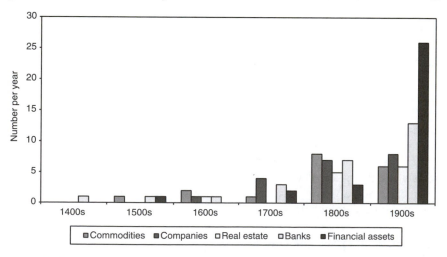

Figure 7.12 Selected major financial crises, 1400–2000.

Source: World Bank, 2001.

triggered by a fundamental deterioration of these fundamentals, to which investors responded in a rational manner.[11]

The most important international financial crisis of recent decades is undoubtedly that which occurred in East and Southeast Asia between 1997 and 1999. Before distinguishing between different forms of crisis, Box 7.2 below sets out the chronology of the Asian crisis, where many of these different elements came together with devastating results.

Box 7.2 A chronology of the Asian crisis

July 2, 1997: In the face of huge speculative pressure, Thailand devalues the baht. The government requests technical assistance from the IMF.

July 8, 1997: Malaysia's central bank intervenes to support the ringgit.

July 11, 1997: The Philippine peso is devalued. Indonesia widens the trading band for the rupiah.

July 18, 1997: The IMF releases US$1 bn from its 'emergency funding mechanism' for the first time to assist the Philippine authorities in supporting the peso.

August 5, 1997: Thailand agrees strict economic austerity conditions from the IMF in return for a $17 bn loan from the international lender and Asian nations.

August 14, 1997: Indonesia allows the rupiah to float freely. The currency plummets in value.

Oct. 8, 1997: Indonesia requests assistance from the IMF and World Bank after the rupiah loses a third of its value.

Oct. 31, 1997: The IMF approves a $40 bn to a loan package for Indonesia. The government closes sixteen financially insolvent banks as part of a swingeing reform programme.

Nov. 17, 1997: The Bank of Korea abandons its effort to prop up the value of the won. It falls to a record low against the US dollar.

Nov. 21, 1997: South Korea requests IMF assistance. Critics call proposed terms of the agreement 'humiliating'. A key component is large numbers of redundancies.

Dec. 3, 1997: The IMF approves a $57 bn package for South Korea, the largest in history.

Dec. 8, 1997: The Thai government announces the closure of fifty-six insolvent finance companies. Thirty thousand workers lose their jobs.

Dec. 18, 1997: Kim Dae Jung becomes South Korea's first opposition to be elected president.

Dec. 23, 1997: The World Bank releases an emergency loan of $3 bn to South Korea.

Dec. 24, 1997: Korea receives $10 bn in loans from the IMF and G7 to avoid a default on its short-term loan. It agrees to open its domestic financial markets to foreign institutions.

Jan. 7, 1998: Chief economist of the World Bank, Joseph Stiglitz openly questions the IMF 'medicine' of strict austerity.

Jan. 8, 1998: The Indonesian rupiah plummets further after President Suharto unveils his state budget plan, which is seen as incompatible with the IMF reform program.

Jan. 12, 1998: Hong Kong-based Peregrine Investments – Asia's largest private investment bank – files for liquidation.

Jan. 13, 1998: Students protest in the Indonesian capital against the IMF policies.

Jan. 15, 1998: President Suharto agrees to eliminate the country's monopolies and state subsidies and signs a new deal with the IMF.

Jan. 28, 1998: International banks and South Korea agree to exchange $24 bn of short-term debt for longer-term loans.

Feb. 6, 1998: South Korean unions, government and businesses reach a landmark agreement to make redundancies legal.

March 9, 1998: The IMF delays a $3 bn instalment of loans to Indonesia, and criticises Suharto's failure to implement agreed reforms.

March 23, 1998: Russian President Boris Yeltsin dismisses his entire cabinet.

April 8, 1998: Indonesia and the IMF reach a third agreement.

May 5, 1998: Students in Indonesia hold demonstrations across the country about fuel and food price rises.

May 12, 1998: Indonesian troops fire on a student protest, killing six and sparking riots.

May 21, 1998: President Suharto resigns after thirty-two years in power and is succeeded by Vice President Habibie.

May 22, 1998: The IMF postpones aid disbursement to Indonesia until political stability is restored.

May 27–28, 1998: A two-day general strike is held in South Korea to protest against 10,000 redundancies.

June 1, 1998: Russia's stock market crashes and foreign exchange reserves fall to $14 bn.

June 25, 1998: Indonesia and the IMF announce a fourth agreement.

July 13, 1998: The IMF announces a package of $23 bn of emergency loans for Russia.

August 11, 1998: Trading on the Russian stock market is suspended.

August 17, 1998: Russia announces a devaluation of the rouble and defaults on debt payments. Latin American stock and bond markets plunge.

Sept. 23, 1998: The Fed orchestrates a $3.5 bn bailout to Long Term Capital Management (LTCM)

Sept. 29, 1998: The Fed cuts interest rates by a quarter point and again in October. World markets rally.

7.4.1 Banking crises

One area where it has long been accepted that crises can occur even without such a deterioration in fundamentals is in the banking sector. However, unlike the other forms of financial crisis covered in this chapter, banking crises can and do occur without any external financial influences. As we have seen previously, banks are inherently susceptible to 'runs', where depositors with concerns over the solvency of the bank rush to withdraw their deposits. However, because banks have assets that can be liquidated instantly but use these assets to lend on a longer-term basis, a 'run' of this kind can lead to the closure of a bank, regardless of whether the bank really did have a solvency problem.[12]

There is also the possibility of 'contagious' bank runs, where the 'run' spreads from one bank to the rest of the system, threatening the viability of the entire banking sector – again, the long-term solvency of the system is largely irrelevant, as contagious bank runs can produce liquidity crises on a scale sufficient to undermine the entire banking sector regardless of the 'soundness' of the banks concerned. We have seen that banks play a pivotal intermediation role in the economy, and it is therefore not surprising that banking crises are associated with significant costs to the economy, as banks' ability to perform this function is undermined.

The full cost to society of a banking crisis far exceeds the losses to the banks' own balance sheets, however. For the World Bank (2001) there are three components of the true economic cost that need to be factored in:

1   The *stock component* is the 'accumulated waste of economic resources that is revealed by the insolvency'. That is, instead of channelling savings to the most productive investments, banks have effectively wasted these funds by channelling them into uneconomic activities.

2   The *public finance component* can result as governments tend to assume at least some direct responsibility for the crisis, in order to bail out depositors and others affected. In many instances, the government has little option but to intervene in this way, though there are obviously fiscal implications of doing so in terms of (a) expenditure cuts elsewhere, (b) tax increases, and/or (c) inflation arising from the printing of money to fund the intervention.

3   The *flow component* is a result of the reduced economic output with which banking crises are usually associated. This impact may be felt through any or all of the following channels:

    • A sharp fall in investment and/or consumer spending due to a loss of confidence;
    • A sharp fall in investment and/or consumer spending due to a lack of credit;
    • A reduction in loans due to the loss of information on creditworthy investment opportunities;
    • A failure in the centralised payment and settlement system.

Clearly, the larger the initial capital shortfall of the banks, the greater will be the final economic impact. In developing countries alone, the World Bank (2001) estimates that the combined cost of banking crises from 1980 to 2000 was more than $1 trillion.

Figure 7.13 below details the estimated fiscal cost of banking crises in individual countries over the past two decades. As we can see, even the smallest impact – in Sweden – amounted to 3% of GDP, while the largest – in Indonesia – wiped out almost 50% of national wealth. For all countries, the average impact of a banking crisis was a reduction in GDP of 17.5% and, as the reference to Sweden makes clear, such crises are not restricted to developing countries. Rather, as discussed in previous chapters on the domestic financial system and financial liberalisation, countries that deregulate their banking systems without first establishing a robust and effective framework of prudential regulation and supervision greatly increase the likelihood of a banking crisis occurring.

In many ways it could be argued that having a banking crisis is something of a 'rite of passage' that must be undergone if a liberalised financial system is to develop successfully, though the cost of this transition would seem to most reasonable people to be extremely high – possibly higher than any benefits that liberalisation might ultimately bring.

Although banking crises can and do happen in both developed and developing countries, it is also the case that concerns about the solvency of banks are associated with situations of weak prudential regulation and supervision, which are more likely to pertain in developing countries. In addition to this factor, the World Bank (op. cit.) gives the following reasons why banking crises are more likely to occur in developing than developed countries:

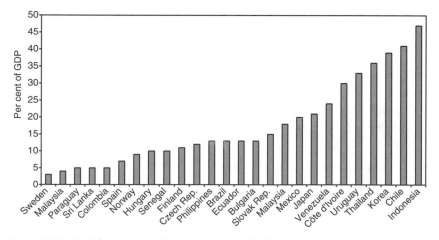

Figure 7.13 Total fiscal costs of banking crises, 1980–2000.

Source: World Bank, 2001.

1   Inadequate prudential regulation and supervision of the banking sector does not prevent banks taking on excessive risks, as they will tend to do otherwise.[13]
2   They experience more severe information problems, which lead banks to make suboptimal lending decisions.
3   Developing country banks have less diversified investment portfolios, reflecting the more concentrated economies in which they operate. This leaves them more vulnerable to economic shocks.
4   The higher volatility of financial assets (equities, bonds, exchange rates etc.) in developing countries leads to higher banking sector fragility, as developing country banks are largely invested in their own domestic markets.
5   Financial markets in developing countries are dominated by banks. As a result, companies tend to be highly leveraged and therefore more vulnerable to economic shocks. Lower access to longer-term capital also increases the vulnerability of firms to shocks.
6   State ownership of banking assets is linked to banking sector vulnerability.
7   There is poor sequencing of financial liberalisation.

Clearly, the costs of banking crises are such that every effort should be made to prevent them. In this regard, robust regulation and supervision is crucial, as is the legal and commercial framework in which banks operate. However, because of the features of developing countries listed above, there remains a higher probability of banking crises in developing than in developed markets even if regulation and supervision were perfect. The volatility and concentration of the financial system of many developing economies increases the probability of genuine insolvencies, whilst the often poor information available also increases the possibility of unfounded fears of insolvency sparking bank runs. We have seen how banking crises can occur independently of any external financial involvement. However, it is also the case that domestic banking crises can also be precipitated by sharp movements of externally driven financial variables, and that these movements may be driven more by perception than reality. This mixture of reality and perception is most readily seen in a second important aspect of financial crises: currency crises.

7.4.2 Currency crises

As described by Dani Rodrik at the start of Section 7.4, there has been a sharply increased incidence of currency crises, particularly though not exclusively in developing and emerging economies, since the collapse of the system of fixed exchange rates in the early 1970s.

If we recall that the key theoretical pillar in support of the switch to fixed exchange rates was that 'rational arbitrageurs' would ensure that exchange rates remained close to their equilibrium/fundamental/'fair' values (Friedman, 1953), then this would suggest that currency crises are caused by a sharp deterioration in the economic fundamentals of the country concerned. Indeed, as we shall see, early attempts to model and explain currency crises broadly adopted this position, only for the weight of evidence to lead economists to question whether this perspective could accurately describe these events.

The first major theoretical work in the field was Krugman (1979). Adapting earlier work by Salant and Henderson (1978),[14] Krugman developed the first standard analysis of the process of speculative attack. Krugman demonstrated how inconsistencies between domestic economic considerations and the maintenance of an external exchange rate peg could provoke a speculative attack, resulting in the collapse of the peg. For example, expansionary domestic monetary policy results in balance of payments problems and the central bank finances this shortfall through the use of its foreign exchange reserves. At some point, however, reserves fall below a particular level, triggering a speculative attack. The remaining reserves are then exhausted and the currency is forced to devalue, thereby eliminating the inconsistency of expansionary domestic policy and the maintenance of a fixed currency peg.

Krugman stresses that it is not necessary for reserves to have been completely exhausted for an attack to be successful. Where policy inconsistencies are apparent, an attack will take place at the earliest point that it could be successful: market actors are all attempting to get out just before the attack, and are aware that others are attempting to do the same, as soon as an attack would be sufficient to wipe out the remaining reserves it will therefore be initiated.

This early canonical model places the responsibility for the success of speculative attacks on currency pegs squarely with the governments in question. From this perspective, the market is merely making a rational move in response to inconsistent economic policies, and is therefore responding to, rather than participating in, real-world events. The speculative attacks that have occurred since 1979, however, led many to question the relevance of this 'first-generation' model. It was pointed out that, commonly, the simple case of expansionary domestic policy did not accord with the facts. More complex theories arose in the 1980s which attempted to align theory more closely with reality. These approaches saw the role of markets as far greater than simply reacting to fundamentals; with the markets viewed as perhaps creating, rather than simply responding to, circumstances.

This second generation of models investigated the possibility of the existence of 'multiple equilibria', wherein the perceptions of market actors are crucial. Multiple equilibria may arise where the sustainable level of a currency depends on whether or not a speculative attack occurs. So, whilst current fundamentals are taken into account, so are future fundamentals; however, these differ depending on whether or not a speculative attack occurs. Therefore, it may be that the currency peg is compatible with current and future fundamentals in the absence of a speculative attack, but incompatible with current and future fundamentals after an attack has taken place.

Obstfeld (1986) offers theoretical and empirical evidence in support of the multiple equilibria hypothesis, arguing that a 'grey area' exists where the sustainability of a currency peg is determined by the attitude of market actors. He stresses that where clear incompatibilities in policy exist then the processes identified by Krugman (1979) may be relevant, but that this model does not adequately describe the diversity of real-world situations, and, crucially, underestimates the role that the markets can play in shaping outcomes.

The distinction between these two approaches is very important. The argument rests upon the extent to which markets are rational and objective processors and users of information, and/or the extent to which they act in a self-fulfilling or collectively irrational way. That is, do markets move in response to economic fundamentals – as orthodox theory suggests – or are market movements more driven by market sentiment, which may be decoupled from underlying economic fundamentals but can then come to shape them?

This also relates to the next issue to consider in this section, which is the increasing prevalence of financial crisis contagion.

7.4.3 Financial crisis contagion

It is now generally well accepted that contagion – or spillover effects – from financial crises are not fully explained by fundamental factors alone. The debate on this subject has been conducted since the ERM crises of 1992/3 and intensified after first the Latin American 'tequila crisis' of the mid-1990s and, more recently, the Asian crisis of 1997/8. At issue have been the explanations for the temporal and geographical clustering of financial crises.

On the one hand some have argued that, whilst crises are indeed clustered in both a geographical and temporal sense, there are sound economic reasons for this, with markets discriminating in the countries that come under speculative attack; that is, only countries with weak fundamentals are vulnerable.

The opposing view has held that the primary causes of the observed clustering lie in the behaviour of international investors, rather than in the fundamentals of the countries concerned. One reason why this debate is significant is for its implications for the justification, or not, for international assistance for crisis-affected countries. If the former camp is right, and countries primarily come under speculative attack because of weak and/or declining economic fundamentals, then international assistance to bail out such countries may not be justified. Alternatively, if the primary cause lies in the changing behaviour of international investors, then the countries affected cannot be said to be culpable and thus may be deserving of international assistance (Eichengreen *et al.*, 1996).

Some commentators working in this area have suggested that although contagion can be observed in the aftermath of a number of financial crises, this does not, of itself, indicate shared causes or uniform transmission mechanisms. Just as each financial crisis is, to some extent, a unique event, so contagious episodes may also be relatively heterogeneous in terms of causes and pattern. Thus, it may be that as the financial system has evolved – particularly since liberalisation began in earnest in the 1970 and 1980s – different linkages have become more or less important. For example, given the declining weight of trade in international financial flows, it would seem probable that contagion as a result of trade linkages would be less important now than in the past. Similarly, given the enormous increase in the scale of capital flows in the last two decades, it would seem likely that financial linkages may have increased in importance as a channel for contagion.

One of the first papers to address this question empirically was Eichengreen *et al.* (op. cit.), who define contagion, in the context of currency crises, as: 'a systematic effect on the probability of a speculative attack which stems from attacks on other currencies, and is therefore an additional effect above and beyond those of domestic fundamentals' (p. 2).

Using a panel of quarterly data for twenty industrial countries, for the period 1959–1993, the authors ask whether the probability of a crisis in one country at a particular point in time is correlated with the incidence of crises elsewhere at the same time. After controlling for the impact of political and economic fundamentals, Eichengreen *et al.* find clear evidence that a crisis in one country increases the probability of speculative attack in another by approximately 8%.

The authors identify two major possible channels through which contagion may occur:

- First, trade links between countries suggest that a devaluation in one country may impact upon the relative international competitiveness of other countries, resulting in speculative attacks on the currencies to re-establish equilibrium.
- Second, contagion may result from similar macroeconomic conditions in the countries concerned. Thus, a successful speculative attack on a country employing a currency peg may lead investors to question the ability of countries experiencing similar macroeconomic conditions to maintain their own currency pegs.

Eichengreen *et al.* test for the existence of both potential forms of contagion. Their results suggest that trade links are the most important, and they conclude that this route is the most significant channel for contagion. The authors caution, however, that the findings are suggestive rather than definitive, as the same results could be produced by exposure to a common, but unmeasured, shock.

Since this pioneering study in the mid-1990s, a number of researchers have conducted studies into the existence of contagious crises and the likely channels through which contagion may spread. Nearly all of these studies have confirmed the finding that fundamentals alone are insufficient to explain the temporal and geographical clustering of crises. As well as trade links a number of other potential channels have been investigated.

The suggestion that crises may be clustered as the result of a common external shock has been labelled 'monsoonal effects' by Masson and Mussa (1995) and defined as 'major economic shifts in industrial countries that trigger crises in emerging markets' (Masson 1998: 5). An example often cited in this context is the debt crisis of the early 1980s that was largely triggered by a sharp increase in US interest rates. Similarly, it has been argued that the relative appreciation of the US dollar vis-à-vis the yen in the mid-1990s adversely affected the competitive position of much of Southeast Asia – as their currencies were pegged to the dollar, producing a decline in export growth and paving the way for the Asian crisis in 1997.

Another potential channel for contagion that has been examined in the literature is financial linkages. The argument is that a crisis in one country may impact upon the portfolios of international investors, causing them to reduce their exposure in other countries in order to re-balance their portfolios with regard to risk exposure or liquidity requirements, for example (Calvo, 1999; Goldfajn and Valdes, 1997). Under this scenario, a country with a high degree of exposure to a major lender to a crisis country may face an increased chance of crisis itself. This phenomenon has been labelled the 'common creditor' argument by Kaminsky and Reinhart (1998).

A third possible channel of contagion is related to shifts in investor sentiment, sometimes referred to as 'pure contagion' (Masson, 1998). Masson defines pure contagion as involving changes in expectations that are not related to economic fundamentals, and differentiates this form from 'monsoonal effects' (described above) and 'spillover effects' which he equates with trade linkages.

He argues that a crisis in one country can function as a 'sunspot', coordinating investors' expectations and (drawing on the literature on multiple equilibria in currency crises) causing them to shift from a 'good' to a 'bad' equilibrium for another country; thus initiating a self-fulfilling currency crisis. Also, if a crisis in one country raises concerns of further crises elsewhere, investors may hope to profit by speculating against the currencies that they think most likely to be the focus of speculative attack; thus, again, a crisis could be self-fulfilling in nature.

There may also be a psychological aspect to this phenomenon. Investors may have a mental paradigm that governs their view of a particular country or region and a financial crisis may bring the validity of this paradigm into question. Thus, in Southeast Asia, for example, the 1990s 'paradigm' was that of the 'Tiger economies' and all benefited from the perception that the region was uniquely placed to enjoy sustainable high rates of economic growth; consequently capital flowed in indiscriminately. This could be viewed as a 'good equilibrium'. However, once the crisis began to unfold 'Tiger economies' became debt-ridden bastions of crony capitalism and capital flowed out just as indiscriminately as it had flowed in. Thus, a crisis could serve to alter investors' perceptions, causing a shift from a good to a bad equilibrium in a psychological sense and precipitating a self-fulfilling crisis.

Some have also argued that a crisis in one country may serve as a 'wake-up call' for investors, causing them to reassess the situation in other countries of which they had previously been unconcerned (Goldstein, 1998).

What is generally accepted, however, is that the contagious nature of financial crises cannot be explained by economic fundamentals alone, but is intimately related to the complexity and interconnectedness of the global financial system, and also to the intricacies of investor psychology under conditions of uncertainty. What are the costs of these crises, however?

Research by Griffith-Jones and Gottschalk (2004) estimates the impact of crises on emerging market output, as shown in Table 7.2. Examining data for eight countries that have suffered serious financial crises, the authors conclude that their combined loss of output following a crisis totalled US$1.25 trillion in 2002 dollars, which corresponds to 65% of the combined GDP of Latin America and the Caribbean, and 54% of that for the East Asia & Pacific region.

Effects of this magnitude clearly impact upon poverty levels in the countries concerned: in Indonesia, for example, poverty levels rose from 7–8% of the population in 1997 to 18–20% in 1998 (Suryahadi *et al.*, 2000).

Looking at the last quarter of the twentieth century, Eichengreen (2004) estimates that currency and banking crises have reduced the incomes of developing countries by approximately 25% from what would otherwise have been the case.

To summarise, we have seen that:

- Certain types of capital flow (FDI) are preferred to others by policy-makers in developing countries.
- The least preferred flows to developing countries (short-term bank and

Table 7.2 Cumulative output loss in crisis-afflicted countries

Country	Period of output loss	Estimated loss (constant 1999 US$ bn)	Estimated loss (constant 2002 US$ bn)
Argentina	2002	25.6	37.1
Brazil	1999–2002	96.7	140.1
Indonesia	1997–2002	238.6	345.9
Korea	1997–2002	122.9	178.1
Malaysia	1997–2002	60.6	87.8
Mexico	1995–2002	78.1	113.2
Thailand	1997–2002	210.5	305.2
Turkey	2001–2002	29.0	42.1
Total		**862.0**	**1249.6**

Source: Griffith-Jones and Gottschalk, 2004.

portfolio flows) are highly volatile, exhibiting procyclical periods of boom followed by rapid reversals, or 'busts'.

- Financial sector crises have been a growing feature of the international financial system for hundreds of years, with the incidence and impacts of crises having grown rapidly since the widespread liberalisation of national and international financial markets began in the 1970s.
- Banking sector crises are more likely to occur in developing countries, and we have given some estimates of the costs of these crises.
- Currency crises can affect any emerging or developing countries, either directly as a result of volatile market sentiment, or indirectly as the result of contagion from another crisis-afflicted country.
- The total costs to developing and emerging economies of all types of financial crises can be extremely high, potentially setting back decades of incremental developmental progress.

The scale of the effects of financial crisis is clearly huge, which places great emphasis on crisis prevention, and also crisis resolution. Accordingly, the next section considers these issues.

7.4.4 Crisis prevention and resolution

There are two aspects to crisis prevention at the international level. First, domestic measures to reduce vulnerability to crisis, and, second, external measures to reduce the build-up of crisis potential.

Domestically, macroeconomic stability is clearly crucial. In this regard, as we have seen in previous chapters, developing countries have been remarkably successful in reducing inflation rates. Similarly, sustainable fiscal balances are also critical – as highlighted by the first-generation currency crisis models described above. Again, however, developing countries have generally made significant progress in this area as well.

Also, developing countries have largely managed to reduce current account deficits to manageable levels, and some regions – notably in East Asia – have generated large current account surpluses, which have enabled them to build up huge foreign exchange reserves as an 'insurance' against speculative attack on their currencies.

On exchange rates, there has also been a shift away from fixed exchange rates towards a more flexible system in many developing countries. For some observers (e.g. Fischer, 2001) this development has greatly reduced the risks of future currency crises. However, it should be stressed that it also has the effect of introducing exchange rate volatility – particularly given the volatility of capital flows – to many emerging and developing economies and, as we saw in Chapter 5, maintaining a fixed or managed exchange rate remains common amongst developing countries.

A genuinely floating exchange rate, of course, presupposes that countries will have fully open capital accounts to allow capital to move in and out of the country without restrictions. However, given the evidence that full capital account liberalisation serves to increase growth volatility, but not necessarily growth itself (Prasad *et al.*, 2003), many countries have chosen to deal with the volatility of capital flows by retaining at least some elements of capital control. In this regard, it is surely no coincidence that the rate at which developing countries have removed capital controls has slowed markedly since 1998 (i.e. the time of the Asian crisis).

The currency mismatches that amplify the effects of currency crises – the burden of dollar denominated debt, for example, rises proportionally as the currency's value falls against the dollar – have also been reduced in recent years. This has occurred in two ways. First, as we have seen, cross-border international bank lending has fallen, to be replaced by domestic currency lending from international banks that have 'crossed the border' and established local subsidiaries in developing countries. Second, there has been an increase in the quantity of local currency debt issued by developing countries, though it should be noted that this remains well short of what it could be potentially, with many countries still suffering the effects of 'original sin'.

Both of these developments have reduced the foreign-currency component of many developing countries' private and public debt, thereby reducing both the vulnerability to crisis and the impact of a crisis if it does occur. That is not to say that the potential for crisis has been removed, however. Far from it. As we have seen, international investors' attitude towards developing and emerging economies is often shaped more by conditions in developed markets than those in the developing world. In the run-up to the Asian crisis, high levels of global liquidity – and low global interest rates and so investment returns – led to 'yield-hungry' investors increasing their allocations to high-yielding – and therefore high-risk – emerging economies. A consequence of this was to push emerging market debt spreads (i.e. the 'risk premium' attached to these financial assets) to historical lows, which greatly increased the incentive for emerging and developing economies to borrow at these rates. Similarly, recent years have also seen very high levels of global liquidity, and the same search for yield has again seen spreads on emerging market debt fall to levels that, for some, underprice the risk of holding these assets.

For example, in October 2002, average emerging market sovereign spreads on J.P. Morgan's EMBI+ reached 1,020 basis point, but by December 2006 the same index was at the historic low of 170 basis points. To clarify, a basis point is 1% of 1%, so that in 2002, emerging market borrowers paid an average of 10% more than the spread on US Treasuries to borrow. By the end of 2006, however, the figure was 1.7%. Given the build-up in crisis potential described above, it is difficult to believe that emerging markets are five times less risky now than was the case in 2002.

Another area of suggested domestic economic improvement in developing countries is the increased recognition of the importance of financial regulation and supervision, where countries have been moving increasingly towards full compliance with international best practice. In banking, this means adherence to the Basel Core Principles for Effective Banking Supervision, for example. However, while these developments are – broadly – to be welcomed, it is not always the case that transporting a set of regulations from developed economies – for which they were explicitly designed – to a very different developing country context will inevitably reduce vulnerability. Indeed, the implementation of inappropriate regulatory frameworks could be expected to do the exact opposite.

As well as these domestic reforms, the Asian crisis and its aftermath encouraged a far greater emphasis on monitoring the situation within developing countries to provide 'early warning signals' of impending crises. The body charged with this 'multilateral surveillance' has been the IMF, which already performs a related function through its Article IV consultations, Financial Sector Stability Assessments, and the reviews of the observance of international codes and standards.

In July 2004, the IMF Executive Board concluded a review of these surveillance activities. The review identified key priorities for further strengthening surveillance. In particular, surveillance activities should be focused on improving analytical tools for early identification of vulnerabilities, particularly with regard to more rigorous assessments of balance-sheet weaknesses and stress-testing with regard to possible macroeconomic shocks (UN, 2005).

Also, the IMF argued for an increased focus on country-specific areas of vulnerability, which requires surveillance that is tailor-made for each country. In this regard, the Fund recognised that there is a need to better understand each country's policy constraints, which relate to institutional, social and political circumstances. The laudable aim is therefore to offer countries realistic advice that they may be in a position to take, rather than taking a dogmatic, one-size-fits-all ideological approach, which the IMF has often been accused of.

The IMF has also been central to the efforts to establish more reliable emergency financing measures for countries facing financial difficulties. As we have seen, domestically, this function has traditionally been undertaken by national central banks. However, internationally, there is no equivalent institution: the role of lender-of-last-resort (LOLR) performed by central banks differs from the emergency financing undertaken by the IMF and other bodies, since there is no automatic right to financing support in the international sphere, whereas this is often the case with a domestic LOLR. Furthermore, a national central bank can, in principle, provide unlimited financial support in its own currency to financial institutions, whereas the support the IMF can offer is by definition limited, as it does not have fiat money-creating powers.

Since its foundation, the IMF has created a number of financing facilities established to help countries deal with macroeconomic shocks. For example, the Compensatory Financing Facility (CFF) was designed in 1963 to help countries deal with terms of trade shocks.[15]

As well as specific initiatives of this kind, the IMF has also taken steps more generally to develop mechanisms to provide emergency liquidity for

(short-term) capital account crises. To deal with this problem the Sup-
plemental Reserve Facility (SRF) was established in 1997 to provide large
amounts of finance to countries affected by a capital account crisis, at a
higher interest rate than that of other Fund facilities.[16]

Following complaints that the criteria for accessing the SRF were not
clearly defined, the IMF agreed the following criteria for access in 2003:

- an exceptionally large need;
- a debt burden that would be sustainable under reasonably conservative
  assumptions;
- good prospects of regaining access to private capital markets during the
  period of the IMF loan; and
- indications that the country's policies had a strong chance of succeeding.

In recognition of the fact that even countries with good fundamentals, a
sustainable debt burden and a sound policy framework could be affected
by liquidity crises akin to a bank run – which is a major admission in any
event, and was largely a response to pressure applied to the Fund – the IMF
also established the Contingent Credit Line (CCL) in 1999. The CCL was
designed to provide rapid emergency support for countries in crisis situations,
with the term 'contingent' referring to the fact that countries had to meet
certain strict criteria in order to be eligible for this assistance. The intention
was to provide support for countries with sound economic and financial
fundamentals, but which were nevertheless affected by contagion from a crisis
in another country or region. However, the CCL was never used and was
discontinued in 2003.

The problem was that countries simply did not wish to apply to the CCL,
even if they were in difficulties, as this would advertise the fact internationally, and so perhaps even precipitate the very crisis they hoped to avoid. Since
the demise of the CCL, the Fund has been exploring other means of achieving the same aim. The debate has centred on the thorny issue of moral hazard, with opponents of explicit financing facilities that provide access in
emergencies arguing that this will lead countries to take excessive risks, knowing that they will be bailed out by the Fund if difficulties emerge. Others
argue that the moral hazard case is overstated and unsupported by empirical
evidence, and that the overwhelming need to avoid the damage caused by
financial crises far outweighs any concerns on moral hazard.[17]

To summarise, there is no doubt that the incidence of financial crises has
increased significantly since the 1970s. Furthermore, it is equally clear that
such crises have real and extremely damaging effects on developing and
emerging economies, leading to loss of output, slower growth and sharply
increased levels of poverty. Whilst there is some agreement on the domestic
measures needed to reduce vulnerability to crises, there is also an acceptance
that this may not, ultimately, be sufficient to prevent a crisis occurring.

If a self-fulfilling liquidity crisis can affect any country, regardless of the strength of its domestic economy, macro stability, regulatory environment, and so on, are there sufficient international, emergency financing measures to enable countries to cope with these events?

At present, the answer to this must be no, which suggests that the decision of some developing countries to slow or stop the removal of capital account controls after 1998 was the correct one. Before considering the issue of external debt and the debt crisis, we shall briefly review options and experience with regard to capital controls.

7.4.5 Prudential capital controls

> The accumulation of risks that developing countries face during capital account booms depends not only on the magnitude of private and public sector debts but also on maturity and currency mismatches on the balance sheets of financial and non-financial agents. Thus, capital-account regulations potentially have a dual role: as a macroeconomic policy tool with which to provide some room for counter-cyclical monetary policies that smooth out debt ratios and spending; and as a 'liability policy' designed to improve private sector external debt profiles.
>
> (UN, 2005: 97)

Thus, for the UN, capital account regulations have the possibility of providing more room for manœuvre with regard to macroeconomic policy – i.e. the set of feasible policy options is not just restricted to those seen as 'market friendly' – and may have the effect of lengthening the 'maturity profile' of external debt. In this regard, the evidence suggests strongly that a higher proportion of longer-term debt in the external debt profile reduces the possibility of a self-fulfilling liquidity type crisis occurring.[18]

What are the options, however? Broadly, capital controls may take one of two forms:

1   price-based controls, such as reserve requirements or taxes;
2   quantity-based controls, such as restrictions on certain types of borrowing.

In addition to these two categories of control that relate to activities in capital markets, policy-makers have a number of further options (UN, op. cit.):

- They can limit banks' ability to borrow short term overseas.
- They can compel banks to match their foreign currency liabilities with foreign currency assets.
- They can prevent banks from lending in foreign currency to firms that do not have a corresponding foreign currency income stream.
- They can impose higher capital adequacy requirements or loan-loss

provisions for short-term lending where a foreign currency is involved, or where there is a currency mismatch.

- They can apply less favourable bankruptcy or tax treatments to institutions borrowing in foreign currencies.

Price-based controls have the advantage of simplicity. A recent example of their success was the introduction in Chile and Colombia in the 1990s of 'unremunerated reserve requirements' that required investors to deposit the reserve requirement (which was therefore effectively a tax on capital inflows) in the central bank for a period of one year. Thus longer-term investors were not discouraged, but shorter-term flows were penalised more heavily.

It is widely agreed (including by the IMF and BIS) that the controls were effective in lengthening the maturity profile of the countries' external debt, though there is less agreement as to their impact on macroeconomic policy flexibility. However, it is likely that the controls allowed them to keep interest rates higher than would otherwise have been the case,[19] which was appropriate for domestic economic circumstances at that time. Box 7.3 below assesses the evidence of the impact of the Chilean 'experiment' with capital controls.

Box 7.3 Chile's experience with capital controls in the 1990s

In September 1991, the Chilean government introduced a targeted form of capital control, which was termed 'the unremunerated reserve requirement' (URR). Under the URR foreign investors are required to hold an unremunerated reserve (i.e. non interest-bearing) at the Central Bank for one year: the URR is therefore equivalent to a tax that falls with the maturity of the form of capital inflow. That is, longer-term investments (those over a year) pay no tax, but the rate rises as the maturity of the investment reduces. Foreign investors have the alternative option of paying an up-front fee based on the relevant international interest rate.

The intention when implementing the URR was threefold: first, to lengthen the maturity of foreign investments in Chile, thus reducing volatility and the risk of sudden withdrawals; second, to increase the effectiveness of monetary policy where the exchange rate is heavily managed (i.e. to overcome, at least in part, the limitations of the 'impossible trinity'; and third, to enable Chile to maintain a lower real exchange rate than would otherwise have been the case.

In May 1999 the Central Bank reduced the rate at which the URR is charged to zero, thus effectively ending the control, but also retaining the option of reinstating it again in the future.

Gallego *et al.* (1999) review the studies that have been undertaken to assess the impact of the URR. Soto and Valdés (1996), Valdés and Soto

(1998) and Eyzaguirre and Schmidt-Hebbel (1997) all find that the URR did succeed in lengthening the maturity profile of foreign investments in Chile, but little evidence was found to suggest impact in the other two areas, although the latter study did find some weak evidence that the effectiveness of monetary policy was enhanced. While Laurens and Cardoso (1998) are reported as finding no impact upon maturities, Gallego *et al.* (op. cit.) conclude that methodological and data problems cast doubt on these findings.

De Gregorio, Edwards and Valdés (1998) take a more comprehensive approach to the issue, which takes account of other changes in regulations regarding the capital account, notably the liberalisation of capital outflows and other inflows. They too find that the URR lengthened maturities and also suggest that there is evidence of greater room for manoeuvre regarding monetary policy. Again, however, no effect on the real exchange rate was found. Furthermore, none of the studies found any evidence that the URR had affected the overall level of inflows.

Other studies which have taken a 'vector auto regression' (VAR) approach have confirmed the findings that the URR led to a relative increase in the proportion of longer-term investments (and decline in short-term holdings) and also that interest rates were higher in Chile (relative to international rates) than would have been possible in the absence of the URR. Again, however, the impact on the real exchange rate was more difficult to identify, though there was some evidence that the URR decreased its volatility.

To summarise, it appears that the URR was able to lengthen investment maturities without reducing overall capital inflows. Furthermore, it afforded the monetary authorities with greater freedom of action when setting interest rates. These are all valuable gains, but perhaps the most important was the lower potential for crisis that the reduction in short-term investment produced. The key here is that controls were targeted at inflows rather than outflows. As Gallego *et al.* (op. cit.) suggest, it is far easier to control capital inflows than capital outflows. Furthermore, it is certainly the case that it is easier to prevent a crisis from happening (by stopping the build up of the potential for crisis) than it is to deal with one when it is in full swing, or to clear up the aftermath.

A final point to make is that, despite the disbelief with which any suggestion that capital controls should be introduced is met by market practitioners, Chile was able to achieve these positive gains and retain full access to the international financial markets.

Despite this seeming success, quantitative restrictions have been more commonly used than price-based controls. The usual approach – perhaps best exemplified by the experience of China today – has been to separate domestic and foreign exchange markets, by quantitatively restricting domestic firms and individuals from foreign currency borrowing and also restricting the ability of non-residents to hold specified domestic financial assets.

Certainly in Asia, experience suggests that countries with such controls – China, India, Taiwan and Vietnam, for example – were considerably less vulnerable to crisis than were the crisis-affected countries that did not have capital controls. Despite this strong empirical evidence, however, the suggestion that a country might decide to impose capital controls is invariably met by howls of protest from 'the market', generally accompanied by dire predictions of the economic collapse that will inevitably ensue.

A good example of this can be seen during the Asian crisis, when in September 1998 Malaysia imposed quantitative capital controls on capital outflows, which aimed to ensure that the local currency – the ringgit – was only used domestically and so prevent a collapse of the exchange rate. Just a few months later these quantitative restrictions were replaced with an 'exit levy', which was a price-based control and was gradually reduced over subsequent years.

At the time of implementation, the move brought tremendous complaints from international investors, who predicted a stampede to withdraw from the country once the controls were lifted. In the event, however, international investors' allocation to Malaysia actually rose following the removal of the restrictions, and Malaysia's approach is now viewed as having being largely successful, particularly in giving the government the macroeconomic freedom to pursue expansionary policies, which accelerated the country's recovery.

To summarise on private flows and crises.

- FDI is still viewed as the 'best' flow due to greater stability and additional benefits.
- Short-term banking flows are just as volatile and dangerous as short-term portfolio flows.
- Macroeconomic and fiscal policy can reduce vulnerability to crisis.
- Good external surveillance can reduce vulnerability to crisis by providing 'early warning signals'.
- Emergency financing from IMF is not sufficient to deal with the scale of the issue.
- Even if all the correct domestic and international measures are taken, however, countries can still be hit by self-fulfilling liquidity-type crises.
- It may therefore be necessary to implement – or at least reserve the right to implement – prudential capital controls.
- Price-based capital controls that penalise short-term inflows are more effective at lengthening maturity profiles of external debt.
- Quantity-based controls that separate domestic and foreign exchange markets are more effective at providing room for macroeconomic policy flexibility.

We have touched on the importance of a country's external debt profile in determining a country's vulnerability to crisis. The final section of this chapter will expand upon this introduction, and consider the issues of external debt, the debt crisis and debt sustainability.

7.5 'Good' debt vs. 'bad' debt

As we saw in Chapter 6, the theoretical benefits of a country taking on external debt are expressed in the 'debt-cycle' hypothesis.[20] This states that external inflows raises total savings, which increases domestic investment rates and therefore spurs higher rates of economic growth. This in turn will allow the foreign debt accrued to be eliminated. There are five requirements for this to occur in practice, however:

1   External flows should be used for investment, rather than consumption purposes.
2   The investment should be efficient.
3   The country must invest in tradable sectors so that a trade surplus can enable foreign debt to be paid off.
4   Domestic savings should be aggressively mobilised.
5   The 'virtuous circle' requires those exporting capital (e.g. from developed countries) to do so in a stable and predictable manner.

Therefore, as long as debt is used for investment purposes, and the investments are efficient and productive enough to produce economic value greater than the cost of the debt, it is rational for developing countries to take on external debt. This can therefore be described as 'good debt'.

Alternatively, 'bad debt' is where the funds raised are ultimately wasted by not being employed productively. In the case of borrowing in an international currency, this raises levels of foreign exchange debt, but does not generate correspondingly higher economic output enabling the debt to be paid off, resulting in a net drain on the economy.

With foreign currency obligations, the issue of 'good debt' is complicated by the currency mismatch that the debt produces, which may fundamentally change the nature of 'debt sustainability', particularly in the event of a currency crisis resulting in a large devaluation. Here, a formerly sustainable debt burden can become unsustainable, as the financial cost of servicing the debt (both in terms of interest and principal) will rise proportionally in relation to the size of the currency devaluation. Thus a 20% devaluation may result in a 20% increase in the burden of external debt, which may be public (e.g. sovereign) debt and therefore entail a large fiscal cost, or private (e.g. corporate) and threaten the viability of private companies in the economy. Thus, if not denominated in domestic currency 'good' debt can easily become 'bad' debt. This is akin to the 'multiple equilibria' approach to currency crisis, where a previously sustainable situation (i.e. a 'good' equilibrium) becomes unsustainable (i.e. a 'bad' equilibrium) following a currency crisis.

Local currency debt, as we have seen, avoids these problems and brings additional benefits to the economy, particularly in the area of domestic savings mobilisation, which may be encouraged by a growing domestic debt market.[21] In these circumstances, the question of whether the debt is 'good' or 'bad' is determined solely by the extent to which the borrowing generates greater economic value than the cost of servicing and repaying the debt. A simpler task certainly. However, 'original sin' has prevented most developing countries from being able to issue local currency debt due to the unwillingness of investors to purchase the paper. This is changing somewhat, as we have seen, but there remains a long way to go.

In addition to the use to which it is put and the possibility of currency devaluations, there are other factors that have historically influenced the sustainability of external debt. In particular, where debt with variable interest rates is taken on, sharp changes to international interest rates can radically change the equation in this regard, as occurred most spectacularly in the LDC debt crisis of the 1980s.

7.5.1 Debt crises and sustainable external debt

For most people, the term 'debt crisis' has become synonymous with the LDC crisis of the 1980s, which in many important ways remains unresolved today, more than thirty years later. However, issues of debt, debt sustainability and default had existed long before this point.[22]

In the post-Second World War period, capital flows to developing countries were dominated by bilateral official donors, private flows and, to a lesser extent, loans and grants from the multilateral development institutions. However, as remains the case today in many instances, there was little coordination between donors in relation to the total level of debt being taken on, and issues of the ability of countries to service their debt obligations were rarely taken into account. It was simply assumed – not least because of the central role of the Harrod-Domar growth model that has been discussed in previous chapters – that the external financial inflows would increase investment, leading to an acceleration of economic growth that would be more than sufficient to generate the funds – including foreign exchange – needed to repay these loans.

As we have also seen, calls from the UN for ODA to increase were not successful in the 1950s and 1960s, as ODA from developed countries steadily fell. A direct result of this was that many developing countries had difficulties servicing their external debts, and the first meeting of the Paris Club (of official ODA donors) was convened in 1956 to agree a rescheduling programme for the debt of developing countries.

The continuing decline of ODA through the 1960s and 1970s created further liquidity and debt servicing problems in developing countries, which seemed to be 'solved' by the sharp increase in private sector flows that was to follow. In the 1970s, however, everything suddenly changed.

In 1973 the Organization of the Petroleum Exporting Countries (OPEC) dramatically increased the price of oil. This had the effect of producing huge current account surpluses in the OPEC countries, surpluses that were deposited in Western banks: thus ensuring that oil-importing developed countries avoided serious balance of payments difficulties. The oil-importing countries of the developing world, however, were not so fortunate. The huge increases in the price of essential oil imports created serious foreign exchange shortages. The Western banks, keen to profitably invest their large extra deposits from the OPEC countries, met this demand with a huge increase in lending channelled through the Eurocurrency market.

In 1970 developing countries borrowed $300 million in Eurocurrency loans. By 1973, however, the figure had reached $4.5 billion, which amounted to more than 20% of all Eurobank loans. At the end of 1973, the outstanding debt of non-oil-exporting developing countries was $78.5 billion. By 1976, the figure was $180 billion, and rose to $600 billion by 1981, following a final surge in lending (UN, 2005).

Following a second OPEC price hike in 1978 the industrialised world sharply tightened monetary policy in an attempt to avoid the inflation that had followed the first price rise. This led to a sudden rise in international interest rates leaving the now heavily indebted countries of the developing world in an impossible position. The first country to threaten default was Mexico in 1982. The US authorities, sensing a threat to the international financial system – and to the US – banking system – intervened. The loans were restructured and a stabilisation programme introduced to instigate economic reforms, which, it was hoped, would increase the likelihood of full repayment of debt. The programme was overseen by the IMF, which had been searching for a new role since its original remit of policing the Bretton Woods system of international fixed exchange rates had become obsolete after the US dollar was floated in 1971.[23]

As a result of the emergence of the LDC debt crisis, the IMF and others began to establish indicators for debt sustainability, the first time this had been done. The main indicators developed at this time were:

- the ratio of debt service or debt service due to exports, to GDP, and to reserves;
- the ratio of amortization to debt;
- the ratio of debt to exports, and to GDP.

The initial response of creditors was to encourage debtor countries to introduce externally designed adjustment programmes, with the aim of generating high rates of economic growth and generating current account surpluses and therefore the ability to meet debt obligations. However, while these policies did generate current account surpluses, this was at the cost of domestic economic stagnation and the 'compression' of imports in many instances. The 1980s came to be known as the 'lost decade' in Latin America, and the resulting numerous defaults by countries in the region changed the nature of the 'negotiations' on debt, however (ibid.).

The Brady Plan, which was introduced in the early 1990s, was a recognition that the debt accrued could not be repaid through the generation of current account surpluses. Creditors were encouraged to write-down (i.e. reduce) debt levels by exchanging the old debts for new instruments: Brady bonds. Creditors accepted this option, and the issuance of Brady bonds enabled Latin American countries to return to the international capital markets, and created a secondary market in Brady bond debt.

The debt reduction (or at least the enhancement of debt sustainability) that this process achieved was focused on middle-income developing countries, however. In contrast, the 1980s and 1990s witnessed a further increase in indebtedness amongst less developed countries.

The increase in private flows to middle-income countries enabled ODA to be targeted more on the least developed countries, particularly in sub-Saharan Africa. The majority of this ODA was in the form of loans, however, which raised debt stocks from $6 billion in 1980 to $11 billion by the end of the 1990s. However, because net official transfers (ODA etc.) remained positive throughout the period (i.e. ODA > debt service payments), the increased level of indebtedness in LDCs did not produce the same difficulties that the previous build-up of private sector debt had done. However, throughout the period, debt service obligations in LDCs constituted more and more of the total ODA coming into countries, therefore leaving progressively less and less for development purposes (UN, 2005).

By the 1990s, therefore, the stock of external debt for both middle-income and LDCs was growing, peaking in 1992 at 65% of GNI for the former, as shown in Figure 7.14 below.

The stabilisation and subsequent decline of the total debt burden was driven by the Brady Plan for middle-income countries, and by the Heavily-Indebted-Poor-Country (HIPC) initiative for LDCs, which was introduced in 1996 and is the subject of the next section.

7.5.2 The HIPC initiative

What distinguishes HIPC from previous initiatives is that it involves multi-lateral creditors (e.g. the World Bank and IMF) for the first time. Bilateral and commercial creditors had, as we have seen, been involved in rescheduling and/or writing-down debt throughout the 1980s and 1990s, but this was not so for the multilateral donors.

It is this which explains why the share of multilateral debt, as a proportion of total debt, rose significantly over this period, particularly for low-income countries. As we can see from Figure 7.15 below, the proportion of middle-income country debt held by the multilateral institutions has remained

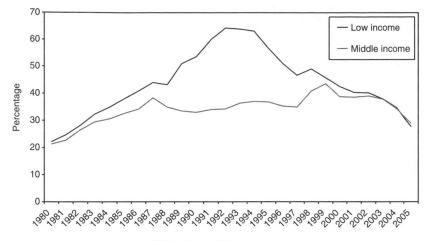

Figure 7.14 External debt to GNI, 1980–2005.

Source: World Bank GDF.

relatively stable since 1980, at a little under or a little over 10%. For low-income countries, in contrast, we see a steady year-on-year increase, so that the 17% of total external debt held by multilateral institutions in 1980 has, by 2005, become almost 40%.

The HIPC initiative was therefore designed to address this issue, and proceeded by placing debt relief within a framework of poverty reduction. In order to qualify for the HIPC process a country's debt burden must be viewed as unsustainable (see below, p. 249) and the country must only be borrowing internationally on concessional terms. That is, it must be unable to access

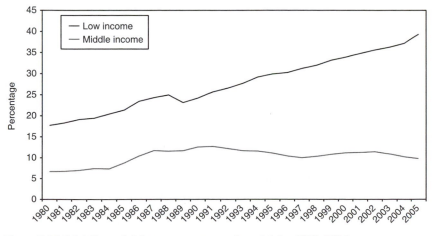

Figure 7.15 Multilateral debt as percentage of total debt, 1980–2005.

Source: World Bank GDF.

private sector finance on commercial terms. Once a country has qualified, there are two stages to the HIPC process.

In the first stage, HIPC countries establish a three-year track record of good economic performance and develop a Poverty Reduction Strategy Paper (PRSP)[24] in conjunction with civil society. The PRSP details the concrete steps that each country will take on poverty reduction and structural adjustment of the economy and must be approved by the executive boards of the Bretton Woods institutions. The consultation process surrounding the development of the PRSP is designed to ensure country 'ownership', not least because of the heavy criticism that the IMF and World Bank have been exposed to for allegedly imposing structural adjustment programmes upon countries.

In addition to this, country ownership is seen as vital if the programme of reform is to be sustained and completed. During stage one, the Paris Club[25] provides rescheduling of debt service commitments falling due during this three-year period, and other bilateral, multilateral and commercial creditors commit to act in the same way.

However, critics have maintained that the PRSP process is just the old structural adjustment programmes repackaged in new clothes.[26] The argument centres on the role of the Bretton Woods institutions (i.e. the IMF and World Bank) and, in particular, the constraints placed on available policy options by the need to have PRSPs approved by the boards of these international bodies. Thus, while a country is 'free' to choose any economic policy in theory, in practice PRSPs are based upon the same policy package of economic and market liberalisation and increased integration into the global economy that the BWIs have long advocated. Indeed, in a 2004 assessment of the PRSP process, the World Bank's Operation Evaluation Department (OED) seems to agree with this critique. The OED argues that the principle of country ownership of PRSPs is undermined by the need for board approval, but that it is also incompatible with ongoing conditionality in World Bank and IMF country programmes. For the OED this often leads to 'self-censorship' and a very limited range of policies being proposed in the PRSPs of very different countries, a view often endorsed by civil society groups in developing countries themselves.

At the end of the three years of stage one a 'decision point' is reached. At this stage, if the rescheduling and other reforms introduced have been successful in making the debt burden sustainable, the country 'exits' the HIPC initiative. Alternatively, if the debt remains unsustainable – as judged by the boards of the IMF and World Bank – the country enters the second stage. At this point, all creditors commit to debt relief to be delivered at the 'floating completion point', with the amount of write-off determined by the reduction needed to bring total debt to sustainable levels.

Following criticisms that the HIPC process was too slow and cumbersome – as well as being unduly stringent on qualification criteria – the initiative was modified in 1999, as the enhanced HIPC (or HIPC2), which entailed three specific changes:

1   *Faster relief*, where the completion point could be reached faster in some instances, and some creditors began to provide debt relief immediately at the decision point;
2   *A stronger link between debt relief and poverty reduction*, where additional resources available following debt relief were earmarked to support poverty reduction strategies in the PRSPs;
3   *Deeper and broader relief* saw sustainable debt thresholds lowered from the original framework of HIPC1, resulting in more countries becoming eligible for the initiative.

This lower level of debt sustainability is defined as follows under HIPC2:

- a Net Present Value (NPV) of public (or publicly guaranteed) debt/exports ratio > 150%;
- a Net Present Value (NPV) of public (or publicly guaranteed) debt/revenue ratio > 250%.

Additional policies accompany this second stage, which the country then implements. These policies are agreed in the relevant PRSP and their successful implementation determines when the 'floating completion point' is reached. During this transitional second stage, the World Bank and IMF provide interim support, and other donors may provide interim debt relief at their discretion. However, all creditors are required to remain committed to supporting the PRSP designed by the government and civil society. When the 'completion point' is reached, all creditors provide the debt relief agreed at the 'decision point', which may be up to 90% of outstanding debt.

At present there are forty countries in the HIPC programme, with thirty of these having reached the decision or completion points (with the latter receiving the full package of committed debt relief) and ten more countries at an earlier stage of the process. Thus far, the 'completion point' countries have seen total debt reduced from US$75 to US$38 billion,[27] a reduction of US$37 billion.

What these figures reveal, however, is that even after the HIPC process has been completed, low-income countries have still been left with significant levels of external debt. Indeed, while the HIPC process succeeded in lowering the NPV of debt/exports ratio of HIPC countries from 317% in 1999 to 147% in 2005, this is perilously close to the threshold of 150% viewed as sustainable, and well above the 81% average ratio for non-HIPC LDCs (World Bank, 2006).

Most of the debt cancelled under HIPC has been that owed to bilateral creditors, with the remaining debt thus largely held by the multilateral development institutions. Following the global 'Make Poverty History Campaign' and the G8 meeting at Gleneagles in 2005,[28] a new debt initiative was announced in an effort to address this, with a particular focus on sub-Saharan Africa.

The multilateral debt reduction initiative (MDRI) is available to all countries that have completed the HIPC process. After its introduction in 2006, twenty-two eligible countries saw substantial debt relief, reducing their debt burden from US$38 billion to US$11 billion, which would appear to be as much as anyone could have expected. However, has this outcome produced the satisfaction that might be supposed?

7.5.3 The HIPC debate

For the World Bank and IMF, the HIPC initiative is largely seen as a great success. Others are far more critical however, particularly international development NGOs such as Jubilee 2000, Oxfam and Christian Aid.

The main criticisms are:

(a) Insufficient consideration for the HIPC's human development needs

The IMF and World Bank undertake their debt sustainability analysis (DSA) by looking at debt/export ratios. The NGOs say that the correct criteria for assessing sustainability is to look at whether the HIPCs have enough resources to meet the MDGs and to service their debt.

In 2006, the UNDP launched a research programme to examine how debt sustainability could be made compatible with countries' efforts to meet the MDGs. As part of this initiative, Spratt (2006) examined the resources required to meet the MDGs and concluded that, if we are serious about meeting the MDGs in the least developed countries, almost no external debt is 'sustainable' in the true sense. That is, the great majority of LDCs will require significant increases in external financial resources if they are to meet the MDGs, even after 100% of debt has been written off.

Table 7.3 compares the estimated expenditure needed to meet the MDGs in low-income countries in 2006, with the available government revenue. As we can see, even if LDCs spent 100% of government revenue on the MDGs, this would still be substantially less than that required. Consequently, within this framework, no external debt is 'sustainable'; rather, what is required is 100% debt relief followed by significantly increased ODA flows.

Table 7.3 Average low-income sustainability estimates for all low-income developing countries in 2006 (US$ bn)

Total GDP	1,391
Total govt. revenue	180.87
Total annual MDG investment needs*	253

Source: Spratt, 2006.

* Estimate from Millennium Project, 2005.

(b) Flawed conditionality

The IMF and World Bank have tended to declare countries 'off-track' because they are not meeting their poverty reduction and growth facility (PRGF) targets, such as reducing fiscal deficits and inflation and pursuing privatisation. However, for the critics, the real issue should be whether countries are successfully implementing their PRSPs and meeting their targets on poverty reduction rather than hitting specific macroeconomic targets.

(c) Too little progress

As of 2004, only fifteen countries had reached completion point, despite the enhanced HIPC initiative having begun five years earlier. Whilst $73 billion of external debt had been cancelled under HIPC and MDRI by 2007, this represents a small fraction of the US$500 billion of total debt owed by LDCs, many of whom are ineligible for the HIPC process.

From the NGO perspective, the complexity of conditionality delays debt relief, although there is consensus that debt relief must carry some conditions.

(d) Creditors are not 'burden-sharing' and the process is too 'creditor-dominated'

NGOs argue that multilateral and commercial creditors have not been carrying their share of the burden, and that some commercial creditors have gone further in attempting to sue the HIPCs for the full debt owed to them. The emergence of so-called 'vulture funds', which buy up discounted debt and then pursue aggressive litigation against the developing countries concerned to collect payment, is just the most blatant example of this trend.

The NGOs have also called for an independent arbitration panel to end creditor domination, and for the IMF and World Bank to allocate more resources to HIPC.

(e) Insufficient allowance is made for economic shocks

For example, as shown in Figure 7.16, commodity prices for many agricultural products saw their seemingly secular fall continue from the 1990s, leading to lower export earnings and tax takes for many HIPCs, but exogenous factors such as this are generally ignored.

Also, the impact of HIV/AIDS has not been fully taken into account, and will undoubtedly lead to lower growth in many HIPC countries.

(f) HIPC may crowd out ODA

The critics argue that HIPC should be provided from additional resources, not from the reallocation of existing budgets.

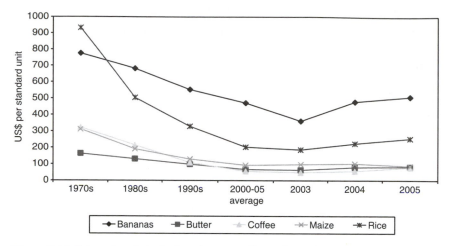

Figure 7.16 Selected real agricultural commodity prices, 1970–2005 (constant 2000 US$).

Source: FAO, 2007.

7.5.4 Debt sustainability

The issue of debt sustainability has become of increasing importance since the debt crisis of the 1980s. We have seen that, recently, critics of the HIPC initiative have called for the definition of sustainability to be changed, so that it is the level of debt (and debt servicing) that is compatible with a country being able to meet the MDGs.

At the same time, and particularly in response to the Asian crisis, the focus has shifted increasingly to the ratio of *short-term* debt, which, if too high, may facilitate a self-fulfilling liquidity-type crisis.

To date, the IMF and World Bank have not moved much on this issue, continuing to base their debt sustainability analyses on the simple quantitative indicators given above. More generally, the IMF (2003) argues that sustainable debt/GDP ratios are much lower in developing and emerging economies than is the case in developed countries. They suggest a sustainable limit for developing countries is 25%, whilst the Maastricht criteria for the EU set the sustainable debt figure at 60%.

There are two reasons for this:

1   Lower revenue/GDP ratios: as we have seen, government revenue as a proportion of GDP is much lower in developing than in developed countries.
2   As well as being lower, revenues are more volatile and more cyclical – countries with greater stability in this regard should be able to sustain higher levels of debt.

The issue of debt sustainability has a wider relevance than the HIPC initiative. There is currently no coherent international mechanism through which countries that are unable to service their debt burden, but do not qualify for the HIPC initiative, can reschedule or restructure their debts. That is, there is no equivalent of bankruptcy for countries.

In an attempt to fill this gap, the IMF published proposals for a Sovereign Debt Restructuring Mechanism (SDRM) in 2001, which would involve debtors and their creditors negotiating a mutually acceptable solution under the auspices of IMF oversight. All creditors would then have to abide by the outcome, which amongst other things would prevent 'vulture funds' from behaving as described above.

A key plank of the initiative was greater Private Sector Involvement (PSI), which was intended to produce a number of effects:

1   to ensure that the private sector felt the real economic effects of their lending decisions;
2   to ensure that the private sector did not assume eventual IMF support for debtor countries that get into trouble, thereby leading to moral hazard and reckless lending;
3   to offer an alternative to debtor countries of outright default;
4   to offer creditors an alternative to 'rushing for the exit' at the first sign of trouble, thereby exacerbating an already difficult decision; and
5   to provide a coherent, credible and transparent mechanism to work out sovereign debt issues in an international context.

Despite high hopes at the outset, the SDRM came to nothing, due to lack of support from (a) developing countries (who feared PSI would lead the private sector to reduce lending), and (b) the private sector (who were wary of the central role granted to the IMF in the process, not least because of the political pressure that the Fund is often subject to). There has also been limited academic support for the proposal, and politically, only the EU was enthusiastic.

Whilst the SDRM currently appears to be dead in the water, there is clearly a need for some mechanism. A variety of proposals have been put forward, with many debt campaigners agreeing that the IMF should not be at the centre of any new system.[29] As yet nothing has been agreed, which is all too often the case in the area of global development finance.

Concluding remarks

In this chapter we have examined the benefits and dangers for developing countries of opening their economies to external capital flows. We have seen that for both benefits and dangers different types of flows have different characteristics. FDI remains the form of capital flow with the most (potential) benefits and the least potential dangers, though even in this case it is by no means certain that the expected benefits will accrue, or the possible dangers be avoided.

The final section of Chapter 8 considers the need for international mechanisms for resolving issues of unsustainable debt in an equitable manner. As we have seen, there is currently no such framework and this points to a wider problem: many of the national mechanisms that have been developed to deal with the negative aspects of the financial system – particularly financial crises in all their forms – have no international equivalent. The reason for this is straightforward: there is no global institution with the democratic mandate needed to legitimately pursue such goals. Furthermore, there is no prospect of such a body emerging in the foreseeable future. However, the sheer scale and complexity of the international financial system means that national level problems are magnified at the international level, which suggests that such a framework is even more needed at the international than at the national level.

What we have instead – as has been touched on this chapter – is a rather *ad hoc* patchwork of institutions responsible for global economic and financial governance, some of which work reasonably well together, many of which do not. At the time of the Asian crisis, this came to be rather grandiosely called the 'International Financial Architecture', and there were many calls for it to be fundamentally reformed.

In Chapter 8 we will consider what has happened in this respect, though it may come as no great surprise to learn that in many ways the answer is: not much. As we shall see, this is not through the lack of sensible proposals, of which there have been many. Furthermore, the lack of major progress to date should not be taken to mean that attempts should just be abandoned. Reform of the international financial architecture is perhaps the most urgent task facing the financial world: the 'architecture' we have today is looking very creaky indeed.

8 The international financial architecture

Evolution, key features and proposed reforms

Introduction

In Chapter 7 we examined issues surrounding the impact of external capital flows to developing countries. We saw that the opportunities these inflows bring invariably entail risks, though the level of both opportunities and risks will vary by both the type of capital flow and the nature of the domestic financial system in different countries.

An important part of this nexus is the framework for global economic and financial governance within which these capital flows move. This has been termed the 'international financial architecture' (IFA), and is the subject of this chapter.

In its broadest sense, the IFA is comprised of global and regional bodies, particularly the Bretton Woods institutions (IMF and World Bank), the World Trade Organisation (WTO), the Bank for International Settlements (BIS), and the regional development banks (RDBs) in Africa, Asia and Latin America.

More narrowly, the IFA may be seen as those institutions and mechanisms that have developed to prevent, manage and resolve financial crises at the international level, and as such attention is largely focused on the Bretton Woods institutions.

The past decade has seen much talk of reform of the IFA, which has largely focused on the respective roles of the IMF and World Bank. This quite narrow focus is understandable, however, since the impetus for the rash of reform proposals we have seen was the shock of the Asian financial crisis of the late 1990s.

Everyone, it seems, agrees that the IFA is in need of major structural work, rather than a cosmetic lick of paint, though it should be noted that the volume of these calls for change has steadily reduced in more recent years, and is now barely a whisper compared to the situation in the wake of the Asian crisis.

In this chapter we will examine the evolution and current structure and activities of the main institutions of the IFA, before considering the varying arguments in favour of reform and concluding with an analysis of what all this talk of reform has actually produced.

8.1 The Bretton Woods institutions

Although representatives of forty-four countries gathered at Bretton Woods in New Hampshire in 1944, there were, in reality, only two key figures: John Maynard Keynes from the UK and Harry Dexter White of the US. The aim was to construct an international economic and financial system that would reduce instability, particularly in relation to the competitive currency devaluations that had marked the inter-war years, and the prevalence of restrictive bilateral trade agreements at that time. These factors, it was thought, had contributed directly to the Wall Street Crash, the Great Depression and so, ultimately, to the onset of the Second World War.

The time was one of faith in the power of the state to achieve desirable goals that the market, left to itself, was now seen as incapable of producing. The earlier faith in the ability of unfettered markets to produce optimal outcomes had been shattered by events, and the ability of governments to successfully manage capitalist economies directly had been demonstrated by the recent wartime experience.

At this time, the United States was the only major developed economy that remained intact – and was even strengthened – by the events of the war. This greatly enhanced the US's bargaining position – not least as it was the only major source of reconstruction funds in the then foreseeable future – which ensured that its viewpoints were largely reflected in the institutional structures that resulted.

These negotiations resulted in the birth of the three key Bretton Woods institutions[1] the International Monetary Fund (IMF), the International Bank for Reconstruction and Development (IBRD, which was to become the World Bank) and the General Agreement on Trade and Tariffs (GATT), which was to become the World Trade Organisation (WTO).[2] Each of these institutions had a specific function within the new system for international economic governance.

However, it should not be assumed that these institutions emerged into a vacuum: at their inception, they were just three institutions within a network of around 300 organisations, which were designed to address international economic matters, both regionally and globally. The most significant of these were: the Organisation for Economic Cooperation and Development (OECD), the European Economic Community (EEC) and the Bank for International Settlements (BIS).

8.1.1 The International Monetary Fund

The role of the International Monetary Fund (IMF) was to create a stable environment for international trade through encouraging the coordination of member countries' monetary policies and ensuring exchange rate stability. This latter function entailed the oversight of the post-war system of fixed exchange rates, where international currencies were pegged to the US dollar, which was in turn pegged to gold at US$35 per ounce. To support these efforts, the Fund was mandated to provide short-term financial support to countries experiencing temporary balance of payments difficulties.

The IMF was born in December 1945, when the first twenty-nine countries signed its 'Articles of Agreement'.[3] Member countries of the IMF were required to pay a 'quota' to the Fund, the size of which was based on the country's GDP. Each country's quota determined the amount of IMF financing it could access and, as well, its voting weight within the Fund. For voting rights, each member had 250 'basic votes' plus one additional vote for each US$100,000 of quota (later changed to 100,000 Special Drawing Rights [SDRs]).

The allocation of basic votes was designed to ensure that smaller member countries still had an audible voice within the IMF's decision-making bodies. In 1945, these forms of voting rights accounted for 11.3% of total votes. As the number of members grew, this initially caused the size of this block of votes to rise. For example, by 1956 the Fund's membership had risen to sixty-eight and the block of 'basic votes' then accounted for 15.6% of total votes, giving smaller countries greater influence. However, subsequently, the growth of the world economy and inflation combined to massively increase the relative importance of 'quota votes' (i.e. those based on a country's shareholding in the IMF, which is based on its relative economic size). By the turn of the twenty-first century, these factors had reduced the block of basic votes to around 2% of total voting, greatly reducing the influence of smaller countries and increasing that of the Fund's economically largest members (Buira, 2002).

The IMF's Articles of Agreement have been modified on a number of occasions since 1945. Today there are thirty-one Articles of Agreement, which cover a range of issues including: membership, quotas and voting rights, members' obligations, financing, IMF operations, special drawing rights (SDRs), emergency provisions and so on.

While there have a series of modifications of different Articles, Article I, which describes the purposes of the IMF, remains unchanged:

(i)   To promote international monetary cooperation through a permanent institution which provides the machinery for consultation and collaboration on international monetary problems.

(ii) To facilitate the expansion and balanced growth of international trade, and to contribute thereby to the promotion and maintenance of high levels of employment and real income and to the development of the productive resources of all members as primary objectives of economic policy.

(iii) To promote exchange stability, to maintain orderly exchange arrangements among members, and to avoid competitive exchange depreciation.

(iv) To assist in the establishment of a multilateral system of payments in respect of current transactions between members and in the elimination of foreign exchange restrictions which hamper the growth of world trade.

(v) To give confidence to members by making the general resources of the Fund temporarily available to them under adequate safeguards, thus providing them with the opportunity to correct maladjustments in their balance of payments without resorting to measures destructive of national or international prosperity.

(vi) In accordance with the above, to shorten the duration and lessen the degree of disequilibrium in the international balances of payments of members. [4]

Point (iv) above, might suggest that membership of the IMF precludes the use of capital controls. However, this is not the case today, and historically the opposite was *almost* true: at its inception, there was a concerted effort from Keynes for the IMF to *require* members to implement controls of capital flows. This was rejected by the US, however, and the final Articles gave countries the option of doing so.

Article IV, which deals with 'Obligations regarding exchange arrangements', states that:

> Recognizing that the essential purpose of the international monetary system is to provide a framework that facilitates the exchange of goods, services, and capital among countries, and that sustains sound economic growth, and that a principal objective is the continuing development of the orderly underlying conditions that are necessary for financial and economic stability, each member undertakes to collaborate with the Fund and other members to assure orderly exchange arrangements and to promote a stable system of exchange rates.

But the more specific references to capital transfers in Article VI, which deals with 'Capital transfers', clarifies:

> Members may exercise such controls as are necessary to regulate international capital movements, but no member may exercise these controls in a manner which will restrict payments for current transactions or which will unduly delay transfers of funds in settlement of commitments, except as provided in Article VII, Section 3(b) and in Article XIV, Section 2.

Under Article IV, the Fund has always been charged with the task of 'surveillance' of members' exchange rate regimes, in order to ensure the effective functioning of the international financial system. However, the key issue to bear in mind is that in this respect – as in many others – the IMF's role in the international financial system has changed radically since its inception. The focus at the outset was ensuring that the system of fixed exchange rates inaugurated at Bretton Woods was maintained, thus facilitating the growth of the international trading system. However, with the collapse of the fixed exchange rate system in the early 1970s, the IMF has sought a new rationale for its existence.

In the early 1980s, the LDC debt crisis provided an opportunity in this regard, and the Fund was instrumental in organising the Mexican rescue package that was described in Chapter 7. Since then, the IMF has retained its focus on ensuring the stability of the international monetary system, but what has led to major changes in the way the Fund approaches this has been an evolving understanding of what is needed to achieve this goal. In particular, the areas of interest to the Fund have progressively broadened since the 1970s.

In 1977, for example, the IMF's remit with regard to surveillance was considerably expanded, after the Executive Board decided that, in order to undertake a complete appraisal of exchange rate policy, the Fund would need to perform a comprehensive analysis of the general economic situation and policy strategy of each member country. This entailed an amendment to the IMF's Articles, which: 'also emphasized that the ultimate objective of surveillance is to help member countries achieve financial stability and sustainable economic growth' (IMF, 2005b).

IMF surveillance takes the form of 'Article IV consultations', which usually take place once a year. IMF staff visit the member country to gather information and hold discussions with government and central bank officials, and often private investors and labour representatives, members of parliament and civil society organisations.

In recent years, surveillance has become more transparent than was previously the case. Ninety per cent of member countries now agree to publication of a Public Information Notice (PIN), which summarises the staff's and the Board's views, and 80% to publication of the staff report itself.

Today, IMF surveillance covers the following areas:[5]

1   *Exchange rate, monetary and fiscal policy issues.* In this area, 'the IMF provides advice on issues ranging from the choice of exchange rate regime to ensuring consistency between the regime and fiscal and monetary policies'.
2   *Financial sector issues.* In 1999, the IMF and the World Bank created a joint Financial Sector Assessment Program (FSAP) to assess the strengths and weaknesses of countries' financial sectors; and FSAP findings provide important inputs into surveillance. This initiative was a direct result of the Asian financial crisis of 1997/8, which led to a greater understanding of the role that the financial sector can play in building up vulnerabilities to crisis and to transmitting the effects through the economy.
3   *Assessment of risks and vulnerabilities* from capital flows have become much more important in recent years. Again, this is a direct result of the increased incidence and severity of financial crises, as detailed in Chapter 7.

That is, the IMF has always been concerned with financial crises, but the attention paid to this issue has increased in tandem with the scale of the problem.

4   *Institutional and structural issues.* As with surveillance of the financial sector, the role of institutional issues (e.g. central bank independence, financial sector regulation, corporate governance and policy transparency and accountability) as well as structural policies (e.g. trade policy, labour market and energy policy) have also gained importance in the wake of financial crises and in the context of some member countries' transition from planned to market economies. In this regard:

The IMF and World Bank play a central role in developing, implementing, and assessing internationally recognized standards and codes in areas crucial to the efficient functioning of a modern economy such as central bank independence, financial sector regulation, and policy transparency and accountability.

While the BWIs have been the major players in the development of codes and standards (C&Ss), as well as assessing the extent to which they are being met in developing countries, the body charged with setting C&Ss is the Financial Stability Forum (FSF), which was also established in 1999. The FSF has promulgated twelve key standards in areas ranging from economic policy transparency, corporate governance, accounting and banking regulation, but each of these categories contains a much larger number of detailed 'recommendations'. As is discussed in some detail in Box 8.1 below, critics have argued that the C&S approach is inherently asymmetrical, as it places the responsibility for global financial stability and the elimination of crisis vulnerability squarely with developing countries, ignoring the role that the developed countries play in this process. Furthermore, as has been discussed in previous chapters, it is rarely the case that standards that have evolved to be appropriate for developed markets can simply be transplanted wholesale into a developing country situation.

Box 8.1 Codes and standards and the Financial Stability Forum (FSF)

In the aftermath of the Asian crisis there was a strong sense that 'something should be done'. Despite the differences of opinion on the primary causes of the crisis, there was a sense that economic and financial weaknesses in the domestic economies of affected countries, as well as shortcomings in financial regulation and supervision, had played a part in the onset of the crisis. Importantly, as well as the objective condition of these variables, the view was that greater transparency was needed. As we have seen, financial markets work on the basis of information and – in principle – should therefore be able to perform their theoretical functions well to the extent that this information is accurate.

In February 1999 Finance Ministers of the G7 agreed the establishment of the Financial Stability Forum (FSF), and the FSF was charged with promulgating international codes and standards (C&S) to establish a benchmark for best practice in areas thought to be of most importance.

Codes & Standards

1. Macroeconomic policy and data transparency

C&Ss under this heading cover: monetary and financial policy transparency; fiscal policy transparency; and data dissemination, with the benchmarks in each case being the codes of 'good practice' issued on these subjects by the IMF.

2. Institutional and market infrastructure

C&Ss under this heading cover: insolvency procedures; corporate governance; accounting and auditing; payment and settlement systems; and money laundering. The respective codes of best practice are those issued by: the World Bank; OECD; IASC; IFAC; CPSS; FATF.

3. Financial regulation and supervision

C&Ss under this heading cover: banking supervision; securities regulation; and insurance supervision. Issuing bodies for best practice are: BCBS; IOSCO; IAIS.

Within these three headings there are more than sixty specific standards, which are seen as reflecting international best practice. Following the promulgation of these C&Ss, the IMF established a review system – Reports on the Observation of Standards and Codes (ROSCs) – which countries could voluntarily agree to participate in. The ROSC process has also become intertwined with the IMF/World Bank Financial Sector Assessment Programs (FSAPs). ROSCs have focused on emerging and developing countries – it is generally assumed that developed economies are compliant, though as Schneider (2003) points out this is far from being the case in many instances.

While most people would support the idea of spreading international best practice in these important areas, the C&Ss have come in for considerable criticism:

- First, it is not clear what they are actually for. The impetus behind the C&S initiative was to reduce the potential for major financial crises, yet the level of detail in some cases goes well beyond what most would consider essential in this respect.
- Second, if the aim is to reduce the potential for crises many critics have highlighted the asymmetric nature of C&Ss. That is, while deficiencies in crisis-affected countries certainly play a part in the onset of crises, many have pointed to the influence of the sources of

speculation (highly leveraged hedge funds in developed markets, for example) as well as the highly volatile nature of the international financial system. In the way they are currently organised, the assumption seems to be that crises are entirely and solely the fault of the countries affected.

- Third, as is clear from the bodies which issue codes of best practice in each area, the process is generally an extension of how these have evolved in developed markets, and particularly in the United States. As Honohan and Stiglitz (2001) have argued, the financial sectors and institutional capacity in many developing countries are such that introducing models of financial regulation and supervision used in very developed financial systems may be ineffectual and even counterproductive.

- Finally, despite their breadth and depth, do C&Ss capture what they are supposed to? For example, prior to the default on its international debt, Argentina received a glowing report regarding its implementation of C&Ss.

As well as these changes to its surveillance activities, the IMF has, as we saw in Chapter 7, moved away from providing short-term financing to support members' balance of payments stability, to providing longer-term funds through a variety of funding facilities, and to imposing (or negotiating) various policy conditions attached to this lending.

However, as we shall see later in this chapter, critics argue that the Fund's role has developed in an *ad hoc* manner, lacking strategic direction, so that today it does many things that it should not, and does not do some things that it should.

8.1.2 The World Bank

As was the case with the IMF, the United States was an important player in the establishment of the IBRD, later to be known as the World Bank. However, unlike the Fund, the eventual structure of which was something of a compromise between the US and UK, the IBRD was almost entirely devised by the US in all its important respects.

Although the Bretton Woods institutions were formally a part of the United Nations system, there were important differences from the outset, and those differences largely remain. In particular, while the UN General Assembly operates a 'one member one vote' system, the Bretton Woods institutions are structured more like a private company, where members receive 'shares' in proportion to the funds they put into the institutions, with the size of these contributions being proportional to each member's status in the world economy. As with a private company, the proportion of 'shares' that each member holds is translated into 'shares', so that the largest economies become the largest shareholders with the largest voting rights.

In the previous section we saw how this structure has led to the IMF being increasingly dominated by its largest members, and the same is true for the World Bank. For example, at its foundation, the USA received 35.07% of the voting rights in the World Bank, with the UK being the second largest shareholder with 14.52% – together they therefore controlled almost 50% of the voting rights within the World Bank.

However, at its foundation, major decisions taken by the World Bank board required an 80% majority to pass. Uniquely, therefore, this gave the US an effective veto over policy, ensuring that only policies of which it approved were given serious consideration.

Over time the number of countries that are shareholders in the World Bank has increased, which has led to a dilution of the voting power of the founding members. For example, by the mid-1960s, the US's shareholding had fallen to around 25%, but this still gave it a power of veto. In 1987, however, a major reallocation of voting rights saw Japan granted additional shares – in reflection of its status in the global economy – with the US's shareholding falling to a little over 16%. An end to the veto then? Not really. In exchange for this dilution, the US raised the threshold on majority decision making from 80% to 85%, thus retaining its veto and therefore its firm grip on World Bank policy. This grip, of course, has also been supported by the fact that the President of the World Bank is 'nominated' (though never then rejected) by the US President and must be a US citizen – as a quid pro quo the head of the IMF is always a European, originally agreed by the European powers, and more recently by the European Union.

For many, this state of affairs has enabled the developed economies, particularly the US, to dominate the IMF and World Bank, which has led to the marginalisation of the UN, which could not be controlled in the same way. Indeed, at the inception of the Bretton Woods system, Keynes had argued strongly that the IMF and World Bank should be located in New York, to maintain close links with the UN, and avoid being overly influenced by political institutions based in Washington.[6] Henry Morgenthau – the US Treasury Secretary – insisted that the institutions should be based in Washington, however, and so they were and so they remain.

Although the size of shareholdings in the World Bank were determined by each country's 'subscribed capital', only 20% of this capital was ever actually paid to the Bank, with the remaining 80% remaining 'callable' if required. In effect, this capital guaranteed the operations of the Bank.

The Bank was (and is) permitted to lend up to 100% of its *subscribed* capital, with the conditions for lending set out in Article III of its constitution:

1   The recipient government must fully guarantee interest payments and repayment of the principal.
2   Borrowers must be creditworthy.

3   Funds must not be available elsewhere at reasonable cost.

Furthermore, Article IV stipulates that the Bank should not interfere in the political affairs of its members and that only economic considerations should be relevant to its decisions.

As its original name suggests, the IBRD was originally designed with the post-war reconstruction of Western Europe in mind. The 'development' aspect was, in general terms, secondary to this. For example, the Bank's first loan was made to France in 1947. This was for US$250 million and in real terms remains the largest that the Bank has made. However, the introduction of the Marshall Plan in the same year largely removed this reconstruction role from the Bank.

A second early change in the Bank's approach related to its lending. Originally, the intention was that the Bank would not make loans directly, but would focus on guaranteeing the issuance of bonds from developing countries. The aim was to restart the flow of private capital from developed to developing countries, which had been sharply reduced in the Great Depression and then eliminated by the Second World War.

However, it became clear very early on that the private sector was simply not interested in such investments, and the Bank decided by 1947 that it would be more effective to provide loans directly itself (Culpeper, 1997).

While the conditions described above set out the circumstances under which the Bank would lend, these only relate to one part of its activities: 'hard' lending (i.e. on broadly commercial terms). From the beginning the World Bank did not loan its own capital, but issued bonds in the international capital markets and used the financing to provide loans. It took the Bank some time to convince the markets of the worth of these bonds, but over time this was achieved. Following this acceptance, the World Bank launched the International Finance Corporation (IFC) in 1956, with the remit to lend to the private sector in developing countries without government guarantees, and thereby to complement the World Bank's focus on lending to governments.

However, in order to convince the US Treasury to permit the establishment of the IFC, the Bank agreed to two conditions: the IFC could not offer equity finance and also had a quite small founding level of capital. These conditions – as well as other factors such as lower demand for IFC services than had been expected and difficulties in obtaining private partners to co-invest – kept the IFC's transactions at a much lower level than had been anticipated. It was only after the IFC's Charter was modified in 1961 to allow it to provide equity financing, as well as other structural and operational reforms, that it began to increase its financial activities.

As mentioned above, 'hard' loans from the World Bank to governments are also offered on broadly commercial terms.[7] However, because the Bank has (and retains) a Triple-A credit rating (the highest that can be obtained) it is able to borrow very cheaply in the capital markets. This very high rating is a function of the fact that the Bank's 'callable' capital from its shareholders effectively guarantees the repayment of any bond issued by the Bank.

However, it became clear relatively early on that many of the poorest countries could not support debt service and repayment on commercial terms, and were therefore not eligible for World Bank support under the loan conditions given above. To address this, the World Bank established the International Development Association (IDA) in 1960, which was charged with providing 'soft' loans and grants of long maturities to the poorest LDCs. IDA issued its first loans (or credits) in 1961 to Chile, Honduras, India and the Sudan.

Unlike its hard loan facility, the Bank did not (and does not) raise the funds for this purpose on the international capital markets. Instead, donors provide direct financing to the IDA, which forms the basis of its soft – or concessional – lending programmes. IDA's capital base has therefore required regular 'replenishments', of which there have been fourteen to date.[8]

For the first quarter of a century of its operations, the World Bank's lending focused on large-scale product lending on infrastructure, particularly power and transport. From 1960 to 1970, for example, 55% of the Bank's total lending went to these sectors, 31% went to the productive sectors (agriculture had 15% and industry 16%), with the social sectors accounting for just 5% (Culpeper, 1997).

In general, this focus on infrastructure, agriculture and industry lending was, at least in part, a function of the requirement on the Bank under Article IV to not interfere in the politics of its member countries and to focus solely on economic issues.

By the 1970s, however, a major shift had taken place in the Bank's thinking, where under the presidency of Robert McNamara there was a shift away from the overwhelming focus on economic growth with the Bank's primary objective now being to alleviate poverty in developing countries. Reflecting this, the Bank's lending patterns shifted significantly towards 'social' areas. As we have seen, social lending constituted just 5% of all World Bank lending in the 1960s. By the mid-1990s, in contrast, the figure was 13.5% (ibid.).

In a further development, the World Bank introduced 'policy-based' structural adjustment lending in 1980, which saw its influence over the internal politics and policy stance of borrowers increase dramatically. To qualify for World Bank financial support, borrowing countries had to sign up to an agreed package of structural reforms. Continuing support was then conditional on their fulfilling these obligations.

From the start, structural adjustment programmes (SAPs) were based on the premise that growth – and therefore poverty reduction – could only be achieved by deep structural reforms in the economy. In many ways this is analogous to the contemporaneous financial liberalisation programme that was discussed in detail in Chapter 3. Indeed, financial liberalisation was very often a key component of SAPs. Financial liberalisation aimed to establish the free market mechanism as the setter of prices in the financial system. Similarly, SAP effectively extended this to the real economy. The standard formulae were therefore price liberalisation (exchange rates, input/output prices, wages, etc.), fiscal probity (tax increases and/or expenditure cuts) and the more general removal of the state from active intervention in the economy, so as to make space for the private sector to (dynamically) fill the gap, now provided with the 'correct signals' due to the price liberalisation described above.

Very early on, however, it became clear that SAPs could have very negative impacts upon poverty and human development, as government spending was cut, government employee numbers sharply reduced, and price caps on many essential items removed. For the Bank and the Fund, this was a transitional issue, which would be resolved as the reforms generated accelerated growth, but the increasingly vociferous critics were either unconvinced that this was true or, even if they were, were unprepared to wait.

Responding to this, the Bank introduced the 'social dimensions of adjustment' programmes in 1987, which aimed to improve social outcomes by protecting important programmes in these areas. However, this was seen as a transitional measure, to be tagged on to the implementation of structural adjustment programmes, which remained unchanged in all key respects.

Structural adjustment programmes thus became 'enhanced structural adjustment programmes' (ESAP), which in turn became the 'poverty reduction and growth facility' (PRGF) in the mid-1990s. This evolution saw issues of poverty and human development (notably relating to education and health) become increasingly important, at least in rhetorical terms. Critics argued that the underlying policies of economic and financial liberalisation remained largely unchanged, however.

More recently, there has been a greater focus on country 'ownership' of these reform programmes, with countries wishing to access financial support from the IMF or the World Bank being required to draw up 'poverty reduction strategy papers' (PRSPs). These national PRSPs are supposed to be the result of wide consultation with civil society groups, thus ensuring legitimacy and encouraging governments to stick to the reform programme. As with the changes on poverty, this stance would appear to be related to the widespread criticism that the Bank and the Fund have received for imposing policies on countries.

Despite these changes, the Bretton Woods institutions are still the recipients of trenchant criticism for their role in developing countries, particularly with relation to the imposition of structural adjustment programmes in all their guises. One of the first countries to implement an SAP in the early 1980s was Ghana, which has subsequently been hailed – by the BWIs – as an exemplar of the success that such reform programmes can achieve. Box 8.2 below examines these claims.

Box 8.2 Structural adjustment in Ghana

At the time of independence in 1957 the consensus was that, in relative terms, the British had left Ghana with a better legacy than many other countries in sub-Saharan Africa. In 1957 Ghana was the largest producer and exporter of cocoa in the world, exported one-tenth of the world's gold and had substantial foreign exchange reserves. Moreover, its infrastructure was relatively well developed, in human capital terms the country had the best-trained and skilled workforce in sub-Saharan Africa, and Ghana's per capita income identified it as a middle-income country, comparable with South Korea.

By the mid- to late 1960s, however, the situation had changed radically: growth had fallen to 0.4%, foreign exchange reserves had been largely exhausted and external debt had reached unsustainable levels. Living standards plummeted, with the minimum wage at half the level of independence, and poverty levels considerably higher. The economic decline continued throughout the 1970s: between 1970 and 1983, import volumes fell by 33%, export earnings – in real terms – halved and the domestic savings and investment rates fell from 12% of GDP to effectively zero. By the early 1980s, inflation stood at more than 100% and per capita incomes had fallen from US$1,009 in 1960, to US$739 (Konadu-Agyemang, 2000).

In 1983, the IMF arrived in a country on the verge of economic collapse. Together with the World Bank, the Fund was to have a pivotal role in shaping Ghana's economic policy in the subsequent decades, with the country being something of a testing ground for the Bretton Woods Institutions' (BWI) framework of economic reform, embodied in the evolving structural adjustment programmes of the 1980s.

Economic Reform Programme 1 (ERP1): 1983–1986

In what was to become the common pattern of structural adjustment programmes, the first Economic Reform Programme (ERP1) was aimed at halting the decline and stabilising the economy of the country. The overall aim was to correct the internal and external imbalances in the economy and realign incentives to make an increase in the trend rate of growth possible.

Specific policies: exchange rate devaluation; removal of trade barriers; price liberalisation; tightened monetary and fiscal policy (i.e. increased interest rates and tax increases/expenditure reductions). The reforms were successful in the sense that negative growth became positive.

ERP2: 1987–1990

The second stage of the reform process saw deeper changes in the economy, focusing on removing remaining price distortions, agriculture-led development, 'retrenching' public sector workers, introducing competition to all sectors of the economy and building institutional capacity to sustain high rates of growth over the longer term, particularly with regard to the liberalisation of the financial sector. The reforms were not successful in maintaining the target growth rate of more than 5%, as the economy stalled in the late 1980s.

ERP3: 1993–2000

As with its predecessor, the third ERP emphasised the importance of boosting long-term growth as the key means of reducing poverty. To this end, the Accelerated Growth Strategy (AGS) of 1993 listed the following objectives: growth to 8%; inflation to 5%; savings and investment rates to above 20%; tax revenues to 18%. Of these objectives, only increasing the tax take and investment rates were met.

The Poverty Reduction Strategy Paper (PRSP)

With a per capita income level of less than US$300 Ghana was eligible for the IMF's Poverty Reduction and Growth Facility (PGRF), which was the latest incarnation of the Fund's structural adjustment programmes. However, to qualify for access to this facility – and to the World Bank's 'soft loan' (IDA) window – Ghana was required to prepare a Poverty Reduction Strategy Paper (PRSP).

The PRSP was ostensibly designed to mark a step-change in the development process, with a determined emphasis on poverty alleviation. However, this is to be achieved by increasing growth rates based on liberalisation and agricultural development, the benefits of which will trickle down to the poor. As the Ghanaian NGO ISODEC (2002) points out, however, these are the same policies that have been implemented consistently since the reforms began:

> the sources of the modest growth projections themselves are not so apparent and may well be dependent policies that have failed in the past to deliver growth such as trade and capital account, liberalization and a financing of growth model resting too heavily on foreign resource expectations especially private foreign income.
>
> (2002: 4)

In 2006, real GDP per capita in Ghana was $300 up from $200 in 1981, but the same as in 1970.

As with the IMF, therefore, the World Bank has changed its approach significantly since its inception (though not to the same extent). In both cases, this can partly be explained by changing perceptions of how its key role should be performed.

For example, the IMF is charged with ensuring a stable international financial framework. Initially this was largely achieved through the maintenance of a fixed exchange rate regime. However, with the collapse of this regime, and the increase in financial volatility and complexity that has subsequently occurred, the IMF has widened its role to incorporate ever more elements that might be relevant to achieving its function.

Similarly, the World Bank's original focus on economic growth was increasingly augmented with the aim of alleviating poverty. This represents a recognition that, although the Bank still sees growth as the primary engine of poverty alleviation,[9] it now recognises – or has been forced to recognise – that it must be more explicit about its poverty-reducing aim. The original understanding that the Bank would focus on purely 'economic' matters remains relevant. However, the perception of what factors impact upon poverty alleviation and growth has changed substantially over the past decades, so that the perceived importance of 'social issues' has risen significantly.

As we saw in Chapter 2, the dominant Harrod-Domar model saw growth as driven by increased investment. However, more recent work on endogenous growth models[10] has increasingly emphasised the importance of factors such as financial sector development and, importantly, human capital development. Thus, while growth may lead to reductions in poverty, investments in education and health, for example, were increasingly seen as important factors in generating growth.

Therefore, for both the Fund and the Bank, it seems that the understanding of how to achieve their (broadening) roles has changed, so that by the 1980s it came to be believed that neither economic stability nor poverty alleviation could be achieved without fundamental reform of many aspects of borrowing countries' economies, that would formerly have been seen as beyond their remit.

Whilst the World Bank is the pre-eminent global development finance institution, it has three regional 'cousins'. The next section will briefly consider these regional development banks in Latin America, Asia and Africa.

8.1.3 The regional development banks

The first RDB to be launched was in Latin America in 1960. The Inter-American Development Bank (IDB) had been proposed by Latin American developing countries as early as the 1890s, but was rejected by the US. Despite this, a later, similar proposal in 1940 formed the basis of the original structure of the World Bank. Following the Bank's launch, the US remained hostile to the creation of the IDB until the late 1950s, when anti-US sentiment in Latin America, coupled with the Cuban revolution and missile crisis, caused a change of mind in the US administration. Once the US was supportive, the negotiations were quickly concluded, and the IDB was launched in 1960 (Culpeper, 1997).

It was six more years before the other two regional banks were established. Like the IDB, the catalyst for the establishment of the Asian Development Bank (AsDB) was a shift in US geopolitical policy. Before 1965, the US had been against the proposal, but this viewpoint was altered by the escalation of the Vietnam War, which again suggested the need for regional capitalist institutions to offset support for communism. Such an institution, it was thought, could promote capitalist economic development, and so facilitate the emergence of successful capitalist economies, as an example to any potential 'dominoes' in the region that might be tempted by the lure of communism.

The African Development Bank (ADB) was also launched in 1966, but uniquely owed little to US support. The concept of the ADB was first floated in 1961 by post-colonial African politicians themselves, and negotiations between the African states that were to be the bank's members lasted for three more years. These were finally concluded in 1964, and the ADB began operations two years later.

In organisational terms, there are many similarities between the RDBs and the World Bank, but also clear differences in some regards. For example, all these institutions have both a 'hard' lending facility – established on similar terms to that of the World Bank – and 'soft' lending programmes funded directly by donors. As we have seen, the World Bank's soft lending is conducted through the IDA; for the IDB, the relevant body is the 'Fund for Special Operations' (FSO), which was incorporated in the IDB from the outset. The ADB launched a soft loan facility in 1973, under the title of the 'African Development Fund' (ADF), with the AsDB amalgamating its soft lending operations as the 'Asian Development Fund' (AsDF) in 1974 (ibid.).

A major organisational difference, however, lies in the relationship between borrowers and non-borrowers (i.e. developing countries vs. developed countries). The World Bank categorises non-borrowers as 'Part 1' members, and borrowers as 'Part 2' members. In terms of voting rights, Part 1 members control 60% of World Bank votes, and thus can block any initiative from borrowing countries. As a result, the Bank has traditionally been dominated by non-borrowing, developed countries – given the distribution of votes, the World Bank's Board only proposes initiatives which it knows have the support of Part 1 members.

Like the World Bank, the AsDB was established as a donor initiative, in this case Japan. From the outset, non-borrowing members of the AsDB have had majority voting rights within the bank – by tradition, the bank's president is Japanese.

The IDB in contrast, established a minimum voting block for borrowing countries (i.e. developing countries) of 53.5% from the outset, and this remains the case today. Therefore while the US may be the largest financial contributor, it cannot secure a voting majority without the support of developing countries. The IDB is therefore 'borrower-dominated and controlled', a situation reflected with the ADB (ibid.).

Unlike the other development banks described here, the ADB had no developed country members when it was launched. Indeed, non-regional countries were not allowed to join the ADB until 1982. Whilst this gave the ADB more autonomy than the other RDBs, it did leave them with significantly fewer resources than the others that had developed country members from the outset.

For example, by 1969 the ADB had only disbursed US$1 million over the first three years of its existence. Things did pick up a little subsequently, but remained tiny in relation to the other RDBs: in the 1970–1972 period the ADB's average disbursement was US$21 million, compared with US$685 million for the IDB and US$172 million for the AsDB.

Prior to 1973, the ADB had only offered non-concessional lending. External donations of US$83 million enabled the bank to open the ADF in 1973, however. These soft-loan resources were boosted further in 1976 with a US$89 million donation from Nigeria – reflecting sharply higher oil revenues following the OPEC price hikes – but it was increasingly clear that the external sources of revenue were needed. Consequently, the ADB's constitution was amended in 1982 to admit non-regional members but, as with the IDB, non-regional members were not permitted to hold a majority voting share in the Board's decisions (Hafsi and Le-Louarn, 1999).

As we have seen, the first few decades of the World Bank's lending were dominated by infrastructure, agriculture and industry lending with a very limited social component. This pattern was mirrored in the lending practices of the AsDF and the ADB, which also largely avoided social lending. In contrast, the IDB focused on social development from the outset, which was a very heterodox approach in the context of the 1960s. By the end of the 1970s, however, lending patterns between all the development banks had largely converged, with all recognising the importance of lending to the social sectors of their respective regions.

This convergence became divergence in the 1980s, however, as the World Bank pursued policy-based structural adjustment lending programmes throughout the decade. The RDBs, in contrast, avoided this form of lending until the end of the decade, but by the 1990s lending patterns had largely converged again (Culpeper, 1997).

This distribution of lending of course says nothing about the scale of lending by each of these institutions. Figure 8.1 below details this, and breaks down the figures into capital available for 'hard' lending, and that available for 'soft' lending.

As we can see, the resources available to the World Bank dwarf those of the RDBs. One would certainly expect this to be the case for any individual regional bank, but the World Bank's resources are also greater than the combined capital resources of the RDBs. For hard lending, the difference is not

Table 8.1 Sectoral distribution of cumulative lending, 1995 (percentage)

Sector	IBRD/IDA	IDB/FSO	AsDB/AsDF	ADB/ADF
Agriculture	20.9	15.7	22.8	27.7
Transport	15.8	13.5	19.9	18.9
Energy	17.4	19.9	25.9	24.3
Industry	15.7	13.0	14.0	18.4
Social	13.5	16.6	15.5	10.8

Source: Culpeper, 1997.

particularly great – US$176 billion vs. 133 billion – but in the soft lending category, the World Bank's capital resources are more than double that of the combined resources of the RDBs.

This strongly suggests that donor governments – i.e the source of capital for the soft lending institutions – prefer to channel their resources through the World Bank than through its regional cousins.

A final comparison of their relative regional influence is given by the amount of resources that the RDBs have pumped into their region, relative to the resources supplied by the World Bank. These are illustrated in cumulative form to 1995 in Figure 8.2 below.

As we can see, the World Bank is dominant (in resource terms) in all the regions. However, the extent of this varies widely. For example, while the IDB has approved loans to 86% of the value of World Bank loans in Latin America, the figures for the AsDB and ADB are 39% and 38% respectively. These differences are largely explained by the relative capital resources held by each of the RDBs, as shown in Figure 8.1 below. As we see, the IDB has

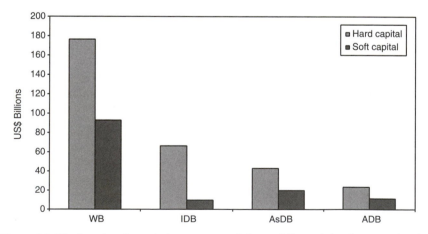

Figure 8.1 Hard and soft capital resources of the multilateral development banks, 1995.

Source: Culpeper, 1997.

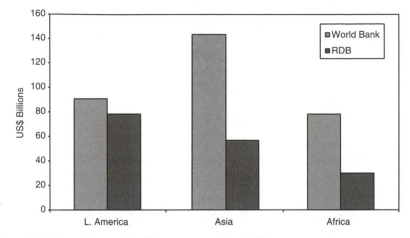

Figure 8.2 Cumulative regional loan approvals to 1995.

Source: Culpeper, 1997.

more than double the capital resources held by the ADB, and considerably more than its Asian counterpart as well.

It is perhaps unsurprising, given the relative dominance of the World Bank, that borrowing countries have tended to place more importance on their relationship with the Bank than with their respective RDBs. Furthermore, this financial clout is augmented by political muscle, so that developing countries which maintain good relations with the World Bank (and the IMF of course) are also more likely to obtain other benefits, notably – but not exclusively – debt relief.

To summarise, we have seen that the Bretton Woods institutions have seen their roles changed significantly since they were founded in 1944. In part, this has been a result of changing circumstances (such as the collapse of the system of fixed exchange rates that the IMF was established to 'police'), but it has also been influenced by changing perceptions of how their objectives – stability, growth and poverty reduction – should best be realised.

The IMF, for example, has come to view issues of financial stability in a much broader sense than was originally conceived. Similarly, the World Bank's initial focus on economic growth (encouraged by the requirement that the Bank did not intervene politically) came to be increasingly accompanied by a focus on poverty alleviation, with poverty and growth – to some extent – being seen as two sides of the same coin, where progress on one side was dependent upon progress on the other.

By the 1980s this had become highly prescriptive, as the IMF/World Bank (and later the RDBs) implemented lending programmes conditional on particular policy reforms, under the 'stabilisation' or 'structural adjustment' programmes. More recently, the emphasis on country 'ownership' has seen the Bank and the Fund attempt to respond to claims that they have imposed policies on countries in no position to object. However, critics claim that the strict parameters placed around the 'set' of policy options available to countries – and recall that all PRSPs must be approved by the Boards of the Fund and the Bank – results in the same policies being followed, regardless of the packaging.

Before moving to issues of reform of the international architecture, however, the next section reviews the evolution of the third pillar of the Bretton Woods system: GATT and the World Trade Organisation.

8.1.4 From GATT to the WTO to the Doha Trade Round

We have seen that the primary aim of the Bretton Woods conference of 1944 was to restore stability to the system of international trade, the disturbance of which – resulting from trends such as competitive currency devaluations and the imposition of trade restrictions – was seen as having been a major contributor to the onset of the Second World War.

As well as the IMF and IBRD, a key plank of this effort was originally to have been the establishment of the International Trade Organisation (ITO). Negotiations on the remit and structure of the ITO culminated in the 'Havana Charter', which was signed by fifty-three countries in 1948. The Charter was a combination of idealism and realism, with some proponents seeing free trade as an essential component of long-term peace and prosperity. To guarantee this, the ITO was to have far-reaching powers that moved beyond simple tariff reduction, incorporating issues of domestic policy such as employment law, for example. However, others – notably the British – insisted on being able to maintain their preferential trading system based on the British Empire.

This uneasy alliance, however, ultimately came to nothing. Increasing Cold War tensions and the now Republican-dominated US Congress made it increasingly clear that the ITO would not be ratified in the US. The project – it seemed – was dead in the water (Narlikar and Williamson, 2004).

Initially, GATT had been envisaged as a transitional measure that would establish a framework for international trade to operate until the ITO came into being. In practice, GATT itself became *the* international framework for trade negotiations and reform for the better part of half a century. GATT came into force in January 1948 with twenty-three original signatories. The Agreement was a far looser and less formal framework than that envisaged under the ITO, which largely restricted itself to government-to-government tariff negotiations regarding the trade in physical goods. Importantly, GATT steered clear of interference in domestic policy and was essentially just a forum for negotiations with no powers of compulsion and a very limited dispute settlement mechanism. Again, this is in sharp contrast to the mooted ITO.

Of the original twenty-three signatories, eleven were developing countries. However, they were marginalised in the negotiating process, which enabled the developed countries to protect sectors where the developing countries would have had a comparative advantage. Consequently, agriculture and textiles were excluded from the start (ibid.).

Since 1947, there have been a number of 'rounds' of negotiations, which saw tariff levels in developed countries fall from an average of 40% in 1947 to 5–6% by the early 1980s. Until recent times, developing countries had not been asked to make major cuts to their tariff levels, with the result that tariffs on trade remain substantially higher in developing countries than is the case in the developed markets. However, developing countries did not benefit as much as the developed nations from greater access to export markets, as many of the products in which they have tended to specialise – agriculture and textiles, in particular – remained outside the sectors covered by GATT agreements.

The number of countries that are signatories to GATT has increased steadily from its inception, so that by the time of the conclusion of the Uruguay round in the mid-1990s there were 123 participating countries. The Uruguay Round from 1986 to 1993 changed the nature of trade negotiations substantially. In the first few rounds, negotiations had focused purely on tariff reductions in physical goods. However, the Uruguay round saw the inclusion of services,[11] as well as 'trade related investment measures' (TRIMS),[12] and 'trade related intellectual property rights' (TRIPS).[13] As was the case in the 1940s, this represented efforts by developed countries to push for liberalisation in areas where they had a comparative advantage, such as the service sector. The round resulted in the replacement of GATT with the World Trade Organisation (WTO), which came into being in 1995 with 128 founding members.

Unlike previous Rounds, developing countries were also asked to commit to significant tariff reductions. This pill was sweetened, though the concept of 'special and differential treatment' – whereby poorer countries are not expected to fully comply with all WTO rules – was retained. This was – and is – seen as a transitional measure, however, with the longer-term goal being equal treatment for all countries, developed and developing alike.

Also, in return for agreeing to the incorporation of TRIMS and TRIPS, and the establishment of the WTO with much greater powers than its predecessor, the developing countries saw previously excluded areas such as agriculture and textiles being incorporated into the new body (Narlikar, op. cit.).

As well as this broader remit, the WTO differs from GATT in some important ways:

1   It is a legally established, permanent global body.
2   Countries are no longer able to avoid implementing agreements if they are incompatible with existing domestic regulation – the so-called 'grandfather clause'.
3   Members must accept all WTO agreements in their entirety.
4   The WTO has a very strong dispute resolution mechanism, with the power to adjudicate on disputes and, if necessary, to authorise countries

to take retaliatory action commensurate with the level of the discrimination against them (ibid.).

The Uruguay Round therefore bought fresh challenges to developing countries, but also opportunities in terms of scope for increasing access to the markets of the developed world. This potential is illustrated in Table 8.2 below, which shows the remaining tariffs that existed in developed markets after the Uruguay Round.

As can be seen, average tariffs for manufactured goods remained at 4% for the high-income countries covered, and 12.9% for middle-income countries. The corresponding figures for agriculture were 10.7% and 26.2% respectively, though maximum tariffs in the agricultural sector remaining in place were as high as 500% for the EU and 350% for the US. Thus, even after the Uruguay Round was concluded, the large number of developing countries that rely on agricultural exports continued to find their access to developed country markets greatly restricted.

Furthermore, whilst average tariff levels remained significant they also rose progressively as you progress upwards through the 'value-added' chain. That is to say, tariffs become progressively higher as production moves through the stages of processing. As can be seen in Table 8.3 below, this 'tariff escalation' is certainly not restricted to developed countries, however.

Thus, although increasing the quantity of manufactured exports and moving up the value chain is a key component linking trade to higher economic growth,[14] developing countries will find their ability to move up to the next 'link' of the chain greatly impeded by tariff escalation of this kind. Also, as Table 8.3 highlights, this is particularly true for sectors such as food and tobacco and textiles, clothing and leather, where one would expect many developing countries to have a potential advantage. Lastly, even getting this process started is likely to prove very difficult of course, due to the very high tariffs on agricultural exports.

The current stage of WTO negotiations – the Doha Round – was launched in 2001. Perhaps as a result of pressure from developing country governments,

Table 8.2 Average tariffs applied to agriculture and manufactures, 1999–2001

	Manufactures	Agriculture	
Country or group	Average tariff	Average tariff	Maximum tariff
Quad	4.0	10.7	—
Canada	3.6	3.8	238.0
EU	4.2	19.0	506.3
Japan	3.7	10.3	50.0
United States	4.6	9.5	350.0
Middle-income countries	12.9	26.2	—

Source: World Bank, 2004.

Table 8.3 Tariff escalation, 2001–2003

Process	US	EU	Japan	Canada	China	India	Brazil	S. Africa
Total								
1st stage	4.4	8.1	14.5	5.0	11.3	28.6	7.9	5.5
Semi-processed	4.8	4.9	4.9	3.9	9.7	32.3	9.6	12.9
Fully processed	5.5	7.0	7.8	8.9	14.0	33.0	13.4	11.5
Food, beverages and tobacco								
1st stage	3.6	13.2	23.6	10.2	15.3	36.3	9.4	10.7
Semi-processed	8.8	19.1	20.3	6.8	28.1	36.6	12.6	10.3
Fully processed	12.5	18.7	22.6	34.1	21.5	48.2	15.0	15.4
Textiles, clothing and leather								
1st stage	3.8	1.0	10.2	1.1	13.0	25.9	9.1	5.0
Semi-processed	9.3	6.7	6.8	6.9	15.1	28.4	15.8	22.1
Fully processed	10.1	9.8	12.0	13.5	20.4	34.2	19.3	32.4

Source: Acharya and Daly, 2004.

NGOs and other interest groups – but also, one would hope, in recognition of the remaining trade-related obstacles to development – the Doha Round was described as a 'development round' from the outset.

Negotiations have not gone smoothly to date, however, suffering numerous breakdowns with different sides blaming the other. Developing countries, particularly the larger ones such as Brazil, India and China, have been able to form powerful coalitions to forward their interests. Their agenda has focused on securing fair access to developed markets for the products described above as being of most importance to developing countries. Developed countries, in contrast, have tried to link these negotiations to wider issues such as the liberalisation of services.

In July 2004 some progress was made, when a framework for negotiations was agreed – that is, all sides agreed what they would negotiate on. At that stage, the aim was to have made concrete progress by the Sixth Ministerial Conference of the WTO in Hong Kong in December 2005, and to have concluded negotiations by the end of 2006. This has long since been and gone.

The Hong Kong Conference did not bring the breakthrough that was hoped for, however, with many criticising developed countries, particularly the EU, for refusing to make substantive changes to agricultural tariffs. In response the EU trumpeted the commitment to end export subsidies by 2013, but it needs to be borne in mind that it is not export subsidies that do the real damage, but subsidies to the domestic producers in developed countries: while export subsidies for EU cereals were reduced from €2.2 billion to €121 million in 2002, domestic subsidies that benefited cereal exporters rose from €117 million to €1.3 billion in the same year.

The Doha Round continues to grind on, but there is, at present, little sign of the breakthrough that would be required to secure real progress. For all countries, trade negotiations are worthwhile to the extent that countries expect to benefit from the outcome. Box 8.3 below gives some estimates on the predicted distribution of benefits that could result from a successful conclusion of the Doha Round.

Box 8.3 Estimated regional distribution of welfare benefits from Doha Round

Source	Unit	50% tariff cut	50% domestic support cut	Removal of export subsidies
Hoekman, Ng and Olearraga, 2003	$ 1985 bn			
World		16.8	0.2	–
Industrialised		14.5	0.5	–
Developing		2.3	–0.3	–
LDCs		0.0	0.0	–
Francois, van Meigl and van Tongeren, 2003	$ 1987 bn			
World		57	8.7	–
EU		9.8	8.4	–
N America		2.7	2.2	–
High income Asia		16.1	–0.5	–
Middle, low income Asia		7.5	–0.3	–
C. & E. Europe		1.7	0.0	–
Mediterranean		15.0	–0.6	–
S. America		2.0	–0.2	–
SS Africa		2.7	–0.1	–
Others		–0.5	–0.2	–
Laird, Cennart and Turrini, 2003	$ 1985 bn			
World		30.3	–	–4.7
Developed		11.1	–	1.9
Transition		0.2	–	–0.9
Developing		9.5	–	–2.9
NIEs & China		4.4	–	–0.2
S. Asia		0.3	–	0.0
SS Africa		0.2	–	–0.4
N. Africa & M. East		3	–	–2.2
L. America		1.3	–	0.1
Other		0.3	–	–0.2
Dimamaran, Hertel and Keeney, 2004	$ 1985 bn			
Developing		–	–0.4	–
Asia		–	–0.1	–
L. America		–	0.1	–

N. Africa & M. East	–	–0.3	–
SS Africa	–	–0.1	–
Other	–	0.0	–

Source: UN (2005).

Although some estimates of the total gains from full liberalisation of world trade can run into the hundreds of billions, the table above looks at the more feasible objectives of a halving of import tariffs, a halving of support for domestic producers and the elimination of export subsidies. When we compare the impact of tariff cuts vs. cuts in domestic support (i.e. subsidising domestic producers) we see that higher benefits result from the former, but that the bulk of these benefits would accrue to developed economies.

Conversely, the poorest parts of the developing world are expected to benefit least from these tariff reductions. It is also important to note that developing regions are generally estimated to lose from cuts in domestic support in developed markets.

The point to bear in mind is that, while the theoretical benefits of free trade are broadly accepted, these are not distributed evenly. In particular, those countries with a large, internationally competitive export sector able to take full advantage of the new opportunities are likely to benefit most. Also, while the 'infant industries' argument has fallen out of favour (though it is showing signs of a comeback) it is important to bear in mind that exposing countries to the full force of competition at an early stage may prevent them from ever developing internationally competitive companies in many sectors.

As we have seen, the Bretton Woods conference on 1944 spawned the three pillars of the international finance and trading system we have today: the IMF, the World Bank and the WTO. Many – though as we shall see, not all – of the recent proposals to reform the international financial architecture have focused on the role of the first two of these institutions, and particularly that of the IMF. This proposed reform is the subject of our next section.

8.2 The creaky international financial architecture in the 1990s

By the mid-1990s the international financial architecture (IFA) as it had developed was a decidedly *ad hoc* affair, with different international and regional institutions having different responsibilities and practices. These were sometimes compatible (or even overlapping in the case of the World Bank and the RDBs) and sometimes not.

However, this IFA, and particularly the Bretton Woods institutions that sit at the heart of it, were heavily criticised, from both the Left and the Right. What were these criticisms, however?

8.2.1 Critics from the Left

Box 8.4 The Washington Consensus

The phrase the 'Washington Consensus' was first used by the economist
John Williamson at a conference at the Institute of Development Studies
in 1989. Williamson (1990: 3) later set out ten policy areas that he
thought there was general consensus on amongst the Washington-based
institutions, notably the IMF and World Bank:

- 'Fiscal discipline.
- A redirection of public expenditure priorities toward fields offering
  both high economic returns and the potential to improve income
  distribution, such as primary health care, primary education, and
  infrastructure.
- Tax reform (to lower marginal rates and broaden the tax base).
- Interest rate liberalization.
- A competitive exchange rate.
- Trade liberalization.
- Liberalization of FDI inflows.
- Privatization.
- Deregulation (in the sense of abolishing barriers to entry and exit).
- Secure property rights.'

Williamson (1999) complains that the term 'Washington Consensus'
has come to mean something very different to that which he originally
intended:

> I have realized that the term is often being used in a sense signifi-
> cantly different to that which I had intended, as a synonym for what
> is often called 'neoliberalism' in Latin America, or what George
> Soros (1998) has called 'market fundamentalism'. When I first came
> across this usage, I asserted that it was erroneous since that was
> not what I had intended by the term. Luiz Carlos Bresser Pereira
> patiently explained to me that I was being naïve in imagining that
> just because I had invented the expression gave me some sort of
> intellectual property rights that entitled me to dictate its meaning:
> the concept had become the property of mankind.

Williamson raises an interesting point here. He saw the 'consensus'
as a gradual convergence in thinking on the best ways to approach
particular economic and financial policies, rather than the imposition
of a 'neo-liberal agenda'. However, it is also the case that the 'intellectual convergence' he speaks of does indeed represent such an agenda

for many people. Furthermore, it is one that many fundamentally disagree with. Most importantly, the 'consensus' has not remained an intellectual exercise by any means, but has formed the basis of structural adjustment programmes implemented by the IMF and World Bank throughout the developing world. If it were the case that, in all cases, policy-makers in these countries completely agreed with the 'suit' of policies we could then talk meaningfully of a 'consensus'.

However, where this has not been the case, the 'consensus' may indeed appear to be more like the imposition of a particular set of liberalising – or 'neo-liberal' – policies.

We have seen how the World Bank and IMF (and the RDBs to a lesser extent) increasingly focused on conditional, policy-based lending in the 1980s and 1990s, and it was this that was at the heart of criticisms of these institutions from the Left.

The major criticisms can be described as follows:

- It was (and is) argued that the IMF and World Bank are dominated by developed countries (particularly the United States) and the policies associated with their lending programmes reflect the interest of the dominant shareholders.
- The 'Washington Consensus' (see Box 8.4) of economic policies imposed by the BWIs – often described as 'neo-liberal' – were seen as serving Western interests.
- The IMF and World Bank were accused of having a one-size-fits-all approach to development, where the same policies were recommended to all countries regardless of their circumstances.
- For critics, the power and influence of the Bretton Woods institutions enabled them to force countries to implement these reforms, not least because financial support was conditional upon their doing so, regardless of their unpopularity with their citizens and negative social consequences that were seen to result.
- The lending programmes of both institutions resulted in increasing levels of debt in developing countries, particularly the least developed ones. As shown in Table 8.4 below, the servicing of these debts (for which further

Table 8.4 Net transfers on debt owed to multilateral lenders, 1987–1994

	1987	1988	1989	1990	1991	1992	1993	1994
World Bank	2.01	−0.71	−0.38	1.76	−1.50	−3.24	−1.19	−3.15
RDBs	1.85	2.28	2.79	2.27	3.37	2.70	2.09	−0.50

Source: Culpeper, 1997.

loans were often provided) resulted in negative resource transfers from
the World Bank in the 1980s and 1990s.
*   As can be seen, debt transfers over the period between the World Bank
    and developing countries were negative (–US$6.5 billion), but these were
    offset by positive flows from the RDBs (+US$16.85 billion).

More generally, critics argued that rather than reducing poverty levels, the
actions of the World Bank and IMF have served to exacerbate the problem.
For example the 'high water mark' of structural adjustment programmes was
in the mid-1980s, when many developing countries implemented Bank and
Fund-inspired structural adjustment programmes.

Figure 8.3 shows that, for all developing countries, the percentage of the
population of developing countries living in absolute poverty (i.e. less than
US$1 per day) declined between 1981 and 1987. However, this does not tell
the whole story by any means. In particular, the aggregate data is heavily
skewed towards Asia because of the size of the population: the decrease in
aggregate poverty levels therefore reflects the decline in poverty in the Asian
region.

However, of all the developing regions, Asia was the least affected by
the IMF/World Bank's structural adjustment-type conditionality, so that the
poverty reductions in this region cannot reasonably be ascribed to the implementation of policies recommended by the Bretton Woods institutions.
In contrast, the regions that did implement many painful reforms – i.e.
Latin America and sub-Saharan Africa – at the instigation of these institutions saw poverty levels rise. In Latin America, the 1980s is known as the 'lost
decade'.

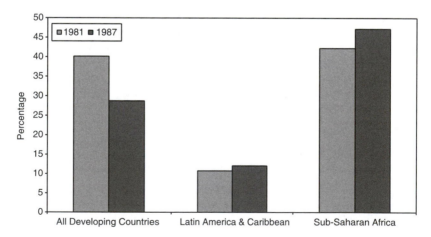

Figure 8.3 Absolute poverty, 1981 vs. 1987 (% of population on less than US$1
        per day).

Source: World Bank WDI.

8.2.2   Critics from the Right

As well as being attacked from the Left, the Bretton-Woods institutions have also long been attacked from the Right. There are numerous reasons for this, ranging from the extreme position that the institutions represent a pseudo-world government in the making and have no legitimacy,[15] to the specific policy recommendations where 'supply-side' economists argue that the IMF, in particular, recommends policies that are likely to be counterproductive to their aims.

Furthermore, and particularly since the LDC debt crisis of the 1980s, critics of the IMF have argued that its very existence promotes moral hazard among both borrowers and lenders, who make reckless lending and borrowing decisions in the knowledge that the IMF will arrive to bail them out in the event of a crisis occurring. As we shall see below, however, there is often a marked asymmetry in this argument, with moral hazard being seen as a more serious issue with regard to reckless borrowers (i.e. developing countries) than for reckless lenders (i.e. international financial institutions).

It was issues of this nature that underpinned debates on the reform of the IFA that occurred in the aftermath of the Asian crisis. This is the subject of the next section.

8.2.3   Reform of the IFA: the proposals

Following the turmoil of the Asian and Russian financial crises, there was much talk of fundamental reform. The international financial architecture as it had developed was widely viewed as inadequate to cope with the demands placed upon it by the modern financial system. Root and branch change was urged, though the 'roots' and 'branches' were often of very different forms.

In this environment, influential actors commissioned reports and proposed reforms. Although each of these reports and statements produced different proposals, they all focused on the role that lenders and borrowers had played in creating the major financial crises of the late 1990s. As discussed above, much was made of 'moral hazard': it was argued that when lenders (borrowers) are protected from the potential downside consequences of their lending (borrowing) decisions – by the probability of an IMF package that ensures they are bailed out in the event of a crisis, for example – they are liable to take insufficient account of risks and lend (borrow) recklessly.

There was considerable debate as to whether the crises had been largely triggered by reckless lending or reckless borrowing, however. The influential Meltzer Report (Meltzer, 2000),[16] for example, repeatedly stressed the role of moral hazard in influencing borrowers' behaviour. The Commission proposed numerous reforms, notably to the workings of the IMF, to rectify these problems, but the report was far more sanguine on the role of lenders.

The Council on Foreign Relations (CFR)[17] and US Treasury Reports[18] were both more balanced in this respect, with the former in particular arguing strongly for more private sector involvement (PSI) in post-crisis workouts: the argument was, and is, that if a private financial institution knows it will have to shoulder some of the costs of resolving post-crisis problems, they will take more care to avoid getting into such a situation in the first place.[19]

Other major studies commissioned at this time included the Geneva Report (1999),[20] which was jointly published by the International Centre for Monetary and Banking Studies in Geneva and the Centre for Economic Policy Research (CEPR) in London, and the Ahluwalia Report, which was commissioned by the G24 and written by the economist Montek Ahluwalia in 1999. A further major report was also published in 2000 by the Washington-based Overseas Development Council (ODC).[21]

The most obvious point to make at the outset is that the events of the Asian crisis and its aftermath were clearly being taken very seriously indeed. Furthermore, all of these reports focus – to a greater or lesser extent – on the role of the IMF. The Meltzer Report also considers the role of the World Bank, the RDBs, the WTO, and the BIS, but it too focused primarily on the IMF. Clearly the role of the Fund was viewed as being of primary importance, both in terms of avoiding financial crisis in the first place, and of resolving crises if they do occur.

Williamson (2000) reviewed these reports, separating their findings into recommendations of different aspects of the IMF's activities. Below, we briefly consider the conclusions.[22]

(a) Scope of the IMF

In one respect there was broad agreement that the IMF's activities exhibited pronounced 'mission creep', with the Fund having taken on more and more functions. All the reports recommend that the IMF should therefore narrow its approach and focus on its 'core competencies', such as surveillance, the promulgation of financial standards and the maintenance of macroeconomic stability. The view that the Fund should retain a key role in preventing and managing financial crises was also broadly expressed.

Whilst there is common ground in some regards there is certainly no unanimity. For example, while the Meltzer Report calls for a fundamental reduction in the Fund's activities, the other reports argue that the IMF should have a major role in (a) promoting macroeconomic coordination between its members, for reasons of global economic stability, and (b) preventing the development of crisis potential in developing and emerging economies. The Meltzer Report, in contrast, starts from the proposition that IMF lending promotes moral hazard (suggesting that the importance of this 'cannot be overstated'). Indeed, a dissenting majority within the committee argued that the IMF should be disbanded.

The other area of disagreement relates to the role of the 'Poverty Reduction and Growth Facility' (PRGF), which is overseen by the IMF. For some

(Ahluwalia; ODC) the facility should be moved to the World Bank. For the Meltzer Report, the PGRF should be simply disbanded.

(b) Surveillance

The IMF undertakes two forms of surveillance:

1 surveillance of the world economy, as published in the World Economic Outlook reports;
2 surveillance of individual member countries.

All the reports were happy for the Fund to continue with (1), and despite differences of emphasis, broadly agree with surveillance of individual countries as well. Most wanted to see greater transparency in this area though, with a particular emphasis on all surveillance reports being published.

(c) Lending

The main questions in this regard were: (a) whether the IMF should provide financing to members affected by crisis; (b) on what terms this financing should be provided; and (c) whether countries should have to 'pre-qualify' for assistance, which would then replace the conditionality associated with IMF lending today.

The last of these points (pre-qualification) encapsulates the nature of the debate. In the Meltzer Report, for example, pre-qualification is essential in order to reduce the moral hazard associated with IMF lending – if a country ignored warnings about the risks of its activities, and therefore could not pre-qualify, it would not be entitled to IMF support.

The Meltzer Commission suggested the following criteria for pre-qualification:

- freedom of entry and operation for foreign financial institutions;
- well-capitalised commercial banks, preferably with part of the capital in the form of uninsured subordinated debt;[23]
- regular and timely publication of the maturity structure of outstanding sovereign and guaranteed debt and off-balance sheet liabilities; and
- a sustainable fiscal position (though it was not specified what this means in practice).

Countries that were able to meet these criteria would be entitled to borrow freely, but at a high rate and for short durations – 120 days maximum, with only one rollover permitted. The 'penalty rate' would be 'a premium over the sovereign yield paid by the member country one week prior to applying for an IMF loan'. However, as Williamson (op. cit.) points out, given that sovereign yields are almost certain to rise sharply prior to the onset of a crisis, this seems implausible.[24] Those who did not meet the criteria would be entitled to no assistance at all.

More broadly, the Meltzer Commission argued that the IMF's lending role should be restricted to this lender-of-last-resort function, which would only be available to solvent, middle-income countries – that is, the Fund should not lend to the poorest developing countries, nor to developed countries.

The other reports listed above agreed that the Fund should focus on lending in crisis situations. However, they were by no means as restrictive as the Meltzer Commission in this respect. The Geneva Report, for example, expressed scepticism on the merits of pre-qualification, which it viewed as being solely designed to prevent moral hazard. For the authors, the moral hazard issue certainly can be 'overstated'[25] – given the hugely negative impact of a financial crisis, it was argued, no government would risk such an event occurring with or without IMF support.

The ODC report also argued that the Fund should focus on lending in crises, but that all countries should be able to borrow in the event of a macroeconomic crisis: the pre-qualification approach was therefore rejected.

The CFR Report suggested that the Fund could distinguish between 'country crises' and 'systemic crises'. In the former case, financial support would be restricted to the usual IMF quota limits (see above, p. 257), whereas systemic crises – where countries affected by contagion through no fault of their own – would be able to access a newly established 'contagion fund', based on newly allocated SDRs. For country crises, IMF conditionality would apply. For contagious, systemic crises, this would not be the case.

The CFR and Geneva Reports both stress the importance of involving creditors in restructuring of debts as a condition of IMF support. In this regard, the Geneva Report argues that IMF financing should be available on more favourable terms to those countries whose bond contracts contain 'collective action clauses', which enable the terms of the bonds to be restructured in the event of a crisis, as negotiated between debtors and a given *majority* of creditors.[26]

Just as the Meltzer Report stressed the moral hazard associated with reckless borrowing, these two reports emphasise the other side of the equation: that is, moral hazard-induced reckless *lending*. It is noteworthy that the Meltzer Report is almost silent on the issue of 'private sector involvement' (PSI) in this regard: it would appear that the Commission considered that moral hazard only affects borrowers, whereas lenders seemingly make rational, economically objective decisions in every instance and are therefore immune to moral hazard.

(d) Governance

Williamson (op. cit.) also considers the reports' views on IMF governance, which we have discussed previously in this chapter. Despite the importance of the issue, they have little to say, beyond calls for greater transparency.

(e) Non-IMF related proposals

As pointed out above, the Meltzer Commission did not restrict its proposals to the IMF. Recommendations for other international and regional institutions were as follows.

THE WORLD BANK AND THE REGIONAL DEVELOPMENT BANKS

> All resource transfers to countries that enjoy capital market access (as denoted by an investment grade international bond rating) or with a per capita income in excess of $4000, would be phased out over the next 5 years. Starting at $2500 (per capita income), official assistance would be limited. (Dollar values should be indexed.) Emergency lending would be the responsibility of the IMF in its capacity as quasi lender of last resort. This recommendation assures that development aid adds to available resources (additionality).
>
> (Meltzer, 2000: 11)

Beyond this, the World Bank and RDBs should focus on technical assistance, the provision of regional and global public goods, and the facilitation of an increased flow of private sector resources to middle-income countries. Furthermore, loans to the poorest countries should be replaced by grants, with the important proviso that a country's ability to access these grants depends on their record of delivery: '. . .poverty is often most entrenched and widespread in countries where corrupt and inefficient governments undermine the ability to benefit from aid or repay debt. Loans to these governments are, too often, wasted, squandered, or stolen.' (p. 12)

To reflect this change in focus, the Commission recommends that the World Bank's name be changed to World Development Agency.

In terms of division of responsibilities between the Bank and the RDBs:

> All country and regional programs in Latin America and Asia should be the primary responsibility of the area's regional bank. The World Bank should become the principal source of aid for the African continent until the African Development Bank is ready to take full responsibility. The World Bank would also be the development agency responsible for the few remaining poor countries in Europe and the Middle East.
>
> (p. 13)

The report also argued that all bilateral and multilateral debt to the HIPC countries should be written off, for countries that 'pursue effective economic development strategies,' as judged by the Bank.

THE BANK FOR INTERNATIONAL SETTLEMENTS

The BIS is generally approved of by the report, which proposed that 'the BIS remain a financial standard setter'.

THE WORLD TRADE ORGANISATION

In contrast, the WTO was seen as going beyond its remit, with the report arguing that the 'grandfather clause' discussed above should be reinstated, with national legislation regaining primacy over WTO rulings:

> As WTO decisions move to the broader range of issues now within its mandate, there is considerable risk that WTO rulings will override national legislation in areas of health, safety, environment, and other regulatory policies. The Commission believes that quasi-judicial decisions of international organizations should not supplant national legislative enactments. [In particular:] Rulings or decisions by the WTO, or any other multilateral entity, that extend the scope of explicit commitments under treaties or international agreements must remain subject to explicit legislative enactment by the U.S. Congress and, elsewhere, by the national legislative authority.
>
> (p. 14)

To summarise, the majority of the reports described here argued in the post-Asia context that the IMF should narrow and focus its activities to crisis prevention and management, and restrict its lending activities to these areas. However, there were strong differences as to the form this lending should take. The majority proposed a refinement of current practice, whereas the Meltzer Report argued for a dramatic reduction in the Fund's activities, so that it would only lend to solvent emerging economies at penalty rates and for short durations. Furthermore, to be eligible for this facility, countries would have to pre-qualify. The overriding aim of the report is to eliminate the moral hazard related to IMF lending, which it sees as the primary cause of reckless borrowing. In contrast, the Meltzer Report has little to say on reckless lending caused by moral hazard, a subject picked up on in two of the other major reports, which argued for greater PSI in crisis resolution to address this issue.

Another feature that these reports share is a very developed country focus. Indeed, it is narrower than that, in being a largely Washington focus. For comparative purposes, we also consider the 2001 report of the Emerging Market Eminent Persons Group (EMEPG), which provides a broader view.[27]

(f) An emerging market perspective

The EMEPG Report takes a much broader view of the issues, taking a considerably more holistic view of the 'international financial architecture'. Eight particular areas are considered:

1   capital account liberalisation;
2   appropriate exchange rate regimes;
3   the regulation of highly leveraged institutions (HLIs);
4   the setting of international financial codes and standards;
5   private participation in crisis prevention and resolution;
6   social protection mechanisms;
7   social protection mechanisms for financial stability;
8   the reform of international financial institutions (IFIs), and regional monetary and financial cooperation.

Unlike the reports covered thus far, the EMEPG Report sees the incidence of financial crises as being inextricably linked to weaknesses in the functioning of the international financial markets in general, not just to deficiencies in the crisis-affected countries:

> Financial fragility in many emerging market economies has been exacerbated in the past by poor corporate governance in (domestic) financial institutions and corporations (both state-owned and private), inadequate financial regulation and supervision, weak institutions and insolvent fiscal systems. Much progress has been made – often under adverse circumstances – to correct these deficiencies by almost all emerging market governments in recent years. However, stronger prudential standards, sound macroeconomic fundamentals, enhanced risk management and improved transparency, although necessary, are not sufficient to provide an assurance of market stability. International action on a coordinated basis is clearly also required.
>
> (EMEPG, 2001: 7)

Unlike the largely developed country perspectives described above, the EMEPG Report also stresses the role of governance, or 'voice'. In this regard it was stressed that although the proposed reforms of the IFA are likely to affect developing and emerging economies more than developed countries, there is little or no representation in international standard-setting bodies for these countries.

On the specific areas above, the report argues the following:

- Capital account liberalisation is a means to an end rather than an end in itself, and should be taken slowly with necessary reforms put in place at each stage before proceeding to the next.
- Governments should not be prevented from using capital controls to address issues of short-term capital flows and encourage longer maturities of their external debt.
- Choice of exchange rate regime should be left to governments and not restricted to 'corner solutions'.
- G7 supervisors should regulate bank lending to HLIs, to 'reduce their

ability to mount speculative attacks on emerging markets.' There should also be more transparency as to their activities and outstanding market positions of HLIs.

- Although the implementation of sound codes and standards (C&S) are important in all countries, a single one-size-fits-all approach should be avoided. Crucially, developing country perspectives should inform the setting of any such standards, particularly in the Financial Stability Forum (FSF).

- 'Over borrowing by emerging market governments, banks and firms is logically matched by voluntary overlending by private investors in advanced economies' (p. 13). The report therefore stresses the importance of PSI in crisis resolution, and raises the possibility of developing an international bankruptcy framework,[28] which could form the basis of sovereign debt restructuring, as well as the need for collective action clauses in bond contracts.

- The EMEPG argues that it is important to recognise the importance of social protection systems and therefore that the increased use of fiscal resources in these areas should be accepted – and indeed, welcomed – by creditors, so long as it is consistent with fiscal stability.

- The report identifies many recent crises as being of liquidity rather than solvency, and therefore argues that the IMF should increase its lending ability to deal with liquidity crises. IMF conditionality should be tailored to the circumstances of each country, and the Fund should focus its lending on crisis situations.

- For its part, the World Bank should focus on longer-term developmental lending, particularly in the funding of social and economic infrastructure where private funding is not available.

- On governance: 'Emerging market countries' representation in the share capital and executive boards of the International Financial Institutions (IFIs) should reflect more accurately their respective importance in the world economy' (p. 15).

- The EMEPG Report ends by calling for greater regional financial and economic cooperation, including the option of countries pooling foreign exchange reserves to repel speculative attacks.

Others have taken a similarly broad approach, arguing that international financial stability can be seen as a global public good,[29] and that the 'public bad' of financial instability and crises disproportionately affects developing countries. As with the EMEPG Report, these types of perspectives tend to view excessive volatility (i.e. its 'public bad' component) as inherent to modern financial markets, and thus argue that coordinated international public measures are needed to offset these tendencies and promote the global public good of financial stability.

To summarise, the Asian crisis and its aftermath provoked a flood of reports from various commissions, committees and eminent groups. Above we have given only a flavour of this outpouring of comment and proposals for reform. At this time, the international financial architecture was widely seen as incapable of preventing, managing or resolving financial crises, though the reasons for this deficiency varied greatly, with some seeing the Fund itself as a major factor in the generation of crises.

At one extreme, the Meltzer Report pinned much of the blame on reckless borrowing inspired by the moral hazard resulting from expected IMF bailouts. Other reports originating from the developed countries saw the importance of moral hazard as overplayed in general terms, but also emphasised the symmetrical nature of the issue – i.e. the role of moral hazard in encouraging reckless lending. To this end, greater 'burden-sharing' and 'private sector involvement' in crisis resolution was seen as essential.

The EMEPG report gave a much broader perspective, arguing that:

- Domestic reforms are insufficient to prevent crises on their own, and reforms to the international financial system are also needed, as indeed is the option of imposing capital controls.
- Highly leveraged institutions (i.e. 'hedge funds') should be regulated to restrict their abilities to undertake speculative attacks.
- Internationally agreed C&S – and reform of the IFA more generally – should have a major input from developing countries and be applied flexibly.
- The IMF should focus on crisis lending, with the World Bank concentrating on its core competency of long-term developmental lending in areas not attractive to private capital but vital for development.
- Developing and emerging economies should be represented in international standard-setting institutions in accordance with their standing in the world economy today.

Clearly the speed with which these various reports were produced suggests that reforms were urgently needed, which would suggest that major reforms would have followed hard on their heels . . .

8.3 Reform of the IFA – what has happened since?

With the benefit of some distance from the Asian crisis that was the catalyst for the debate on reform described above, Griffith-Jones and Ocampo (2003) argue that the architecture has – or should have – five functions.

Specifically, it should:

1 guarantee the consistency of national macroeconomic policies with stability and growth at the global level as a central objective;
2 ensure appropriate transparency and regulation of international financial loan and capital markets, and adequate regulation of domestic financial systems and cross-border capital account flows;

3   ensure the provision of sufficient international official liquidity in crisis conditions;
4   create and maintain accepted mechanisms for standstill and orderly debt workouts at the international level;
5   develop appropriate mechanisms for development finance.

With the possible exception of point 5, all of these have seen recommendations for reform, many of which are described above. The authors go on to give four reasons why progress on reforms has been so disappointing:

(a) No agreed upon international reform agenda

As we have seen there are considerable differences in the proposals for reform. However, as demonstrated by the difference between the EMEPG Report and the others in the previous section, the largest gap – in terms of agreeing an agenda – appears to be between developed countries, on the one hand, and emerging and developing countries, on the other. Clearly, if there is no agreement on what the problems are, there can be little hope of progress on finding solutions.

(b) Progress has been asymmetrical

To date the focus of reforms has been on strengthening national economic, financial and regulatory frameworks within developing and emerging economies. For example, developing countries have broadly accepted the implementation of internationally recognised codes and standards for macroeconomic and financial regulation, as designed by the Financial Stability Forum. However, there has been little if any progress in reforming the international aspects of the IFA. This would only be sufficient if the sole cause of financial instability and crises were policy deficiencies in developing countries. However, as is broadly accepted, this is not the case: a country with perfect fundamentals and regulation can still be affected by a self-fulfilling crisis, and/or by contagion from another crisis.

Similarly, there has been no real progress on macroeconomic coordination (particularly among G7 countries as called for by the EMEPG Report) to reduce the build-up of crisis potential. This situation has improved somewhat in recent years, with the launch of the IMF's 'Multilateral Consultation Process' in 2006. The initiative brings together relevant countries – depending on the nature of the issue – to discuss mutually beneficial solutions and increase the prospect of cooperative action to resolve problems. The first Consultation focused on correcting global economic imbalances, and saw five countries (or country groups) take part: China, the Euro Area, Japan, Saudi Arabia and the United States.

It is too early to say what the outcome of this process will be. The fact that the Fund cannot compel countries to change their economic policies (not least as these countries do not borrow from the IMF and cannot therefore have conditions imposed) suggests that prospects of success turn on whether the Fund can convince participants that change is in their common interests. Intuitively, it is likely that this will be the case in some instances but not in others. For example, perhaps the largest imbalance the global economy faces today is the trade surpluses in East Asia, the trade deficit in the US and the resulting build-up of foreign exchange reserves in the former. However, many have argued that the recycling of these reserves into US Treasuries has effectively been a process where the East Asian economies lend the US the funds needed for it to purchase their imports. In many ways, therefore, this situation suits both parties and, although it may not suit the others at the table, consensus will surely be needed before major change occurs.

Also, while considerable effort has been put into developing and modifying the various IMF financing facilities (which was the focus of the Washington-based reports described above) there has, as we saw in the previous chapter, been far less progress on international debt workout agreements that involve 'burden-sharing' between creditors and debtors.

A second asymmetry that is identified is the focus on crisis prevention and management in middle-income countries, at the expense of developing mechanisms to encourage stable, long-term financial flows to the poorest LDCs.

The reforms that have occurred, such as the introduction of codes and standards, for example, reflect the perspective of developed countries. Those that have a more developing country slant – burden-sharing, regulating hedge funds, and so on – have made little or no progress in comparison.

(c) The IMF may not have sufficient resources to perform its key task

Despite the fact that most commentators (even Meltzer) agree that the IMF needs access to more funds to manage crises better, there has been a growing reluctance amongst developed countries to support large-scale IMF lending. The primary rationale for this is the desire to avoid moral hazard which was central to the Meltzer Report, as we have seen.

The crises of recent decades have demonstrated that the scale of international financial markets today is such that to provide sufficient resources to enable a country to (a) deter a speculative attack, and/or (b) rebuild their financial infrastructure following a crisis requires a far greater level of financing than was the case in the past.

Figure 8.4 below shows that although the resources available to the Fund have increased steadily since its foundation, in relative terms – i.e. as a percentage of the size of the global economy – the opposite has been the case. Thus, while in 1944, IMF resources were equivalent to more than 3.5% of its members' GDP, by 2003 this had fallen to 0.9%.

As Buira (2006) points out, IMF members – particularly emerging markets

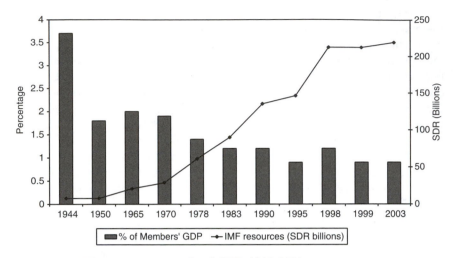

Figure 8.4 IMF resources vs. members' GDP, 1944–2003.

Source: IMF WEO.

– that face severe external financing difficulties do not typically have access to private capital markets at these times. The burden therefore falls directly on the Fund.

Furthermore, contagious or region-wide crises – of the kind seen in Asia in the late 1990s – have the potential to stretch these resources to the limit. A fundamental difference between a national central bank acting as a lender-of-last-resort and the IMF taking on a similar role, is that the Fund does not have the ability to issue its own fiat currency. Thus, while a national central bank can – in theory at least – provide as much support as is required, the support that the IMF can offer is limited to that which its members can provide.

As is shown in Figure 8.4, in relative terms this has been falling steadily, while at the same time the size of the potential call on IMF resources has risen hugely. Given the current disagreements on the role of the Fund, and even the fact of its existence – particularly in the political circles of its largest contributor, the US – there seems little chance of this trend being reversed in the foreseeable future.

(d) Reform of IFA characterised by insufficient developing country representation

The international bodies responsible for reforming the IFA (IMF, World Bank, FSF and BIS) have very limited representation for developing and emerging economies. In the case of the IMF and World Bank this is a function of historical precedents, the time lag in adjusting voting rights to reflect modern economic realities, and the unwillingness of developed countries to dilute their control over these institutions.

The BIS, in contrast, started out as a forum for developed country central bankers, and while its edicts – particularly those of the Basel Committee on Banking Supervision – have come to be the international standard adopted by all countries regardless of their level of development, developing and emerging economies are generally only afforded 'consultant' status, rather than being full members. A similar, semi-detached status is afforded to developing countries in the FSF, which is perhaps even more unreasonable than the case of the BIS, since many of the codes and standards promulgated by this body are directed almost exclusively to low- and middle-income countries.

Griffith-Jones and Ocampo (op. cit.) describe the following areas where good progress on reform has been made:

- the development of C&S and standards for crisis prevention in capital recipient countries;
- the design of new IMF financial facilities;
- the HIPC Initiative aimed at bringing external debts of low-income countries to sustainable levels.

Areas of limited progress are:

- macroeconomic surveillance and mechanisms to guarantee the coherence of macroeconomic policies;[30]
- improvements in worldwide regulatory standards;
- the redefinition of IMF conditionality.

Areas of no progress are:

- the use of SDRs as an instrument of IMF financing;
- the design of international standstills and workout procedures;
- development finance;
- regional schemes in all areas of the financial architecture.

The factor that may, at least in part, explain the asymmetric nature of these reforms is the lack of developing country participation in the relevant international bodies that determine reforms and set standards. Without a seat at the table – and therefore an effective veto over decision-making – the concerns of developing and emerging economies are very unlikely to be prioritised. This is basic political economy and it has been ever thus.

Concluding remarks

In this chapter we have examined the birth, evolution and current state of what has come to be known as the international financial architecture. As we have seen, the current patchwork of international and regional institutions that we have today was widely viewed as being incapable with dealing with the realities of modern financial crises in the period after the Asian crisis. Root and branch reform was proposed from many different directions, often in ways that were mutually incompatible.

Since that time, however, not much has actually happened, and what has happened has largely focused on reducing the vulnerability to crises in developing countries. Furthermore, as the scale, duration and impact of financial crises has risen sharply, the measures deemed necessary for a country to protect itself from such events have widened commensurately.

This would be fine if the sole cause of such events lay in policy errors in countries that are recipients of capital flows. However, with the exception of a very limited number of commentators, nobody, it seems, thinks this is the case.

As well as the recipients of capital flows, it is surely the case that countries that are the source of these outflows have a greater role to play. However, as we have seen, there is little agreement on what measures should be taken, with perhaps the most marked divide being between commentators from recipient countries and those from source countries.

A final point to make relates to the political economy of this situation. Financial crises disproportionately affect low- and middle-income countries, while richer countries – which are the source of most international capital flows – receive considerable benefits from the financial centres which they host. Similarly, while richer countries may provide the bulk of the financing for the multilateral financial and development institutions, it is in poorer countries that they largely operate.

9 Development finance and the private sector

Driving the real economy

Introduction

We have seen throughout this book how ensuring an appropriate level of development finance requires both domestic resource mobilisation and a suitable level of external capital inflows, from both the private and official sectors. Furthermore, we have seen that it is not just the level of total finance available but the composition of this financing that determines the ultimate developmental impact.

As was stressed from the outset, financial sector development is not an end in itself. Its sole purpose – which must always be borne in mind, but is too often forgotten – is to facilitate developmentally beneficial activity in the real economy, and so contribute to national economic progress and poverty reduction. Success or failure should thus be judged purely against this criterion.

In this regard, a fundamental issue to consider is the mechanisms through which this financing – and its ancillary benefits and/or costs – is transmitted to the private sector in developing countries. Accordingly, in this penultimate chapter we will consider these issues, with a particular focus on financing small-and-medium-enterprises (SMEs) which, as we have seen, are of paramount importance in developing and emerging economies.

When we consider financing options for the private sector, a very important issue relates to the capital structure of firms. Of course this is something of a chicken and egg situation: the financing is available in different environments is likely to shape the capital structures that firms adopt. Conversely, the capital structures that prevail will also be influenced by factors other than the availability of particular forms of finance, and this in turn will influence the type of financing that is desired.

Accordingly, the first section will consider some broad issues regarding differences in financial structures internationally.

9.1 General determinants of firms' capital structure

It has long been accepted that the capital structure of a firm will be influenced by the industry in which it operates. Empirically, Bradley *et al.* (1984) find that debt ratios show distinct differences between particular industries, and a number of theoretical explanations have been given as to why this should be so.[1] Whilst there may be some effects in this regard, more recent research strongly suggests that a far more important determinant than industry affiliation is the country in which the firm operates.[2]

This suggests that it is public policy and institutional differences between these countries that are the major determining factors in capital structure. In a survey of capital structures across thirty-nine developed and developing economies, Fan *et al.* (2003) identify the following determinants as the most important:

- *Tax effects:* in countries where dividends on shares are highly taxed, companies tend to have higher levels of debt finance.
- *Macro effects:* in countries with high macroeconomic instability (i.e. high inflation) companies tend to have a lower proportion of debt in their capital structures, and the debt that they do have is of short maturities.[3]
- *Legal environment effects:* in countries with high levels of corruption, firms tend to take on higher levels of total debt, but again the debt structure is very short-term.[4]
- *Institutional effects (1):* in countries with high levels of bank deposits, firms tend to have much more short-term debt structures, due to the relative abundance – and therefore relative cost – of debt financing.
- *Institutional effects (2):* in countries with high levels of life insurance assets, companies tend to have debt structures of longer maturities, reflecting the preference of life insurance companies to hold long-term debt, and the fact that life insurance penetration in developing countries is positively correlated with the supply of equity finance.

The evidence also suggests that the more access companies have to long-term debt and equity finance, the higher their ability to make long-term investments, which ultimately leads to higher economic growth.[5]

In contrast, a preponderance of short-term debt financing is associated with (a) underdeveloped financial systems, (b) financial systems dominated by banks, (c) macro instability, and (d) weak legal frameworks (and high levels of corruption). This is of course unsurprising: in such conditions where uncertainty is very high, investors will prefer to keep their commitments as 'revocable' – and thus short-term – as possible, while given the short-term nature of their liabilities, banks will generally prefer to provide shorter-term financing.

As we have seen, these features tend to be associated with the economies of developing countries, particularly the poorest LDCs. It therefore comes as no surprise that debt maturities are, in general terms, shorter in developing countries than is the case in developed countries.

9.2 The SME sector

The majority of studies that have compared countries' corporate financing structures have, understandably, focused on the largest firms, for which data is more readily available. Thus, while the findings given above have relevance for developing and emerging economies, they are derived from one specific part of the corporate landscape in these countries.

However, in practice, developing countries tend to have an 'hour-glass-shaped' corporate structure, with a limited number of very large companies, large numbers of SMEs, but with few medium-sized companies between the two. This phenomenon, which is often referred to as the 'missing middle', is widely accepted[6] but is backed with very little internationally comparable data, not least because of the very different ways that an SME – as well as corporate entities of other size categories – is defined (UNCTAD, 2006).

Notwithstanding this paucity of data, the 'missing middle' argument has led to much research into the obstacles to the growth of small firms in developing countries. In this regard, particular focus has surrounded the financing of the SME sector: is there a financing constraint to the growth of smaller enterprises and, if so, how can it be overcome?

The rationale for this emphasis on SMEs, of course, is based on a number of assumptions regarding the positive economic functions that SMEs may perform. The World Bank (2004) described these assumptions as follows:

1   SMEs enhance competition and entrepreneurship and thus have economy-wide benefits in efficiency, innovation and productivity growth.
2   The growth of SMEs boosts employment more than the growth of large firms because SMEs are more labour intensive.
3   SMEs are generally more productive than large firms but are impeded in their development by failures of financial markets and other institutions.

The impetus for research into the financing constraints facing the small business sector is therefore based on two things. First, the assumed benefits of a strong and vibrant SME sector, as described above; and, second, the lack of effective financing mechanisms in many developing countries to facilitate this expansion, thus preventing small firms becoming medium-sized, and medium-sized firms becoming large.

9.2.1 SMEs: the financing gap

The World Bank (2002) builds on the research on the capital structures of larger firms cited above. The Bank's approach combines the finding that access to different forms of finance is strongly determined by factors such as a country's legal system, with research that demonstrates that access to external financing, in general, is shaped by these same factors.

That is, not only does a country's legal system – and financial sector development, more generally – strongly influence the sort of financing available, it also has a strong impact on the availability of external finance of any sort. From a development perspective, this is a crucial issue: 'A direct implication of these studies is that in countries with weak legal systems, and consequently, weak financial systems, firms obtain less external financing and that this results in lower growth.'[7]

The key findings from the World Bank study are as follows:

1   SMEs in developing countries finance a significantly smaller proportion of their investments from external sources, particularly from banks.
2   Whilst it would be expected that SMEs would compensate for this shortfall by increasing their access to financing options such as leasing and trade finance, this is not in fact the case. For the World Bank this is explained by the fact that access to such financing mechanisms is itself a function of financial sector development (2002: 5): 'Financing from these sources does not fill in the financing gap of small firms in countries with underdeveloped institutions since the use of these financing sources is positively associated with the development of financial institutions and equity markets.'
3   Surprisingly, SMEs also access government and development bank finance less than do larger firms.
4   Finally, although SMEs do access finance from the informal sector more than do large firms, this represents less than 2% of their total investments, and therefore has little impact on the financial constraints facing these firms.

The mention of trade finance above merits a digression at this stage. Although the Bank does not see trade finance as filling the funding gap facing SMEs in developing countries, it is an extremely important source of finance for poorer countries, particularly the least developed. Accordingly, Box 9.1 below outlines the key issues and trends in relation to this subject.

Box 9.1 Trade finance

Trade finance – as the name suggests – refers to the financing of imports and exports. An effective system of trade finance, however, requires the development of a trade finance infrastructure, which relates to the following three activities:

- provision of capital to firms that are engaging in international trade transactions;
- provision of support services to manage the risk involved in these transactions;

- provision of international payment mechanisms (UNESCAP, 2000).

UNESCAP describes three benefits of effective systems of trade finance:

- Reduced capital outlay – where 'Trade finance provides companies with the necessary capital and liquidity and helps them to better manage their cash flow, allowing them to expand and grow.'
- Reduced risks – 'The development of a sound and secure trade finance infrastructure will increase the number of options available to traders to reduce or eliminate risks associated with non-payment or payment delays, fluctuation in exchange rates, changes in trade and financial regulations and political unrest, among others.
- Increased competitiveness – 'Terms of payment are increasingly used as competitive tools during contract negotiation. Buyers would generally favour a contract that provides certainty and attractive credit terms. Traders with access to a wide array of trade finance tools and instruments are better equipped.'

Key issues and trends for developing countries

- Trade finance is particularly beneficial to the poorest developing countries, who may not be able to access straight commercial finance, yet may still be in a position to obtain finance for trade, as banks are more willing to lend when traded goods provide security for the loan: while trade finance constitutes up to 80% of loans to non-investment grade borrowers, the figure for investment grade borrowers is 20–40%.
- As with other forms of bank lending, trade finance is strongly pro-cyclical: in the early 1990s trade finance rose from 10% of total bank lending to almost 30%, before falling back sharply to around 12% in the mid-1990s and rising again to 25% by 2002.
- Despite these fluctuations the trend line is one of growth, where trade finance grew, on average, by 11% per year from 1988 and 2002.
- The role of the private sector – particularly private insurers – has increased enormously over the past two decades. In 1990 the private sector provided virtually no trade finance; by 2004 it accounted for almost half of new commitments.
- The growth of private sector involvement, however, is almost entirely due to short-term commitments: in the medium- to long-term business, private insurers constitute only 0.2% of new commitments. In contrast, the IMF (2001) estimates that between 85 and 95% of short-term credit insurance business within and beyond the European Union is now under written by private insurers.

From a policy perspective, this funding shortfall[8] is a critical obstacle to development: if SMEs are the key driver of innovation, entrepreneurship, employment and therefore poverty reduction that is generally supposed, their lack of access to finance will prevent this function being fulfilled, as even successful SMEs will have difficulty expanding due to lack of access to external finance.

For this reason, development organisations – notably the World Bank/IFC but also bilateral donors – have channelled significant funding into supporting the SME sector in developing countries. For example, the World Bank alone approved US$10 billions' worth of SME support programmes from 1992 to 2002 and US$1.3 billion in 2003 alone (World Bank, 2002).

Before considering the wisdom of this expenditure, the next section will deal with the obstacles to filling this financing gap with private sector finance and consider mechanisms through which they could be overcome.

9.2.2 *Financing SMEs from the private sector: the institutional perspective*

A relatively well-developed literature has emerged that sees SME financing from the private sector from the perspective of the type of institutions providing the finance.[9] That is, different financial institutions were viewed as having a comparative advantage in the provision of different forms of finance.

Two major financing mechanisms are described in the literature:

1   '*Transactions lending*' forms refer to arm's-length financing based on 'hard' quantitative data, which is objectively verifiable and available to all market participants. Examples of the variables used are: financial ratios from balance sheets; credit scores from third-party agencies; or information about 'cash receivables' from creditable customers of the company, which can serve the function of collateral.
2   '*Relationship lending*', in contrast, is based on qualitative information gathered through contact with the borrower over time. Examples include: the character and prospects of the SME's owners and managers; the company's payment record; and future prospects for the SME based on strong knowledge of the company's position in the local market in which it operates (Berger and Udell, 2004).

From this perspective, a common finding in the literature is that large financial institutions have a comparative advantage in 'transactions lending', whilst smaller financial institutions have a similar advantage in the financing of 'relationship lending' (ibid.).

The reasons generally give for this are:

1   Large institutions are likely to be in a better position to exploit economies of scale in the processing of quantitative data, but may be less

good at processing qualitative information because it is difficult to quantify and therefore transmit through the communication channels of large institutions (Stein, 2000).

2   With relationship lending, the loan officer has direct contact with the SME and is therefore the 'repository of soft information', but this cannot be readily communicated to the senior staff of the institution.

3   This may provide advantages in relationship lending to small institutions because they will generally have fewer overall layers of management (Berger and Udell, 2002).

4   Large institutions may also be disadvantaged at relationship lending to SMEs because the organisation is geared toward providing transaction lending and wholesale financial services to large corporate clients (Williamson, 1988, cited in Berger and Udell, 2006).

The empirical literature suggests that, because of these features, large financial institutions tend to:

- base their decisions on financial ratios rather than on prior relationships;
- focus on arm's-length, short-term transaction lending, rather than developing longer-term relationships;
- only lend to older, established and financially secure SMEs that are able to provide the 'hard' data needed to facilitate transaction lending;
- lend at lower interest rates than do smaller financial institutions;[10]
- avoid lending to 'opaque' SMEs that are not transparent enough to obtain transaction type lending (Berger and Udell, 2006).

From a policy perspective, these viewpoints have resulted in a focus on ensuring that there is a sufficient quantity of small financial institutions in the economy, so as to ensure that SMEs (even 'opaque' ones) have access to external finance. That is, a broad consensus had developed that only small financial institutions were suited to lending to the SME sector, which in turn suggested that the lack of available finance was – at least in part – a function of an inadequate supply of relatively small financial institutions. Is this correct, however?

9.2.3 Financing SMEs from the private sector: a more nuanced perspective?

In general terms, the assumptions underlying this perspective have been inferred rather than proven. That is, actual lending patterns of private institutions are not available for analysis, as this is proprietary, commercially sensitive material. As a result, researchers have started from the theoretical position that large financial institutions *should* focus on transaction lending, moved on to the assumption that SMEs cannot readily access this kind of finance, added the assumption that small financial institutions may be better placed to provide relationship lending, and concluded that it is necessary to have a high proportion of small financial institutions in an economy to finance the SME sector.

However, more recent research contends that many of these assumptions are unfounded (Berger and Udell, 2006). The authors point out, although the evidence is quite limited, that there is not a statistically significant relationship between the size of financial institutions and the funding of the SME sector, which they suggest is because large institutions do lend to SMEs, and that they could lend more if the financial framework in which they operate were altered.[11]

In particular, it is argued that defining 'transaction lending' as a homogeneous category is overly simplistic. Instead, they identify five forms of transaction lending, and argue that only the first of these may be inappropriate for SMEs. The five categories described are as follows:[12]

1   financial statement lending;
2   lending based on small business scoring;
3   asset-based lending;
4   factoring;
5   trade credit.

(a)   Financial statement lending

As the name suggests, this form of lending entails the provision of loans on the basis of the strength of a borrower's financial statements. For this to be feasible, there are two requirements.

First, the financial statements must be genuinely informative, in the sense that audited statements are prepared by independent and credible accounting firms on the basis of internationally accepted accounting standards, such as the European International Accounting Standards (IAS) or the US system of Generally Accepted Accounting Principles (GAAP). The issue of accounting standards has become increasingly prominent in recent years, with efforts being made to bring these two global frameworks together. This process has significant implications for developing countries looking to adopt an internationally credible accounting framework, which are discussed in Box 9.2 below.

Box 9.2 IAS vs. GAAP

As we saw in Chapter 8, the introduction of the system of international codes and standards in the aftermath of the Asian crisis was an attempt to establish best practice benchmarks in a number of key areas. One such area is accounting. The body listed by the Financial Stability Forum as the issuer of international accounting standards is the International

Accounting Standards Commission (IASC), which has now been recast as the IASB, with the 'commission' becoming a 'board'. Its guidelines are termed the International Financial Reporting Standards (IFRS).

While it is surely sensible for all countries to use approaches to accounting that are as similar as possible, this is not as straightforward as it might appear. Indeed, the IASC(B) has been working for many years in an attempt to harmonise its approach to that used in the United States: Generally Agreed Accounting Principles, or US GAAP. While this may seem a little arcane, the issue has exercised some of the finest minds in the profession intensely. At least in part, disagreements stem from differing understandings of what accountancy is primarily for at the national level.

For example, the primary purpose of GAAP is to provide accurate information to participants in capital markets (investors, creditors) and the general public. The UK's Accounting Standards Board (ASB) has traditionally had a narrower distinction, with accounting primarily geared towards the providers of risk capital. In other European countries – while these factors are relevant – they are not necessarily primary. In France and Germany, for example, accounting has traditionally served primarily as the basis for contractual arrangements and for tax purposes. The French government also uses accounting to make macro-economic policy decisions (Gebhart, 2000). Furthermore, in countries with a common law tradition (e.g. US and UK) responsibility for formulating accounting standards is generally delegated to a self-governing private sector body, such as the (Federal) ASB in the US and ASB in the UK. In countries with a tradition of civil code law such as France, however, such issues are established in law with no discretion given to other bodies.

In 2002, the IASB and the US FASB agreed to work towards reducing differences between IFRS and US GAAP and in 2006 the two bodies agreed to reach a deal by 2008. At present companies listing in the US markets are required to either use GAAP, or to formally reconcile their accounting procedures with this system. If successful, the harmonisation process will allow companies issuing accounts according to IFRS to list in US markets with no further requirements.

For developing countries, with equally unique historical experience – as well as the added issue of colonialism in some instances, which entailed the imposition of the approach used by the coloniser – it is necessary to take account of these developments. For those wishing to access international capital markets and/or seeking listings on stock exchanges in developed countries, there is no alternative. As we have seen, the IASB standards are specified as the international benchmark by the FSF – a problem to date, however, has been that compliance with these standards does not mean compliance with US GAAP. The additional costs of reconciling these two systems, particularly in circumstances where there have been huge costs and efforts made to implement the IASB standards, have further worsened the situation.

If we assume that IFRS and US GAAP are to be harmonised, however, what are the implications for developing countries of implementing the former?

As is the case in the United States, the IFRS's approach to accounting focuses on the needs of participants in capital markets. The first difficulty, therefore, is that almost universally, accounting traditions in developing countries will not have been established on this basis, and are generally directly related to the tax system. Furthermore the complexity of IFRS, particularly with regard to exotic financial instruments such as complex derivatives, are not particularly relevant for many developing countries, particularly the poorer ones.

Samaha and Stapleton (2008) argue that this complexity, whilst problematic in itself, also raises the possibility of compliance being more *de jure* than *de facto*, where formal compliance can disguise the lack of a real harmonisation in approaches. They also raise the issue of the training of accountants in many developing countries, which may be a matter of lack of resources in part, particularly in a rapidly changing international environment.

What does all this add up to? Well, it is clearly the case that if countries (and their companies) want to participate in international capital markets there is no option but to adopt the accounting rules that are accepted in this arena. However, it is also important that these guidelines be streamlined and made relevant to the different conditions faced by different countries. Finally, countries should be allowed to go through a relatively lengthy transition to IFRS harmonisation, perhaps with interim – or bridging – mechanisms in the meanwhile. It is not feasible to expect instant compliance: American and European accounting experts have been discussing, debating and arguing about these issues for years. The outcome should not just be presented as a *fait accompli* that developing countries must immediately implement.

Second, to be helpful in obtaining external finance – as opposed to being a hindrance – a company's financial statements must obviously demonstrate a robust financial position, reflected in the relevant financial ratios that can be fed into a financial institution's lending model. The strength of these ratios, in combination with risk mitigation elements such as collateral, will then determine the precise nature of the loan contract to be offered.

Unlike the other forms of transaction lending listed above, financial statement lending is only possible where firms are transparent in terms of information: i.e. they can produce the necessary 'hard' quantitative data to support their loan application. For firms that are in a position to do so, financial statement lending has two clear advantages:

- The 'informativeness' of the financial statements addresses information problems in a very low-cost manner.
- Because financial statement lending and monitoring is based on 'hard' information, it can be offered by large and complex financial institutions at relatively low cost due to: (a) the ease with which this information can be used in lending models to produce the initial decision to lend (or not), and (b) the fact that the financial variables upon which this decision is based change regularly and transparently ensures that changes to a borrower's circumstances can be rapidly – and cheaply – incorporated into the monitoring process.

(b) Lending based on small business credit scoring

This type of lending is also based on 'hard' information about the potential borrower, which is largely of the personal consumer data form in the case of SMEs. Examples include data such as personal income, levels of debt, financial assets or home ownership, and may be obtained from a third-party public or private credit bureau.

This data is then fed into a 'loan performance prediction model', which results in a credit score for the loan. Some financial institutions may lend (or not) purely on the basis of this score, while others may use supplementary data from other areas, including qualitative data.

Mester (1997) gives a number of advantages of this approach, drawing on the US experience:

- Credit scoring greatly reduces the time taken to process a loan application.
- This produces time (and thus cost) savings for both lenders and borrowers.[13]
- Transparent criteria increase the objectivity of loan decisions.

Mester (op. cit.) does give some drawbacks of the credit scoring process, however:

- First, the process is only as effective as the criteria (and the data) upon which it is based. Therefore, if credit scoring does not accurately reflect actual creditworthiness – particularly the probability of default – then cost savings are likely to be more than offset by higher losses to the financial institution.
- The model must be rigorously tested through the economic cycle, so that it accurately predicts defaults in both good times and bad.[14]

These sorts of models are relatively new, having first appeared in the US in the 1990s, with the key innovation being the use of personal credit histories to produce the credit score. Unlike financial sector lending, however, there is no requirement for the SME itself to be informationally transparent, since the loan is made on the basis of the personal creditworthiness of the owner, not the company itself.

However, while not necessarily requiring formal financial statements, the process is based on information on creditworthiness – either of the small enterprise or its owner – in either an individual (the particular SME or person) or pooled (i.e. by risk category of borrowing entity) form. As shown in Figure 9.1, these forms of information are far more readily available in high-income than in middle-income countries, which in turn have a far greater level of credit information than that found in low-income countries. For example, while more than half of adults in high-income countries have credit information stored with a private, third-party credit bureau – which potential lenders can immediately access to ascertain creditworthiness – the corresponding figure for low-income countries is 0.16%.

Thus, while small business scoring models may be an attractive option in the longer term, for less developed countries in particular there will clearly need to be a significant upgrading of the informational infrastructure of the financial sector before it is feasible on any meaningful scale.

(c) Asset-based lending

With this form of lending, the financial institution depends on the assets of the SME as the guarantor of repayment. The use of collateral is not unique to this form of lending, however, as collateral may be used to mitigate the risk (and therefore improve the terms) of other forms of lending such as financial statement or small business credit scoring. The difference with asset-based

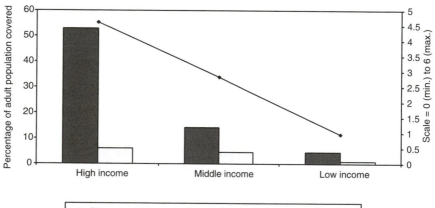

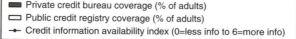

Figure 9.1 Availability of credit information: high-, middle- and low-income countries, 2006.

Source: World Bank WDI.

lending, however, is that the collateral is pledged as the *primary* method of repayment.

Asset-based lending is also a transaction form of lending based on hard data, since the size of the loan available is a quantitative function of the value of the assets pledged as collateral. As with the other forms of lending described, it can therefore also be undertaken by large financial institutions in a way that exploits economies of scale.

At present, pure asset-based lending only occurs in four countries, which suggests that there are significant obstacles to its development, which we discuss below. However, in the countries where it is used, it forms an important part of total lending – in the US, for example, asset-backed lending, at US$300 billion, is a third as large as the total level of commercial and industrial lending of US$900 billion.

However, a note of caution should be sounded with respect to lending based purely on collateral. While lenders perceive this as an ideal way of minimising – or even eliminating – risk, this is far from being the case. That is, the size of the loan offered is a direct function of the estimated liquidation value of the asset in question. However, this value will move – to a greater or lesser extent depending on the type of asset – in a procyclical manner in relation to the business cycle. Thus in times of booming asset prices, lenders will be willing to lend increasing amounts as the liquidation value of the assets is seen to rise. This is fine unless the situation is one of an asset price bubble, which if pricked will lead to a sharp fall in asset prices and thus a commensurate fall in the liquidation value of the collateral that has been used to support the increase in lending. Consequently, increased use of collateral-based lending has the potential to prolong asset price bubbles, making the eventual correction all the more painful.[15] It is often the case in finance that risks are in fact high and rising when lenders perceive them to be very low.

(d) Factoring

Factoring involves the purchase of accounts receivable, which are known as a 'factor'. Factoring has similarities with asset-based lending – in that finance is provided on the basis of an asset 'owned' by the borrower, rather than an assessment of creditworthiness – but also significant differences:

- First, asset-based lending may entail inventories and physical equipment as well as expected flows of finance. In contrast, factoring only entails the last of these.
- Second, with factoring, the accounts receivable are formally *sold* to the lender, so there is an *ex ante* transfer of ownership.
- Third: '... factoring is essentially a bundle of three financial services: a financing component, a credit component and a collections component. Essentially, under most factoring relationships the borrower outsources

its credit and collections activities in addition to obtaining financing'
(Berger and Udell, 2004: 25).

Therefore, as with the previous three examples, factoring is a form of 'hard'
transaction lending form, since it is based on quantitative – and verifiable –
data, and can therefore – in theory at least – be provided by large as well as
small financial institutions.

As we shall see below, factoring can be a particularly useful lending tech-
nique in countries with a weak commercial law and enforcement framework,
which is often the case in developing countries. For example, even in the event
of bankruptcy the ownership of the accounts receivable has already been
transferred to the creditor.

Furthermore, while there is some risk of procyclicality in the sense of
fluctuating values of 'accounts receivable', this is likely to be far less of an
issue than is the case with broader forms of asset-based lending, where price
volatility will be considerably higher.

Factoring is also a powerful tool in enabling SMEs to smooth their expend-
iture/payment cycle. That is, while an SME incurs cost in the production and
transport of a good, the buyer will typically not pay for thirty to ninety days.
Such delays can be terminal for an SME without a financial cushion to fall
back on. The factoring process therefore enables the SME to sell the
'accounts receivable' immediately – at some discount – thereby overcoming
this time lag. Furthermore, the institution that purchases the factor need not
assess the creditworthiness of the SME – which may in any event be rather
opaque – but can focus attention of the creditworthiness of the entity that
owes the SME (Klapper, 2005).

Factoring has become of increasing importance in both developed and
developing countries. By 2005, global factoring volume exceeded US$1 tril-
lion, including more than US$5 billion in China, Mexico, Turkey and Brazil.
Whilst this may seem insignificant relative to the global turnover – and it
remains the case that the use of factoring is dominated by developed countries – there has been a sharp increase in its usage in emerging economies in
particular. For example, the four emerging economies listed above saw a 50%
rise in the use of factoring in the first five years of the twenty-first century,
and there is every sign of this continuing (ibid.).

(e) Trade credit[16]

Many of the techniques described above are employed in the provision of
trade credit, where credit scoring and the analysis of financial statements are
a standard part of the process, for example.

Similarly, factoring has become an increasingly important aspect of trade
facilitation and trade credit. For example, of the US$1 trillion of factoring
volume seen globally in 2005, US$90 billion related to the cross-border
receivables of exporters. The problems caused by the time lags often involved

in receiving payment that many SMEs face are generally more pronounced in the export sector. That is, SMEs from developing countries may have to wait a considerable time to receive payment, as the purchasing firm in a developed economy may want to wait and ensure product quality before issuing payment. However, as purchasers in developed markets are more likely to have a publicly available credit history, the SME can arrange ahead of time to sell these accounts receivable to a financial institution, thus alleviating its potential liquidity constraints (Klapper, 2006).

Some countries have adopted a formal, state-run framework to oversee this process. For example, the Bank of China's 'Export Factoring Service' buys up the credit risk of local exporters' international sales, and then provides credit cover for importers from the US, UK and Hong Kong (ibid.).

However, while trade credit is closely related to other forms of financing described above, it is also the case that it is generally viewed as a distinct lending mechanism, particularly given its importance to the SME sector.[17] For example, in the US, trade credit provides a third of all debt financing to SMEs, the same proportion as that provided by commercial banks (Robb, 2002, cited in Berger and Udell, 2004).

(f) Relationship lending

All of the transaction lending forms described above are designed, in different ways, to overcome problems of information. In circumstances where there remain unresolved information problems, however, relationship lending may be the only – and most probably the best – way for financing to be provided.

Unlike transaction lending, lending based on relationships does not use hard, quantitative data, but depends on 'soft' qualitative data that may be proprietary to the loan officer. This form of information may relate to the individual concerned (e.g. character, past record with repayments), or the small enterprise (e.g. repayment record, current and anticipated financial status), or the area in which the enterprise is based (e.g. potential market size, disposable income levels), or the business sector in which the SME operates (e.g. current and anticipated demand for products, competitors, market share).

One consequence of this is that as the gathering of this sort of data is likely to be relatively expensive and time-consuming, it may result in higher interest rates being attached to these forms of loans.

It has often been assumed that informationally 'opaque' SMEs have no option but to access lending based on relationships, as they cannot produce the 'hard' data needed for transaction lending. However, as Berger and Udell (2004) point out, this may indeed be the case for lending based on financial statements, but is not so for the other forms of transaction lending described above.

To summarise:

- Financial statement lending requires credible, audited financial statements and accounts.
- Small business credit scoring requires high levels of information on the creditworthiness of potential borrowers.
- Asset-based lending requires borrowers with high-quality (i.e. valuable) collateral, to which they have demonstrable rights of ownership.
- Factoring requires the borrower to provide credible 'accounts receivable' ideally from a client with a publicly available credit record.
- Trade credit may entail many of these lending mechanisms, particularly collateral and factoring, and is likely to require the involvement of a credible public body to facilitate, coordinate and provide guarantees.

We have also seen that many of these mechanisms are rarely used in developing countries, particularly the poorest, which must therefore rely on relationship lending. However, this lack of variety of lending forms does not reflect their inherent unsuitability for financing the private sector, particularly SMEs, but may instead be crucially determined by deficiencies in a country's 'lending infrastructure'.

9.3 The lending infrastructure

A country's 'lending infrastructure' refers to the environment in which lending takes place, and in particular to the institutions (broadly defined) that facilitate or constrain such lending. For the World Bank, Berger and Udell (2004) identify three components of the lending infrastructure:

1   the information environment;
2   the legal, judicial and bankruptcy environment;
3   the tax and regulatory environment.

The authors suggest that these frameworks can affect the availability of credit to SMEs in two ways:

- First, there may be direct effects, where the characteristics of each of these components of the lending infrastructure influence the extent to which different lending instruments are readily available.
- Second, there may be indirect effects, whereby the lending infrastructures constrain the development of different types of financial institution, which in turn influences the level and type of credit available.

9.3.1 The information environment

We have already seen how the availability of information – particularly, though not exclusively, relating to the creditworthiness of borrowers – can determine the extent to which different forms of lending can be used. Thus, in an information-rich environment, small business credit scoring is possible and has many advantages. Without such information, however, it is an impractical option.

This aspect of the lending infrastructure has strong direct effects on the availability of credit to SMEs. In particular, good accounting standards and credibly independent accounting firms are an essential prerequisite for the production of timely and informative financial statements. Consequently, poor accounting standards and the absence of independent and trusted accounting firms is a strong constraint on transaction lending on the basis of financial statements.

Second, the extent to which creditors share information about the payment history of borrowers also directly affects the type of credit available to SMEs. That is, it is not possible for third-party credit bureaus to develop in the absence of information sharing, which clearly constrains the availability of credit based on small business credit scoring. More generally, the argument is often made that the lack of credit bureaus (a) significantly increases the time taken to process loan applications, (b) increases the cost of loans, and (c) raises the level of defaults (Miller, 2003, cited in Berger and Udell, 2004).

Given this, one would expect there to be a strong positive correlation between the supply of credit to the private sector and the coverage of credit bureaus, and that developing countries eager to increase the supply of credit to the private sector should therefore target growth in the coverage of credit bureaus as a priority.

However, as can be seen from Figure 9.2 below, there is no such clear-cut

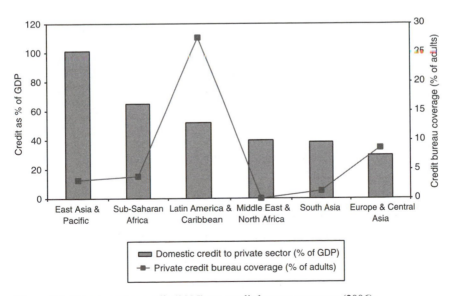

Figure 9.2 Private sector credit (2005) vs. credit bureau coverage (2006).

Source: World Bank WDI.

relationship. For example, the region with the highest level of domestic credit to the private sector – at more than 100% of GDP – is East Asia, but private credit bureaus only enjoy a 3.2% coverage rate. It might be thought that the explanation lies in the fact that public credit bureaus are performing this role, but the figure here is about the same, at 3.6%. Furthermore, if we look at the figures for Middle East and North Africa, we see that credit equivalent to 40% of GDP is achieved with no private credit bureaus at all, and only 4% coverage from their public equivalent. At the other extreme, Latin America boasts the highest level of credit bureau coverage of 27.6% and 7.5% for the private and public components respectively. This combined 36% coverage results in a supply of credit to the private sector of a little over 50% of GDP, which is a reasonable outcome, but far less than that achieved in East Asia – and also sub-Saharan Africa – with a minimal credit bureau infrastructure.

Clearly, while credit bureaus – private or public – can play a valuable role in facilitating an increase in the supply of credit to the private sector, not least to SMEs, it is perfectly possible to channel high levels of funds in their absence. That said, it is certainly the case that the sharing of (useful) information between lenders on the characteristics of borrowers will increase the efficiency of the lending infrastructure and, all other things being equal, increase the supply of credit. The regional exceptions given above are likely to have their own peculiarities, which facilitate the provision of credit to the private sector in ways that may not be replicable. For example, the dominant role played by oil revenues in the Middle East, the role of donors in the provision of credit in sub-Saharan Africa, and the importance of the state in providing and directing credit in China should not be underestimated.

Moreover, as well as the overall level of credit, there is also the question of its allocation. That is, the sharing of information on borrower's creditworthiness can only improve assessments on the riskiness of loans, allowing lenders to price their loans correctly to take account of this risk and supporting the long-term health of the financial sector, and thus its ability to continue to make loans in the future. Consequently, the finding in Miller (2003) that the absence of credit bureaus raises the levels of default is not surprising.

The more general point to stress, however, is that while developing this aspect of the lending infrastructure is important it is certainly not a solution in itself, and is clearly not the only means of channelling high levels of financing to the private sector.

9.3.2 The legal, judicial and bankruptcy environment

For the World Bank – as described in Berger and Udell (2004) – the key features of the legal environment that affect the availability of credit and its composition are, first, commercial laws that specify property rights, and second, the framework for enforcing these laws. That is, while it is vital to have strong property rights, they are of little use in the absence of effective enforcement.

For the Bank, recent empirical work[18] has demonstrated a link between the strength of property rights and their enforcement and the level of external finance used for investment purposes. Countries that do not have these positive features, in contrast, tend to have a greater reliance on less efficient financing from development banks, the state or the informal sector.

Figure 9.3 examines this linkage for a group of emerging and developing economies from different regions of the world. The figure shows the degree of confidence that managers surveyed had in their countries' courts' ability to uphold property rights[19] compared with the countries' level of FDI in 2004. The findings from the World Bank would suggest a positive correlation between these two variables, and in simple terms this is the case though not in any significant sense. A simple correlation yields the coefficient of 0.03, which although positive is hardly compelling.

Comparing the same survey data on managers' confidence with aid flows as a proportion of gross capital formation also yields the expected negative sign on the correlation coefficient. In this case this is –0.05: again, this is a very weak relationship, if it is one at all.

What this would seem to suggest is that, while there may be some tendency for investment flows to be positively correlated with the reality – as opposed to the official, legal position – of property rights enforcement, there are plenty of countries that buck this trend. For example, Bulgaria has a relatively low level of confidence in the property rights being upheld (43%), but combines this with the highest level of FDI as a proportion of GNI (10.9%). Conversely, Burundi, Cameroon and Malawi have relatively high levels of confidence in property rights (63%, 62% and 71% respectively), but negligible levels of FDI as a proportion of national income (0.006%, 0.001% and

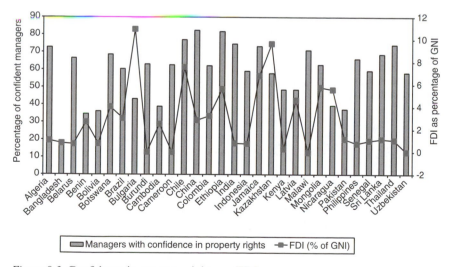

Figure 9.3 Confidence in property rights vs. FDI.

Source: World Bank WDI and author's calculations.

−0.03% respectively). Indeed, there does appear to be something of a pattern in this data, whereby countries from sub-Saharan Africa with strong and enforced property rights do not benefit from the direct investment flows that the findings from the World Bank would seem to predict and that theory would suggest. This is clearly a significant problem, as it is safe to assume that many developing countries have placed great store in improving their 'investment infrastructure', not least in the area of property rights, with the aim of increasing investment flows. That these inflows have not emerged in many countries, while other countries with weak property rights have seen large inflows, could understandably lead them to question the advice that they have been given.

In theoretical terms, another important issue in this area is that the lack of secure property rights largely prevents the banking sector from being able to compensate for incomplete information. Thus the features that serve to mitigate the problems of moral hazard and adverse selection – such as covenants, collateral and personal commitments – are rendered ineffective in the absence of clear and enforceable property rights. The nature of the bankruptcy process is also viewed as similarly important by the Bank. For example, the length of time that a company remains classified as bankrupt affects the speed with which creditors can be compensated.[20] Also, the details of the bankruptcy system are very important, particularly in areas where principles such as 'absolute priority' are enforced, which upholds the priority rights of secured lenders (Berger and Udell, 2004).

Enforcement is clearly fundamental in all of these areas. The World Bank (2003b) cites the case of the Czech Republic in this regard, where the time taken to enforce loan contracts, and the cost of doing so, are very high relative to its competitors. The Bank finds that, as a result, 'unsecured creditors can expect little or nothing for their claims and that secured creditors encountered limited rights, long delays with no compensation, and a poor environment for selling collateral assets'.

Clearly, a framework such as this is not conducive to most forms of lending, particularly asset-based lending, though it may in turn encourage others, such as factoring.

9.3.3 *The tax and regulatory environment*

The tax and regulatory environment facing lenders and borrowers is also seen as having a direct effect on the availability of credit to SMEs, with taxes on particular products or processes providing a disincentive for their use and an incentive for the use of alternatives.[21]

The tax and regulatory environment will also have significant indirect effects, through its impact on the ease with which different forms of financial institution can establish themselves. For example, Berger and Udell (2004) argue that:

- Government restrictions on the entry of foreign financial institutions may indirectly restrict the availability of credit to SMEs, as countries with a mix of domestic and foreign-owned institutions have been shown to lend to the SME sector more than do countries without the foreign component.
- More generally, constraints on the functions which different financial institutions can perform (for example, as under the Glass-Steagall Act in the USA) are also associated with the development of a fragile financial sector, and with lower levels of credit than would otherwise be available.
- The extent of government ownership of financial institutions affects the availability of credit. For example, high levels of state ownership are correlated with lower levels of credit availability to SMEs, despite the fact that many governments explicitly target the SME sector.

While there is certainly evidence to support these arguments, in the form of large aggregated regressions, it is not clear that all countries should therefore:

- remove all restrictions on the participation of foreign financial institutions;
- remove all functional boundaries between different forms of financial institutions; or
- remove all vestiges of state ownership from the financial sector.

For the first point, it is certainly true that the presence of efficient, technologically sophisticated international banks has the potential to force up standards in the financial systems of many countries. However, it is also the case that – by definition – such banks tend to be very large and, as we have seen, large financial institutions are less likely to lend to SMEs than are smaller banks.

What evidence there is suggests that this is the case: large foreign banks lend less to SMEs than do *small* domestic banks, but no less – and possibly more – than do *large* domestic banks. Ultimately, there is a strong argument for liberalising entry restrictions, but this does not mean that countries at all levels of developments should do so. Clearly, the domestic banking sector will struggle to compete with such large financial conglomerates, particularly in countries at low levels of development. As a consequence, overly hasty liberalisation raises the real possibility that the domestic financial sector will be unable to compete and thus unable to evolve into the fully developed *domestic* financial sector that might otherwise have evolved. For some, of course, this does not matter at all – others may well conclude that the development of a vibrant and effective domestic financial sector is a prerequisite of genuine development.

For the second point, it is generally forgotten that the Glass-Steagall Act was introduced in the US for a specific reason. In particular, the Act was implemented in response to the Wall Street Crash of 1929, where conflicts of interest, insider dealing and flagrant breaches of trust by banks – which were often on 'both sides of the deal' and therefore could not deal impartially with their clients – were seen by many as being at the heart of the problem. After repeal, as a result of unrelenting pressure – with proponents arguing that the US banking system could not compete on equal terms with other international banks that did not face such restrictions – we are today largely back in a pre-1929 world, where functional boundaries are a thing of the past.

Now the distinctions between commercial banks, investment banks, securities brokers and securities dealers, for example, are only enforced with 'Chinese walls' within institutions, rather than by a separation of institutions by function. While this may be more efficient in a narrow sense, it also raises genuine conflicts of interest issues. One interesting point in this regard is a trend for large banks to buy up successful niche players in each of these sectors, and many others. The question that this begs is why do they think they can turn more profit from these companies than their – already successful – owners and managers, if the Chinese walls that they erect are to remain intact?

When the actual behaviour of countries is examined with respect to the restrictions they impose on the activities of banks, we see that only very few have no restrictions at all. Of the 150 countries included in the World Bank's *Bank Regulation and Supervision Database,* only 11 countries[22] impose no controls. The activities detailed in the database are banks' involvement in:

- securities dealing and broking;
- insurance;
- real estate;
- owning non-financial firms.

The most common restriction is on bank involvement in the real estate sector, which both Australia and the United States prohibit. It seems, therefore, that the majority of countries – developed and developing alike – see significant potential disadvantages from the removal of all functional boundaries for financial institutions. The key point to make, which is too often ignored, is that 'efficiency' is not everything, and, if it comes at the cost of generating damaging asset price bubbles, can hardly be described as 'efficient' in any meaningful sense.

Finally, it is also certainly true that state involvement in the financial sector will, on average, lead to inferior outcomes in terms of the availability of credit and its allocation. However, this is not always so.

Table 9.1 lists the ten countries with the highest level of state ownership in the banking system in 2003. The most obvious point to make is that this list clearly does not equate with the ten least developed countries in the world.

Rather, what we see are some of the richest (Germany, Liechtenstein),

Table 9.1 Proportion of banking assets owned by state, 2003*

India**	75%
Togo	51%
Tunisia	43%
Germany**	42%
Russia	36%
Liechtenstein	32%
Argentina	32%
Taiwan	28%
Poland	24%
Mali	22%

Source: World Bank Financial Structure Database.

* State has more than 50% stake.
** As of end 2002.

some high- to middle-income countries (Taiwan, Poland, Argentina), some rapidly developing emerging markets (India, Russia), and some less developed countries (Togo, Mali).

The conclusion therefore must be that, while high levels of state ownership of the banking system may be associated with negative economic outcomes when looked at in terms of aggregated global data, this certainly does not mean that this must always be so. As with much else we have covered in this book, it seems to be the case that actual outcomes depend on *how* state-owned banks function in practice.

Furthermore, the example of Germany also suggests that it does not necessarily follow that as countries develop, the level of state ownership must always fall towards zero: Germany has built one of the most successful economic systems in the world with more than 40% of its banking system owned by the state.

9.4 Is the focus on SME financing in developing countries justified?

We have seen that considerable effort and resources have gone into addressing the financing gap for SMEs in developing countries, and that these efforts are justified on the basis of the unique contribution that the SME sector is supposed to make to the economy. In particular, the consensus has been that:

1   SMEs are responsible for the bulk of new job creation. Stimulating the sector can therefore have a disproportionate impact on employment and poverty levels.
2   SMEs are a fundamental source of entrepreneurship and innovation, and a vibrant SME sector is therefore likely to result in higher future growth rates.

3   A well-developed SME sector increases levels of competition in the economy, by raising the degree of dynamism and flexibility therein.

Although this has long been the received wisdom, some relatively recent research has begun to question these assumptions. Biggs (2002) sets out to test the evidence on each of these claims, with interesting results.

9.4.1 Do SMEs create the bulk of new jobs?

Much of the evidence on SMEs' role in job creation comes from studies in the US. In particular, the work of Birch (1979, 1981, 1987) is the key source in this regard. Birch's research into the US economy in the 1970s produced the eye-catching finding that 80% of all new jobs in the US during this decade were created by companies with less than 100 employees. However, the validity of this finding has been questioned on a number of grounds.

First, Birch's classification of SMEs included small establishments started by larger companies. For example, the opening of a new Wal-Mart with around eighty employees would be classified as job creation by SMEs.[23]

Second, Birch's analysis focused on *gross* job creation, rather than *net* job creation. It is widely accepted that SMEs do create a large proportion of jobs; however, due to the high failure rate in the SME sector, they also destroy a large number of jobs. When net job creation is considered, the evidence suggests that large companies create more permanent, stable jobs than does the SME sector[24] (Biggs, 2002).

Although the majority of the data on this issue pertains to the US market, the limited number of developing country evidence also supports this conclusion. Biggs and Shah (1998) examined the experience of four sub-Saharan countries in the 1980s and found that large enterprises (>500 employees) were the dominant source of net job creation. The precise figures were 56% in Ghana, 74% in Kenya, 76% in Zimbabwe and 66% in Tanzania.

As well as the quantity of net jobs, large firms are also responsible for the highest-quality job creation. In both developed and developing countries, large firms pay significantly higher wages (35% premium in developed countries and up to 50% in developing countries), and offer better benefits such as pensions, as well as providing superior working conditions (ibid.).

9.4.2 Are SMEs 'seedbeds' for entrepreneurship and innovation?

First, do SMEs disproportionately contribute to innovation within the economy? For Biggs (2002) it entirely depends on the sector. That is, SMEs are indeed more innovative in the hi-tech, skill-intensive sectors such as computing, but large enterprises produce the majority of innovations in lower-technology, capital-intensive sectors such as food and chemicals.

However, it is likely that even in the narrow hi-tech sector, these findings from the US are not transferable to developing countries: 'At earlier stages of development technology transfer from abroad is the force driving technological progress, not innovation. Very little investment in basic R&D is undertaken by either large or small firms in low-income countries.'[25] That is, the focus in most developing countries is on acquiring and adapting foreign technology. The example of the East Asian economies, starting with Japan and later incorporating Singapore, Taiwan and South Korea in particular, is instructive in the regard.[26]

Figure 9.4 illustrates this discrepancy in R&D spending, as seen from the late 1990s. As we can see, spending on R&D in high-income countries averages a little under 2.5% of GDP, compared to a little over 0.5% in middle- and low-income countries.

Within the developing world, the East Asian region had the highest relative research expenditure (0.9%), followed by Eastern Europe (0.88%), South Asia (0.75%) and Latin America (0.56%). The World Bank holds no data on North or sub-Saharan Africa in this area, but it is safe to assume that the level of R&D expenditure must be lower than the other regions for which data is available, as presumably this is what pulls down the low- and middle-income averages to the levels shown above.

One of the principal means through which technology transfer can be achieved is via linkages with international TNCs operating in the country concerned. Indeed, research in sub-Saharan Africa,[27] Asia and Latin America[28] suggest that it is these linkages that give larger firms a productivity advantage over SMEs in these regions. It is therefore difficult to see SMEs themselves as 'seedbeds' of innovation in the developing world. Furthermore, to the extent that SMEs are involved in the export sector, this is in an indirect

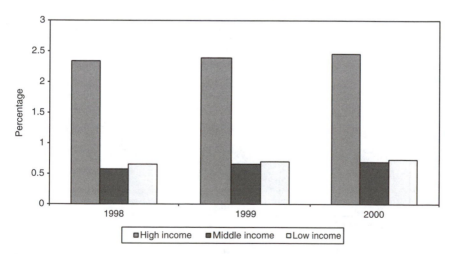

Figure 9.4 R&D expenditure as percentage of GDP, 1998–2000.

Source: World Bank WDI.

form through their role in the supply chain of larger companies, which are often also TNCs (ibid.).

The argument that SMEs are responsible for the majority of new firm formation has already been considered in the context of job creation, but a similar argument holds for firms' survival and longer-term growth prospects. That is, SMEs create lots of new firms, but a high proportion of these fail and/or are unable to grow into medium-sized enterprises. For example, fewer than 10% of African firms with fewer than ten employees ever grow to employ more than fifty people (Biggs, 1999). In part, these low survival and growth rates may be because the establishment of a small enterprise is often a last resort. That is, the lack of alternative forms of employment may drive the desperate to set up on their own, which is supported by evidence from both developed and developing countries that the level of SME start-ups increases in economic downturns.[29]

9.4.3 SME dynamism vs. large companies economies of scale

It is certainly the case that SMEs add to the dynamism and flexibility of an economy, particularly in hi-tech sectors. Historically, this has led many to conclude that SMEs therefore also contribute to higher levels of growth – a subject we shall return to below. However, as well as this dynamism and flexibility, an economy also needs an appropriate quantity of larger firms that are able to benefit from the exploitation of economies of scale.[30] There is thus a balance to be struck. In developing countries, on average, 60% of economic activity is generated by the SME sector. For developed countries, the corresponding figure is 30%. This suggests that, if anything, developing countries need to increase the proportion of larger firms within their economies.

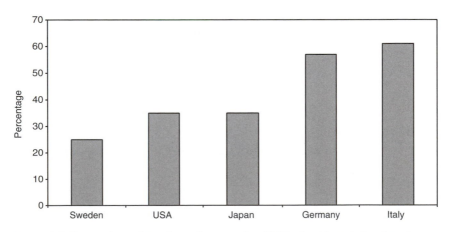

Figure 9.5 Proportion of total employment by SMEs in selected developed economies, 2001.

Source: Biggs, 2002.

However, as shown in Figure 9.5, even within developed countries there are wide differences in the size of the SME sector, which this average figure disguises. For example, in the US small firms have an employment share of 35%, which is the same level as in Japan. Sweden, in contrast, has 25% of jobs in the SME sector, whilst Germany has 57% and Italy has 61%.

At the other extreme, in Eastern Europe in the early 1990s as few as 1% of jobs were in the SME sector, reflecting the legacy of the communist era, when the focus was on large-scale, centralised production and the exploitation of economies of scale. Conversely, in many developing countries, the problem has been too little focus on large-scale production, which may be an after-effect of widespread import-substitution-industrialisation, where the monopoly position of a few large but inefficient firms was protected, preventing other firms reaching a large size. At the same time, excessive regulation and high tax levels encouraged many small firms to remain in the informal sector (ibid.).

9.4.4 SMEs and growth

The findings presented above – largely from Biggs (2002) – suggest that the focus on SME development may not be quite as justified as has been thought. However, much of the evidence is somewhat anecdotal and/or *ad hoc*, and cannot be said to be conclusive evidence against the importance of the SME sector in the aggregate sense.

In an attempt to address this, the World Bank developed an internationally comparable database of the size of SME sectors in a range of developed and developed countries, and sought to develop statistically robust evidence on their impact upon employment, growth and poverty reduction.[31] The study finds that:

- Contrary to the data provided in Biggs (op. cit.), the size of the SME sector – in terms of contributions to employment and GDP – shows no variability across countries at different income levels. However, this is only so if the informal sector is included, which was not the case in previous studies. If one strips out the informal sector the findings – which again run counter to those presented above – show that the relative importance of the SME sector increases in line with per capita incomes. As countries develop, however, the (informal) SME sector declines and the (formal) SME sector increases (Ayyagari *et al.*, 2003).
- While there is a statistically significant correlation between the size of the SME sector and economic development and growth, causality tests suggest that it is not that a strong SME sector causes economic growth, but rather than as a country develops this tends to lead to an increase in activity in the SME sector (Beck *et al.* 2004b).
- Furthermore:

    When the analysis focuses on income growth among the lowest

income quintile rather than the overall population, it again finds no evidence for the importance of SMEs. Nor does it find any statistically significant relationship between the importance of SMEs and the depth and breadth of poverty across countries.

(ibid.: 3)

Figure 9.6 illustrates this variable 'relationship', by comparing GDP per capita and the relative size of the SME sector in terms of employment in the manufacturing sector. As we can see, the countries considered do not, as the conventional wisdom might have predicted, exhibit any clear, positive relationship between these two variables. Furthermore, as pointed out above, causality tests suggest that to the extent that any relationship exists between the size of the SME sector and growth, this runs from growth to SMEs, and not in the other direction – again, this is contrary to what the conventional wisdom would predict.

To summarise, the case for the unique benefits that SMEs can bring to the economy would appear to be overstated, particularly in developing countries. However, it is clearly important for an economy to develop a vibrant and diverse economy. That is, a combination of competitive and efficient small, medium and large firms must be optimal. In this regard the real problem facing developing countries is that of the 'missing middle' described above, not necessarily the lack of SMEs *per se*. In this regard, SMEs do appear to face particular issues in growing their firm size and market share.

For Biggs (2002) an important obstacle to this process is 'institutional failure':

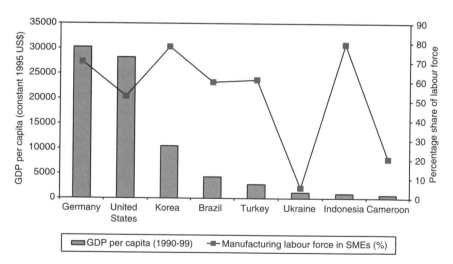

Figure 9.6 GDP per capita vs. SME manufacturing labour force share.

Source: Beck, Demirgüç-Kunt and Levine, 2004.

The failure of public institutions in many developing countries to properly enforce business contracts and property rights, and to provide adequate information on markets, raises the costs of governing market exchanges, sometimes prohibitively. In such high transaction-cost environments, the extent of the market for individual business firms is limited by the number of business transactions that can be governed by relational contracts. Firms often cannot take advantage of profitable opportunities outside their local networks of personal relations because of information and enforcement problems.[32]

However, it should be remembered that, as we have seen, these factors are no guarantor of economic success, nor is development necessarily dependent upon them in all instances.

However, it is surely the case that difficulties in obtaining finance are not the only constraints on the growth of small firms. The aggregated data does clearly show a relationship between the business environment and growth in this respect, which is what one would broadly expect: for firms to invest and grow they need to have confidence that (a) they can enforce their ownership rights, (b) contracts will be upheld, and (c) the business environment in which they operate is relatively stable. Economies characterised by high levels of uncertainty and minimal enforcement of the rule of law are unlikely to facilitate this process.

Large firms are often able to surmount these problems by protecting their own property and investing in the acquisition of information. However, in most cases such expense is beyond the reach of the SME sector.

Empirical research in developing countries suggests that the economic success of SMEs is directly connected with the extent to which they have been able to overcome these institutional failures by becoming 'embedded' in these private institutional support systems developed by large firms (UNCTAD, 2000).

In this regard, the success or failure of an SME to prosper and expand may be strongly related to its ability to forge linkages with larger firms. One such sector, of course, is foreign TNCs operating in developing countries, particularly where TNCs are relatively large compared to the size of the national economy, as is the case in many least developed countries, for example.

9.5 TNC–SME linkages

At the global level, the stock of FDI to world GDP stood at 22.7% in 2005. For developing countries, the average was slightly above this at 26.6%, compared to a figure of 21.6% for developed economies.

The countries with the highest ratio of FDI to GDP are generally small island states, particularly those in the Caribbean that have become financial services centres – or tax havens depending on your perspective, of course. For

Table 9.2 FDI stock as a proportion of GDP in five African countries, 2005

Liberia	719%
Equatorial Guinea	130%
Chad	78%
Congo	63%
Gambia	60%

Source: UNCTAD FDI Database.

example, the Cayman Islands and Bermuda have stocks of FDI to GDP of 2,743% and 2,498% respectively. However, a number of sub-Saharan African countries also have extremely high ratios, as shown in Table 9.2. In such circumstances, where TNCs dominate the economic activity of a country, building strong and sustainable linkages with domestic SMEs may well be essential to the growth and development of the economy.

Economies of developing countries are often characterized by polarized enterprise structures where only large and small, but no middle-sized firms exist, along with technological heterogeneity, and segmented goods and labor markets between them. A stronger integration of their SMEs into modern supplier chains can make an important contribution towards improving the enterprise size structure. A well-balanced structure of enterprise sizes may emerge where the economies of scale in production are ideally combined with the flexibility of small enterprises.[33]

For UNCTAD (2000) there are a number of different type of linkages that SMEs in developing countries can, in principle, forge with TNCs. Furthermore, the benefits to SMEs from this process are likely to be determined by the nature of these linkages, which in turn will be determined by the strategic stance of the TNC, the skills and characteristics of the SME sector, and the policies of the government in question.

Four types of linkages are described:

1   *Backward linkages with suppliers*: Here the SME becomes a part of the TNC's supply chain, and may source and/or provide parts, components, materials and services from domestic suppliers. The benefit of these backward linkages to the SME, however, will depend on the quantity and types of supplied inputs, and the extent to which the TNCs transfer technology and knowledge in the process of building a long-term relationship with the SMEs. In this regard, linkages of this form range from arm's-length market transactions to long-term partnerships between the TNC and SME in question.

2   *Linkages with technology partners*: In some circumstances TNCs may launch common projects in conjunction with SME partners. These

projects may take a variety of forms, which may or may not include equity linkages. Examples include: joint ventures, licensing agreements and broader strategic alliances. Technological alliances are common among developed countries and, although increasing, remain relatively rare between TNCs and SMEs from developing countries.

3 *Forward linkages with customers*: The primary forward linkages developed by TNCs are with marketing (or retail) outlets. For example, TNCs that wish to outsource the distribution of branded goods may invest in the outlet concerned. The second form is with industrial buyers, where TNCs producing inputs may offer after-sales services on how to use and maintain the purchased goods. The third form refers to linkages in which a TNC produces goods for secondary processing by an SME with a forward linkage.

4 *Other spillover effects*: These include:

(a) 'Demonstration effects', which occur as TNCs introduce innovative working practices that may be replicated by local entrepreneurs, resulting in an upskilling of local industry. At the other extreme, however, the TNC may 'outcompete' local businesses.

(b) 'Human capital spillovers' can occur when TNCs' trained and newly experienced local personnel move to local firms or form their own companies.

From UNCTAD's perspective, the most important of these linkages – for the SME and the local economy – is backward linkages in the supply chain. The potential benefits to the SME from these linkages are clear: 'The large enterprises, being their customers, open up new markets for them, often facilitate regular sales and growth, which permits economies of scale. Such links may relieve them of marketing tasks and provide an important impetus for modernization' (UNCTAD, 2000: 5–6).

However, it is important to stress that these benefits do not follow automatically from the forging of the relationship – the extent of the actual benefits will be, in part, determined by the reasons behind the TNC's wish to forge such links, which will influence both its relative bargaining power and the advantages it hopes to obtain. In this regard, the report describes four possible advantages to the TNC of forging these linkages:

1 *Productivity gains*: The primary motivation of a TNC for outsourcing the production of goods and services is that the SME is able to produce better or cheaper products than itself:

> If the underlying rationale of the customer is to make use of technological specialization and/or economies of scale of the supplier, the latter has a relatively high autonomy over product design and will be responsible for improvements. Since the supplier produces a specialized complementary input for the customer, the latter cannot easily

play one supplier off against another. This gives the SME a certain bargaining power.

(ibid.: 6)

Relationships of this form will tend to be long-term, strategic partnerships from which much benefit to the SME and local economy will be derived.

2 *Factor-cost advantages*: SMEs in developing countries generally have access to cheaper labour than does the TNC. However, if a TNC establishes a relationship with the sole aim of reducing wages, the terms are usually far less beneficial for the supplier since it is based on the SME retaining a cost advantage in the face of strong competition. Such linkages can lead to a 'race to the bottom', as SMEs compete to offer ever-lower wages. Box 9.3 describes this process whereby outsourced manufacturing/assembly has moved from low-cost bases in East Asia, to yet cheaper bases in Southeast Asia, and more recently to China, with its huge pool of low-cost workers.

Box 9.3 'Flying geese' and new trade theory

The 'flying geese paradigm' was coined to describe a process of industrial upgrading allowing countries to 'catch up' with the industrial world. Akamatsu (1961) saw Japan as the first of the 'geese', where the country could import technology and use relatively cheap labour to produce internationally competitive goods. As labour costs rise, however, the viability of this strategy diminishes and the production of the cheaper goods moves to the next 'geese' in the pattern – in this case, the Newly Industrialising Countries (NICs) of Hong Kong, Korea, Singapore and Taiwan.

At the same time the lead 'goose' – Japan – moves to the production of higher-value goods. The process then countinues, with lower-end production moving to the next wave of geese – i.e. the South East Asian economies, while the process of upgrading continues to ripple down from the lead country. The move to the final wave of countries – Vietnam and, particularly, China – can be seen as the most recent stage of the process.

What differentiates this approach from orthodox international trade theory is that comparative advantage is dynamic rather than fixed. That is, although each successive 'goose' uses its relative advantage of cheap labour costs, this is in the context of upgrading and the creation of comparative advantage at higher points on the value chain. In this respect, Meier (1988) argues that dynamic gains from trade can be incorporated into the Heckscher-Ohlin (H-O) model of international trade. That is, a country's initial comparative advantage may be determined,

---

as in the H-O model, by the relative abundance of the different factors of production – e.g. abundant cheap labour. However, as a country develops it accumulates more capital and experiences improvements in skills and technological development:

> As these changes occur, the country's comparative advantage changes from an initial comparative advantage in natural resource-intensive exports through other stages of comparative advantage in exports that are successively unskilled-labor intensive, skilled-labor intensive, capital-intensive, and knowledge-intensive. The progression nullifies the constraint of foreign demand for a given export from a given country. As a country progresses through the stages of comparative advantage, another country can then replace the exports previously produced by the country that has graduated along the comparative advantage scale.

Thus, while the path that each country takes through this 'progression' will be influenced by factors such as the initial degree of land scarcity, for example, there is the possibility of influencing the trajectory of the progression. This perspective is central to New Trade Theory (NTT), which is based on the work of Paul Krugman.

Krugman's (1986) major insight was to remove the assumption of constant returns to scale that is central to the H-O model. Krugman argued that the reality of economies of scale within firms is incompatible with the perfect competition assumed in orthodox trade theory. Rather, a more realistic assumption is one of 'monopolistic competition', where as the market expands (through trade, for example) it does so through a mixture of more firms (providing product variety) and larger firms with greater scale economies. This perspective helped economists to explain some puzzling facts: rather than what would be expected on the basis of comparative advantage, much trade takes place between developed countries with very similar endowments of the factors of production, and consists of broadly similar goods.

Importantly, however, it also helped to restore credibility to the idea that a country could pick 'national champions'. For example, it is not clear why South Korea should have a comparative advantage in much of its heavy industrial production. However, from an NTT perspective, the government was able to identify the area in which it wished to develop 'champions' (steel production, for example) and then allow the industry to develop to a critical size before exposing it to international competition. It may be that the benefits of economies of scale are such that, in certain sectors, it is not feasible for there to be more than a very small number of global producers. The countries that are able to bring their companies to the size where these economies of scale allows them to compete globally are therefore able to out-compete smaller competitors, bringing clear benefits to the national economy.

Although Krugman supported this perspective in principle, he was doubtful that, in practice, countries would be able to accurately select and effectively support 'national champions'. Regardless of this, however, many have seized on the theory to support just such a policy.

3   *'Passive' (numerical) flexibility*: such relationships entail occasional subcontracting to increase production in periods of high demand – i.e. 'just in time' production. The benefits to the SME and local economy from such links are likely to be weak, however. In particular, the (financial) risks of having capacity (both human and physical) standing idle for long periods, coupled with short bursts of intense activity, is passed entirely to the SME in question.

4   *'Active' (functional) flexibility*: This form of linkage is likely to be more beneficial, however. With 'functional' flexibility, suppliers are able to respond to changes in functional (i.e. not numerical) demand by rapidly switching production processes and/or modifying the composition of inputs and outputs. However, to be possible, such a system of production requires multi-skilled workers and may require programmable multi-purpose machines.

In terms of realising the benefits to the SME and local economy, a key point to make is that the TNC and SME (and government of the country concerned) are highly likely to have very different objectives. As described above, there are a number of reasons why a TNC would wish to forge linkages with a local SME, and the nature of this motivation has a strong impact on the relative bargaining power as each party tries to fulfil its objectives (UNCTAD, 2000).

For example, the SME (and certainly the government) will wish there to be as much technology transfer as possible. However, from the TNC's perspective, it is likely that its technological 'know-how' is central to the maintenance of its market position. As a result, it will wish to minimise 'leakage' in this regard (ibid.).

If the motivation for the TNC is just to secure cheap labour, or to access local knowledge, for example, these objectives are relatively easy to obtain from a variety of sources. In such a situation, an SME (and its government) seeking the transfer of as much technology as possible will be in a very weak bargaining position. In these circumstances, the TNC is most likely to be able to meet its objectives. Conversely, if the TNC wishes to take advantage of specialised production techniques developed by the SME, or to exploit its advanced 'active (functional) flexibility' the SME has far greater bargaining power, and is therefore much more likely to see its objectives realised.

Such partnerships are most common between developed countries and are now very rare in the case of a TNC and a developing country. In the past, the catalyst for such relationships has often been government regulations that require the TNC to forge local partnerships. However, as we have seen in previous chapters, WTO regulations – particularly the trade-related-investment-measures (TRIMS) – now largely prevent developing countries from implementing such 'local content requirements'.

Without such requirements, technological partnerships of this kind are likely to remain the province of TNCs operating in other developed economies, as SMEs in the developed world – particularly the least developed countries – are highly unlikely to have the level of technology required, and thus have very limited bargaining power. However, there is of course a 'chicken and egg' element here: one means of obtaining such technological advancement is by requiring TNCs to develop a domestic SME supply base, but this has now been largely closed off by the WTO regulations described above.

Perhaps recognising this reality, UNCTAD (2000) suggests that governments should adopt a carefully targeted approach. That is, if the government aims to attract all forms of FDI, perhaps on the basis of labour costs, the types of linkages formed are unlikely to bring significant benefits to the economy, other than low-wage employment of course. Alternatively, if a government adopts a more focused approach, beginning with the identification of sectors in which the country may have a comparative advantage, and followed by a targeted strategy to attract TNCs with expertise in this sector, more benefits are likely to accrue.

In this regard, a vital element is the availability of a group of highly-skilled local workers that the TNC can draw upon, therefore increasing the bargaining power of the country's SME sector, and raising the possibility that the form of the relationship will be of significant benefit to both parties. For human capital formation of this kind, the identification of the country's potential areas of comparative advantage should go hand in hand with developing a pool of labour for these sectors. For example, countries can focus on increasing the proportion of engineering, science, logistics and business graduates, before developing a more specialised group from this pool of labour.

The experience of the economies of East and Southeast Asia is highly instructive in this regard, where the importance of human capital development was appreciated very early on, and significant government expenditure was devoted to developing national levels of human capital.

UNCTAD lists TNC strategies that are themselves compatible with the development of deepening, long-term linkages. These are as follows:

- The investment is driven by the search for strategic capabilities and assets rather than for cheap natural resources, low wages or protected local markets.
- The TNC looks to expand the pool of skilled workers through in-house education and training.

- The TNC is involved in public–private partnerships, which help develop the skill-base of the host region.
- Local personnel are incorporated into senior management structures.
- Decision-making is largely devolved to the local subsidiary by the parent company.
- New business opportunities are developed beyond the scope of the initial investment, which would not have been possible without the involvement of the TNC.
- Business models used are based on networking and the use of SME clusters.
- Outsourcing is significant and locally oriented.
- Suppliers and affiliates are supported with R&D capacity.

However, to be in a position to take advantage of these strategies, however, SMEs in developing countries are seen as needing:

- to have a commitment to continuous learning;
- to achieve minimum efficiency standards and focus on maintaining and improving them;
- to analyse their strengths and weaknesses;
- to proactively identify and form relationships with suitable TNC partners;
- to negotiate contracts with great care;
- to be able and willing to change as the needs of the relationship change;
- to contribute specific assets, beyond familiarity with local politics, regulations and local markets. That is, to bring something unique 'to the table' (UNCTAD, 2000).

To summarise, the benefits that SMEs and developing countries will obtain from relationships with TNCs are dependent on the nature, depth and duration of these linkages.

As we have seen, this will be influenced by a number of factors, which can be divided into four categories:

1   the possibility (or not) of insisting on 'local content' in relation to the TNC's supply chain;
2   the existence and efficiency of supporting public policies and measures that increase domestic SME investment and facilitate technology transfer and skills development;
3   the TNC corporate strategy, which may (or may not) be conducive to local SME development; and
4   the existence of SMEs which are able to meet high TNC standards or at least have the potential to achieve such standards within a short learning period.

Clearly, governments are in a position to directly influence both (1) and (2), but obviously have little or no influence on a TNC's corporate strategy. One increasingly important element in this regard, however, is the growing emphasis on corporate social responsibility (CSR), which is explored in Box 9.4 below.

Box 9.4 CSR, SRI and TNCs: compatible acronyms?

Government can enlist the support of certain TNCs in building linkages because many profit-seeking TNCs are concerned with the issues of corporate responsibility since they live in a media-driven world. They understand that they need an implicit license to operate in their societies. All societal groups are expected to perform certain roles and functions that can change overtime. Expectations related to TNCs are undergoing unusually rapid change due to the expanded role of these enterprises in the global economy. The social contract stipulates that with power and rights go certain, responsibilities.

(UNCTAD, 2000: 13)

Corporate social responsibility (CSR) has become of increasing importance to both TNCs and domestically oriented companies. To date, much of this has been focused on companies in developing markets, but increasingly, it is spreading to the developing world. In particular, companies' activities – particularly in relation to the pay and conditions of their workers and their environmental impact – in developing countries have become increasingly scrutinised, and they have been pressurised to account for their actions. We have seen the export processing zones (EPZs) often compete on the basis of low wage or minimal labour restrictions: there would therefore appear to be a direct tension between CSR and commercial issues, though this is not so straightforward as it might at first appear.

Most large companies are very conscious of the value of their 'brand' and are therefore anxious to avoid lurid newspaper headlines, for example, that show them in a bad light. Indeed, most major companies now have a dedicated department focusing on CSR issues. In this respect, CSR can indeed impact directly upon the 'bottom line' if a company's brand is damaged by adverse publicity. For some, however, CSR is nothing but a marketing exercise, with some companies that can afford the trappings of CSR investing heavily in doing so, regardless of the nature of their main business activity.

Various bodies – from the UN to the Commonwealth – have developed guidelines and codes of practice, to which many large companies have signed up. In relation to TNCs' activities in developing countries these codes of conduct stress the importance of issues such as working conditions, the environment and forging meaningful links with local SMEs. However, it is one thing to sign up to such guidelines and quite another to proactively seek to forge and deepen these relationships. A crucial driver in this regard – at least potentially – is the socially responsible investment (SRI) movement. SRI entails investing according to socially responsible or ethical principles and seeks to encourage better behaviour. The size of the SRI sector is such that it now has real potential clout.

	US$ billions	*UK£ billions*	*Euro billions*
United States	2332.0	1630.2	2621.7
United Kingdom	326.0	224.5	370.0
Canada	31.4	21.6	35.0
Europe	17.6	12.2	19.8
Japan	1.9	1.3	2.2
Australia	1.1	0.7	1.2
Total	**2710.6**	**1863.5**	**3049.9**

Global SRI universe 2001

Source: Sparkes, 2002.

As we can see, by 2001, there was more than US$2.5 trillion of global SRI assets. To date, very little emphasis has been put on development issues by the SRI movement, and what emphasis there has been has tended to be negative rather than positive – i.e. avoiding 'bad' companies rather than encouraging positive behaviour. However, there is enormous untapped potential. The role of TNCs has expanded hugely in many developing countries, and there is the possibility of this being of significant benefit to the host countries, but only if TNCs behave in such a way (i.e. forging deep, long-term linkages in the economy) that make this a reality. While policy-makers can develop their SME sector to be able to exploit these opportunities, concerned investors in developed countries – of whom there are many – have significant influence over the activities of these companies, given the proportion of their shares held by parts of the SRI sector. They need to use this influence.

Concluding remarks

In this penultimate chapter we have examined the relationship between the financial sector and the development of the private sector, with a particular emphasis on small and medium-sized enterprises.

As was stressed at the outset, this is of course the primary purpose of the exercise: financial sector development is not an end in itself, but is valuable to the extent that it facilitates the development and growth of the real economy, and thus leads to poverty alleviation in developing and emerging economies. To the extent that it does not achieve this, it is just an abstract debate, which may be interesting in itself, but is ultimately a case of angels dancing on the head of a pin.

The final chapter will attempt to draw together the lessons that have been learned throughout this book and, it is hoped, provide a little more light than heat than is often to be found in the field of development finance.

10 Finance for development
What do we know?

Introduction

Throughout this book we have examined various aspects of the financial sector and its relationship with economic growth, development and poverty alleviation:

- First, the context for the book was set out in the form of a theoretical overview;
- Second, evidence on the nature of the relationship between financial sector development (FSD), growth and poverty reduction was assessed;
- Third, we considered issues surrounding financial liberalisation, again focusing on the linkages with growth and poverty reduction;
- Fourth, we looked in some detail at the domestic financial system, covering issues such as government finances and policy, and the development of different aspects of the financial system infrastructure;
- Fifth, we examined issues of domestic financial reform;
- Sixth, the external financial system was introduced, comprising both private and official flows;
- Seventh, the relationship between external financial flows and the incidence of financial and debt crises in developing countries was considered;
- Eighth, we examined the relationship between FSD and the 'international financial architecture', particularly the Bretton Woods institutions, the regional development banks and GATT and the WTO; and
- Ninth, we considered issues surrounding the financing and development of the private sector – particularly SMEs – and assessed linkages between TNCs and SMEs in developing countries.

In this last chapter, we will bring these various strands together, with an examination of the issues facing governments in developing countries who are seeking to develop their financial systems with the aim of spurring higher rates of economic growth and reductions in poverty levels. The point of departure in this respect will be the 'official advice', which is offered to developing countries by the multilateral development institutions, particularly the World Bank. To this end, we will be asking: where is the 'received wisdom' on these issues correct, and where not? Where does it go too far, and where not far enough? Where does the evidence support a particular course of action, and where is this not the case?

There are three stages to the process of financial sector development, before we reach the ultimate objective:

1   The government needs to mobilise sufficient levels of domestic savings to provide the financial sector with the resources to perform its role, and attract appropriate levels and compositions of external capital flows to augment these domestic savings as needed, while avoiding the risk of being hit by a financial crisis.
2   The financial sector must be structured so that it is able to process and channel these resources to the most potentially productive parts of the private sector.
3   The private sector must invest these external financial resources – in combination with its own internal resources – so as to a) increase economic activity, b) create high and stable levels of employment (therefore reducing poverty directly), c) raise levels of productivity, and therefore d) produce high and sustainable levels of economic growth.

10.1 Mobilising savings

Levels of savings, as a proportion of GDP, vary widely between developing countries and regions. Furthermore, even within each region or country, savings rates are not stable over time. We have seen in previous chapters that rates of savings are positively associated with investment and ultimately growth rates. However, we have also seen that the direction of causality in this regard is ambiguous, with some empirical results suggesting that growth causes savings rates to rise, rather than a rise in savings rates producing higher rates of economic growth.

However, we have also seen that financial sector development (FSD) does not necessarily lead to increased savings rates. Indeed, there is some evidence – particularly from higher-income countries – to suggest that FSD may actually reduce savings rates, at least over the shorter term. Furthermore, as described in Box 10.1 below in the case of Japan, it is also the case that savings rates can be too high: in some countries, a very high propensity to save can result in consumption being too low, which depresses growth rates. As with much else that has been covered in this book, what is needed is the correct balance between savings, investment and consumption.

Box 10.1 Savings rates, domestic demand and deflation in Japan

The historical trajectory of Japan's economy has, in many ways, prompted a rewriting of the textbooks. Eschewing the laissez-faire approach to economic development, Japan was the first modern example of a 'developmental state', where extensive government intervention in the economy steered industrial policy through a process of export-led growth. The model was later replicated – to a greater or lesser extent – by the Asian 'tiger economies', most notably South Korea and Taiwan. A key was sustained investment, based on high levels of domestic savings, which in turn was facilitated by the separation of the domestic and international aspects of the economy. That is, domestic demand (in terms of consumption) remained low with disposable incomes instead being saved and used for investment purposes.

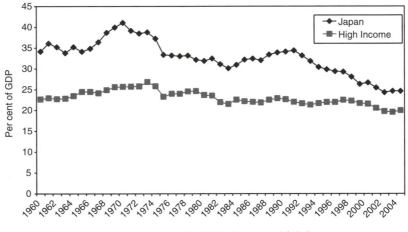

Gross domestic savings rates 1960–2005: Japan vs. high-income average.

Source: World Bank WDI.

Some of this story is part of the 'normal' development process, where poorer countries tend to have high rates of savings and investment as they catch up with the richer economies. At early stages of development profitable investment opportunities are relatively easy to come by, leading to high rates of return on such investment and so encouraging savings and investment. As the economy develops, however, such opportunities become harder to find and rates of return drop accordingly, with people switching instead to consumption, thus building domestic demand in the economy.

The table above shows the domestic savings rate for Japan compared with the average for high-income countries from 1960. As we see, Japan's saving rate has been consistently above that of their peers – often by as much as 10 percentage points – for most of this period, and it is only in recent years that what looks like a consistent downward trend can be seen. Why is this?

Madsen (2005) argues that the normal rate of domestic investment in an advanced economy is around 10–11% of GDP – when a country exceeds this, as the US did in the late 1990s, for example – the usual outcome is an oversupply of productive capacity. By the early 1980s, Japan's investment rates had fallen to 13.4%, but a number of factors prevented it from falling further (ibid.):

- Japanese corporations distributed lower profits to shareholders than in other comparable economies, so that the sector could finance its own investment and did not require extra finance.
- The aging Japanese population saw a large proportion of citizens enter the 40–65 age bracket and so increase their savings with a view to retirement.
- The usual response would have been for the excess capital to move overseas (either as financing or as exports), but the sheer size of the Japanese economy, coupled with political tensions – notably with the US – over a persistently large current account surplus made this impossible.
- Instead the capital was channelled into generating huge asset and property price bubbles.
- The bursting of these bubbles in the late 1980s depressed domestic demand yet further, which was compounded by a reduction of investment in additional capacity by Japanese industry.
- In an attempt to take up the slack and boost demand the government began running aggressive fiscal deficits, leading to an increase in the national debt of 100% between 1989 and 2003.
- Excess supply relative to depressed demand pushed Japan into deflation, which further reduced the incentive to consume – even with interest rates at zero, saving still makes money in deflation.
- Japan's saving rate is now falling quite fast, partly as large numbers retire, and domestic demand may in time rise to match supply. But this has taken the best part of twenty years: China beware!

Although we cannot unequivocally say that higher rates of savings produce higher levels of growth, it is undeniably the case that rapidly growing developing economies tend to have relatively high savings rates. In many ways this is intuitively obvious: the availability of a large pool of domestic savings would seem to be a prerequisite to channelling these funds to their most productive domestic use – of course, the existence of such a pool does not, in itself, guarantee that funds *are* channelled to their most productive use, but it does create the conditions where this is at least possible.

Having said that, in a world of free capital movements no country need be constrained by the level of its domestic savings, since it is free to borrow internationally to raise total national savings as required. However, as we have also seen, with a reliance on external capital flows, particularly short-term banking and portfolio flows, such a country may significantly increase its vulnerability to financial crises, with all the negative developmental consequences that these events entail. Consequently, the *social* benefits of increased savings rates (i.e. reduced reliance on external borrowing) are likely to exceed the *private* benefits of these savings, with the result that policy-makers in developing countries are surely right to aim to mobilise domestic savings to the optimal level, as far as is possible.

The differences in domestic savings rates between developing regions are shown in Figure 10.1, which depicts changes in this regard from the end of the 1980s to 2005. As can be seen, the East Asian region has the highest rates by some distance, averaging more than 37% over the period. At the other extreme, savings rates in sub-Saharan Africa are the lowest of any region, averaging just 17% – less than half the figure for East Asia. The other regions average between 20% and 25%, which equates to the average of 22% for high-income countries over the same period.

In terms of changes to savings rates, Loayzu *et al.* (2000) distinguish between drivers influenced directly by policy, and those independent of government policy measures.

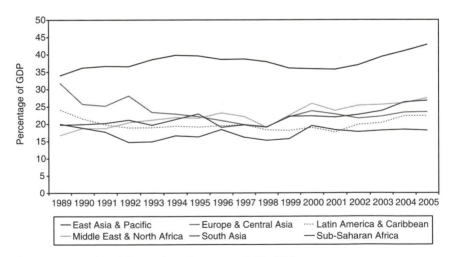

Figure 10.1 Regional domestic savings rates, 1989–2005.

Source: World Bank WDI.

10.1.1 Non-policy drivers of savings rates

1 *Persistence*: despite the major historical changes shown above, savings rates display considerable inertia, in that they are highly serially correlated with previous levels. Therefore any policy measure to raise (or of course lower) savings rates will take a number of years to come to fruition.[1]

2 *Income*: unsurprisingly, there is considerable empirical evidence to demonstrate that savings rates are positively correlated with per capita income, so that as income rises so do savings rates. In developing countries it is estimated that a doubling of income levels leads to an increase in the long-run private savings rate of 10 percentage points. However, the evidence also suggests that these effects taper off as a country's level of wealth rises, so that the correlation no longer holds for developed countries. Studies also distinguish between temporary and permanent increases in income: the 'Permanent Income Hypothesis'[2] states that temporary increases in savings should be entirely saved, whilst permanent increases should be entirely consumed. As described above, the extreme form of this hypothesis is generally rejected by the evidence, however studies do suggest that the impact on savings rates are higher for increases in income that are seen as temporary, than is the case with those expected to be permanent.[3]

3 *Growth*: the Permanent Income Hypothesis also predicts that higher growth rates will result in lower savings rates as individuals save less in the expectation of higher future income. Again, however, the empirical evidence contradicts this prediction, with most studies finding a positive link between growth and savings rates, for example. Loayza *et al.* (op. cit.) find that a 1-percentage-point increase in the growth rate results in a similar rise in the savings rate.

4 *Demographics*: the 'life-cycle hypothesis'[4] predicts that savings will be low amongst the young and amongst the elderly, with a 'hump' of higher savings occurring during middle age. Although some studies have questioned this prediction, most confirm that such a relationship does generally hold.

5 That is, a rise in the young-age or old-age dependency ratios, *ceteris paribus*, leads to a reduction in private savings rates: a rise in the young-age dependency ration of 3.5 percentage points is associated with a fall in the savings rate of 1 percentage point, and the impact of a similar rise in the old-age dependency ratio is likely to be more than double this (ibid.).

When we look at the experience of the developing regions historically, we see that, in some cases, savings rates and the proportion of the population of working age are positively correlated as one would expect. This is true for both South and East Asia, where the correlation is high and positive. However, for both Latin America and sub-Saharan Africa, no such relationship is evident, as illustrated in the case of the latter in Figure 10.2 below. Indeed, if any relationship is discernible, it is a negative one.

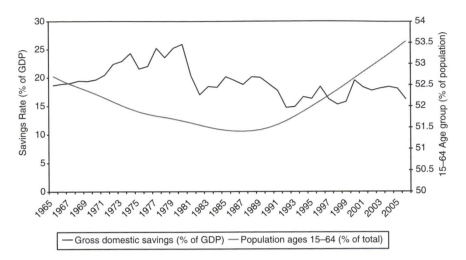

Figure 10.2 Sub-Saharan Africa: working-age population vs. domestic savings rate.
Source: World Bank WDI.

This suggests that, while the dependency ratio may have some impact on savings rates, this can be easily overwhelmed by stronger factors. The obvious candidate in this regard is the growth – or lack of it – of real per capita incomes.

6   *Uncertainty*: theoretically, high levels of uncertainty are expected to lead to higher levels of saving due to the 'precautionary motive', which some studies suggest accounts for a substantial proportion of total household savings. However, it is not possible to measure uncertainty directly, and the proxies that have been used – such as inflation rates, for example – have generally failed to find any significant link with savings rates (ibid.).

10.1.2 Policy-related drivers of savings rates

1   *Fiscal policy*: the 'Ricardian equivalence hypothesis' predicts that an increase in government saving should lead to an offsetting reduction of private saving, so that there is no net impact on total national savings. Most empirical research rejects full Ricardian equivalence, however, and find that the offset predicted is only partial. For example, the 'offset coefficient' is estimated to be just 30% in India, but 80% in Mexico.[5] However, as long as the coefficient remains less than 1, it appears that a straightforward means of raising national savings is through direct government saving. In contrast, tax incentives to raise savings rates have generally proved ineffective in most cases, though there is evidence that they have been successful in raising national savings when linked to mandatory long-term savings programmes.[6]

2 *Pension reform*: from a theoretical perspective the move to 'fully funded' from pay-as-you-go (PAYG) pension systems would be expected to raise national savings. However, again, the evidence is inconclusive, with the method of financing the fiscal costs of 'transition' to a fully funded scheme, and the efficiency of the resulting scheme, largely determining the net impact on savings rates. If the costs of transition are met by reducing government expenditure and/or raising taxes, the savings rates of those affected will fall. In the longer term, however, a positive effect on savings would be expected. For example, Gallego *et al.* (1999) find that a third of the 13-percentage-point increase in Chile's saving rate since 1986 is attributable to the introduction of the fully funded system. In the long run, mandatory savings schemes – such as those in Singapore where 25% of salaries must be saved in a pension scheme – will clearly raise private savings above what would otherwise have occurred, though the net welfare effects of such an approach are ambiguous.

3 *Financial liberalisation*: a usual feature of liberalisation is an increase in real interest rates. Theoretically, this would be expected to raise savings rates – empirical evidence suggests that this is not the case, however.[7] On the other hand, an increase in the availability of credit would be expected to reduce savings rates – empirical evidence is supportive of this prediction, finding that a 1-percentage-point increase in the ratio of private credit to income reduces savings by 0.74 percentage points.[8] In combination, therefore, financial liberalisation is not associated with an increase in savings rates, with most studies that find a significant relationship suggesting that it is a negative one.

4 *External borrowing and foreign aid*: research[9] suggests that an increase of external borrowing by 1 percentage point reduces total domestic savings by about half this amount – the so-called 'crowding out' effect. Studies suggest a similar relationship between aid flows and private savings rates, though these are not conclusive and the correlation may be explained by the fact that aid flows disproportionately go to LDCs with very low savings rates.[10]

Therefore, while some key drivers of savings rates are beyond the control of government, other policy levers do seem to have some effect.

To summarise, the impact on savings rates that have been discussed can be described as follows:

(a) Non-policy

- Higher income = positive impact;
- Higher growth = positive impact;
- Increase in old-age/young-age dependency ratio = negative impact (but not in all instances – other effects may be stronger);
- Higher uncertainty = ambiguous impact.

(b) Policy

- Increased government saving = positive impact;
- Tax incentives = no impact in most instances, but positive effect when related to mandatory savings schemes;
- Pension reform (move to PAYG) = ambiguous short-term impacts; positive long-term impacts;
- Financial liberalisation = negative impacts;
- Higher interest rates = no impact;
- Increased credit = negative impact;
- Increased external borrowing = negative impact;
- Increased aid flows = ambiguous impact, but more likely to be a positive if small effect.

Governments therefore can influence savings rates directly through policy, though not always in the way that might be expected. Furthermore, over the longer term, it may be that encouraging high rates of economic growth (and therefore personal income growth) is the most effective means of raising savings rates. That said, this is by no means a simple linear relationship, as illustrated in Figure 10.3 below, which shows that high per capita incomes are no guarantor of a high savings rate, and vice versa.

As we can see, savings rates in high-income countries have declined on average from 1970 to 2004, at the same time as average rates have tended to rise in middle- and low-income countries

As was pointed out above, however, the propensity to save may be strongly influenced by cultural as well as economic factors and these, of course, are far

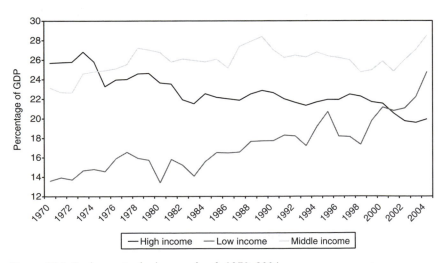

Figure 10.3 Savings rates by income level, 1970–2004.

Source: World Bank WDI.

less amenable to influence by government policy. They may also change over time of course.

Figure 10.4 illustrates well how the average figures given for income levels in the previous figure disguise wide differences. As we can see, in both the US and UK, total domestic savings have been on a downward trend since 1960. In both Malaysia and South Korea, in contrast, there is a steady upward trend, so that by 2005, both countries' domestic savings rates are more than double those in the US and UK.

Conceptually, the two-way causality between savings and growth that has been described in this book is mediated through the financial sector: increasing investment leading to higher growth requires a pool of savings to draw upon; and the higher incomes resulting from growth lead to an increase in the size of this pool of savings, enabling further investment and yet higher growth.

For this nexus to work, however, a robust and efficient financial sector is essential. The next section examines in some detail the 'official line' on what government can (and cannot) do to facilitate the development of the financial sector.

10.2 Financial sector development

When working well, the financial system enables firms to take advantage of profitable investment opportunities when they arise, by reducing their reliance on internally generated finance, as well as informal sector sources such as families and friends. As we have seen, private firms in developing countries have generally less access to external finance of this form than is the case in developed countries, and as Figure 10.5 illustrates, this is a particularly

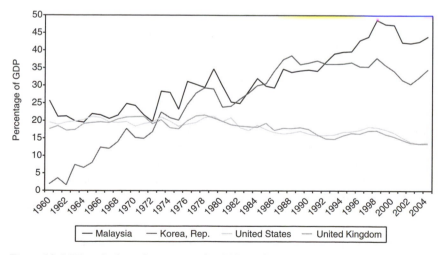

Figure 10.4 Historical savings rates in US and UK vs. Malaysia and Korea, 1960–2005.

Source: World Bank WDI.

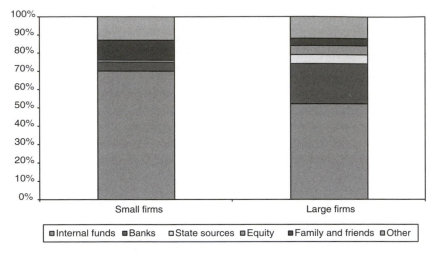

Figure 10.5 Sources of investment funds for small and large firms.

Source: World Bank, 2005b.

important issue for smaller firms in these economies, where 70% of financing may be reliant on internal funds.[11]

However, the lack of access to external forms of finance is considered a severe impediment to business growth throughout the developing world. The largest problems in this respect are reported in sub-Saharan Africa (where almost 70% of firms see financial constraints as a key obstacle to growth), followed by South Asia (47%) and Latin America (33%).[12]

This is crucial, as the ability to access external forms of finance enables entrepreneurs to grow their businesses, despite often being cash-poor, and well-functioning financial markets may also impose discipline upon the behaviour of firms by monitoring the uses to which this finance is put – though poorly functioning markets may do the opposite, of course. In a situation where financial markets function well, shareholders are able to monitor the behaviour of firms to ensure that their investments are being well looked after. Where this is not the case, however, companies may get the benefits of access to finance without the constraining oversight of investors.

Furthermore, effective financial systems provide a range of opportunities for both firms and households to manage risk, particularly through derivatives and insurance markets, thereby ensuring that risky – but potentially profitable – business ventures are more likely to be undertaken. However, these benefits come with dangers. Complex derivative products in particular can be used to obscure as well as to manage risk. The danger, therefore, is that investors perceive instruments to be less risky than they actually are, and act accordingly. A classic recent example of this process can be seen in the US subprime crisis of 2007, which is described in Box 10.2 below.

Box 10.2 The subprime lending crisis

Subprime mortgages – as the name suggests – are those extended to people with credit ratings considered poor by the mainstream market. The subprime sector began in the United States in the 1990s and grew rapidly: by 2004 US$500–600 billion of loans were being issued per year in the US, and by 2007 it was estimated that subprime mortgages accounted for around 13% of all mortgages in the US (i.e. the 'mortgage bond market'). This was US$1,300 billion, or 10% of US GDP. Many of the loans were issued during a period of relatively low interest rates, and borrowers were further cushioned by offers wherein rates were discounted for an initial period, before ramping up sharply thereafter. The fact that the borrowers were considered high-risk meant that the real interest rates on the loans were well above normal market rates. As interest rates in the US rose and the full terms of the loans became apparent, however, many borrowers found themselves unable to service their loans. Huge waves of default began.

If this were all that had happened, the direct consequences might have been restricted to the US. These would have been severe, and the indirect impact of economic slowdown in the US would have certainly adversely affected the global economy. However, as the events unfolded it became increasingly clear that much of the international financial system – particularly its major banks – were intimately involved, and not just directly.

Rather than remaining on the balance sheets of the original lenders, the subprime loans were repackaged as 'Special Purpose Vehicles' (SPVs), which in this instance were termed 'Residential Mortgage-Backed Securities' (RMBSs). These in turn were further 'sliced and diced' and sold on as 'Collateralised Debt Obligations' (CDOs).

This is the heart of the problem. The increasing 'sophistication' and 'complexity' of the financial instruments used to securitise the loans broke the link between lender and borrower. The originators of the loans – knowing that the risks could be bundled up and sold on at a handsome profit – thus had every incentive to keep agreeing more and more loans, regardless of the long-term credit-worthiness of the borrowers in question. The subprime market was driven by mortgage brokers who again could turn a tidy profit by signing people up, regardless of their ability to service the debt. It is alleged that many were convinced to take up subprime loans on false pretences.

Furthermore, the 'collateralised' in CDO was highly important. The fact that the loans were ultimately backed by real assets – i.e. residential property – enabled the CDOs to attract an AAA investment rating, which meant that they were deemed to be suitable for the portfolios of even the most conservative financial institutions. The pool of potential buyers of subprime vehicles thus grew very large indeed, and financial institutions were able to use the instruments as collateral to raise further financing.

In the traditional mortgage market, banks (and building societies in the UK) lent from their base of deposits. By repackaging their subprime loans and selling them on, however, there were no such restrictions on the quantity of loans that subprime lenders could make: the only ultimate limit was the size (and appetite) of the US$7 trillion US mortgage bond market, which had previously been dominated by quasi-government agencies.

From 1998 to 2004, US house prices rose by around 6% per year, before accelerating to more than 12% in 2005/6. Prices fell by 4% in 2007, and are forecast to fall a further 10% in 2008.

The upshot of all this, as subprime lenders go bankrupt in their droves, is that the large financial institutions have been left holding paper that is either worth drastically less than they had thought, or is effectively worthless. As the ripples spread around the world in 2007 – and the UK witnessed its first bank run in more than a century – banks stopped lending to each other, as none knew the real creditworthiness of the other. By 2007, banks had announced losses of US$60 billion, but as the opaque instruments unwind many expect this to inexorably rise. The potential effects of a global credit crunch are only beginning to be glimpsed.

Giants of international finance such as Citigroup and Merrill Lynch have been humbled, turning to Middle Eastern sovereign wealth funds for huge injections of cash. The party would seem to be over: the high water mark of high finance passed. In time, however, this may not prove to be so. As we have seen, throughout history people have failed to remember the lessons of the past, and so have been forced to repeat them.

For the World Bank (2005b) a well-developed financial system may also reduce poverty levels, both directly and indirectly through its positive impact on growth:

- Income inequality is reduced through the alleviation of credit constraints and increased access to investment opportunities for poor households.
- The facilitation of competition between firms that purchase goods produced by poor households helps poor households escape exploitation by those firms.
- The facilitation of competition between firms that supply goods to poor households also helps them avoid exploitation.
- FSD can stabilise the economy by reducing volatility: for example, doubling private credit can reduce the volatility of growth from 4% a year to 3%.

- There is also some evidence that child labour is lower in countries with greater access to financing, as firms have less need to rely on informal and internal resources, including family members as workers.[13]

It should also be remembered, however, that the liberalisation of the financial sector that is often taken as synonymous with financial sector development also increases the probability of a country experiencing a financial crisis, with very severe development and poverty implications. Therefore, it is not just any FSD that counts, but the quality of the FSD that determines outcomes.

However, it is clearly no easy task to develop the financial sector so that it is able to adequately perform these vital functions, while avoiding the dangers inherent in financial liberalisation. For the World Bank (op. cit.), the key problems to overcome are (a) market failure (and, in particular, asymmetric information) and (b) political issues.

For example, when a firm applies for a loan, the expectation is that they will honour their commitment to repay. However, there is the possibility of default in any transaction, and the fact that the lender cannot have as good information as to the borrower's intentions as the borrower does himself greatly complicates this process. The level of interest that is charged on a loan reflects the lender's view of the riskiness of the borrower. If their knowledge in this regard were perfect, interest rates could be perfectly calibrated to protect them from the prospect of default. However, under asymmetric information this is not possible.

As a result, lenders typically ration credit quantitatively,[14] or charge rates of interest that are above those that match the actual credit risk of the lowest-risk borrowers. Consequently, borrowers with low-risk ventures are discouraged from seeking such finance, but those with very high-risk ventures are not discouraged from seeking loans: the so-called 'adverse selection' problem, first described in Akerlof's classic 'market for lemons' paper that described the process in the context of the second-hand car market.[15]

In general terms, therefore, raising interest rates above a certain level *increases* the risks lenders are exposed to, and these problems are further exacerbated by the possibility of dishonesty – i.e. those with no intention of repaying the loan will not be discouraged however high the rate of interest charged – and weak contract enforcement.

These information problems can make it hard for firms to obtain financing unless they have means of mitigating the risks, such as collateral. On the other side of the equation, these problems also make it hard for those with savings (i.e. surplus capital) to find attractive opportunities to either invest in or lend to.

Although these information problems are inherent to all financial systems, they are particularly acute in developing countries, not least because the factors that can mitigate them – third-party credit bureaus; use of collateral; effective contract enforcement and legal sanctions – are often considerably less developed than is the norm in developed countries, if they are developed at all.

They can also be either reduced or exacerbated by government policy, which in turn can often be influenced by political economy factors – particularly the influence of certain interest groups – in ways that are not conducive to broadly effective FSD.

Indeed, these two fundamental issues – market failure and politics – came together in the second half of the twentieth century, where many governments attempted to overcome market failures in the financial system by intervening directly. The form of these interventions ranged from direct ownership of financial institutions, particularly banks, to regulations requiring the private sector to direct credit to particular groups and sectors. The domestic financial sector was also often shielded from competition by government regulations that prevented foreign financial institutions from entering the domestic market.

Unfortunately, political factors – not least 'government failure'[16] as opposed to the market failures described above – too often led to deep distortions, rent-seeking and a general inefficiency of the financial sector. Although direct government intervention in the financial sector has been relatively successful in some instances – such as some East Asian economies, for example – the general record is not encouraging.

That said, there is certainly nothing inevitable about the failure of government intervention to achieve its objectives. As we have seen, the East Asian example shows clearly that it can be done, and the endemic nature of market failure in the financial systems of developing countries suggests strongly that some level of intervention is certainly needed.

However, fears of 'getting it wrong' – coupled with an ideological leaning towards market solutions – has led to a certain rectitude on the part of the international financial institutions (IFIs) in the advice they offer to developing country governments. In this regard, the ('Washington') consensus view has become that governments should focus on 'delivering the basics' – that is, establishing a 'level playing field' within which financial institutions have the freedom to develop. There may be scope for further intervention beyond this – though the IFIs tend to stress the potential downside of such interventions more than any potential upside – but establishing this basic, minimum financial infrastructure is an essential prerequisite for any such measures.

As we can see from Figure 10.6, however, despite the trend towards financial liberalisation that has been ongoing for twenty–thirty years, and the IFIs preference for private ownership in financial systems, state ownership of the banking sector remains substantial in many countries, particularly in India, but also in a range of other countries at very different levels of development.

In practice, therefore, significant state intervention in the financial system is a reality and is likely to remain so for the foreseeable future. Indeed, as the example of Germany illustrates, the move towards the divestiture of state assets in the financial system is by no means an inevitable linear trend that

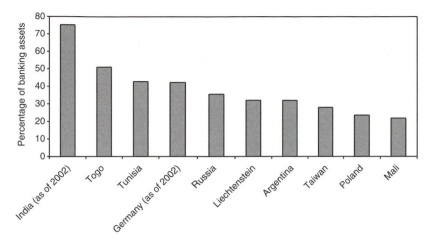

Figure 10.6 State ownership in the banking sector: global 'Top 10'.

Source: World Bank Financial Structure Database.

accompanies more generalised economic development. It is evidently perfectly possible for a country to be highly developed and wealthy, and yet to have a large proportion of its banking sector owned by the state.

Given this context, what other 'basics' does the World Bank argue that policy-makers should focus upon delivering?

10.3 'Delivering the basics?'

According to the Bank, many governments have 'learned the lessons of the past' and are now focusing solely on delivering the basics as a foundation for effective financial sector development. The World Bank (2005b) describes these 'basics' as follows:

- ensuring macroeconomic stability;
- fostering competition;
- securing the rights of borrowers, creditors and shareholders;
- facilitating the flow of information;
- ensuring that banks do not take excessive risks.

10.3.1 Ensuring macroeconomic stability

As we have seen throughout this book, macroeconomic stability is essential to the effective functioning of financial markets, and to economic development more generally. In particular, the key targets are (a) low and stable rates of inflation, (b) sustainable levels of external debt, and (c) appropriate and sustainable exchange rate regimes.

In general terms, macroeconomic instability leads to highly volatile interest rates and exchange rates, which imposes significant costs on both financial institutions and firms and households that borrow from them, making saving, borrowing and investment decisions extremely complex and uncertain. Furthermore, high interest rates also attract speculative capital flows putting upward pressure on the exchange rate and negatively affecting exporting firms.

More specifically, high rates of inflation erode the real value of the capital of financial institutions and greatly complicate the task of mobilising domestic savings. High fiscal deficits lead to higher rates of interest and spreads on government paper. This in turn makes the holding of this paper attractive to financial institutions, which results in the crowding out of the private sector in terms of credit.

There is an important balancing act to bear in mind here, however. While low inflation and a high level of private sector credit are important, they are means not ends. That is, the reason why both are targets of government policy is because of the positive impact that is expected on growth.

In this respect, Figure 10.7 depicts Colombia's experience with these three variables from 1980 to 2006. Perhaps the most striking aspect of the figure is that, although credit and inflation are relatively volatile, with the latter on a long-term downward trend from the early 1990s, it is difficult to observe any appreciable impact upon the real growth rate. Indeed, at 3.45% the average growth rate in the first half of the period when inflation was high and volatile, was higher than that in the second, where growth averaged 3.26% as inflation fell consistently.

There is little difference in either period, of course, but the point to make is that stability may be important for growth, but it clearly is not essential.

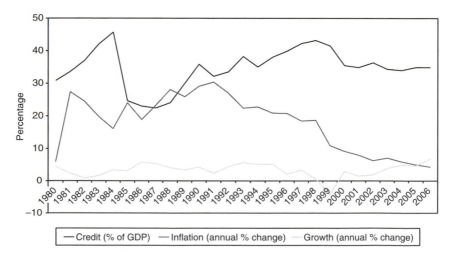

Figure 10.7 Inflation, credit and growth in Colombia, 1980–2006.

Source: WDI and IMF WEO.

Furthermore, it is likely that policy-makers in Colombia might have expected a rather more noticeable impact upon their growth rate after fifteen years of bearing down on inflation and the difficulties that would have caused.

10.3.2 *Fostering competition*

For the World Bank (2005b) there are two aspects to competition in the financial system. First, there is the existence or absence of restrictions on *domestic* financial institutions from competing in different sectors of the financial system. Second, there is the existence or absence of restrictions on *foreign* financial institutions from entering the domestic market.

For the Bank, restrictions on competition between domestic financial institutions (the so-called 'functional boundaries') have been associated empirically with slower economic growth, reduced employment opportunities and concentrated bank markets, leading to fewer large, mature firms developing. Conversely, the Bank argues that removing these barriers is associated with greater stability of the banking sector, greater access to finance for firms and households and lower interest rates charged to borrowers.

Of course, as with all large cross-country studies, there will be many examples where neither of these broad conclusions holds. For example, there are few countries with more restrictions on the activities of financial institutions than China, yet this has not been an impediment to the country's phenomenal growth.

For restrictions on the entry of foreign financial institutions, similar conclusions are drawn by the World Bank. Furthermore, despite concerns that the presence of foreign banks will weaken the domestic financial system, the Bank suggests that the contrary is true: the presence of foreign banks leads to greater efficiency of local banks, as well as the introduction of innovative techniques developed in their home markets.

Table 10.1 provides a snapshot of the extremes of foreign back participation. The fifteen countries on the left are those with the highest level of foreign ownership, while those on the right are the fifteen with the least. As we can see, both sides contain countries at different levels of development. However, it is also the case that, of the countries with the highest level of foreign bank penetration, only one – Luxembourg, which is a special case given its size and history – is a high-income country. In contrast, the group of countries with the least foreign ownership contain a number of the richest countries in the world, including Switzerland, Finland, Italy, Spain and Canada.

Again, therefore, it seems that restricting entry to the domestic banking system is certainly not an absolute bar to successful development. A related point to make is that many of the countries with the highest level of foreign bank ownership are low-income countries that have had borrowing relationships with the multilateral development institutions in recent decades. A typical component of structural adjustment programmes in all their incarnations has been a requirement to open the financial system to foreign banks.

Table 10.1 Proportion of banking industry that is foreign-owned

'Top 15'		'Bottom 15'	
Country	*Proportion*	*Country*	*Proportion*
Guinea Bissau	100	Taiwan	0
Estonia	98.9	Israel	0.012
Luxembourg	94.64	Trinidad & Tobago	0.024
Benin	91	Turkey	0.034
Czech Republic	90	Algeria	0.039
Croatia	89.3	Sudan	0.04
Côte d'Ivoire	84.2	Canada	0.048
Senegal	78.7	Italy	0.057
Lithuania	78.19	Finland	0.062
Niger	73.4	Thailand	0.067
Namibia	90	Spain	0.085
Poland	68.7	Guatemala	0.09
Mali	67	Ukraine	0.105
Burkina Faso	56	Switzerland	0.107
Venezuela	43.22	Greece	0.108

Source: World Bank Financial Structure Database.

As well as bank–bank competition, the World Bank (2005b) argues that it is important to develop competition from non-bank financial institutions (NBFIs), such as leasing and finance companies.

More generally, the Bank suggests that FSD can also be facilitated by relaxing investment rules on financial institutions such as pension funds. That is, many pension funds are highly restricted in terms of the assets in which they can invest, and historically some countries have required pension funds to invest largely in government bonds, which amounts to a pool of cheap funds that the government can use for borrowing purposes. Freeing them so that they can invest more broadly – in equities and corporate bonds, for example – encourages competition as well as broadening and deepening financial markets more generally.

However, it is also the case that there may be good reasons to restrict pension funds, in particular, in terms of their potential investment universe. For example, it took more than five years for UK pension funds to recoup most of their losses following the collapse of the dotcom bubble in 2001. Like other investors, pension fund managers were lured into abandoning many of their previous strictures as internet and technology stocks rose higher and higher and it became impossible to resist climbing aboard the bandwagon. Therefore, investment restrictions are not only related to government wishing to borrow cheaply by insisting pension funds buy government bonds – this is clearly inimical to FSD, but it does not necessarily follow that there should be no restrictions of any kind.

To summarise, while it is clear that the regulation and supervision of financial institutions should be robust and effective, it is equally clear that overly restricting the activities that different financial institutions can undertake reduces competition and innovation and retards the development of an effective financial sector. However, this does not answer the key questions.

'Robust and effective' regulation does not stipulate what form this should take – though the World Bank (2005b) is quite clear on its view about this. Similarly, nobody would want to 'overly' restrict competition and innovation, but this does not determine where the line should be drawn. Competition is not an end in itself: it is a route to developing a more vibrant financial sector that effectively supports the sustainable development of the real economy leading to the maximum level of poverty reduction. To the extent that competition achieves this goal it should be encouraged, but where it does not it should not.

10.3.3 Securing the rights of borrowers, creditors and shareholders

Many of the problems inherent in financial transactions that have been described (e.g. asymmetric information) can be mitigated if the rights of creditors and shareholders are clearly established and effectively enforced. In such a situation, lenders and investors will be far more willing to provide finance than would be the case if there were some level of doubt over the enforceability of these rights.

For the World Bank (2005b), governments have a key role to play in establishing and enforcing this framework, which brings significant benefits. Secure property rights enable borrowers to credibly pledge collateral (including land, for example) as security for a loan, and then allow longer-term borrowing, including external borrowing from foreign institutions. Furthermore, the cost of this external finance is significantly lower in countries with secure and enforceable property rights: a study of thirty-seven countries found that if a country improved its protection of property rights from the 25th to the 75th percentile, spreads on loans would decline by 0.87% (ibid.).

Clearly, however, there is little point in having strong rights if they are not enforced. For example, while Russia has adopted rigorous laws protecting shareholder and creditor rights by importing templates from developed countries, the lack of an effective legal system to enforce these rights is viewed as a major obstacle to the expansion of private credit and financial sector development in general.

For example, there are thirty-one procedures to negotiate with regard to contract enforcement in Russia, with an average of 178 days being required. However, in 2005, 64% of managers in Russia lacked confidence in the courts' ability to uphold and enforce commercial contracts.[17]

Financial liberalisation in developing countries, particularly the high level of privatisations and development of domestic stock markets, has significantly increased the need for effective and efficient shareholder rights. These developments have also brought issues of corporate governance to the fore, not least because of pressure from foreign investors and evidence that improvements in corporate governance are associated with better financial performance by firms. Effective shareholder rights give equity investors both the means and the incentive to monitor firms' corporate governance performance, and thus provide pressure for positive change.

The effectiveness of this monitoring process is of course influenced by the degree of transparency in terms of firms' financial reporting. Requirements in this regard are generally set and enforced by the stock exchange itself, but government can establish the framework in which this process operates and, crucially, ensure that requirements are enforced. Indeed, high disclosure requirements that are effectively enforced are associated with increased levels of market liquidity, lower costs of capital and the higher valuation of firms.[18]

However, while the Bank is certainly right in general terms, this does not mean that transparency and monitoring by shareholders are sufficient to *guarantee* 'good behaviour'. For example, the US is widely seen as being the most advanced market in these areas, yet this did not prevent the corporate abuses perpetrated by Enron and WorldCom. As in the case of UK pension funds described above, bull markets and a sense of 'irrational exuberance' have a tendency to encourage investors and analysts to overlook possible problems and focus on the positives.

10.3.4 Facilitating the flow of information

We have seen that issues of asymmetric information are often at the heart of problems of financial sector development. One means by which lenders can reduce these problems is to collect information themselves – both *ex ante* and *ex post* – about each potential borrower, but this is clearly a very expensive and inefficient method. In developed countries, as we have seen, this problem is overcome through the use of third-party credit bureaus, which collect and collate data on loan payment histories, therefore allowing lenders to more accurately predict the probability of default in a far more cost-effective manner.[19]

Importantly, the widespread use of credit bureaus significantly increases the incentives for borrowers to repay their loans promptly, since a long delay – or a default – with one lender would jeopardise their access to credit from all lenders using the credit bureaus. The World Bank (2005b) presents evidence that, on average, countries that do not have credit bureaus to any meaningful extent have a private credit to GDP ratio of 16%, while those that do have such a network have a comparative figure of 40% if the bureaus are publicly owned, and 67% where they are privately owned.

It is clearly the case that the availability of third-party information of this form is positive in terms of facilitating business activity, particularly in circumstances where other mitigating forces such as the use of collateral are limited, as is the case in many developing countries. However, it is also true that such institutions are not essential to high levels of credit to the private sector: in China, for example, domestic credit provided by the banking sector was 138% of GDP in 2006, at which time there were no private credit bureaus in the country, and the public agencies only covered 10% of the population.

10.3.5 Controlling excessive risk taking

As we have seen at more than one point in this book, banks have a tendency to take on excessive levels of risk. There are a number of reasons for this, most of which are related to issues of moral hazard. For example, limited liability laws ensure that banks do not face the full potential downside of their activities,[20] as does the fact that they may use depositors' funds to 'speculate' but reap any potential upside themselves. Also, due to their systemic importance to the financial system, they may rightly think that governments will not allow them to fail, as a bank run in one institution can rapidly spread through the banking system.

In 2007, the UK witnessed its first full-scale bank run since the 1860s, as savers rushed to withdraw their funds from Northern Rock, which had suffered disproportionately from the US sub prime mortgage market crisis and in which savers had lost confidence that their money was safe. As with all bank runs[21] in a system of 'fractional reserve banking', however, perceptions rapidly became reality, and the UK government was forced to step in and guarantee the deposits of savers. Deposit insurance can obviously reduce the risks of such bank runs, but is itself a major source of moral hazard.

For all these reasons, governments have a role in constraining banks from taking on excessive risks. As we have seen, the main avenue through which governments perform this function is via the prudential regulation and supervision of banks. For example, prudential regulation may require banks to maintain a certain level of diversification, and to hold minimum levels of regulatory capital (i.e. 8%) with respect to their outstanding loans.

As with other elements of the 'basics' described above, however, stringent regulations are of little use without effective supervision. In some instances problems in this area will be a function of limited resources and human capital development. In others, it may be a product of 'capture' where regulators and supervisors come to represent the interests of the institutions they are supposed to be regulating. Of course, 'regulatory capture' is certainly not unique to developing countries, with some suggesting that the outcome of the Basel II reform process is a clear example of developed country regulators being 'captured' by the major international banks.[22]

Partly for this reason, the World Bank (2005b) argues that prudential regulation and supervision needs to be augmented by effective market discipline. This monitoring role may be undertaken by large depositors, subordinated debt holders, shareholders or ratings agencies, for example. Before the 1998 crisis in Argentina, for example, banks were required to issue subordinated debt equal to 2% of their deposits: those that complied paid lower deposit rates, had faster growth in deposits, lower capital ratios and fewer non-performing loans (NPLs); those that did not comply, in contrast, were penalised by the market in that they were forced to increase levels of capital held as well as liquidity ratios (ibid.).

For the Bank (2005b:123): 'The effectiveness of private monitoring depends on how well information disclosure regulations are enforced, whether ratings agencies compete with each other, the proportion of state ownership of banks, and the nature of deposit insurance.'

For example, banks can be required to disclose financial information according to international best practice, as well as information relating to governance such as the remuneration of senior management. Also, ratings agencies will obtain higher levels of credibility if they are required to disclose all relevant business relationships, as well as their historical record in ratings – particularly with regard to upgrades and downgrades.

Although the use of ratings agencies is still in its infancy in many developing countries, the upward trend is clear. However, it is again important to balance the Bank's optimism over and against the effectiveness of market discipline. In theory there is little to fault in the argument, but theory and practice are not always the same thing. Ratings agencies, for example, have been regularly criticised for failing to predict financial crises in general or corporate collapses in particular. From the Asian crisis, to Enron, to the US sub prime crisis of 2007, ratings agencies failed to spot the warning signs.

As was argued above, all market players are liable to get caught up in the waves of euphoria that surround investment bubbles. Furthermore, this is not just a matter of information: in the run-up to the Asian crisis in 1997, there was ample warning about the parlous state of some regional banking systems – the Bank for International Settlements (BIS), in particular, warned investors of the dangers.

In a bubble situation, however, the risk of missing out on the profits being reaped by your competitors may seem a greater risk than a general crisis. There is relative safety in the 'herd': even if large losses are suffered, this is the same for all, with no individual investor being singled out.

The words of John Maynard Keynes seem just as apposite today as they were in 1931: 'A sound banker, alas, is not one who forsees danger and avoids it, but one who, when he is ruined, is ruined in a conventional and orthodox way along with his fellows, so that no one can really blame him.'[23]

This is not to say that market discipline is always and everywhere ineffective. It can and often does function well. However, to assume that all market participants rationally assess all the available information before taking an investment decision in every instance is perhaps a little naïve.

It is certainly true, as the World Bank argues, that it is important for governments to deliver the basics in terms of underpinning the development of an effective financial sector, though the Bank's faith in this limited infrastructure to deliver real benefits may be somewhat optimistic and its view of what the 'basics' are is rather lopsided.

At the beginning of this chapter, three prerequisites were set out if financial sector development is to lead to a virtuous circle of increased real economic activity, sustainable job creation and poverty reduction. The first was to mobilise the maximum level of domestic savings, while the second looked at how the financial sector could be best developed to channel these funds to the private sector. The third and final aspect was that the private sector needs to invest these domestic financial resources – in combination with external financing – as productively as possible.

The next section again critically examines the World Bank's stance on these issues, before bringing these strands together with a more optimistic look at how countries might be able to go beyond 'the basics' and achieve real progress.

10.4 Private sector development: delivering the basics

As with the financial sector, the World Bank (2005b) gives its view as to the 'basics' from a private sector development (PSD) perspective. For the private sector to efficiently and productively invest external finance obtained from the financial sector – or similarly to invest their own internal resources – a number of basic prerequisites are identified. The first and most basic of these is the provision of security and stability.

10.4.1 Security and stability

Clearly, for economic activity to develop effectively, financial institutions, firms and households require a minimum level of security: at the extreme, the outbreak of war will clearly bring lending and investment to a halt in any country. The importance of security, however, goes well beyond the avoidance of war. In particular, just as property rights and enforcement are vital for FSD, they are a similarly essential precondition for private sector development of all forms.

The World Bank (2005b) lists four elements of property rights that should be a priority in terms of implementation:

1   the verification of rights to land and property;
2   the facilitation of contract enforcement;
3   the reduction of crime;
4   the elimination of the uncompensated expropriation of property.

There is clearly a long way to go in many of these areas – as illustrated in Figure 10.8 below, a high percentage of firms in many developing countries lack confidence in the ability (or willingness) of courts to uphold their property rights.

Without such confidence, firms will have great difficulty securing external finance for investment purposes, and even if they are able to do so, may not have the confidence to invest. The Bank is thus correct to stress the importance of establishing an independent, efficient and credible judiciary that is able to swiftly enforce property rights.

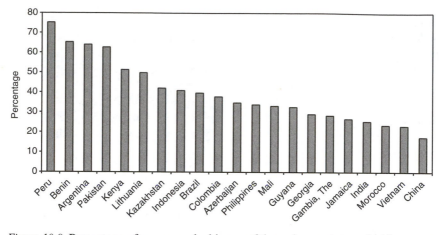

Figure 10.8 Percentage of managers lacking confidence in courts to uphold property rights.

Source: World Bank WDI.

Similarly, high levels of crime are a clear disincentive for investment, as is the risk that even if property rights can be effectively established, the government may arbitrarily expropriate the property. Although the Bank also makes a valid point here, it is difficult to see that low levels of crime are one of the 'basics' in terms of PSD and investment. The United States has long had relatively high crime rates, but also has high rates of investment. Similarly, in the early years of the twenty-first century, Russia has had very high crime rates, combined with high rates of investment. The key point to make is that, while low rates of crime will generally be supportive of investment and therefore growth, they are not a prerequisite to either.

As the Bank points out, property rights are important as they link effort with reward, and thereby encourage further effort. For example, a farmer with secure land rights who invests in machinery and fertilisers to enhance the yield of his crops will capture the rewards (or failure) of this investment. In contrast, if property rights are not clearly established, the farmer will be uncertain as to whether he will be able to capture these benefits and will therefore not be willing to put in the investment (and effort) in the first place. Box 10.3 below explores this issue in the Ethiopian context where the lack of security of land tenure has long been an important issue.

Box 10.3 Land tenure and agricultural productivity in Ethiopia

Since ousting the Marxist 'Derg' regime in 1993, the Ethiopian government's development policy has been centred on agriculture as the main driver of industrialisation. The avowed aim is to raise agricultural productivity and output, to ensure national food security and to provide both the raw materials for industrial development and to build domestic demand for industrial output. As we can see from the figure below, however, agricultural yields remained virtually unchanged from 1993 to 2005.

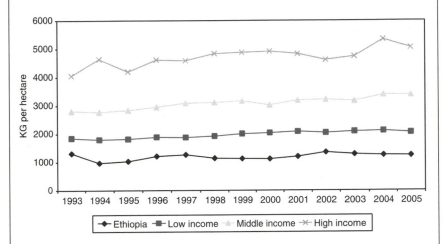

Cereal yields 1993–2005: Ethiopia vs. low-, medium- and high-income country averages.

Source: World Bank WDI.

Not only have agricultural yields remained largely unchanged in Ethiopia, they are also well below the average for other low-income countries. Similarly, other indicators such as agricultural value added per worker have changed little over the same period.

Regardless of repeated government initiatives, agricultural output in Ethiopia remains almost entirely a function of rainfall, so that years of good rains see output, yields and thus productivity rise. Conversely, years of drought see the opposite. Indeed, the IMF (2003) estimates that 93% of total variation in Ethiopia's GDP is determined by climatic conditions. Although the government has prioritised fertiliser use – and retained subsidies in the sector – this has had no impact upon productivity levels. For many commentators, the fundamental obstacle that needs to be overcome is the lack of security of land tenure.

Without security of land tenure there is no incentive to invest in productivity-enhancing measures such as irrigation schemes. Furthermore, without the collateral that land ownership provides, financial institutions are not willing to lend for such purposes.

The issue of land tenure in Ethiopia has been the focus of extensive study and (intensive) debate. To date, however, the government has refused to budge, instead incorporating common ownership of land into the 1994 Constitution, thus retaining the Derg policy of public land ownership.

Individual farmers have the right to farm on particular plots of land, but no right to sell this land in either a lease or freehold form. Furthermore, the right to farm land has been – and remains – conditional on living in particular villages, largely preventing migration away from unproductive areas. Population pressures in rural areas, exacerbated by soldiers returning from conflicts, have seen plot sizes gradually reduce, as more and more people are allocated smaller and smaller plots of land. This has led to lower productivity, as the number of plots of economically viable size declines, as well as skewed incentives: farmers have every incentive to exploit all the natural resources on their land for profit immediately, rather than wait for the land to be possibly taken away from them in a later redistribution.

Furthermore, general population pressure has increased demand for land to such an extent that the historical practice of leaving land fallow and rotating usage has all but disappeared. More and more marginal land is being brought into use, and agricultural land is generally farmed intensively on an ongoing basis. The result: deforestation, soil degradation, declining productivity and reduced incomes for agricultural workers. A major shift in policy would appear to be urgently needed if this vicious circle is to be broken.

The second key element of the basic infrastructure for PSD identified by the World Bank is the area of regulation and taxation.

10.4.2 Regulation and taxation

Good regulation is designed to address the market failures that restrain productive investment and, crucially, to align the interests of firms and society. Whilst the activities of firms can bring huge benefits to societies, the interests and objectives of firms do not necessarily accord with wider societal objectives. The aim of regulation, therefore, is to align these two sets of objectives as far as is possible.

For example, generally speaking most firms would prefer as low a level of regulation as possible. However, firms also tend to seek dominant market positions and to maintain those positions by restricting competition in a variety of direct and indirect ways. From a societal perspective, as we have seen, encouraging competition brings undoubted safeguards and benefits, whereas the restriction of competition inhibits innovation and so improvements in productivity, resulting in higher costs for both firms and consumers.

Although governments can directly influence level of competition through its regulation of the anti-competitive practices of large firms operating in their jurisdiction, the extent to which this is possible in practice will be influenced by the relative bargaining power of the firm and government. For example, the European Union is able to regulate the behaviour of Microsoft's business activities in the EU, not least because Europe is a key market for the company which generates large revenues. An individual developing country, in contrast – particularly a relatively smaller one – has far less relative power over companies such as Microsoft. In such circumstances, the company concerned is more likely to be able to dictate the terms on which it will engage with the country.

For the World Bank, it is important to strike a balance between regulation to address market failure and the possibility of government failure via regulation designed to address this:

> Too often, governments pursue regulatory approaches that fail to achieve the intended social objectives because of widespread informality, yet harm the investment climate by imposing unnecessary costs and delays, inviting corruption, increasing uncertainty and risk, and creating unjustified barriers to competition.[24]

For the Bank, the appropriate striking of this balance requires the government to focus on:

- the removal of unjustified regulatory burdens and the streamlining of procedures;
- the reduction of regulatory uncertainty by reducing the discretion of individual regulators and undertaking regular consultation with industry;
- the reduction of barriers to competition through the reduction of regulatory barriers to entry and the tackling of the anti-competitive behaviour of firms.

Domestic taxes (as well as taxes and regulation 'at the border') also clearly influence the investment decisions and behaviour of firms. The formal/informal sector issue is of major importance in this regard: tax rates in developing countries are broadly comparable with those in developed countries but, as we have seen, the tax take as a proportion of GDP is significantly lower. In large part, this reflects the size of the informal sector in developing countries, which adds substantially to the financial pressure (in terms of extracting taxes) facing those firms that operate in the formal sector and do pay tax.

Clearly, expanding the proportion of economic activity that occurs in the formal sector is fundamental to broadening the tax base and so raising the tax take. This requires, however, that taxes are not so high that they discourage the transition to the formal economy, and that the tax system is efficient and as simple and streamlined as possible.

The Bank is surely right that setting tax rates too high can have distorting and often counterproductive effects. However, the reverse may also be true. That is, 'tax competition' between developing countries seeking to attract FDI, in a world where the demand for inward investment far outstrips its supply, may drive tax rates below the optimal levels. As with much else, therefore, governments need to strike the correct balance in this area.

The situation with taxes 'at the border' is similar. Simplicity, reasonable rates and a swift and efficient collection mechanism will encourage payment. Indeed, the relative ease with which border taxes can be collected is one reason for their continued widespread use. However, governments do need to ensure that this fact itself does not lead it to increase the tax burden in this area too much to compensate for the difficulty of tax collection in other sectors of the economy.

10.4.3 Workers and labour markets

For many firms in developing countries a shortage of skilled workers and labour market regulations are a major constraint on the growth of their firms. To address the first of these problems, governments need to foster a skilled workforce through investment in human capital via education and training. The success of the East Asian 'Tiger economies' is, at least in part, accredited to long-term efforts in this area, where countries such as South Korea invested far more in education and skills training than was usual for countries at similar levels of development.[25]

The World Bank (2005b) also argues that, for labour market regulations, it is important to strike a balance between protecting the rights of existing workers and protecting the rights of the entire, potential workforce. For example, overly strict regulation on 'hiring and firing' may make firms reluctant to take on new workers, disadvantaging those not currently in the work force and increasing (or at least not reducing) the size of the informal sector. Clearly a balance needs to be struck here, since incumbent workers do need protection from unscrupulous employers, particularly in many developing countries where abuses of workers' rights are common.

To summarise, we have seen that the World Bank (2005b) views effective FSD as being dependent upon government 'delivering the basics' in terms of:

1 ensuring macroeconomic stability;
2 fostering competition;
3 securing the rights of borrowers, creditors, and shareholders;
4 facilitating the flow of information;
5 ensuring that banks do not take excessive risks.

However, for the private sector to productively employ the finance available from an effective financial sector, the government also has to provide a number of other basic prerequisites in the following areas:

1 security and stability;
2 regulation and taxation;
3 workers and labour markets.

For the Bank, the ability of government to deliver in these areas determines the nature of the country's 'investment climate', which is viewed as fundamental to levels of investment, growth and poverty reduction. The next section considers these issues.

10.5 The investment climate, investment, growth and poverty reduction

Throughout this book we have considered how different aspects of financial sector development are related to economic growth and poverty reduction. However, it has also been stressed that, whilst FSD is important, it is a means to an end, not an end in itself. That is to say, it is the growth of private firms – that is facilitated by FSD – that potentially leads to these positive effects in terms of growth and poverty reduction.

The centrality of private sector development (PSD) is undeniable: private firms provide more than 90% of all jobs, for example, and the extent that they are able to generate these jobs is strongly influenced by a country's 'investment climate'.

The World Bank (2005b:1) describes the relationship as follows:

> A good investment climate provides opportunities and incentives for firms – from microenterprises to multinationals – to invest productively, create jobs, and expand. It thus plays a central role in growth and poverty reduction. Improving the investment climates of their societies is critical for governments in the developing world, where 1.2 billion people survive on less than \$1 a day, where youths have more than double the average unemployment rate, and where populations are growing rapidly. Expanding jobs and other opportunities for young people is essential to create a more inclusive, balanced, and peaceful world.

As well as providing the overwhelming majority of jobs, the private sector is also the primary source of government tax revenue, either directly, as corporation tax, or indirectly via income taxes and indirect sales taxes on the products that it produces.

Furthermore, despite the increasing importance of external finance – particularly in the form of FDI – the great majority of investment in developing countries is domestic in origin.

Figure 10.9 illustrates this by comparing the relationship between total domestic fixed capital formation (i.e. investment) with FDI, both as a proportion of GDP. As we can see, the largest multiple is found in South Asia, where total domestic investment is more than twenty-five times larger than FDI.

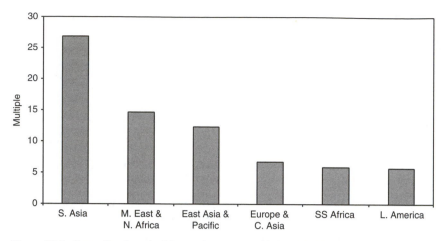

Figure 10.9 Gross fixed capital formation as a multiple of FDI.

Source: World Bank WDI.

The lowest multiple is in Latin America, but even here total domestic investment is still almost six times larger than FDI.

For the World Bank, therefore, a good investment climate encourages higher levels of investments from firms, by removing unnecessary costs, risks and barriers to competition. Why does the Bank consider this to be important?

Low barriers to entry are seen as essential in order to encourage: (a) the diffusion of new ideas, (b) firms' ability to import capital equipment as required, and (c) improvements in working practices and the way that production techniques are organised. In short, a good investment climate fosters a competitive environment where firms have opportunities and incentives to innovate, test their ideas and either succeed or fail (World Bank, 2005b).

Almost a century ago, Schumpeter described the central driver of capitalism as 'creative destruction', and for the Bank this remains true today: firms must be allowed to fail as well as to succeed. A good investment climate facilitates this process by making it easier for firms to enter and exit markets and sectors. Firms innovate to secure a competitive advantage, and it is this innovation that is ultimately the source of higher productivity and economic growth.

However, just as FSD is a means to an end, growth is also not an end in itself. As we have discussed throughout the course, the reason for the emphasis on economic growth is because of the strong relationship between growth and poverty reduction, though as we have also seen the strength of this relationship is far from stable.

As well as this indirect impact on poverty through its impact on growth rates, the quality of the investment climate also affects the lives of the poor through a number of direct channels (ibid.).

First, a good investment climate encourages job creation in the private sector, which directly reduces poverty. However, as pointed out above, the government must strike a balance between protecting the rights of incumbent workers – and so ensuring that jobs are of a high enough quality to have a positive effect on poverty levels – and avoiding regulation so strong that firms choose not to create new jobs.

Second, a good investment climate encourages competition which puts downward pressure on the prices of goods and services, from which the poor benefit. The flip side of this, however, is that this downward pressure on prices will also affect the poor directly in a negative sense, to the extent that they are selling into the market, either as farmers or as suppliers to larger firms.

In general terms, as the Bank points out, FSD enables all firms able to take advantage of profitable investment opportunities, as well as helping poor families cope with exogenous shocks, natural disasters and so on. Furthermore, to the extent that a good investment climate leads to an expansion of economic activity, tax revenues will also rise, providing funds that can be spent on services which benefit the poor. Of course, this does not guarantee that additional government revenues will be used for this purpose, but it does at least create the possibility that this could occur. What can governments do to influence the investment climate directly?

10.6 'Tackling costs, risks and barriers to competition'

10.6.1 Costs

The most obvious example of how governments can affect the cost of doing business is through the tax system. Here 'tax competition' between countries – both developed and developing – has become increasingly common since the 1980s, as countries compete to attract inward investment. This has resulted in a steady decline in corporate tax rates throughout the world, but the rate of fall has been faster in developing than in developed countries, not least because poorer countries may feel a greater relative need to attract FDI, but also that their relative bargaining position vis-à-vis transnational corporations will generally be weaker than with developed economies.

As a result of these forces, average corporate tax rates in developing countries had fallen to 20% by the beginning of the twenty-first century, compared with a figure of 35% for OECD countries (Murshed, 2001).

In addition to tax policy, the World Bank (2005b) also describes a number of other channels through which government policy also has strong impacts on business costs.

First, through the provision of public goods such as education, for example, the government affects the availability of skilled labour and the cost of training that companies face. As we have seen, the countries that have been most successful in terms of development in recent decades – particularly the Asian 'Tiger economies' – have invested relatively high amounts of government spending to education and training. The public good element here is important, since it would not be in the interest of a private business to provide the same level of education and training as the state, since they would have no way of 'capturing' all the returns on their 'investment': once trained, the employee might well decide to go and work for a rival firm, which would then obtain the benefits of the previous training as a 'free rider'. Consequently, with no public provision in this area, education and training would be far below the optimal level for society.

Second, the state of a country's infrastructure also has a strong influence on a firm's costs and the same public good arguments are relevant here: countries that have the best record in development terms have tended to invest heavily in infrastructure development.

Third, by establishing the framework for contract enforcement, the government determines the efficiency, cost and time taken for this process.

In this respect, Figure 10.10 compares the length of time needed to enforce contracts in a number of countries at different levels of development and in different regions. As we can see, it takes around 800 days in Cameroon – i.e. more than two years – to enforce a contract, while the corresponding figure in South Korea, for example, is 230 days. It must surely be the case that this wide divergence will have a significant influence on firms' business decisions.

In all of these areas (other than tax, of course) government activities reduce the cost of doing business, encouraging far higher levels of economic activity than would otherwise be the case. Indeed, this facilitation of business, through expenditure on public goods and the setting and policing of the regulatory and legal framework in which business operates, is essential to the workings of any successful economy. In this respect, there is no such thing

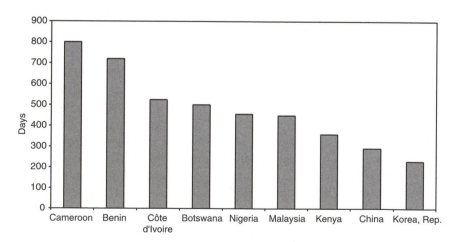

Figure 10.10 Average number of days needed to enforce a contract, 2006.

Source: World Bank WDI.

as a 'free market' of a genuinely laissez-faire form: well-functioning markets are not 'natural', but require a supporting framework of rules in which to operate, and the nature of this framework in turn influences strongly the form that market transactions take.

That said, the Bank rightly points out that excessive or unnecessary regulation can lead to higher costs and stifle business activity. Perhaps more important than the quantity of regulation, however, is the care with which it is crafted and enforced, and the extent to which it is tailored to the circumstances of particular countries. In this regard, the one-size-fits-all approach to regulation in particular may well have led to many developing countries implementing regulatory frameworks that have evolved in very different countries, both in terms of history and culture, but more importantly in terms of levels of development.

A good example of the type of unnecessary regulation that the Bank rightly takes exception to is the excessive time that an unwieldy bureaucracy can produce in this area. For example, it takes two days to register a new business in Australia, but 200 days in Haiti (ibid.).

10.6.2 *Barriers to competition*

As pointed out above, firms will generally prefer less competition rather than more. However, it is certainly the case that high levels of competition can bring great benefits to society. It is therefore important that government policy facilitates competition by eliminating barriers to entry and exit in different sectors, and constrains anti-competitive practices on the part of large, incumbent firms.

However, while the World Bank (2005b) generally sees unfettered competition as optimal in all circumstances, there may be many circumstances where this is not the case. Although not particularly fashionable now, it is undoubtedly the case that most if not all countries that are now 'developed' did not become so by allowing free entry to foreign competitors at all stages of their development.[26]

History would seem to teach that when those competing have very different levels of resources, expertise and experience, the outcome is likely to be in the favour of the stronger party. The 'infant industries' argument remains much criticised, but in many ways this is the result of policies being badly implemented, rather than a fundamental problem with the idea itself: as many countries in East Asia have proved, it is possible to develop very rapidly using this model, but only if it is done well. If it is done badly, as too often has been the case, the results can be devastating from a development perspective.

10.7 The process of reforming the investment climate

It is clearly the case that progress on reform of the investment climate requires more than a change in formal policies, but will stand or fall with regard to implementation – 90% of firms in developing countries report gaps between formal policies and what happens in practice, for example (ibid.).

For the World Bank (2005b) there are four key challenges for governments in this area:

(a) Restraining rent-seeking

The effectiveness of any reform process will be largely determined by the extent to which the government is able to maintain its course and not have the reform process distorted by rent-seeking at senior levels.

(b) Establishing credibility

In order to be prepared to invest for the longer term, firms must have confidence in the future. In this respect, the stability, coherence and credibility of government policies are critical. Firms may suspect that long-term government policies may be abandoned due to short-term political or economic pressures – governments need to allay these fears if it wishes to spur high and sustained levels of investment.

(c) Ensuring policies fit local conditions

To be effective, any policy measures must be appropriate for local conditions. For example, policies that have proved effective in some developed countries may not be appropriate in a developing country context, and should therefore not be simply imported as a package.

More specifically, the direction and speed of reform should also take local capacity into account: there is no point announcing a policy that cannot be feasibly implemented or enforced, particularly as this will serve to undermine government credibility.

(d) Focus on the basics

Finally, the World Bank argues that governments should focus on 'delivering the basics' and avoid more direct interventions in the economy.

Conclusion: going beyond the basics

The World Bank (2005b) is highly sceptical that governments should seek to go beyond the delivery of 'the basics', as described and analysed above. What does the Bank mean by this?

By 'going beyond the basics' the Bank is, to a large extent, referring to efforts to replicate the East Asian 'developmental state' model, where the state was actively involved in 'picking winners'. It did this through the identification of key sectors and firms, the direction of credit and tax advantages to these sectors and firms, and the maintenance of market restrictions to enable these 'infant industries' to develop into strong, internationally competitive industries.

For the Bank:

> The overall experience with government's ability to 'pick winners' is discouraging . . . Even in the best of circumstances, many selective interventions seem to be a gamble. The more ambitious the goal and the weaker the governance, the longer the odds of success. Selective interventions should thus be approached with caution, and not viewed as a substitute for broader investment climate improvements.

While it is certainly the case that interventions of this kind should not be seen as a substitute for investment climate reforms, it is also true that the approaches are not necessarily mutually exclusive.

Many of the 'basics' proposed by the Bank are sensible, though others display a puzzling faith in the 'magic of the market' to resolve complex difficulties, when there is ample evidence that this is far from being sufficient in many instances.

For example, it is difficult to find an example of a country that has followed the 'basics' policy line faithfully – and importantly not gone beyond it as proposed by the Bank – that has prospered to anything like the extent that countries which have chosen a different path.

At the start of this book, and throughout it, the point has been repeatedly made that financial sector development is not an end in itself. The real goal of course, is to facilitate increased and beneficial economic activity and so promote development and poverty reduction. Ultimately, all policies in the financial sphere – as well as all other economic areas – must be judged on their performance in this regard.

Clearly, as the World Bank rightly points out, many countries have tried and failed to replicate the success of the Asian 'Tiger economies', often making things worse in the process than would otherwise have been the case. However, the scale and persistence of poverty in many countries and regions in the world is such that it is very difficult to see how simply sticking to the 'basics' can hope to succeed in any meaningful sense.

To reiterate: where are the countries – either today or historically – that have achieved a step-change in development and poverty reduction by following the minimalist path proposed by the World Bank?

Figure 10.11 below depicts the scale of poverty reduction by developing region from 1981 to 2004.

As we see, the relatively low levels of poverty in the Middle East and North Africa have fallen steadily throughout. Europe and Central Asia ends the period with a similarly low incidence of absolute poverty to that which it began, after experiencing a quite large rise due to the transition from communism from the late 1980s onwards.

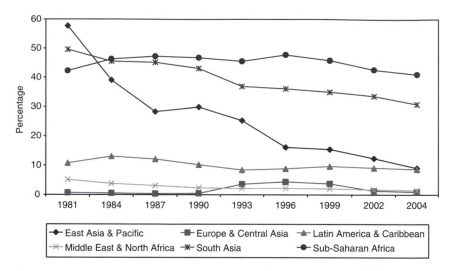

Figure 10.11 Regional poverty levels (percentage living on less than US$1 per day).
Source: World Bank WDI.

Two other regions showing little change are Latin America and sub-Saharan Africa: in the first instance about 10% of the population was living on less than US$1 per day throughout the period; for sub-Saharan Africa, however, between 40% and 50% of the population remained in absolute poverty for this twenty-five-year period.

In contrast, both South and East Asia saw significant falls in poverty levels, which is particularly marked in the latter. The proportion of the East Asian and Pacific population living on less than a dollar a day in 1981 was 57.7%, the highest of any of the regions. By 2004 this had fallen to 9%.

When considering lessons to be learned on the effectiveness of differing development strategies these trends are telling. The oil wealth of the Middle East makes comparisons difficult, and the transition economies experience is also unique – including accession to the European Union in many instances. Of the four remaining regions, however, it would be reasonable to assume that sub-Saharan African and Latin America have most closely followed the World Bank line, whether willingly or as part of the conditions of structural adjustment programmes.

In contrast, the East Asian economies – and to a lesser extent those of South Asia – have taken a far more heterodox stance, which entailed 'going beyond the basics' consistently. Furthermore, in some countries – particularly China – many of the 'basics' have been largely ignored. China has virtually none of these elements in place, yet it has been growing at more than 10% a year for a decade, has recently overtaken the USA as the world's largest recipient of FDI and is now the world's second largest economy by some estimates based on purchasing-power parity. Most importantly, China has witnessed the greatest reduction in poverty in human history.

Clearly, not every country has the advantages of China – its sheer size makes it attractive to investors wishing to access the domestic Chinese market. However, as we have touched upon in earlier parts of this book, the evidence appears to be that a country's 'room for manœuvre' is largely determined by its relative bargaining power in the world. Smaller developing countries cannot hope to match China's status in this regard: not individually anyway.

However, the relative bargaining power of each country would clearly be greatly enhanced through closer regional ties and enhanced regional cooperation. We have considered this with regard to the development of capital markets, but the point may be more broadly applicable.

For example, the terms upon which FDI are attracted to an economy – and the benefits the country therefore derives from the investment – will be determined by the relative bargaining power of the parties. Larger regional groups taking a common stance with regard to FDI will see their bargaining power greatly increased. The same argument holds for tax competition with regard to transnational corporations of course.

Domestically, the same picture emerges. All the aspects of financial and private sector development we have seen would lead to greater societal benefits in a larger economic area, offering a greater range of investment opportunities and more scope for specialisation, innovation, higher productivity and economic growth. It is clearly an essential prerequisite for governments to improve their country's investment climate, thereby spurring growth FSD, PSD and poverty reduction – the ultimate aim of the whole exercise.

It is also very clear that this may not be enough though: governments can – and perhaps must do more if the scourge of poverty is to be finally resolved. However, we must also recognise that each country's ability to do so is dependent on (a) appropriate policy design and implementation, (b) the size and diversity of the domestic economy, and (c) the relative bargaining power of the country vis-à-vis the rest of the world. Both (b) and (c) would of course be greatly enhanced by ever closer regional cooperation and greater South–South links in general.

As we conclude this journey it is clear that the approach taken to financial sector development in developing countries needs to be far more ambitious than that proposed by the World Bank. Focusing on the 'basics' may of course prevent policy errors in terms of intervention, but surely we can and must move further than this 'counsel of despair' if the step-change in development that is so sorely needed is to be achieved.

Notes

1 An introduction to the financial system in theory and in practice

1 That is, financial institutions such as pension funds and insurance companies into which individuals deposit savings on a 'contractual' basis.
2 On 26 June 1974 at 15:30 CET, the German authorities closed Bankhaus Herstatt, a middle-sized bank with a large FX business. Prior to the closure, however, a number of Herstatt's counterparty banks had irrevocably paid deutschmarks into Herstatt but, as US financial markets had just opened, had not yet received their dollar payments in return. This failure triggered a ripple effect through global payment and settlement systems, particularly in New York. Ultimately, this fed into New York's multilateral netting system, which over the following three days, saw net payments going through the system decline by 60% (BIS, 2002).
3 That is, the Bank of England is charged with ensuring that inflation is 2.5%, neither higher nor lower. The ECB, in contrast, aims for inflation to be *below* 2%. For some commentators, this difference, though seemingly arcane, builds in a deflationary bias to the ECB's operations, which may have negative effects on growth.
4 Although many countries have an official floating exchange rate, in many instances this is actually a 'dirty float', where the central bank (or other official institution) intervenes in the market to 'manage' the floating of the exchange rate.
5 This point is illustrated with his famous analogy of the beauty contest, wherein the aim is not to choose the most beautiful contestant, but rather to select that contestant who one thinks the other 'judges' will select. As all are in the same position, the aim is to decide what average opinion will expect average opinion to be.
6 See Stiglitz and Weiss (1981) for the seminal paper in this respect.

2 Finance, poverty, development and growth

1 Environmental (or ecological) economists have long argued that policies geared towards generating ever-higher levels of growth – particularly at the global level – are incompatible with environmental sustainability, and ultimately with the elimination of poverty. See Daly (1997) *The Limits to Growth: The Economics of Sustainable Development*, for an account of this perspective.
2 Dollar and Kraay (2001).
3 See Chen and Ravallion (1997), Deininger and Squire (1996), Dollar and Kraay (2001) and Easterly (1999), for example.
4 See Li and Zou (1998) and Forbes (2000), for example.
5 See Barro (2000) and Lopez (2004), for example.
6 See Easterly and Rebelo (1993) and Perotti (1996), for example.
7 Easterly (2001) finds that IMF/World Bank structural adjustment programmes

tend to reduce the growth elasticity of poverty. The author suggests that this may be because the poor are unable to take advantage of the opportunities afforded by these programmes, leading to growing inequality.

8 Ravallion and Chen (2004) and Arbache *et al.* (2004), for example.

9 With the notable exception of neo-Marxist thought, which takes classical theory in the direction pioneered by Marx in the nineteenth century.

10 This section draws extensively on Easterly (1997), which gives an excellent – and fascinating – account of the impact of the Harrod-Domar model, particularly the concept of the 'financing gap', on development economics and the pattern on ODA from the 1950s to the late 1990s.

11 Schumpeter (1911).

12 Lewis (1955).

13 Goldsmith (1969).

14 See Levine *et al.* (2000) for evidence of causality in this respect.

15 Measured as the ratio of liquid liabilities to GDP, which describes the level of financial intermediation in the economy.

16 See DFID (2004).

17 DFID (2004: 5).

3 Financial repression, liberalisation and growth

1 See McKinnon (1973) and Shaw (1973).

2 Though it should be noted that liberalisation in this respect was not always entirely voluntary, as the conditions attached to international 'rescue packages' during the Asian crisis often included a requirement to remove restrictions on the entry of foreign financial institutions.

3 In terms of the money supply: M1 = cash in circulation and current accounts; M2 = M1 + time-related deposits savings deposits and non-institutional money-market funds; M3 = M2 + large time deposits, institutional money-market funds, short-term repurchase agreements and larger liquid assets.

4 See Greenword and Jovanovic (1989), for example.

5 See Siregar (1992), for example.

6 Reported in Williamson and Mahar (1998).

7 The *q* ratio is simply the market value of a company as measured by its stock market valuation, divided by the replacement value of the firm's assets.

8 See Díaz-Alejandro (1985), 'Good-bye Financial Repression, Hello Financial Crash', *Journal of Development Economics*.

9 See Stiglitz (1994) for the seminal account of the extent of market failures in financial markets and the resultant scope for welfare-enhancing government intervention in markets.

10 See Glick and Hutchison (2000) and Bordo *et al.* (2001), for example.

11 Bertolini and Drazen (1997) quoted in Eichengreen and Leblang (op. cit.)

12 The countries considered are: Argentina, Australia, Brazil, Canada, Chile, Denmark, Finland, Greece, Italy, Japan, Norway, Portugal, Spain, United States, Belgium, France, Germany, the Netherlands, Switzerland and Great Britain.

13 Key features of such a system are: the independence of regulators and supervisors – both from government and the private sector; adequate remuneration of staff, so as to reduce incentives for corruption; and adequate training of staff.

14 Principal–agent problems refer to the fact that often the incentives and objectives of the 'principal' are not mirrored in the 'agent' through which these objectives are pursued. In financial systems virtually all actors are both principals and agents in certain circumstances. Thus, in a democracy the government is the 'agent' to the voters' 'principal', but the government is the principal to its regulatory body's agent. Similarly, when dealing with the financial sector, the regulator is the

principal, while banks are agents, but at the level of the bank, the managers are agents and the shareholders are the principal. This overlapping – and often contradictory – network of incentives and objectives affect all financial systems, but the difficulties are more acute within developing countries with relatively immature financial sectors characterised by concentrations of power and rent-seeking.

15 See Chapter 1.
16 See Stiglitz and Weiss (1981).
17 Bankers are reluctant to raise interest rates to market clearing levels, as this exacerbates problems of adverse selection and moral hazard (ibid).

4 The domestic financial system

1 See Demirgüç-Kunt and Levine (1999).
2 The mitigation of asymmetric information is often cited as one of the key functions of banks within the financial system, or even the explanation for their continued existence. In this regard, Ben Bernanke has convincingly argued that the severity and length of the Great Depression in the 1930s was, at least in part, the result of widespread bank failures that sharply increased problems of asymmetric information in the financial system (Bernanke, 1984).
3 Krugman (1998) described this process, where Asian assets were bought at very low prices, as 'Firesale FDI'.
4 See the World Bank Firm Informality research programme (2006).
5 Indeed, much of the modern banking sector in Germany evolved from its original community-based 'microfinance' institutions, which displaced the inefficient incumbent banks.
6 See Rousseau and Wachtel (2001) for an overview on the link between inflation, financial sector development and economic growth.
7 Mundell (1972).
8 See Levine *et al.* (2000), for example.
9 See La Porta *et al.* (1998), for example.
10 See Acemoglu *et al.* (2001) and Bloom and Sachs (1998), for example.
11 See Levine *et al.* (op. cit.), for example.
12 Honohan and Stiglitz (2001).
13 See Vittas (1998) for a good overview of the potential role of institutional investors on financial sector development.
14 See Gerschenkron (1962).
15 It should be noted that banks too perform a similar function in the financial system. Individual depositors are able to withdraw their funds on demand – they are therefore provided with liquidity. However, knowing that only a small proportion of depositors are likely to do so at any one time, in the absence of a bank run, banks are able to transform these short-term liabilities by lending for longer-term investment projects.
16 See Markowitz (1952) for the seminal work on the role of portfolio diversification.
17 The first fundamental theorem of welfare economics holds that competitive market equilibriums are, by definition, Pareto efficient outcomes. See Arrow and Debreu (1954) for the formal proof of the first theorem.
18 See Greenwald and Stiglitz (1986), for example.

5 Reforming the domestic financial system

1 See Mundell (1962), for example.
2 These issues will be covered fully in subsequent chapters on the external system and financial crises. In this regard, the example given above is a description of a classic first-generation currency crisis (Krugman, 1979).

3 See Kydland and Prescott (1977, 1982, 1988) for their seminal contributions to this field, for which they were awarded the Nobel Prize in 2004.
4 See the works of James Buchanan for a US-focused perspective on public choice.
5 See Alesina and Tabellini (1987), for example.
6 This argument can be related back to the Harrod-Domar growth model discussed in Chapter 2, which relies on capital expenditure to kick-start growth.
7 See Tanzi (1987), for an early example.
8 This is particularly the case with corporation tax revenues, where profits expand more than average economic growth rates and vice versa.
9 There is some evidence to suggest that (a) compliance costs are far higher than administrative costs, and that (b) compliance costs in developing countries are far higher than is the case in developed countries (Bird and Zolt, 2003).
10 The logical conclusion in this line of thinking is the increasing popularity of the flat tax, where a uniform rate is levied across the economy.
11 See Box 5.2 on tax reforms in Ethiopia.
12 See Guttentag and Herring (1986) for an excellent account of why banks may be prone to excessive risk-taking and therefore need to be restrained.
13 A bank is solvent if the value of its assets exceeds its liabilities, after taking into account expected losses.
14 A bank is liquid if it can fund its current expenditure and meet customers' demands to withdraw deposits.
15 These concerns were primarily focused on banks in developed countries, particularly in Japan. It was feared that international competition in the banking sector was leading to increasing banking fragility, as banks held less and less capital in reserve to cover future losses in attempts to compete internationally.
16 One means of protecting independence is to ensure that agencies are not dependent upon the state for funding, but obtain their financing from an independent source.
17 The old-age dependency ratio is the number of pensioners drawing benefit divided by the working population.
18 This is exactly the option recommended to the UK government by the Turner Report on pension sustainability in the UK.
19 And particularly since 1994, when the Bank published *Averting the Old Age Crisis*. The World Bank approach to pension reform is perhaps set out most clearly in Holzmann and Stiglitz (2001).
20 See Zalewska (2006) for evidence in this regard with respect to pension reforms in Poland.
21 See North (1990).

6 The external financial system (I)

1 As was examined in Chapter 2, the underlying theory behind this reasoning relies heavily on the Harrod-Domar growth model, which links investment rates with growth. Where domestic savings are insufficient to fund the rate of investment estimated as being necessary to generate a target rate of growth – as is the case in most developing countries – external financial inflows are required to boost the investment rate.
2 The Organisation for Economic Cooperation and Development.
3 The G8 Summit in Heiligendamm, Germany in 2007 saw politicians come under pressure from campaigners to honour the pledges made at Gleneagles. Despite the clear need to accelerate disbursements, no binding commitments emerged, though all agreed that it was 'vital' to make progress.
4 For example, see Ovaska (2005) for an econometric study that finds a 1% increase in ODA (as a proportion of GDP) results in a reduction of real per capita growth of 3.65%.

5 See Burnside and Dollar (2004), for example.
6 However, Rajan and Subramanian (2005) control for these effects in their study and still find no systematic relationship between aid and growth, regardless of the type of aid and irrespective of institutional quality or standards of governance.
7 See Clemens *et al.* (2004), for example.
8 This phenomenon is known as the 'Dutch Disease', after the sharp rise in the Dutch exchange rate following large finds of natural gas. An overvalued exchange rate of this kind can lead to a 'hollowing out' of the economy, as formerly competitive export sectors are no longer able to compete.
9 PDAE (2005).
10 The 'Global Fund to Fight AIDS, Tuberculosis and Malaria' was established in 2002, following agreement at the G7 summit in Genoa.
11 The Clinton Foundation, as the name suggests, was established by former US President Bill Clinton after leaving office.
12 The SDR is an artificial currency that serves as the official monetary unit of the IMF. For members of the IMF, SDRs can be used to settle balances with other members, as well as with the Fund itself. An IMF member country has to supply its own currency to another member country in exchange for SDRs.
13 See Stiglitz (1989) and Summers and Summers (1989), for example.
14 These issues will be discussed in more depth in Chapter 7, where we consider the currency crises that have resulted from such speculative attacks.
15 Whereas a unilateral CTT may not have been possible historically this is no longer the case. The increasing automation and centralisation of foreign exchange transaction now ensures that trades in any major currency can be tracked and identified by the relevant central bank, and a CTT levied through settlement accounts held at the central bank by major financial institutions.
16 See Spratt (2005) for an account of how a CTT could be implemented on sterling transactions.
17 Kregel (2004) argues that such periods of net financial transfer from developing to developed countries are not exceptions but, historically, have been the norm.
18 See Persaud (2000), for example.
19 Eichengreen *et al.* (2003).
20 See Blanchard and Fischer (1989), Obstfeld and Rogoff (1994) and Obstfeld (1994), for example.
21 See Bende-Nabende *et al.* (1997) and de Mello (1999), for example.

7 The external financial system (II)

1 We will be examining in more detail what this means in practice later in the book.
2 Transaction exposure risk relates to the actual cash flow involved in settling transactions in foreign currencies.
3 The risk that financial statements of overseas subsidiaries of a company will gain or lose value because of exchange rate movements when translated into the currency of the parent company upon consolidation.
4 See Chapters 4 and 5 for a discussion of TNCs and domestic tax revenues in developing countries.
5 See Minsky (1982) for an excellent account of how these processes can lead to inherently fragile financial systems.
6 See Clarke *et al.* (2002), for example.
7 See Clarke *et al.* (2001).
8 See Berger and Udell (1995), for example.
9 See Reisen and Von Maltzan (1999) for evidence in this regard.
10 Indeed, for a lengthy period there was a very strong correlation between move-

ments in the NASDAQ equity index of hi-tech stocks and the levels of spreads in the J.P. Morgan emerging market bond index (EMBI).

11 See Schiller (2000) for an excellent analysis of how and why movements in market prices can become decoupled from changes in economic fundamentals of the underlying asset.

12 See Diamond and Dybvig (1983) for the seminal theoretical paper on the nature of banking crises.

13 See Chapters 4 and 5 for a discussion of the factors driving this phenomenon.

14 Salant and Henderson (1978) developed a model to demonstrate how the attempt to peg the price of gold with a government stock would ultimately result in a speculative attack that would eliminate the stock in question. Krugman (1979) subsequently adapted this model to currency crises analysis.

15 That is, the relative price of their exports versus their imports. Terms of trade shocks are a particular issue for countries dependent on a limited number of primary commodity exports, the value of which can fluctuate sharply.

16 The SRF is available at higher rates of interest to encourage IMF members to see it as a 'last resort' rather than a first port of call. In this, the Fund is following the advice of Walter Bagehot in the nineteenth century, where he argued that the central bank operating as lender-of-last-resort should 'lend freely' but at 'punitive rates of interest', so as to provide a strong incentive to institutions to avoid getting into difficulties of this kind in the first place.

17 Issues of moral hazard – for both lenders and borrowers – will be addressed in Chapter 8, where we consider the reform of the 'international financial architecture'.

18 See Williamson (1999), for example.

19 Developing countries with fully open capital accounts may be unable to raise interest rates as high as the domestic economy may require, as higher rates can attract short-term speculative inflows, which will distort other key macro variables.

20 Ffrench-Davis and Reisen (1998).

21 See IMF (2005a), for example.

22 Indeed, the first recorded sovereign default was as long ago as 1343, when the English King Edward III defaulted on his 'sovereign' debt to a group of Florentine merchant banks, leading to a collapse in confidence in Florence's merchant banking system. The resulting bank run – where depositors rushed to remove their funds – led to the closure of a number of prominent merchant banks, and has been described as the 'Great Crash of the 1340s' (Kohn, 1999).

23 The changing nature of the IMF's international role will be examined in depth in Chapter 8.

24 Conditionality of the IMF's Enhanced Structural Adjustment Facilities (ESAF) was replaced in 1999 by that of the Poverty Reduction and Growth Facilities (PRGF). PRSPs were introduced at the same time.

25 The Paris Club is the informal group of official creditors of developing countries, which includes the multilateral development institutions. It is the public sector equivalent of the London Club group of private sector creditors.

26 See Stewart and Wang (2003), for example.

27 This figure is the net present value (NPV) of outstanding debt in constant 2005 US$.

28 See Chapter 6.

29 See the proposal for a sovereign bankruptcy framework modelled on the US bankruptcy codes Chapter 9 (for government agencies) or Chapter 11 (for corporations). In these proposals debtor countries can call for a standstill of debt service payments if they are deemed unsustainable, with the decision then moving to an independent, international insolvency court.

8 The international financial architecture

1 In the planning for the post-war world, the Bretton Woods organisations were linked to the United Nations, which was born at the same time and would be responsible for the maintenance of peace in the post-war world. The IMF and the World Bank are therefore 'Specialized Agencies of the United Nations' under Article 57 of its Charter.

2 In the original Bretton Woods agreement, the IMF and IBRD were to be joined as a triumvirate by the International Trade Organisation (ITO). However, this body was never ratified by the US Congress, and many of its functions were subsequently taken up by the less formal GATT, agreed in 1948.

3 The Articles were adopted at the United Nations Monetary and Financial Conference, Bretton Woods, New Hampshire, 22 July 1944.

4 http://www.imf.org/external/pubs/ft/aa/aa01.htm

5 The quoted passages in this summary of surveillance activities are taken from: http://www.imf.org/external/np/exr/facts/surv.htm

6 Keynes had first argued that the IMF and World Bank should be based in London, but having no support for this position turned to the second-best option – in his view – of New York.

7 However, from the start, the Bank has offered loans of much longer maturity than commercial banks would be prepared to do.

8 At its inception IDA's capital base was approximately US$1.1 billion. In nominal terms this has increased by a little under 10% per year since then, so that by the 14th IDA 'replenishment' (2006–2008) US$33 billion will be disbursed. However, in real terms IDA resources only increased up to the early 1980s, and have since remained broadly flat at between US$5 and 10 billion (Weiss, 2007).

9 See Dollar and Kraay (2001) for a more recent exposition of the Bank's position in this respect.

10 See Romer (1986) and Lucas (1988) for the seminal early contributions.

11 Services were incorporated as the General Agreement on Trade in Services (GATS).

12 TRIMS require countries that are recipients of FDI to treat domestic and non-domestic economic entities in the same way, and so prohibit them from requiring foreign investors to source at least a proportion of inputs locally, for example.

13 TRIPS internationalises the protection of intellectual property rights, requiring countries to uphold patents, copyrights, industrial designs, trademarks etc.

14 See Krugman (1986) for an introduction to the 'New Trade Theory' that this represents.

15 Arguments of this form have been most often made by US-based right-wing think tanks such as the Heritage Foundation and American Enterprise Institute.

16 The Meltzer Report is that of the International Financial Institutions Advisory Commission established by the US Congress and chaired by Allan Meltzer, with an additional ten members who included academics Charles Calomiris, Jerome Levinson and Jeffrey Sachs, businessmen, politicians and think tank Directors C. Fred Bergsten of the Institute for International Economics and Edwin Feulner of the Heritage Foundation. The report was issued in March 2000.

17 The CFR Report is that of an Independent Task Force sponsored by the US Council on Foreign Relations (1999). This task force was jointly chaired by Carla Hills and Peter Peterson, with Morris Goldstein as project director and twenty-three other luminaries of the American internationalist establishment (including C. Fred Bergsten, director of the Institute for International Economics) as members.

18 The US Treasury Department Response to the Meltzer Report (US Treasury Report [2000]).

19 See Chapter 7 for an account of the evolution and ultimate demise of the mooted 'sovereign debt workout mechanism', which sought to address this issue.

20 The authors were Jose De Gregorio, Barry Eichengreen, Takatoshi Ito and Charles Wyplosz (1999).

21 This was co-chaired by John Sewell and Sylvia Saborio, directed by Kevin Morrison, and comprised a further eleven members from academia, think tanks, including John Williamson, Nancy Birdsall and Joseph Stiglitz.

22 The following sub-sections summarise the points made in Williamson (2000).

23 The insistence on subordinated debt is that in the event of bank failure, holders have a lower claim on the assets of the institution than do holders of 'senior debt'. As a result, spreads in the subordinated debt can provide a good indication of the soundness of the bank.

24 This problem is exacerbated by the issue of crisis contagion discussed in Chapter 7. That is to say, a crisis in one country can lead to a sharp increase in spreads in another country, which may precipitate a contagious crisis for which the country concerned cannot reasonably be held accountable. For example, the Russian sovereign debt default of August 1998 caused a sharp widening of emerging market spreads throughout the world. In Latin America, this saw spreads rise from 450 basis points over US Treasuries in August to 1,600 basis points in September (Goldstein, 2005). In the event, this did not trigger a Latin American crisis, but it could very easily have done so. In such circumstances, would it have then been reasonable to insist that Latin American countries should be provided financial support at a 'penalty rate' of more than 1,600 basis points, when just a few weeks earlier their sovereign debt had been trading at less than a third of this?

25 See Chang (2000) for an excellent examination of the role of moral hazard in the Asian crisis. The author argues that there is little evidence to support the contention that the crisis was the result of moral hazard. Furthermore, he contends that the issue of moral hazard is generally misunderstood and can have positive as well as negative consequences. Notable examples are the role of limited liability in facilitating the capitalist development and the insurance industry, both of which are clear examples of moral hazard.

26 Collective action clauses (or 'cacs') enable a majority of bondholders to agree to restructure the terms of the debt, with the restructuring then being binding on all bondholders, including those who had voted against the restructuring. The initiative – which was strongly resisted by creditors until relatively recently – is designed to ensure that a small number of bond holders cannot veto a restructuring, as is the case with straight bonds that require 100% of creditors to agree before a restructuring can take place. Recent years, particularly since the Argentine default, have seen a significant increase in the number of bonds issued with collective action clauses.

27 Members of the group are: Il SaKong (chair), Korea; Edmar Bacha, Brazil; Kwesi Botchwey, Ghana; Solita Collas-Monsod, Philippines; Ruth de Krivoy, Venezuela; Mar'ie Muhammad, Indonesia; Jaime Serra-Puche, Mexico; Manmohan Singh, India; Noordin Sopiee, Malaysia; Chalongphob Sussangkarn, Thailand; Roberto Zahler, Chile.

28 See Chapter 7.

29 See Wyplosz (1999), for example.

30 Though as described above, there has been some progress in this area since 1996, with the establishment of the Multilateral Consultative initiative for systemically important countries.

9 Development finance and the private sector

1 For example, Titman (1984) argues that firms which produce relatively unique products will tend to have low levels of debt. The rationale is that consumers will be less inclined to purchase the goods of firms that may have only a limited life-span, and that this is more likely in firms that produce unusual, niche products, leading them to keep leverage down so as to signal longevity.

2 In this regard, Fan *et al.* (2003) point out that, while firms from the same industry within particular countries tend to have similar capital structures, there is no evidence that firms from the same industry but located in different countries do likewise. For example, Brazilian chemical companies have an average leverage ratio of 0.57 while the corresponding figure for chemical firms in the UK is 0.16. Both display a relatively low standard deviation, indicating considerably intra-country uniformity. This distinction appears to reflect a broader pattern, where chemical companies in developing countries tend to take on more leverage than do their counterparts in developed countries.

3 As debt contracts are generally written in nominal – as opposed to real – term, and inflation reduces the value of this nominal debt, investors will be less willing to purchase debt in a high inflation environment, as its value will be rapidly eroded. Short-term debt suffers less in this regard, but the ideal instruments for dealing with this issue are inflation-linked, or indexed bonds.

4 Where corruption is a problem, outsiders (i.e. investors) will wish to hold assets that protect them against insiders (i.e. managers/owners). In this regard, debt – and particularly short-term debt – offers considerably more protection than does, for example, equity investment. See Chapter 4 for a review of the impact of the colonial legacy of different developing countries in this respect, particularly to whether their system is based on (English) common law, or (French) civil law.

5 Though the literature suggests that an over-reliance on long-term debt also has drawbacks, with shorter-term debt structures being – at least in theory – preferable under certain conditions. See Caprio and Demirgüç-Kunt (1997) for an excellent review of the literature in this area.

6 See UNCTAD (2001), for example.

7 World Bank, 2000: 1.

8 The finding that SMEs have less access to external sources of finance is not particular to developing countries, but is also the case in the developed world. See Berger and Udell (1998) and Galindo and Schantiarelli (2003), for example.

9 For example, Beck *et al.* (2006) show that institutional development is the most significant country characteristic that can explain variations in the availability of financing for firms in different countries.

10 See Berger *et al.* (2003) and Carter *et al.* (2004), for example. It is suggested that this is because (a) larger institutions lend to the more creditworthy SMEs, and that (b) they employ lower-cost lending technologies (Berger and Udell, 2006).

11 Much of the evidence in this regard comes from the United States. For example, Jayaratne and Wolken (1999) and Berger *et al.* (2003) show that there is no rela-tionship between the availability of credit to the SME sector and the relative market shares of large or small banks in particular regions of the US.

12 The following sub-sections that consider the five distinct categories of transaction lending is based on Berger and Udell (2006).

13 For example, the price per loan of a standard 'off the peg' credit scoring model averages US$1.50 to US$10 per loan (Muolo, 1995).

14 As we have seen in previous chapters, banks have long had a tendency to under-estimate risk in booms and overestimate it in economic downturns. This same tendency is also apparent in many credit risk models, particularly those which rely on relatively short runs of historical data. That is, if the model assumes that

conditions in the near future will replicate those in the near past – as many do – there is a built-in risk of procyclical assessments of risk. The downturn in the US sub-prime mortgage market in 2007 is a very good recent example of such a phenomenon, where lenders' credit risk models appeared to have assumed that the benign economic conditions – particularly with regard to low interest rates and high liquidity – would continue. When this changed, as of course it had to at some point, many were seemingly caught unawares, with dire financial consequences.

15 See Menkhoff *et al.* (2006) for an analysis of this process with respect to the Thai property market in the mid-1990s.
16 See Box 9.1 for an overview of key issues and trends in the provision of trade credit.
17 Though, as we have seen, access to trade credit has not been sufficient to offset the funding shortfall faced by the SME sector in developing countries.
18 See Beck *et al.* (2004a), cited in Berger and Udell (2004).
19 The survey data is from 2002 to 2006 depending on the country.
20 While these arguments apply to private corporations, a similar point can be made with regard to countries. As we saw in Chapters 7 and 8, campaigners have argued strongly that some form of international bankruptcy procedures are needed to deal with countries that have unsustainable levels of debt. Just as with private companies, the same arguments hold: a clean break is needed to enable creditors and debtors to move on, with prolonged disputes over essentially unpayable debts being in neither party's interests.
21 For example, taxes on factor invoices will negatively affect the use of factoring (Berger and Udell, 2004).
22 These are: Antigua and Barbuda, the British Virgin Islands, Canada, Hong Kong, New Zealand, Poland, St Lucia, St Vincent and the Grenadines, Turkey and the UK.
23 See Armington and Odle (1982).
24 See Dunne *et al.* (1988).
25 Biggs (2002: 7).
26 For example, in 1985 South Korean residents made just 2,700 patent applications – compared to 275,000 in Japan, which had long-since assimilated foreign technology and was then developing its own innovations. By 2004, South Korean residents made more than 100,000 patent applications.
27 Biggs *et al.* (1996).
28 Pack (1992) and Rodriguez-Clare (1996) respectively, cited in Biggs (2002).
29 See Storey and Jones (1987) for evidence in this regard from the UK, Liedholm and Mead (1987) for Africa and De Soto (1987) for Latin America. All cited in Biggs (2002).
30 Thurik (1994).
31 See Ayyagari *et al.* (2003) for the full paper, and Beck, Demirgüç-Kunt and Levine (2004) for a summary of the findings.
32 Biggs (2002: 25).
33 UNCTAD (2000).

10 Finance for development

1 In part, of course, these differences are culturally determined. As can be seen from Figure 10.1, there are clear regional differences in the propensity to save, which are likely to reflect cultural norms on the importance of saving, as well as just the availability of surplus funds.
2 Friedman (1957).
3 See Loayzu *et al.* (2000).
4 Modigliani and Brumberg (1954).

5 That is, an increase in government savings in India of £100 would be expected to reduce private savings by £30. The corresponding figure for Mexico would be £80.

6 Jappelli and Pistaferri (2002).

7 See Chapter 3 for evidence in this respect.

8 Loayza *et al.* (2000).

9 See Loayza *et al.* (2000).

10 Doucouliagos and Paldam (2006) review more than ninety studies of aid effectiveness conducted since the 1960s. They find that aid flows do indeed 'crowd out' private investment, but this is only partial.

11 See Chapter 9 for a fuller discussion on the financing obstacles facing small and medium-sized firms.

12 World Bank (2005).

13 See Dehejia and Gatti (2004) for evidence in this respect.

14 See Stiglitz and Weiss (1981) for the seminal paper on credit rationing in conditions of asymmetric information.

15 Akerlof (1970).

16 See Nesslein (2003), for example.

17 World Development Indicators.

18 Woo-Cumings (2001).

19 In contrast, the early microfinance movement pioneered by the Grameen Bank in Bangladesh was able to overcome these informational problems with the use of peer group selection and monitoring. Here the peer group, of course, did not suffer from the same informational problems due to their local knowledge (in an *ex ante* sense) and the borrower's fears of local stigma (in an *ex post* sense).

20 See Chang (2000) for an excellent account of how moral hazard has historically been a source of much positive economic development, particularly in areas such as corporate limited liability and the insurance market.

21 See Diamond and Dybvig (1983) for the seminal theoretical paper on the genesis of bank runs.

22 See Griffith-Jones and Persaud (2003).

23 Keynes (1936).

24 World Bank (2005b).

25 As discussed previously in this book, investment in 'human capital' of this kind may have a positive impact on growth, as human capital is a driver of endogenous growth.

26 See Gerschenkron (1962) for the seminal paper on this subject, and Chang (2007) for a more recent treatment.

References

Abiad, A. G., Oomes, N. and Ueda, K. (2004) 'The Quality Effect: Does Financial Liberalization Improve the Allocation of Capital?', IMF Working Paper No. 04/112.

Acemoglu, D., Johnson, S. and Robinson, J. (2001) 'The Colonial Origins of Comparative Development', *American Economic Review*, 91, 5: 1369–1401.

Acharya, R. and Daly, M. (2004) 'Selected Issues concerning the Multilateral Trading System', WTO Discussion Paper No. 7.

Aghion, P., Caroli, E. and Garcia-Peñalosa, C. (1999) 'Inequality and Economic Growth: The Perspective of the New Growth Theories', *Journal of Economic Literature*, 37, 4: 1615–1660.

Ahluwalia, M. (1999) 'The IMF and the World Bank in the New Financial Architecture', in *International Monetary and Financial Issues for the 1990s*, vol. XI, New York and Geneva: United Nations; referred to as 'the Ahluwalia Report',

Akamatsu, K. (1961) 'A Theory of Unbalanced Growth in the World Economy', *Review of World Economics*, 86: 3–25.

Akerlof, G. A. (1970) 'The Market for 96 "Lemons": Quality Uncertainty and the Market Mechanism', *Quarterly Journal of Economics*, 84, 3: 488–500.

Alesina, A. and Perotti, R. (1996) 'Income Distribution, Political Instability, and Investment', *European Economic Review*, 40, 6: 1203–1228.

Alesina, A. and Rodrik, D. (1994) 'Distributive Policies and Economic Growth', *Quarterly Journal of Economics*, 109, 2: 465–490.

Alesina, A. and Tabellini, G. (1987) 'A Positive Theory of Fiscal Deficits and Government Debt in a Democracy', NBER Working Paper No. W2308.

Alesina, A., Grilli, V. and Milesi-Ferretti, G. M. (1994) 'The Political Economy of Capital Controls', in L. Leiderman and A. Razin (eds) *Capital Mobility: The Impact on Consumption, Investment and Growth*, Cambridge: Cambridge University Press.

Aliber, R. Z., Chowdhry, B. and Yan, S. (2003) 'Some Evidence that a Tobin Tax on Foreign Exchange Transactions May Increase Volatility', *European Finance Review*, 7, 3: 511–514.

Anderson, B. (1998) 'From Miracle to Crash', *London Review of Books*, 16 April: 3–7.

Arbache J. S., Dickerson, A. and Green, F. (2004) 'Trade Liberalization and Wages in Developing Countries', *The Economic Journal*, 114: 73–96.

Armington, C. and Odle, M. (1982) 'Small Business: How Many Jobs?', *Brookings Review*, Vol. 1, No. 2 (Winter): 14–17.

Arrow, K. (1962) 'The Economic Implications of Learning by Doing', *Review of Economic Studies*, 29, 3: 155–173.

Arrow, K. and Debreu, G. (1954) 'The Existence of an Equilibrium for a Competitive Economy', *Econometrica*, 22, 3: 265–290.

Arteta, C., Eichengreen, B. and Wyplosz, C. (2001) 'When Does Capital Account Liberalization Help More than it Hurts?', NBER Working Paper No. 8414.

Arthur, B., Holland, J. H., LeBaron, B., Palmer, R. and P. Tayler (1996) 'Asset Pricing under Endogenous Expectations in an Artificial Stock Market', Sante Fe Institute Paper No. 96-12-093.

Asian Development Bank (2004) *Asian Development Outlook 2004*, Manila: Asian Development Bank.

Atiyas, I. (1992) 'Financial Reform and Investment Behavior in Korea: Evidence from Panel Data', mimeo, Washington, DC: World Bank.

Ayyagari, M., Demirgüç-Kunt, A. and Beck, T. (2003) 'Small and Medium Enterprises across the Globe: A New Database', World Bank Policy Research Working Paper No. 3127.

Bagehot, W. (1978) *The Collected Works: Economics Essays*, Vol. 9, London: The Economist.

Banerjee, A. and Iyer, L. (2002) 'History, Institutions and Economic Performance: The Legacy of Colonial Land Tenure Systems in India', in MIT Department of Economics Working Paper No. 02-27.

Bank for International Settlements (2002) 'Settlement Risk in Foreign Exchange Markets and CLS Bank', *BIS Quarterly Review*, 6, Basel: BIS.

Barberis, N. and Thaler, R. (2003) 'A Survey of Behavioral Finance', in G. Constantinides, M. Harris and R. Stulz (eds) *Handbook of the Economics of Finance*, Vol. 1b, Amsterdam: Elsevier.

Barr, N. (2000) 'Reforming Pensions: Myths, Truths and Policy Choices', IMF Working Paper No. 00/139.

Barro, R. (2000) 'Inequality and Growth in a Panel of Countries', *Journal of Economic Growth*, 5: 5–32.

Barth, J. R., Caprio, G. and Levine, R. (2004) 'Bank Regulation and Supervision: What Works Best?', *Journal of Financial Intermediation*, 13, 2: 205–248.

Baulch, B. (2003) 'Aid for the Poorest? The Distribution and Maldistribution of International Development Assistance', CPRC Working Paper No. 35.

Bayoumi, T. (1993) 'Financial Deregulation and Household Saving', *Economic Journal*, 103, 421: 1432–1443.

Beck, T., Demirgüç-Kunt, A. and Levine, R. (2003) 'SMEs, Growth and Poverty: Do Pro-SME Policies Work?', *World Bank Public Policy Note* No. 268.

Beck, T., Demirgüç-Kunt, A. and Levine, R. (2004) 'SMEs, growth, and poverty: cross-country evidence', available at: www.worldbank.org/research/projects/sme/Beck-SMEs_Growth_and_Poverty.pdf

Beck, T., Demirgüç-Kunt, A. and Maksimovic, V. (2004a) 'Bank Competition and Access to Finance: International Evidence', *Journal of Money, Credit, and Banking*, 36: 627–648.

Beck, T., Demirgüç-Kunt, A., and Maksimovic, V. (2004b) 'Financing Patterns around the World: Are Small Firms Different?' World Bank Working Paper.

Beck, T., Demirgüç-Kunt, A., Laeven, L. and Maksimovic, V. (2006) 'The Determinants of Financing Obstacles', *Journal of International Money and Finance*, 25: 932–952.

Bencivenga, V. R., Smith, B. D. and Starr, R. M. (1995) 'Transactions Costs, Technological Choice, and Endogenous Growth', *Journal of Economic Theory*, 67: 153–177.

Bende Nabende, A., Ford, J. L. and Slater, J. (1997) 'The Impact of FDI and Regional Economic Integration on the Economic Growth of the Asean-5 Economies, 1970–1994: A Comparative Analysis from a Small Structural Model', Department of Economics Discussion Paper 97/13, University of Birmingham.

Berg, A., Borensztein, E. and Mauro, P. (2002) 'An Evaluation of Monetary Regime Options for Latin America', *North American Journal of Economics and Finance*, 13: 213–235.

Berger, A. N. and Udell, G. F. (1995) 'Relationship Lending and Lines of Credit in Small Firm Finance', *Journal of Business*, 68: 351–382.

Berger, A. N. and Udell, G. F. (1998) 'The Economics of Small Business Finance: The Roles of Private Equity and Debt Markets in the Financial Growth Cycle', *Journal of Banking and Finance*, 22, 6–8: 613–673.

Berger, A. N. and Udell, G. F. (2002) 'Small Business Credit Availability and Relationship Lending: The Importance of Bank Organisational Structure', *Economic Journal*, 112: F32–F53.

Berger, A. N. and Udell, G. F. (2004) 'The Institutional Memory Hypothesis and the Procyclicality of Bank Lending Behavior', *Journal of Financial Intermediation*, 13, 4: 458–495.

Berger, A. N. and Udell, G. F. (2006) 'A More Complete Conceptual Framework for SME Finance', *Journal of Banking and Finance*, 30, 11: 2945–2966.

Berger, A. N., Rosen, R. J. and Udell, G. F. (2003) 'Does Market Size Structure Affect Competition? The Case of Small Business Lending', *Journal of Banking and Finance*, 57, 6: 2533–2570.

Berger, A. N., DeYoung, R., Genay, H. and Udell, G. F. (2000) 'The Globalization of Financial Institutions: Evidence from Cross-border Banking Performance', Brookings-Wharton Papers on Financial Services No. 3: 23–158.

Bernanke, B. S. (1984) 'Non-monetary Effects of the Financial Crisis in the Propagation of the Great Depression', *American Economic Review*, 73, 3: 257–276.

Bertolini L. and Drazen A. (1997) 'Capital Account Liberalization as a Signal', *American Economic Review*, 87: 138–154.

Besley, T. J. and Burgess, R. (2000) 'Land Reform, Poverty Reduction and Growth: Evidence from India', *Quarterly Journal of Economics*, 115, 2: 389–430.

Biggs, T. (2002) *Is Small Beautiful and Worthy of Subsidy?* Washington, DC: International Finance Corporation.

Biggs, T. and Shah, M. (1998) 'The Determinants of Enterprise Growth in Sub-Saharan Africa: Evidence from the Regional Program on Enterprise Development', RPED Discussion Paper, World Bank.

Biggs, T., Ramachandran, V. and Shah, M. (1999) 'The Growth of African Firms', RPED Discussion Paper, World Bank.

Biggs, T., Shah, M. and Srivastava, P. (1996) 'Technological Capability and Learning in African Firms', Technical Paper, World Bank.

Birch, D. L. (1979) *The Job Generation Process. Final Report to Economic Development Administration*, Cambridge, MA: MIT Program on Neighborhood and Regional Change.

Birch, D. L. (1981) 'Who Creates Jobs?', *The Public Interest*, 65: 3–14.

Birch, D. L. (1987) *Job Creation in America: How our Smallest Companies Put the Most People to Work*, New York: Free Press.

Bird, G. (2004) *International Finance and the Developing Economies*, Basingstoke: Palgrave Macmillan.

Bird, R. M. and Zolt, E. M. (2003) *Introduction to Tax Policy Design and Development*, Washington, DC: World Bank.

Blanchard, O. J. and Fischer, S. (1989) *Lectures on Macroeconomics*, Cambridge, MA: MIT Press.

Bloom, D. E. and Sachs, J. (1998) 'Geography, Demography and Economic Growth in Africa', Brookings Papers on Economic Activity No. 2.

Bodnar, G. M. and Gebhardt, G. (1998) *Derivatives Usage in Risk Management by US and German Non-Financial Firms: A Comparative Survey*, Cambridge, MA: National Bureau of Economic Research.

Bordo, M. D. and Eichengreen, B. (1998) 'Implications of the Great Depression for the Development of the International Monetary System', NBER Working Paper No. 5883.

Bordo, M. D., Eichengreen, B., Klingebiel, D. and Martinez-Peria, S. M. (2001) 'Is the Crisis Problem Growing More Severe?', *Economic Policy*, 16, 32: 51–82.

Bosworth, B. P. and Collins, S. M. (1999) 'Capital Flows to Developing Economies: Implications for Saving and Investment', Brookings Papers on Economic Activity No. 1, Brookings Institution, pp. 143–169.

Boyd, J. and Prescott, E. C. (1986) 'Financial Intermediary Coalitions', *Journal of Economic Theory*, 38, 2: 211–232.

Bradley, M., Jarrell, G. and Kim, E. H. (1984) 'On the Existence of an Optimal Capital Structure: Theory and Evidence', *Journal of Finance* 39, July: 857–878.

Buira, A. (2002) 'An Analysis of IMF Conditionality', Oxford University, Dept. of Economics, Discussion Paper Series No. 104.

Buira, A. (2006) 'Does the IMF Need More Financial Resources?', in Edwin M. Truman (ed.), *Reforming the IMF for the 21st Century*, Washington, DC: Institute for International Economic Policy.

Burgess, R. and Pande, R. (2005) 'Can Rural Banks Reduce Poverty? Evidence from the Indian Social Banking Experiment', *American Economic Review*, 95, 3: 780–795.

Burnside, C. and Dollar, D. (2004) 'Aid, Policies and Growth: Revisiting the Evidence', World Bank Policy Research Working Paper No. 3251, World Bank.

Calderon, C. and Liu, L. (2003) 'The Direction of Causality between Financial Development and Economic Growth', *Journal of Development Economics*, 72, 1: 321–334.

Calvo, G. (1999) 'Contagion in Emerging Markets: When Wall Street Is a Carrier', mimeo, University of Maryland.

Campbell, J. Y. and Mankiw, N. G. (1990) 'Permanent Income, Current Income, and Consumption', *Journal of Business and Economic Statistics*, 8, 3: 265–279.

Caprio Jr., G. and Demirgüç-Kunt, A. (1997) 'The Role of Long-term Finance: Theory and Evidence', Policy Research Working Paper Series, No. 1746, World Bank.

Caprio, G., Honohan, P. and Stiglitz, J. E. (eds) (2001) *Financial Liberalization: How Far, How Fast?* Cambridge: Cambridge University Press.

Carter, D., McNulty, J. and Verbrugge, J. (2004) 'Do Small Banks Have an Advantage in Lending? An Examination of Risk-Adjusted Yields on Business Loans at Large and Small Banks', *Journal of Financial Services Research*, 25, 2/3: 233–252.

Chang, H.-J. (2000) 'The Hazard of Moral Hazard: Untangling the Asian Crisis', *World Development*, 28, 4: 775–788.

Chang, H.-J. (2007) *Bad Samaritans – The Myth of Free Trade and the Secret History of Capitalism*, New York: Bloomsbury Press.

Chapple, S. (1991) 'Financial Liberalization in New Zealand, 1984–90', United Nations Conference on Trade and Development Discussion Paper No. 35, UNCTAD.

Chari, A. and Henry, P. B. (2002) 'Capital Account Liberalization: Allocative Efficiency or Animal Spirits', NBER Working Paper No. 8988.

Chen, S. and Ravallion, M. (1997) 'Household Welfare Impacts of China's Accession to the World Trade Organization', World Bank, Policy Research Working Paper No. 3040.

Chwieroth, J. (2007) 'Neoliberal Economists and Capital Account Liberalization in Emerging Markets', *International Organization*, 61, 2: 443–463.

Clarke, G., Cull, R. and Peria, M. (2001) 'Does Foreign Bank Penetration Reduce Access to Credit in Developing Countries? Evidence from Asking Borrowers', Policy Research Working Paper No. 2716, World Bank.

Clarke, G., Cull, R., Peria, M. and Sánchez, S. (2002) 'Bank Lending to Small Businesses in Latin America: Does Bank Origin Matter?', Policy Research Working Paper No. 2760, World Bank.

Clemens M., Radelet, S., and Bhavnani R. (2004) 'Counting Chickens when they Hatch: The Short-term Effect of Aid on Growth', Working Paper No. 44, Washington, DC: Center for Global Development.

Coady, D. P. (1997) 'Fiscal Reform in Developing Countries', in C. K. Patel (ed.), *Fiscal Reforms in the Least Developed Countries*, Cheltenham: Edward Elgar, pp. 18–50.

Council on Foreign Relations Independent Task Force (1999) *Safeguarding Prosperity in a Global Financial System: The Future International Financial Architecture*, Carla Hills and Peter Peterson, Co-Chairs, Morris Goldstein, Project Director, Washington, DC: Institute for International Economics.

Cull, R. and Peria, M. (2007) 'Foreign Bank Participation and Crises in Developing Countries', Policy Research Working Paper Series, No. 4128, World Bank.

Culpeper, R. (1997) *The Multilateral Development Banks: Titans or Behemoths?*, Boulder, CO: Lynne Rienner, and Ottawa: The North-South Institute.

Daly, H. (1997) *The Limits to Growth: The Economics of Sustainable Development*, Boston: Beacon Press.

Damodaran, A. (2002) *Investment Valuation: Tools and Techniques for Determining the Value of Any Asset*, New York: John Wiley.

Davidson, P. (1998) 'Volatile Financial Markets and the Speculator', *Economic Issues*, 3, September: 1–18.

De Gregorio, José, Edwards, Sebastian and Valdés, Rodrigo (1998) 'Capital Controls in Chile: An Assessment', Paper presented at the Interamerican Seminar on Economics, Rio de Janeiro, Brazil.

De la Torre, Augusto and Schmukler S. L. (2004) 'Coping with Risk through Mismatches: Domestic and International Financial Contracts for Emerging Economies', Policy Research Working Paper Series, No. 3212, World Bank.

De Mello, L. R. (1999) 'Foreign Direct Investment-led Growth: Evidence from Time Series and Panel Data', Oxford Economic Papers 51, pp. 133–151.

De Soto, H. (1987) *The Other Path*, New York: Harper and Row.

Dehejia, R. and Gatti, R. (2004) 'Why Should we Care about Child Labor? The Education, Labor Market, and Health Consequences of Child Labor', NBER Working Paper No. 10980, National Bureau of Economic Research.

Demetriades, P. and Devereux, M. (1992) 'Investment and "Financial Repression", Theory and Evidence from 63 LDCs', Working Paper in Economics No. 92/16, Keele University.

Demirgüç-Kunt, A. and Levine, R. (1999) 'Bank-Based and Market-Based Financial Systems: Cross-Country Comparisons', manuscript, World Bank, Washington.

Demirgüç-Kunt, A., Levine, R. and Beck, T. (2000) 'A New Database on the Structure and Development of the Financial Sector', *World Bank Economic Review*, 14, 3: 597–605.

Deininger, K. and Squire, L. (1996) 'A New Data Set Measuring Income Inequality', *World Bank Economic Review*, 10: 565–591.

DFID (2004) 'The Importance of Financial Sector Development for Growth and Poverty Reduction', Policy Division Working Paper.

Diamond, D. and Dybvig, P. (1983) 'Bank Runs, Deposit Insurance, and Liquidity', *Journal of Political Economy*, 91: 401–419.

Díaz-Alejandro, C. (1985) 'Good-Bye Financial Repression, Hello Financial Crash', *Journal of Development Economics*, 19, 1/2: 1–24.

Dollar, D. and Kraay, A. (2001) 'Growth is Good for the Poor', Policy Research Working Paper Series, No. 2587, World Bank.

Doucouliagos, H. and Paldam, M. (2006) 'Aid Effectiveness on Accumulation: A Meta Study', *Kyklos* 59, 2: 227–254.

Dunne, T., Roberts, M. J. and Samuelson, L. (1988) 'Firm Entry and Post-Entry Performance in the U.S. Chemical Industries', Papers 0–88–4, Pennsylvania State University, Department of Economics.

Easterly, W. (1997) 'The Ghost of Financing Gap: How the Harrod-Domar Growth Model Still Haunts Development Economics', Policy Research Working Paper Series, No. 1807, World Bank.

Easterly, W. (1999) 'Life during Growth', *Journal of Economic Growth*, 4, 3: 239–276.

Easterly, W. (2001) 'The Effect of IMF and World Bank Programs on Poverty', WIDER Discussion Paper 2001/102.

Easterly, W. and Rebelo, S. (1993) 'Fiscal Policy and Economic Growth: An Empirical Investigation', *Journal of Monetary Economics*, 32, 3: 417–458.

Eatwell, J. (1997) 'International Financial Liberalisation: The Impact on World Development', UNDP Office of Development Studies Discussion Paper Series.

Ebrill, L., Keen, M., Bodin, J. and Summers, V. (2001) *The Modern VAT*, Washington, DC: International Monetary Fund.

Edison, H., Levine, R., Ricci, L. and Slok, T. (2002) 'International Financial Integration and Economic Growth', *Journal of International Money and Finance*, 21, 6: 749–776.

Edwards, S. (2001) 'Capital Mobility and Economic Performance: Are Emerging Economies Different?', NBER Working Paper No. 8076 (January), National Bureau of Economic Research.

Eichengreen, B. (2004) 'Financial Instability', Paper written on behalf of the Copenhagen Consensus.

Eichengreen, B. and Leblang, D. (2003) 'Capital Account Liberalization and Growth: Was Mr. Mahathir Right?', *International Journal of Finance and Economics*, 8, 3: 205–224.

Eichengreen, B. and Mody, A. (1998) 'What Explains Changing Spreads on Emerging Market Debt: Fundamentals or Market Sentiment?', RMC Discussion Paper 123. World Bank, Resource Mobilization and Cofinancing Vice Presidency, Washington, DC.

Eichengreen, B., Hausman, R. and Panizza, U. (2003) 'Currency Mismatches, Debt Intolerance, and Original Sin: Why they are not the Same and why it Matters', National Bureau of Economic Research Working Paper No. 10036.

Eichengreen, B., Rose. A. K. and Wyplosz, C. (1996) 'Contagious Currency Crises', NBER Working Paper Series, No. 5681, July.

Emerging Market Eminent Persons Group (2001) *The Seoul Report: Rebuilding the International Financial Architecture*. Seoul.

Escudé, G., Burdisso, T., Catena, M., D'Amato, L., McCandless, G. and Murphy, T. (2001) 'Las Mipymes y el mercado de crédito en Argentina', Documento de Trabajo No. 15, BCRA.

Eyzaguirre, N. and Schmidt-Hebbel, K. (1997) 'Encaje a la Entrada de Capitales y Ajuste Macroeconómico', Unpublished paper, Santiago: Central Bank of Chile.

Fan, J., Titman, S. and Twite, G. (2003) 'An International Comparison of Capital Structure and Debt Maturity Choices', Working Paper, AFA 2005 Philadelphia Meetings.

Fantahun, B. (2002) 'Tax Reform Program in Ethiopia', in G. Ageba, J. Mohammed and S. Tesfay (eds), *Policy Reform, Implementation and Outcome in Ethiopia*. Proceedings of the 11th Annual Conference on Ethiopian Economy, Nazareth, Ethiopia. Addis Ababa: Ethiopian Economic Association and Department Economics, Addis Ababa University.

FAO (2007) *The State of Agricultural Commodity Markets 2006* (Part 2: Review of Agricultural Commodity Markets), Rome: FAO. http://www.fao.org/docrep/009/a0950e/a0950e00.htm

Ffrench-Davis, P. and Reisen, H. (1998) *Capital Flows and Investment Performance in Latin America*, Paris: OECD Development Centre.

Fischer, S. (2001) 'Exchange Rate Regimes: Is the Bipolar View Correct?', *Journal of Economic Perspectives*, 15, 2: 3–24. (Repr. in Fischer (2004) *IMF Essays from a Time of Crisis*, Cambridge, MA: MIT Press).

Fisher, I. (1933) 'The Debt Deflation Theory of the Great Depression', *Econometrica*, 1, 4: 227–257.

Forbes, K. (2000) 'A Reassessment of the Relationship between Inequality and Growth', *American Economic Review*, 90: 869–897.

Foster, D. and Rosenzweig, M. (2003) 'Economic Growth and the Rise of Forests', *Quarterly Journal of Economics*, 118, 2: 601–637.

Friedman, M. (1953) 'The Case for Flexible Exchange Rates', in *Essays in Positive Economics*, Chicago: University of Chicago Press.

Friedman, M. (1957) *A Theory of the Consumption Function*, Princeton, NJ: Princeton University Press, for the National Bureau of Economic Research.

Fry, M. (1978) 'Money and Capital or Financial Deepening in Economic Development?' *Journal of Money, Credit, and Banking*, 10, 4: 464–475.

Fry, M. (1980) 'Saving, Investment and Growth, and the Cost of Financial Repression', *World Development*, 8: 317–327.

Fry, M. (1995) *Money, Interest, and Banking in Economic Development*, 2nd edn., Baltimore, MD: Johns Hopkins University Press.

Galindo, A. and Schiantarelli, F. (eds) (2003) *Credit Constraints and Investment in Latin America*, Washington, DC: Inter-American Development Bank publications.

Galindo, A., Schiantarelli, F. and Weiss, A. (2007) 'Does Financial Liberalization Improve the Allocation of Investment? Micro Evidence from Developing Countries', *Journal of Development Economics*, 83, 2: 562–587.

Gallego, F., Hernandez, L. and Schmidt-Hebbel, K. (1999) 'Capital Controls in Chile: Effective? Efficient?', Working Paper No. 59, Central Bank of Chile.

Galor, O. and Zeira, J. (1993) 'Income Distribution and Macroeconomics', *Review of Economic Studies*, 60, 1: 35–52.

Gebhardt, G. (2000) 'The Evolution of Global Standards in Accounting', Brookings-Wharton Papers on Financial Services, pp. 342–368.

Gelb, A. (1989) 'Financial Policies, Growth, and Efficiency', World Bank Research Working Paper No. 202.

Gelos, G. (1997) 'How Did Financial Liberalization in Mexico Affect Investment? Evidence from the Manufacturing Sector', Department of Economics, Yale University.

Geneva Report (1999) *An Independent and Accountable IMF: Geneva Reports on the World Economy*, Geneva: International Center for Monetary and Banking Studies.

Gerschenkron, A. (1962) *Economic Backwardness in Historical Perspective. A Book of Essays*, Cambridge, MA: Harvard University Press.

Gerxhani, K. (2004) 'The Informal Sector in Developed and Less Developed Countries: A Literature Survey', *Public Choice*, 120, 3/4: 267–300.

Glick, R. and Hutchison, M. (2000) 'Capital Controls and Exchange Rate Instability in Developing Countries', *Federal Reserve Bank of San Francisco Economic Letter*.

Goldfajn, I. and Valdes, R. O. (1997) 'Are Currency Crises Predictable?', IMF Working Paper No. 97/159.

Goldsmith, R. W. (1969) *Financial Structure and Development*, New Haven, CT: Yale University Press.

Goldstein, M. (1998) *The Asian Financial Crisis: Causes, Cures, and Systemic Implications*, Washington, DC: Institute for International Economics.

Goldstein, M. (2005) 'What Might the Next Emerging-Market Financial Crisis Look Like?', Working Paper No. WPOG-7, Institute for International Economics.

Greene, J. and Villanueva, D. (1991) 'Private Investment in Developing Countries: An Empirical Analysis', *IMF Staff Papers*, 38, 1: 33–58.

Greenwald, B. C. and Stiglitz, J. (1986) 'Externalities in Economies with Imperfect Information and Incomplete Markets', *Quarterly Journal of Economics*, 101, 2: 229–264.

Greenword, J. and Jovanovic, B. (1989) 'Financial Development, Growth, and the Distribution of Income', National Bureau of Economic Research Working Paper No. 3189.

Gregorio, J. de and Guidotti, P. E. (1992) 'Financial Development and Economic Growth', IMF Working Paper No. 92/101.

Griffith-Jones, S. and Gottschalk, R. (2004) *Costs of Currency Crises and Benefits of International Financial Reform*, Brighton: Institute of Development Studies.

Griffith-Jones, S. and Ocampo, J. A. (2003) 'What Progress on International Financial Reform? Why so Limited?', Report prepared for the Expert Group on Development Issues, Sweden.

Griffith-Jones, S. and Persaud, A. (2003) *The Political Economy of Basle II and Implications for Emerging Economies*, Port of Spain: ECLAC.

Grilli, V. and Milesi-Ferretti, G. M. (1995) 'Economic Effects and Structural Determinants of Capital Controls', *IMF Staff Papers*, 42, 3: 517–551.

Grossman, G. and Helpman, E. (1991) 'Quality Ladders in the Theory of Growth', *Review of Economic Studies*, 58, 1: 43–61.

Guttentag, J. and Herring, R. (1986) 'Disaster Myopia in International Banking', *Essays in International Finance*, Vol. 164, Princeton, NJ: Princeton University Press.

Habermeier, K. and Kirilenko, A. (2001) 'Securities Transaction Taxes and Financial Markets', IMF Working Paper No. WP/01/51, Washington, DC: IMF.

Hafsi, T. and Le-Louarn, J.-Y. (1999) *The African Development Bank: Hope for Africa (A), (B) et (C)*, Montreal: Centre d'étude en administration internationale.

Hausmann, R. and Fernández-Arias, E. (2000) 'Foreign Direct Investment: Good Cholesterol?', IADB, Research Department Working Paper No. 417.

Herring, R. J. and Chatusripitak, N. (2000) 'The Case of the Missing Market: The Bond Market and Why it Matters for Financial Development', ADB Institute Working Paper No. 11.

Hicks, J. (1969) *A Theory of Economic History*, Oxford: Clarendon Press.

Holzmann, R. and Stiglitz, J. (eds) (2001) *New Ideas about Old Age Security*, Washington, DC: World Bank.

Honohan, P. and Stiglitz, J. (2001) 'Robust Financial Restraint', in G. Caprio, P. Honohan and J. E. Stiglitz (eds) *Financial Liberalization: How Far, How Fast?* Cambridge: Cambridge University Press.

IMF (2001) 'How Beneficial Is Foreign Direct Investment for Developing Countries?', *Finance and Development*, Washington, DC: IMF.

IMF (2003) *World Economic Outlook September 2003: Public Debt in Emerging Markets*, Washington, DC: IMF.

IMF (2005a) *Global Financial Stability Report, 2005*, Washington, DC: IMF.

IMF (2005b) *IMF Surveillance: A Factsheet*, Washington, DC: IMF.

ISODEC (2002) Ghana Poverty Reduction Strategy Paper (GPRS): ISODEC's Position Paper, Ghana: ISODEC.

Jalilian, H. and Kirkpatrick, C. (2002) 'Financial Development and Poverty Reduction', *International Journal of Finance and Economics*, 7, 2: 97–108.

Jappelli, T. and Pistaferri, L. (2002) 'Tax Incentives for Household Saving and Borrowing', CSEF Working Paper No. 83, Centre for Studies in Economics and Finance (CSEF), University of Salerno, Italy.

Jaramillo, F., Schiantarelli, F. and Weiss, A. (1992) 'The Effect of Financial Liberalization on the Allocation of Credit: Evidence from a Panel of Ecuadorian Firms', World Bank Working Paper No. 1092.

Jayaratne, J. and Wolken, J. (1999) 'How Important Are Small Banks to Small Business Lending?: New Evidence from a Survey of Small Firms', *Journal of Banking and Finance*, 23: 427–458.

Kaldor, N. (1956) 'Alternative Theories of Distribution', *Review of Economic Studies* 23, 2: 83–100.

Kaminsky, G. and Reinhart, C. (1998) 'On Crises, Contagion and Confusion', mimeo, George Washington University and University of Maryland.

Keynes, J. M. (1936) *The General Theory of Employment, Interest and Money*, London: Macmillan.

Kindleberger, C. (1978) *Manias, Panics and Crashes: A History of Financial Crises*, New York: Basic Books.

King, R. and Levine, R. (1993) 'Finance and Growth: Schumpeter Might Be Right', *Quarterly Journal of Economics*, 108, 717–737.

Klapper, L. (2005) 'The Role of Factoring for Financing Small and Medium Enterprises', Policy Research Working Paper Series, No. 3593, World Bank.

Knight, M. (1999) 'Developing and Transition Countries Confront Financial Globalization', *Finance and Development*, IMF.

Koch, D. J., Westeneng, J. and Ruben, R. (2007) 'Does Marketisation of Aid Reduce Country Poverty Targeting of Private Aid Agencies?' *European Journal of Development Research*, 19, 4: 635–656.

Kohn, M. (1999) 'Merchant Banking in the Medieval and Early Modern Economy', Department of Economics Working Paper No. 99–05, Dartmouth College.

Konadu-Agyemang, K. (2000) 'The Best of Times and the Worst of Times: Structural Adjustment Programs and Uneven Development in Africa: The Case of Ghana', *Professional Geographer* 52, 3: 469–483.

Kraay, A. (2004) 'When is Growth Pro-Poor? Cross-Country Evidence', IMF Working Paper No. 04/47, International Monetary Fund.

Kregel, J. (2004) 'External Financing for Development and International Financial Instability', G-24 Discussion Paper Series, No. 32.

Krugman, P. (1979) 'A Model of Balance of Payments Crisis', *Journal of Money, Credit and Banking,* 11, August: 311–325.

Krugman, P. (1986) 'Increasing Returns and the Theory of International Trade', in T. Bewley (ed.), *Advances in Economic Theory*, Cambridge: Cambridge University Press.

Krugman, P. (1997) 'Are Currency Crises Self-Fulfilling?', *NBER Macroeconomics Annual*, Cambridge, MA: MIT Press.

Krugman, P. (1998) 'Fire-sale FDI', prepared for NBER Conference on Capital Flows to Emerging Markets, February 20–21, 1998, MIT, mimeo.

Kuznets, S. (1955) 'Economic Growth and Income Inequality', *American Economic Review*, 45, 1–28.

Kydland, F. and Prescott, E. (1977) 'Rules rather than Discretion: The Inconsistency of Optimal Plans', *Journal of Political Economy*, 85, 3: 473–492.

Kydland, F. and Prescott, E. (1982) 'Time to Build and Aggregate Fluctuations', *Econometrica*, 56, 2: 1345–1371.

Kydland, F. and Prescott, E. (1988) 'The Workweek of Capital and its Cyclical Implications', *Journal of Monetary Economics*, 21, 2–3: 343–360.

La Porta, R., Lopez-de-Silanes, F., Shleifer, A. and Vishny, R. (1998) 'Law and Finance', *Journal of Political Economy*, 106, 6: 1113–1155.

Laurens, B., and Cardoso, J. (1998) 'Managing Capital Flows: Lessons from the Experience of Chile', IMF Working Paper No. 98/168.

Levine, R. (1991) 'Stock Markets, Growth, and Tax Policy', *Journal of Finance*, 46, 4: 1445–1465.

Levine, R. (1997) 'Financial Development and Economic Growth: Views and Agendas', World Bank Policy Research Working Paper No. 1678.

Levine, R. and Zervos, S. (1998) 'Stock Markets, Banks, and Economic Growth', *American Economic Review*, 88, 3: 537–558.

Levine, R., Loayza, N. and Beck, T. (2000) 'Financial Intermediation and Growth: Causality and Causes', *Journal of Monetary Economics*, 16: 31–77.

Levy-Yeyati, E. and Sturzenegger, F. (2002) 'To Float or to Fix: Evidence on the

Impact of Exchange Rate Regimes on Growth', *American Economic Review*, 93, 4: 1173–1193.

Lewis, A. (1955) *The Theory of Economic Growth,* London: George Allen & Unwin.

Li, H. and Zhou, H. (1998) 'Income Inequality is not Harmful for Growth: Theory and Evidence', *Review of Development Economics*, 2, 3: 318–334.

Liedholm, C. and Mead, D. (1987) 'Small Scale Industries in Developing Countries: Empirical Evidence and Policy Implications', International Development Papers 9, Department of Agricultural Economics, Michigan State University.

Loayza, N., Schmidt-Hebbel, K. and Servén, L. (2000) 'What Drives Private Saving across the World?', *Review of Economics and Statistics*, 82, 2: 165–181.

Lopez, J. H. (2004) 'Pro-poor-Pro-growth: Is there a Trade Off?', World Bank, Policy Research Working Paper No. 3378.

Lopez, J. H. (2005) 'Pro-poor Growth: A Review of what we Know (and of what we Don't)', mimeo, World Bank.

Lopez, J. H. and Servén, L. (2004) 'The Mechanics of the Growth-poverty-inequality Relationship', mimeo, World Bank.

Lucas, R. E. (1988) 'On the Mechanics of Economic Development', *Journal of Monetary Economics*, 22, 1: 3–42.

Lucas, R. E. and Sargent, T. J. (1981) *Rational Expectations and Econometric Practice*, London: Allen & Unwin.

Luna-Martinez, J. de and Rose, T. (2003) 'International Survey of Integrated Financial Sector Supervision', World Bank Policy Research Working Paper No. 3096.

Madsen, R. (2005) 'The Silver Lining of an Aging Japan', *Far Eastern Economic Review,* 168, 9: 33–37.

Malkiel, B. (1987) 'Efficient Market Hypothesis', in J. Eatwell, M. Milgate and P. Newman (eds), *The New Palgrave: A Dictionary of Economics*, London: Macmillan.

Mann, A. J. (2002) *Estimating the Administrative Costs of Taxation: A Methodology with Application to the Case of Guatemala*, Arlington, VA: DevTech Systems.

Markowitz, H. M. (1952) 'Portfolio Selection', *Journal of Finance*, 7, 1: 77–91.

Masson, P. R. (1998) 'Contagion: Monsoonal Effects, Spillovers, and Jumps Between Multiple Equilibria', IMF Working Paper No. 98/142.

Masson, P. (2006) 'New Monetary Unions in Africa: A Major Change in the Monetary Landscape?', *Economie Internationale*, 107, 3: 86–105.

Masson, P. and Mussa, M. (1995) 'The Role of the Fund: Financing and its Interactions with Adjustments and Surveillance', Pamphlet Series No. 50, IMF.

McKinnon, R. (1973) *Money and Capital in Economic Development*, Washington, DC: Brookings Institution.

Meier, G. (1988) 'Theoretical Issues Concerning the History of International Trade and Economic Development', Stanford University Research Papers No. 992, https://gsbapps.stanford.edu/researchpapers/library/RP992.pdf

Meier, G. (1991) *Politics and Policy Making in Developing Countries,* San Francisco: International Center for Economic Growth.

Meltzer, A. H. (Chair) and others (2000) *Report to the United States Congress of the International Financial Institutions Advisory Commission*, Washington, DC.

Menkhoff, L., Neuberger, D. and Suwanapor, C. (2006) 'Collateral-Based Lending in Emerging Markets: Evidence from Thailand', *Journal of Banking and Finance,* 30, 1: 1–21.

Mester, L. (1997) 'What's the Point of Credit Scoring?', *Federal Reserve Bank of Philadelphia Business Review*, September/October: 3–16.

Miller, M. (2003) *Credit Reporting Systems and the International Economy*, Cambridge, MA: MIT Press.

Minsky, H. (1982) 'The Financial Instability Hypothesis, Capitalist Processes and the Behaviour of the Economy', in C. Kindleberger and J.-P. Laffargue (eds), *Financial Crises, Theory, History and Policy,* Cambridge: Cambridge University Press.

Mirrlees, J. (1971) 'An Exploration in the Theory of Optimum Income Taxation', *Review of Economic Studies*, 38, 2: 175–208.

Mishkin, F. (1991) 'Asymmetric Information and Financial Crises: A Historical Perspective', in R. Hubbard (ed.) *Financial Markets and Financial Crises,* Chicago: University of Chicago Press.

Modigliani, F. and Brumberg, R. (1954) 'Utility Analysis and the Consumption Function: An Interpretation of Cross-section Data', in K. K. Kurihara (ed.), *Post-Keynesian Economics*, Piscataway, NJ: Rutgers University Press.

Moguillansky, G. (2002) 'Investment and Financial Volatility in Latin America', *CEPAL Review*, 77: 45–63.

Montiel, P. and Servén, L. (2004) 'Macroeconomic Stability in Developing Countries: How Much is Enough?', World Bank Policy Research Working Paper Series, No. 3456.

Morisset, J. (1993) 'Does Financial Liberalization Really Improve Private Investment in Developing Countries?', *Journal of Development Economics*, 40: 133–150.

Mundell, R. (1961) 'A Theory of Optimum Currency Areas', *American Economic Review*, 51, 4: 509–517.

Mundell, R. (1962) 'The Appropriate Use of Monetary and Fiscal Policy for Internal and External Stability', IMF Working Paper No. 9.

Mundell, R. (1972) 'African Trade, Politics and Money', in R. Tremblay (ed.), *Africa and Monetary Integration*, Montreal: Les Editions HRW.

Muolo, P. (1995) 'Building a Credit Scoring Bridge', *US Banker*, May: 71–73.

Murshed, S. (2001) 'Conditionality and Endogenous Policy Formation in a Political Setting', Discussion Paper No. 2001/92, WIDER.

Muth, J. F. (1961) 'Rational Expectations and the Theory of Price Movements', *Econometrica*, 29: 315–335.

Narlikar, A. (2005) *The World Trade Organization – A Very Short Introduction*, Oxford: Oxford University Press.

Nesslein, T. (2003) 'The Theory of Government Failure', in *The Encyclopedia of Public Administration and Public Policy,* London: Routledge.

North, D. C. (1990) *Institutions, Institutional Change and Economic Performance*, Cambridge: Cambridge University Press.

Obstfeld, M. (1986) 'Rational and Self-fulfilling Balance of Payments Crises', *American Economic Review*, 76, 1: 72–81.

Obstfeld, M. (1994) 'International Capital Mobility in the 1990s', CEPR Discussion Papers No. 902.

Obstfeld, M. and Rogoff, K. (1994) 'The Intertemporal Approach to the Current Account', NBER Working Paper No. 4893.

Obwona, M. and Mutambi, B. (2004) 'Foreign Direct Investment in Africa: Trends, Determinants and Linkages with Growth and Poverty', Paper presented at AERC Senior Policy Seminar Seminar on Growth and Poverty Reduction VI in Kampala, 2–4 March.

Orszag, P. R. and Stiglitz, J. (2001) 'Rethinking Pension Reform: Ten Myths About

Social Security Systems', in R. Holzmann and J. Stiglitz (eds), *New Ideas about Old Age Security*, Washington, DC: World Bank.

Ovaska, T. (2005) *More Aid Less Growth*, London: Globalisation Institute.

Overseas Development Council (2000) *The Future Role of the IMF in Development*, Washington: ODC.

Pack, H. (1992) 'Learning and Productivity Change in Developing Countries', in *Trade Policy, Industrialization and Development*, Oxford: Oxford University Press.

Patel, C. K. (1997) *Fiscal Reforms in the Least Developed Countries*, Cheltenham: Edward Elgar.

PDAE (2005) *Paris Declaration on Aid Effectiveness*, Paris: OECD.

Pehlivan, H. (1996) 'Financial Liberalization and Bank Lending Behaviour in Turkey', *Savings and Development*, 20, 2: 171–187.

Perotti, R. (1996) 'Growth, Income Distribution and Democracy', *Journal of Economic Growth*, 1: 149–187.

Persaud, A. (2000) 'Sending the Herd off the Cliff Edge: The Disturbing Interaction between Herding and Market-sensitive Risk Management Practices', Institute of International Finance Competition in Honour of Jacques de Larosiere, First Prize Essay on Global Finance for 2000, Washington, DC.

Prasad, E., Rogoff, K., Wei, S. J. and Kose, A. (2003) *Effects of Financial Globalization on Developing Countries: Some Empirical Evidence*, New York: International Monetary Fund.

Pritchett, L. (2006) 'The Quest Continues', *Finance and Development*, 43, 1: 18–22.

Quinn, D. (1997) 'The Correlates of Change in International Financial Regulation', *American Political Science Review*, 91, 3: 531–551.

Rajan, R. G. and Subramanian, A. (2005) 'Aid and Growth: What Does the Cross-Country Evidence Really Show?', NBER Working Paper No. 11513, National Bureau of Economic Research.

Ravallion, M. (2004) 'Pro Poor Growth: A Primer', World Bank, Policy Research Working Paper No. 3242.

Ravallion, M. and Chen, S. (2004) 'China's (Uneven) Progress against Poverty', World Bank, Policy Research Working Paper No. 3408.

Ravallion, M. and Datt, G. (2002) 'Is India's Economic Growth Leaving the Poor Behind?', *Journal of Economic Perspectives*, 16, 3: 89–108.

Reisen, H. and Von Maltzan, J. (1999) 'Boom and Bust and Sovereign Ratings', OECD Development Centre Working Paper No. 148, OECD Development Centre.

Reynoso, A. (1989) 'Financial Repression, Financial Liberalization, and the Interest Rate Elasticity of Developing Countries', Ph.D dissertation, MIT.

Ricardo, D. (1817) *On the Principles of Political Economy and Taxation*.

Robb, A. M. (2002) 'Small Business Financing: Differences between Young and Old Firms', *Journal of Entrepreneurial Finance and Business Ventures* 7, 2: 45–65.

Rodriguez-Clark, A. (1996) 'Multinationals, Linkages, and Economic Development', *American Economic Review*, 86.

Rodrik, D. (ed.) (1998) 'Who Needs Capital-Account Convertibility?', *Essays in International Finance*, 207, Princeton: Princeton University Press.

Rodrik, D. and Velasco, A. (1999) 'Short-term Capital Flows', NBER Working Paper No. 7364, National Bureau of Economic Research.

Rodrik, D., Subramanian, A. and Trebbi, F. (2004) 'Institutions Rule: The Primacy of Institutions over Geography and Integration in Economic Development', NBER Working Paper No. 9305.

Rojas-Suarez, L. (2001) 'Can International Capital Standards Strengthen Banks in Emerging Markets?', Institute for International Economics, Working Paper No. WP01–10.

Romer, P. (1986) 'Increasing Returns and Long-Run Growth', *Journal of Political Economy*, 94, 5: 1002–1037.

Rostow, W. W. (1960) *The Stages of Economic Growth: A Non-Communist Manifesto*, Cambridge: Cambridge University Press.

Rousseau, P. and Wachtel, P. (2001) 'Inflation, Financial Development and Growth', in T. Negishi, R. Ramachandran and K. Mino (eds), *Economic Theory, Dynamics and Markets: Essays in Honor of Ryuzo Sato*, Boston, MA: Kluwer Academic Press.

Sakakibara, E. (2002) 'Regional Cooperation in Asia', Paper prepared for the FONDAD Conference on Financial Stability in Emerging Economies: Steps Forward for Bankers and Financial Authorities, De Nederlandsche Bank, Amsterdam, June 3–4.

Salant, S. and Henderson, D. (1978) 'Market Anticipation of Government Policy and the Price of Gold', *Journal of Political Economy*, 86, 4: 627–648.

Samaha, K. and Stapleton, P. (2008) 'Compliance with International Accounting Standards in a National Context: Some Empirical Evidence from the Cairo and Alexandria Stock Exchanges', *Afro-Asian Journal of Finance and Accounting*, 1, 1: 40–66.

Schiller, R. (2000) *Irrational Exuberance*, New York: John Wiley.

Schmidt, R. (2001) 'Efficient Capital Controls', *Journal of Economic Studies*, 28, 3: 199–212.

Schumpeter, J. (1911/1965) *The Theory of Economic Development*, Oxford: Oxford University Press.

Shaw, E. (1973) *Financial Deepening in Economic Development*, Oxford: Oxford University Press.

Shleifer, A. and Vishny, R. W. (1986) 'Large Shareholders and Corporate Control', *Journal of Political Economy*, 94, 3: 461–488.

SIDA (2008) History of Swedish Development Cooperation, http://www.sida.se/sida/jsp/sida.jsp?d=733&language=en_US

Siregar, M. (1992) 'Financial Liberalization, Investment and Debt Allocation', Ph.D. dissertation, Boston University.

Smith, A. (1776) *An Inquiry into the Nature and Causes of the Wealth of Nations*.

Soto, M. and Valdés, S. (1996) 'Es el Control Selectivo de Capitales Efectivo en Chile? Su Efecto sobre el Tipo de Cambio Real', *Cuadernos de Economía* (Latin American Journal of Economics), Instituto de Economía, Pontificia Universidad Católica de Chile, 33, 98: 77–108.

Spahn, P. B. (1996) 'The Tobin Tax and Exchange Rate Stability', *Finance and Development*, 33, 2 (June): 24–27.

Sparkes, R. (2002) *SRI: A Global Revolution*, New York: John Wiley.

Spratt, S. (2005) 'A Sterling Solution: Implementing a Stamp Duty on Sterling to Finance International Development', Paper prepared for the Stamp Out Poverty campaign.

Spratt, S. (2006) 'External Debt and the Millennium Development Goals: A New Sustainable Framework', Expert Paper commissioned by the UNDP.

Stein, J. C. (2000) 'Information Production and Capital Allocation: Decentralized vs. Hierarchical Firms', NBER Working Paper No. 7705, National Bureau of Economic Research.

Stewart, F. and Wang, M. (2003) 'Do PRSPs Empower Poor People and Disempower the World Bank, or Is it the Other Way Round?' QEH Working Paper Series, University of Oxford.

Stiglitz, J. E. (1989a) 'On the Economic Role of the State,' in A. Heertje (ed.), *The Economic Role of the State*, London: Basil Blackwell.

Stiglitz, J. E. (1989b) 'Using Tax Policy To Curb Speculative Short-Term Trading', *Journal of Financial Services Research*, 3, 2/3: 101–115.

Stiglitz, J. (1994) 'The Role of the State in Financial Markets', *Proceedings of the World Bank Annual Conference on Development Economics 1993*, Washington, DC: World Bank.

Stiglitz, J. and Uy, M. (1996) 'Financial Markets, Public Policy, and the East Asian Miracle', *World Bank Research Observer*, 11, 2: 249–276.

Stiglitz, J. and Weiss, A. (1981) 'Credit Rationing in Markets with Imperfect Competition', *American Economic Review*, 71, 3: 393–410.

Stiglitz, J., Ocampo, J. A., Spiegel, S., French-Davies, R. and Nayyar, D. (2006) *Stability with Growth*, Oxford: Oxford University Press.

Storey, D. and Jones, A. (1987) 'New Firm Formation – A Labor Market Approach to Industrial Entry', *Scottish Journal of Political Economy*, 34, 1: 37–51.

Summers, L. H. and Summers, V. P. (1989) 'When Financial Markets Work Too Well: A Cautious Case for a Securities Transactions Tax', *Journal of Financial Services*, 3: 163–188.

Suryahadi, A., Sumarto, S., Suharso, Y. and Pritchett, L. (2000) 'The Evolution of Poverty in Indonesia, 1996-99', Unpublished manuscript, Country Economics Department, Washington, DC: World Bank.

Tanzi, V. (1987) 'Quantitative Characteristics of the Tax Systems of Developing Countries', in D. Newbery and N. Stern (eds), *The Theory of Taxation for Developing Countries*, Oxford: Oxford University Press.

Tanzi, V. (2004) 'Fiscal Policy: When Theory Collides with Reality', CEPS Working Paper, Center for European Policy Studies.

Thurik, A. (1994) 'Between Economics of Scale and Entrepreneurship', Research Report 9404, EIM.

Titman, S. (1984) 'The Effect of Capital Structure on a Firm's Liquidation Decision', *Journal of Financial Economics*, 13, 1: 137–151.

Tobin, J. (1978) 'A Proposal for International Monetary Reform', *Eastern Economic Journal*, 4, 3/4: 153–159.

Tobin, J. (1984) 'On the Efficiency of the Financial System', *Lloyd's Bank Review*, 153, July: 1–15.

Tversky, A. and Kahneman, D. (1974) 'Judgement under Uncertainty: Heuristics and Biases', *Science*, 185: 1124–1131.

Umlauf, S. R. (1993) 'Transaction Taxes and the Behavior of the Swedish Stock Market', *Journal of Financial Economics*, 33: 227–240.

UN Millennium Project (2005) *Investing in Development: A Practical Plan to Achieve the Millennium Development Goals*, London: Earthscan.

UNCTAD (2000) *TNC-SME Linkages for Development: Issues-Experiences-Best Practices*, New York: United Nations Publications.

UNCTAD (2001) *The 'Missing Middle' in LDC's. Why Micro and Small Enterprises are not Growing*, New York: United Nations Publications.

UNCTAD (2006) *World Investment Report*, New York: United Nations Publications.

UNESCAP (2000) 'An Introduction to Trade Finance', in *Trade Finance Infrastructure Development Handbook for Economies in Transition*. http://www.unescap.org/tid/publication/tipub2374_chap1.pdf

United Nations (2005) *World Economic and Social Survey 2005: Financing for Development*, New York: United Nations Publications.

United States Department of the Treasury (2000) *Response to the Report of the International Financial Institutions Advisory Commission*, Washington, DC: US Department of the Treasury.

Valdés, S. and Soto, M. (1998) 'The Effectiveness of Capital Controls: Theory and Evidence from Chile', *Empirica*, 25, 2: 133–164.

Vittas, D. (1998) 'Institutional Investors and Securities Markets: Which Comes First?', World Bank Policy Research Working Paper No. 2032.

Wei, S. J. and Kim, J. (1997) 'The Big Players in the Foreign Exchange Market: Do they Trade on Information or Noise?', NBER Working Paper No. 6256.

Weiss, M. (2007) *The World Bank's International Development Association (IDA)*, Washington, DC: World Bank.

Westerhoff, F. and Dieci, R. (2006) 'The Effectiveness of Keynes-Tobin Transaction Taxes when Heterogeneous Agents Can Trade in Different Markets: A Behavioral Finance Approach', *Journal of Economic Dynamics and Control*, 30: 293–322.

White, H. and Anderson, A. (2000) 'Growth vs. Redistribution: Does the Pattern of Growth Matter?', DFID White Paper on Eliminating World Poverty: Making Globalisation Work for the Poor.

Williamson, J. (1990) 'What Washington Means by Policy Reform', in J. Williamson, (ed.), *Latin American Adjustment: How Much Has Happened?*, Washington, DC: Institute for International Economics.

Williamson, J. (1993) 'A Cost-Benefit Analysis of Capital Account Liberalisation in Developing Countries', in B. Fischer and H. Reisen (eds), *Financial Opening: Policy Issues and Experiences*, Paris: OECD.

Williamson, J. (1999) 'Implication of the East Asian Crisis for Debt Management', mimeo, University of Warwick.

Williamson, J. (2000) 'The Role of the IMF: A Guide to the Reports', Institute for International Economics Policy Brief No. 00-5.

Williamson, J. and Mahar, M. (1998) 'A Survey of Financial Liberalization', *Essays in International Finance*, No. 211.

Williamson, O. (1988) 'Corporate Finance and Corporate Governance', *Journal of Finance*, 43, 3: 567–591.

Woo-Cumings, M. (2001) 'Diverse Paths toward "the Right Institutions": Law, the State and Economic Reform in Asia', ADB Working Paper No. 18.

World Bank (1989) *World Development Report*. Washington, DC: World Bank. World Bank (2001) *Finance for Growth: Policy Choices in a Volatile World*, Washington, DC: World Bank.

World Bank (2003) *World Development Report 2003*, Washington, DC: World Bank.

World Bank (2004) *SMEs, 'Growth, and Poverty. Do Pro-SME Policies Work?' The Public Policy for the Private Sector, Note N. 268*, Washington, DC: World Bank.

World Bank (2005a) *Whither Latin American Capital Markets?*, Washington, DC: World Bank.

World Bank (2005b) *World Development Report: A Better Investment Climate for Everyone*, Washington, DC: World Bank.

Wyplosz, C. (1999) 'International Financial Stability', in I. Kaul, I. Grunberg and M. A. Stem (eds), *Global Public Goods: International Cooperation in the 21st Century*, New York: Oxford University Press, pp. 152–189.

Zalewska, A. (2006) 'Is Locking Domestic Funds into the local Market Beneficial? Evidence from the Polish Pension Reforms', *Emerging Markets Review* 7, 339–360.

Index